IDENTITY AND POWER IN THE ANCIENT ANDES

CRITICAL PERSPECTIVES IN IDENTITY, MEMORY, AND THE BUILT ENVIRONMENT
HELAINE SILVERMAN, UNIVERSITY OF ILLINOIS AT URBANA-CHAMPAIGN, SERIES EDITOR

Places in Mind: Archaeology as Applied Anthropology
edited by Paul A. Shackel and Erve Chambers

Identity and Power in the Ancient Andes:
Tiwanaku Cities Through Time
John Wayne Janusek

The Ecology of Power: Culture, Place, and Personhood
in the Southern Amazon, AD 1000–2000
Michael J. Heckenberger

IDENTITY AND POWER IN THE ANCIENT ANDES

TIWANAKU CITIES THROUGH TIME

JOHN WAYNE JANUSEK

Routledge
New York • London

Published in 2004 by
Routledge
270 Madison Avenue
New York, NY 10016
www.routledge-ny.com

Published in Great Britain by
Routledge
2 Park Square
Milton Park, Abingdon
Oxon OX14 4RN
www.routledge.co.uk

Routledge is an imprint of the Taylor & Francis Group.
Printed in the United States of America on acid-free paper.

10 9 8 7 6 5 4 3 2 1

Library of Congress Cataloging-in-Publication Data

Janusek, John Wayne, 1963-
Identity and power in the ancient Andes: Tiwanaku cities through time/
John Wayne Janusek.
p. cm.
Includes bibliographical references.
ISBN 0-415-94633-6 (hb : alk. paper) — ISBN 0-415-94634-4 (pb : alk. paper)
1. Tiwanaku culture. 2. Indians of South America — Urban residence — Bolivia — Tiwanaku River Valley. 3. Indians of South America — Ethnic identity — Bolivia — Tiwanaku River Valley. 4. Indians of South America — Bolivia — Tiwanaku River Valley — Social life and customs. 5. Tiwanaku Site (Bolivia) 6. Lukurmata Site (Bolivia) 7. Tiwanaku River
Valley (Bolivia) — Antiquities. I. Title.
F3319.1.T55J36 2004
984;1201 — dc22 2004015539

For Felipe "Papi" Choque, whose expertise, patience, and good humor has ensured the success of many archaeology projects, his wife Paulina, his daughter Elsa, and his son, my godson, Wilson

Contents

Part 4

List of Figures

Acknowledgments

In producing this book I have incurred enormous personal and scholarly debts, and I can only hope to acknowledge a few of them here. This book draws on research I conducted in the southern Lake Titicaca Basin over fifteen years, beginning in July, 1987. Having just arrived that year, I excitedly descended by taxi down the perilous *autopista* (imagine a vertical autobahn) into La Paz from the airport in El Alto. I was a recent graduate of the University of Illinois at Chicago, eager to work in Lukurmata with Alan Kolata and the Proyecto Wila Jawira. Alan had been my professor at University of Illinois–Chicago and for the next seven years, while at the University of Chicago, he served as my principal advisor. It is to Alan, my friend, mentor, and advisor-*cum*-colleague, that I owe my most profound professional gratitude. He introduced me to the Andes, put up with me over countless field seasons, and graciously provided academic, logistical, and personal support over the years. His contagious enthusiasm inspired my love for Andean archaeology and Bolivia. Our interpretations of Tiwanaku differ in some respects, but he always graciously accepts my ideas and steps in when I'm being overly foolish. All in all he has truly, as he once put it, "saved me from myself."

I cannot imagine what life in ensuing years would have been like without my Wila Jawira cohort—more sane, perhaps, but infinitely poorer in friendships, memories, and ideas. For my early years at Lukurmata, I am grateful to Marc Bermann, Howard Earnest, Chip Stanish, and Karen Wise for sharing their expertise in various aspects of archaeology, and to Robert Coffman for his careful excavations in the Misiton sector. For my later years in Lukurmata and Katari, I am indebted to Sonia Alconini, who helped supervise excavations in Misiton, and to Matthew Seddon, who worked with me on a particularly challenging project in the surrounding Katari Valley. For Tiwanaku, I am grateful for the unflagging support, enlightened advice, and humbling sarcasm of my peers-turned-field siblings, including Juan "Ernie" Albarracin-Jordan, Sonia Alconini, Chris Begley, Deborah Blom, Nicole Couture, Howard Earnest, Martin Giesso, Claudia Rivera, Kathryn Sampeck, Cheryl Sutherland, Ann Webster, and Melanie Wright. Wittingly or not, they and others are collaborators in this research (although, of course, I am entirely responsible for any bad interpretations!). Many of them and others supervised excavations in areas treated here: Nicole Couture, Howard Earnest, Kathryn Sampeck, Javier Escalante, and the late Max Portugal excavated in Putuni; James Mathews, Ann Webster, and Martin Giesso excavated in Akapana East 1; and Chris Begley excavated in Akapana East 2.

I am equally grateful to many Bolivian archaeologists who offered advice or support over various field seasons. Oswaldo Rivera Sundt, former director of the Instituto Nacional de Arqueología (INAR), provided permits for various phases of this research and went far beyond the call of duty to ensure that the project ran smoothly, expeditiously jumping in when it did not. Over the past several years, Javier Escalante has generously done the same as director of the Unidad Nacional de Arqueología. Waldo Villamor shared his extensive ethnohistorical knowledge and library, and Carlos Ponce Sanginés shared his profound knowledge of Tiwanaku archaeology. Many other archaeologists at INAR and at the Universidad Mayor de San Andres were generous with their knowledge, in particular the late Max Portugal, whose remarkably positive spirit I truly miss.

Writing itself has indebted me to a number of tolerant colleagues and friends. Since 1998 Vanderbilt University has provided critical research support and an ideal academic environment, granting the leave in 2001–2002 that allowed me to write this manuscript. Discussions with Beth Conklin, Arthur Demarest, Francisco Estrada-Belli, Ted Fischer, Bill Fowler, Tom Gregor, and Annabeth Headrick, in particular, have helped sharpen my ideas and broaden my theoretical and regional interests. Tomi Castle helped transform portions of the manuscript into a coherent, readable text. Outside of Vanderbilt, Art Joyce and Chip Stanish read various manuscript drafts and, with great fairness and thinly veiled sarcasm, made invaluable critical suggestions. Late night phone conversations with several close colleagues also shaped the manuscript, and I am especially grateful to Deborah Blom and Melissa Vogel for listening and offering ideas. A special note of gratitude goes to Helaine Silverman, a supportive colleague and amazing series editor who enthusiastically facilitated publication in a timely and efficient manner.

Many other colleagues and friends have helped shape and sharpen the ideas presented here, whether in person, at conferences, at hazily remembered parties, or in writing. The list is long and I have inevitably forgotten to mention some names (apologies in advance!), but among them are Matthew Bandy, Brian Bauer, Chris Beaule, Marc Bermann, David Browman, Larry Coben, Amanda Cohen, Sergio Chavez, the late Karen Mohr-Chavez, Mickey Dietler, Clark Erickson, Paul Goldstein, Ramiro Gutierrez, Christine Hastorf, Cynthia Herhahn, William Isbell, Elizabeth Klarich, Linda Manzanilla, Michael Moseley, Donna Nash, Carlos Osterman, Johan Reinhard, Andy Roddick, Katharina Schreiber, Wolfgang Schüler, William Sillar, Alexei Vranich, P. Ryan Williams and Karen Wise. I also thank many Bolivian students and colleagues for their sharp minds and relentless wit, especially Dante Angelo, Carlos Lemuz, Pilar Lima, Marcos Michel, Jose Luis Paz, and Claudia Rivera.

A profound note of gratitude is owed Wolfgang Schüler, world's foremost high-altitude anthropological photographer and *cholologist.* Many of the excellent photos in this and other Proyecto Wila publications are his. Wolf has consistently put me up in La Paz, and has disinterestedly helped my research projects at various turns and in many, many ways. Great thanks also go to Don Rene Irahola, my Cochabambino "father away from home" and expert auto mechanic, who keeps me running, honest, and laughing.

Much of the research synthesized in this book was funded by the National Science Foundation (BNS# 9021098) and a Fulbright-Hays Dissertation Research Fellowship. It also benefited from serial grants to Alan L. Kolata provided by the National Science Foundation and the National Endowment for the Humanities. A note of gratitude goes to Dr. Robert Gelbard, former U.S. Ambassador to Bolivia, and his family for their support in the 1990s and for facilitating wonderful relations with embassy personnel.

Most fundamental to the archaeology treated in this book are many Bolivian Aymara who skillfully conducted the excavations and helped make the altiplano my home. Through them I have learned to appreciate the value they have for their past and the hope they have for archaeology in drawing the past into their lives. Perhaps more than anything else in my life, living and working with many Aymara friends and colleagues has exploded my worldview, fostering the education of a lifetime. I am grateful to all of the members of the Associación de Arqueólogos in Tiwanaku (the *chojos*), and to Don Cesar Calisaya, who with unsurpassable diplomacy and eloquence continues to facilitate positive relations with members of communities across the southern Lake Titicaca Basin. Mario Loza generously offered his mapping expertise time and again, and Eulogio Mayta, who tragically died of typhoid fever in February 1996, drafted many of the original ceramic illustrations published here. I am especially grateful to archaeology *maestros* Celso "Celio" Chura and Felipe "Papi" Choque. Working and living with Papi, my *compadre*, is an amazing, often humbling experience. His love for archaeology is surpassed only by his ability to take everything—I mean *everything*—in stride. Excavation is his art, and like many artists he receives little credit for his work aside from daily wages, occasional photos, and lasting memories. Papi is an inspiring friend and colleague and an incredible human being. I dedicate this book to him, his wife Paulina, his daughter Elsa, and his son—my godson—Wilson.

Finally, I thank my parents for their unwavering support of my nerdy interests and professional pursuits over the years. Because of them I got off my lazy haunches and became an archaeologist.

Note: In the mission of producing a broadly conceived book, I refrain from including detailed quantitative measurements and tables. Such information, which is critical to the results and interpretations, is found in numerous other publications. Where relevant, I refer to those publications. I refer the reader, in particular, to the numerous chapters (written by me and others) that comprise the volume edited by Alan Kolata, Tiwanaku and Its Hinterland: Archaeology and Paleoecology of an Andean Civilization, Vol. 2, *Smithsonian Institution Press, 2003.*

Introduction

Identity and power are critical elements of social relations in all human cultures, and at last they are increasingly subjects of archaeological inquiry. While nonmaterial and relatively abstract, they are, as anthropology demonstrates on a global scale, deeply inscribed in material culture, built environments, and anthropogenic landscapes.

I strive to develop an approach to relations of identity and power and their significance in the rise and fall of archaic states. I focus on Tiwanaku, paying special attention to changing local residential patterns and ritual practices in its two primary cities. Although attention to local livelihoods is still subdominant in the study of past societies, it is critical for understanding the unwritten principles and practical relations involved in the creation, use, significance, and modification of material assemblages and built landscapes. The Andean region offers a particularly intriguing and little studied account of shifting relations of identity and power over the long term.

Tiwanaku, one of the most provocative sites in the high Andes, is an enduring mystery. Situated in the high altiplano near the southern edge of Lake Titicaca, Tiwanaku fascinated an early Spanish chronicler named Pedro Cieza de Leon, just as it continues to fascinate travelers and archaeologists today. Cieza, the young "Chronicler of the Indies," visited the ruins in 1549 and wrote their first known description. Cieza wrote of the ruins, "I would say that I consider this the oldest antiquity in" the Andes (1959:283–284). His account goes on,

> Tihuanacu [*sic*] is not a very large town, but it is famous for its great buildings which, without question, are a remarkable thing to behold.

> Near the main dwellings is a man-made hill, built on great stone foundations. Beyond this hill there are two stone idols of human size and shape, with the features beautifully carved, so much so that they seem the work of great artists or masters. They are so large that they seem small giants, and they are wearing long robes, different from the attire of the natives of these provinces. They seem to have an ornament on their heads. Close by these stone statues there is another building, whose antiquity and this people's lack of writing is the reason there is no knowledge of who the people that built these great foundations and strongholds were, or how much time has gone by since then, for at present all one sees is a finely built wall which must have been constructed many ages ago (Cieza 1959:282–283).

Further, it appears the indigenous inhabitants had no idea who had constructed the monuments or who had once inhabited the site. Cieza continues,

> I asked the natives, in the presence of Juan Vargas (who holds an encomienda over them), if these buildings had been built in the time of the Incas, and they laughed at the question, repeating what I have said, that they were built before they reigned, but that they could not state or affirm who built them. . . . I say that it might have been that before the Incas ruled, there were people of parts in these kingdoms, come from no one knows where, who did these things, and who, being few and the natives many, perished in the wars (Cieza 1959:284).

For Cieza, as for many later writers, neither the native groups inhabiting the ruins and their environs nor their ancestors were capable of creating such impeccable monuments. Until recently, Western explorers and researchers rarely considered a connection between the culture that produced Tiwanaku and the local traditions, daily routines, and periodic festivals of later indigenous groups.

Father Bernabe Cobo, a Jesuit priest who composed a synthetic chronicle of Inca culture and history during the first half of the seventeenth century, reiterated Cieza's assumptions. He noted of Tiwanaku,

> the fact of the matter is that the Indians do not remember any of these things; they all confess that it is such an ancient construction that their information does not go back that far. However, they do agree on one thing. The buildings were already constructed many years before the Incas started to govern. In fact, it is widely reported among the Indians themselves that the Incas made their great

> edifices in Cuzco as well as in other parts of their kingdom on the model of this place (Cobo 1990:103–104).

The local cultural amnesia regarding the ruins of Tiwanaku supported European beliefs in the existence of an ancient, extinct master race of people who built and inhabited the site. Natives' apparent lack of identification with the monuments implicates a social disjuncture sometime in the pre-Colonial past, and shapes a basic line of inquiry in this book. I compare relatively unexplored dimensions of Tiwanaku, its local urban living spaces and ritual activities, in an attempt to understand who the Tiwanaku were and why their memory was already so obscured, according to some chroniclers, by the time of European contact.

Two decades of intensive research in the high plateau, or *altiplano*, of the Bolivian Andes indicates that Tiwanaku was the center of a prehispanic polity that influenced much of the south-central Andes for more than six centuries, from AD 500 to AD 1150. The polity's demographic, cultural, and political core was located in the southern Lake Titicaca Basin, at some 3,800 meters above sea level (see Chapter 1, Figure 1.1). At this altitude, native subsistence and political economy presented unique challenges. The domesticated species most important to humans included llamas, alpacas, and guinea pigs (or *cuy*), and chenopodium (or *quinoa*), tubers, and broad beans (*tarwi*). Many other goods considered significant among high altitude populations, notably maize and coca, were acquired from groups in warmer subtropical valleys to the east and west. Because markets never fully developed in the Andes, as they had in Mesoamerica and Mesopotamia, such goods were acquired through a variety of other mechanisms ranging from llama-caravan exchange to direct colonization. A desire for highly valued exotic goods such as coca and maize, in part, motivated the imperial designs of Tiwanaku leaders and the panregional influence of their ideology.

This book explores Tiwanaku over the long term, a fifteen-hundred-year history beginning just before the onset of the Christian era and ending just before the first Inca imperial expeditions entered the Lake Titicaca Basin in the fifteenth century. It consists of four parts. Part I establishes the theoretical and methodological foundations of the investigation, Part II outlines the emergence and development of the Tiwanaku state, Part III narrates the consolidation and collapse of the polity, and Part IV offers concluding syntheses. Rather than providing a general overview of Tiwanaku history and culture, I focus on Tiwanaku and Lukurmata, the two sites that for several centuries were its principal political, cultural, and ritual centers. The sites occupy adjacent valleys, Tiwanaku and Katari respectively, which together formed Tiwanaku's political and cultural heartland. I trace the history of the two sites from their emergence as independent settlements, through their expansion as prestigious ceremonial cities, to their demographic decline. I elaborate a perspective of the Tiwanaku polity that emphasizes the residential, largely nonelite, and highly diverse populations who inhabited the two centers. This perspective has been neglected in conventional interpretations, which tend to emphasize Tiwanaku's prestigious ceremonial complexes, its integrative state institutions, or its nonurban kin-based organizations.

To investigate identity and power in Tiwanaku, I develop in Chapter 1 a practice perspective, by which I mean an approach that emphasizes the ongoing give-and-take between human actions, strategies, and interests, on the one hand, and their specific generative cultural principles on the other. Such an approach helps steer archaeological interpretation away from the essentialism embedded in concepts such as "group," "chiefdom," and "state." It allows us to detail the dynamic roles played by diverse groups and to ask why they participated in and identified with a polity such as Tiwanaku. I address the means by which political and cultural hegemony are internalized as natural, commonsense understandings of the world, and yet simultaneously questioned, transformed, or openly contested. By emphasizing culturally informed practices and practical intentions as they shifted over time, I illuminate the intricate historical processes involved in state rise, consolidation, and collapse, and in the creation of poststate societies.

Anchoring this approach to an archaeological investigation of the high Andes, Chapter 2 synthesizes documented patterns of sociopolitical organization, ritual activity, and spatial order in the post-Conquest south-central Andes. I believe that, when used critically, ethnohistorical and ethnographic analogy are powerful methods for comprehending archaeological patterns. I discuss later societies to highlight forms of identity, polity, cosmology, urbanism, and regional interaction that characterized the south-central Andean highlands over the past five hundred years. Primarily, these societies are understood on their own terms, and their characteristics form an introduction to patterns of life and society and of ritual and landscape in the region. Secondarily, patterns of post-Conquest society and culture provide useful, historically contingent analogies for the more distant past, and thus provide one element in a more comprehensive epistemology of archaeological interpretation.

In Chapter 3, I evaluate the implications of three general intellectual traditions regarding Tiwanaku's history and character. An old tradition emphasizes the symbolic and ritual significance of Tiwanaku, and in some interpretations the principal site is considered an uninhabited ceremonial center. The dominant tradition holds that Tiwanaku was the densely inhabited center of a centralized native state; following some of these interpretations, state leaders forged an empire by aggressively conquering and controlling much of the south-central Andes. A more recent tradition holds that Tiwanaku was characterized by significant local power and autonomy. According to some interpretations in this vein, Tiwanaku was a federation of autonomous groups.

I argue that relations of state and community were intricate and in flux, always mediated through both shared and contested understandings of the cosmos as well as diverse forms of domestic and ritual practice. While no intellectual tradition is entirely off the mark, none captures Tiwanaku in its history and intricacy, for each ultimately seeks to find in Tiwanaku a fundamental determining essence, whether in symbol, state, or society. Two dimensions that are critical for outlining a more nuanced interpretation of Tiwanaku are social diversity and historical change. Even though the polity cohered through valued symbols, characteristic practices, and ultimately, through profound cultural hegemony, sociopolitical hierarchy, and transformative strategies of integration, Tiwanaku was socially diverse and ideologically syncretic. Further, while certain ideals and practices retained their significance for centuries, the character of the polity and of the predominant relations among its constituent groups changed significantly over time.

Chapters 4 through 9 follow a temporal framework punctuated by three successive chronological periods; Late Formative (100 BC–AD 500), Tiwanaku (AD 500–1150), and Early Pacajes (AD 1150–1450). In Chapter 4, I discuss evidence for residential activity and ritual places at both sites during the Late Formative, when Lukurmata and, in particular, Tiwanaku emerged as major regional centers, each the focus of distinct social networks, shifting political alliances, and diverse ritual activities. I highlight the roles local groups played in promoting Tiwanaku's prestige and legitimacy and in forging the early state. Chapter 5 consists of a comparison of residential and ritual areas dating to the first phase of the Tiwanaku Period, Tiwanaku IV (AD 500–800), during which Tiwanaku emerged as the vast, densely inhabited center of a panregional Andean state. Tiwanaku was, in part, a cosmopolitan city housing groups maintaining vibrant local identities. In Chapter 6 I discuss residential and ritual places dating to Tiwanaku IV in Lukurmata, by which time the site was a major regional center of ritual prestige and political power in the Katari Valley. Lukurmata became Tiwanaku's "second city," but it remained a local center inhabited by groups who continually reproduced a vibrant, common ethnic-like identity.

I investigate transformations in residence and ritual that changed the face of Tiwanaku during Early Tiwanaku V (AD 800–1000) in Chapter 7. Massive urban renewal in Tiwanaku attests to powerful elite factions that sought to legitimize their privileged roles in society and in the cosmos through state ceremonies and sponsored rituals of consumption. Chapter 8 examines Early Tiwanaku V occupations in Lukurmata, which, somewhat paradoxically, declined in population and importance between AD 800 and 900. Diagnostic evidence for the causes of Lukurmata's decline comes from the surrounding floodplain of the Katari Valley, which was simultaneously converted into a centrally managed agricultural estate. Discussion of Tiwanaku influence outside of the core, specifically on the Island of the Sun in Bolivia and in the Moquegua Valley in southern Peru, sheds additional light on the nature of the transformations. Changes in many Tiwanaku peripheral zones demonstrate intensified state influence and an interest in producing certain consumable goods, specifically maize, in mass quantities.

Chapter 9 outlines state fragmentation and the development of post-Tiwanaku society in Late Tiwanaku V (AD 1000–1100/1150). Tiwanaku collapse, I argue, was triggered by the onset of a long-term drought, but it evolved out of the volatile social relations and conflicting ideals that had characterized Tiwanaku throughout the state's history. Contrary to some conventional views, Tiwanaku does not appear to have succumbed to waves of immigrating Aymara. Collapse was a cultural resurgence that involved profound realignment in local identity and power relations, and it produced a heterarchical sociopolitical landscape of polities and communities that maintained certain traditional practices and boundaries. The region experienced many later transformations, including the successive establishment of Inca, Spanish, and Bolivian regimes and their distinctive manners of appropriating Tiwanaku to different hegemonic ends. Nevertheless, Tiwanaku's documented cultural amnesia, a partly intentional rupture in local memory and identity, was an integral part of collapse itself.

Attention to identity and power, elemental in the dynamic historical play of social activity and cultural principles and of novelty and tradition, brings us a little closer to understanding a complex and enigmatic archaeological phenomenon such as Tiwanaku. I believe, in turn, that such a perspective of a past formation such as Tiwanaku offers critical insight into current interpretive emphases in anthropology. It points the way toward a balanced approach to cultural change and continuity and to social diversity and coherence. In reaction to the essentialism inherent in functional, structural, and culturalist approaches in anthropology, it is commonly assumed following certain strands of postmodernism that societies past and present have changed incessantly and profoundly. Such assumptions render attention to continuities in identity, ideology, and many social practices irrelevant and doom the use of ethnohistorical analogy to failure. Hand in hand with this idea goes the critical stance that social coherence, such as that embedded in conventional ideas of culture or polity, is a hegemonic construct that anthropologists conceptually impose on evanescent, inconsistent, and often contradictory social relations and ideals.

This investigation of the Andean polity of Tiwanaku finds a more felicitous balance between continuity and change, social coherence and fragmentation, cultural tradition and strategic action. With its attention to the long term, archaeology is well positioned to outline the contextual specificity of the current stance in the social sciences. A view emphasizing evanescence and fragmentation, like any worldview, is grounded in a particular experience, in this case one that emphasizes the rapid, volatile, and increasingly global transformations in which we are currently engaged. Change is indeed continuous; cultures such as Tiwanaku are inevitably forgotten; and particularly dynamic historical junctures, even times analogous to our current experience, have occurred again and again. This should not blind us to the fact that symbols, ideals, and practices often transcend the rise and fall of civilizations—such as a Christian cross, a patriarchal nuclear family, or a market economy—despite shifts in role and meaning. It should neither blind us to the fact that in many societies, most of the time, continuity—often grounded in the idealized actions of mythical ancestors—held a greater purchase on peoples' ideals and realities than it tends to in our own. While simultaneously transformative, human actions are shaped by cultural principles, principles that to a great extent, in imparting meaning to those actions, are conservative. Nevertheless, out of human activity, and from the mutually generative relations of thought and action, emerge new views and creative ways of living in, acting upon, and transforming the world. Ultimately, it is entirely through situated human activity and social relations, among commoners as much as elites, that states such as Tiwanaku rose, gained prestige, influenced vast regions, and collapsed.

PART 1

CHAPTER 1

Identity and Power in the Past

Theory concerning the rise and constitution of past complex societies has struggled with the relation of *state* and *society*. Many models, and some drawing on Durkheim's concept of *organic solidarity*, have stressed the role of integrative institutions. Seminal in this vein was the work of Elman Service (1975:53), which considered everything in complex societies, including "technological, economic, religious, artistic, and recreational functions . . ." as "depend[ent] on the ability of the political aspect of the culture to integrate and protect the society." Other models have stressed the roles of internal tensions and ranking in the rise of complexity, a broad perspective well-summarized in Morton Fried's remark (1967:27) that "[e]quality is a social impossibility." Models in this tradition, influenced to varying degrees by Marxist social thought, take the position that states fundamentally institute inequality.

While at first blush dissimilar, these two perspectives differ largely in the moral value attributed to the interests of the state, and to the place, fate, and relative power of the people. Different values involve divergent analytical emphases regarding the relative role of political structures, economic redistribution, and religious ideology. Yet, such sweeping approaches to the rise and character of colonial regimes and states—whether viewed from above or below, whether conceptually grounded in organic solidarity or in class divisions, and whether the moral emphasis leans toward central institutions or toward subaltern communities—share common epistemological foundations. Searching for commonalities has fostered an essentialized view of past complex orders as relatively homogeneous formations. Implicit in the sociological category of *state* are shared assumptions regarding the composition of complexity, the dynamics of history, and the significance of power, identity, and cultural practice.

Most archaeologists agree that archaic states were urban societies rooted in agrarian or agropastoral pursuits, and that they maintained a relatively stable (or "non-fissioning") centralized political structure (Claessen 1984; Cohen 1981; Cohen and Service 1978; Wright 1977; Wright and Johnson 1975). Whether emphasizing integration or inequality, conventional approaches to complexity typically invoke societies characterized simultaneously by political integration on the one hand, and social heterogeneity on the other. Social heterogeneity refers to differences in role or occupation, while status, characterized as an expression of integration (Service 1975; Wright and Johnson 1975) or of inequality (Blau 1977; Fried 1967; McGuire 1983), refers to differences in wealth, prestige, or power (following Weber 1947). Dimensions of social difference not necessarily grounded in role or status, including ethnicity, faction, kinship, age group, or gender, are all too frequently underemphasized or altogether ignored (but see Brumfiel 1994, 1995; Crumley 1987, 1995; Demarest 1992, 2004; Feinman 2000; Joyce and Winter 1996; Joyce et al. 2001; Joyce 2000; Pauketat 1994, 2000; among others).

Most models of complexity in the social sciences (not to mention in everyday common sense) are, to one extent or another, rooted in an evolutionary paradigm. Conventional evolutionary approaches narrate a natural progression of increasing cultural complexity that is characterized by either increasingly effective integration or increasing inequality (e.g., Flannery 1972; Fried 1967; Service 1975; Steward 1955; White 1949). In either approach history is largely hypothetical, a mythical exegesis—whether legitimization or critique—of the genesis of a modern Western-dominated civilization of nation states. Recent models elaborate intricate processes of social change and long-term cycles of state rise and fall (Marcus 1992, 1993; Wright 1984), while developing more intricate approaches to the relation between cultural processes, historical events, and individual actions (Flannery 1999). Even in some recent models, however, attention to human strategy and activity in explaining social transformation falls squarely on leaders, chiefs, or other ruling elites—in fact, they verge on heroic narratives. Human motivation is largely one-dimensional and predictable. People, it is assumed, invariably seek wealth, prestige, and power. History is treated as a natural unfolding of the specific moral value attributed to the state, with scant attention to nonelite interests, strategies, and actions on the one hand, or to the particular cultural logics that inform them on the other. Overall, evolutionary models treat complex societies as vast, self-serving systems, whether of benevolent integration or of inequality.

Yet, social systems and structures consist solely of human relations and activities. Of conventional models Lewellen (1983:60) notes, "[o]ne feels the need. . . to reestablish the sense that we are talking about real human beings—living, dying, warring, struggling to make it against the odds." In many models the everyday relations and activities that compose past polities, the "concrete rhythms of daily life" (Ensor 2000), are significant only to the extent that they affect or support the system. Individuals and groups, by the same token, are significant insofar as they fill a rank or a role. Living day to day and doing archaeology or any other work, we have a practical sense that this is not the case. Just as we do not completely live and work for the institutions or political systems in which we find ourselves, and we do not entirely agree with their ideals, methods, and aims, neither did people living in past complex societies. We must assume that, to some degree, life in past complex societies was also multifaceted, and that humans, most of the time, maintained diverse interests and reasons for living and doing.

Pointing out what appears deceptively obvious, Anthony Giddens (1979:7) notes that "social systems have no purpose, reasons or needs whatsoever; only human individuals do so." Societies exist only insofar as they are created, reproduced, reformulated, and destroyed through social relations and activity—relations and activity that shape and are transfigured by enduring "structuring structures" (Bourdieu 1977:22). While much human motivation and activity in past states clearly supported state power and centralizing strategies, most extended well beyond that limited domain, as is resolutely demonstrated in the collapse of many past states (e.g., Demarest et al. 1997). In seeking to illuminate the rise, consolidation, and ultimate fragmentation of past states such as Tiwanaku, we must address a fuller range of cultural logic and social practice.

In this chapter I establish a theoretical foundation for what I consider a deeper understanding of past complex societies such as Tiwanaku, and an epistemological framework for elaborating dynamic models for state rise, consolidation, and collapse. Like Philip Corrigan and Derek Sayer (1985:7–8), I believe traditional and current models attribute too much concreteness to "the *idea* of the state," and take too literally the "message of its domination (emphasis added)," whether celebrating or critiquing its specific interests and ends. Suspiciously resonant with popular (and populist) political ideas and corporate management strategies, many political models take for granted the "noun-ness" of states, and so mirror their politically interested appearance of impenetrability and solidity.

I address such assumptions in two ways. First, and again to quote Corrigan and Sayer (1985:3), the "activities and institutions conventionally identified as 'the State' are cultural forms." States *state* and establish truth. They foster emotional attachment to a range of things both material and ideal, forging a state culture that is in appearance common, global, and timeless. States are, in addition, as Durkheim noted (1904:72) "above all, supremely, the organ of moral discipline," and they seek to normalize, render natural, and establish as obvious, what are, in reality, contextually and historically specific ideological premises. The affective, symbolic, and ideological dimensions of society's power were implicated (in varying senses) in Durkheim's collective conscience, in Weber's legitimacy, and in Marx's ponderous traditions. Yet an approach that weighs in such domains must also consider activity that transcends state functions, symbols, and interests. Thus, and second, we must consider all of society, differentiated as it was in regard to gender, class, ethnicity, territory, lineage, ancestry, and ritual. A long-term perspective may clarify in what ways group identities and local practices emerged and shifted over phases of state emergence, development, consolidation, and collapse. In considering a wide range of social groups and practices in an archaic state, and by paying close attention to transformations at multiple scales, we may understand how a unifying dominant ideology and homogenizing state culture were differentially interpreted, refracted, and even appropriated and reinterpreted in myriad ways, for specific local interests and, perhaps, in some cases, to counterhegemonic ends.

In the following pages I elaborate a theoretical perspective of identity and power as culturally grounded social relations amenable to archaeological research on past states. First, drawing on established ideas, I develop a framework for identifying social activity as cultural production, and generative principles as human activity. Next, I establish a foundation for understanding this relation in the long term, over spans of relative continuity and phases of profound cultural and political change. I then investigate the place of power in complex society by focusing on ideology and what I term "practical hegemony" as two dimensions of state culture and social consciousness. Next, I investigate social identity, expressed as ethnicity and other types of affiliation, as a potent element of power relations in settings of state hegemony. The discussion then turns to power and identity in past cities, the political and ritual centers of archaic states, and their possible expressions in built environments and anthropogenic landscapes. Together, these themes establish a conceptual foundation for appreciating the place of power and identity in the rise and collapse of Tiwanaku.

A Perspective on Practice

In archaeology we often deal with relatively broad scales of human history, the *langue durée*, or "history with a slower pulse rate" (Braudel 1980:95). Much of what we survey, excavate, or analyze is the collective residue of processes that occurred over generations. In treating long-term history, we need not assume that change "just happened," that societies simply evolved into states, or that day-to-day events and real human intentions were insignificant. As cultural anthropology increasingly turns to the particular and the evanescent in its focus on the global present, archaeology is advantageously positioned to highlight relatively enduring principles of social life, and the significance of recurring activity and entrenched relations. To use a visual metaphor, the relation between scales of history is similar to the different ways one experiences a city like Chicago, whether from its gritty, bustling streets or from a place a hundred stories above. As observers in a skyscraping deck we enjoy a unique perspective, and may be able to discern a world of macro-patterns not immediately apparent to a window shopper on State Street. Archaeologists are well positioned to apprehend the significance of phases in which social practices and material culture changed gradually and in subtle ways, and times when, following cumulative transformations, they changed rapidly and profoundly.

Archaeology requires a flexible theoretical approach that considers long-term history as cumulative social practices and historical events. Attention to the long term draws us into the domain of *praxis*, a "situational sociology of meaning" (Sahlins 1985:xiv) in which we can investigate culture through time. So-called practice theory has fostered some understanding of the dialectical relation of cultural principles and human actions, yet no approach effectively grasps all dimensions of this complex relation. Pierre Bourdieu's (1977) concept of *habitus*, as the subliminal "generative schemes" that humans unconsciously draw on while going about life, establishes a foundation. Habitus, according to Bourdieu, is an internalized, malleable system of dispositions— a common sense mastery of situations—that generates particular practices. These practices are similar among people sharing similar circumstances and experiences (a family, community, ethnic group, etc.), appearing harmonized and ordered without recourse to overt rules or laws. The dispositions of habitus are commonsense traditions beyond argument, for "what is essential goes without saying because it comes without saying" (Bourdieu 1977:167). However, in this view there is ultimately little attention to how such dispositions induce social change. Novel human intentions play a relatively minor role in the habitus, for the "conditional freedom it secures is as remote from a creation of unpredictable novelty as it is from a simple mechanical reproduction of things as they are" (Bourdieu 1977:95).

Giddens' (1979) research on structuration, increasingly popular among archaeologists (e.g., Barrett 1994; Joyce and Winter 1996; Joyce et al. 2001; Dobres and Robb 2000), offers more powerful roles for human action and intention. The concept of structuration emphasizes the dialectical relation of "structure" and "action." Less deterministically than humans drawing on habitus, Giddens' humans are knowledgeable individuals who go about life drawing on "tacit stocks of knowledge," a more *informed* common sense. In going about daily life, humans intervene in the world through intentional and continuous flows of activity or "agency," in which they draw on practical knowledge and, to some extent, reproduce the social world. By continually engaging in society "every actor knows a great deal about the conditions of [its] reproduction" (Giddens 1979:5), and so is empowered with some "discursive penetration" of its workings, however limited and incompletely comprehended. Thus, intentional or not, activity often has powerful consequences, and given changing circumstances beyond the control or awareness of any agent, these consequences can produce major—even unexpected—changes. Empowered with knowledge and potential action, all humans, elite and commoner, ruler and subject, can effect profound change, even if, ultimately, the specific, cumulative consequences are unintended.

Following such epistemologies and inhabiting a world of fast-paced change, ephemeral relations, and virtual realities, anthropologists now generally privilege the individual over structure, strategic action over essential order. Anthropologists focus on cultural mutability and multiple voices as part of a shared cultural experience. Culture is a "carnivalesque arena of diversity" (Clifford 1988:46) more than it forms an "integrated ethos" (Ortner 1984:131) or patterned "webs of significance" (Geertz 1973). According to what many now consider outmoded culturalist approaches (Sahlins 1985:47), "culture" too restrictively determines historical reality, and hegemonic representations weigh too heavily on the brains of the living (Obeyesekere 1997). Some suggest leaving behind the concept of culture altogether as an essentialized, colonial construct (Abu-Lughod 1991).

To be sure, increasing interest in diversity and cultural discontinuity challenges a "dominant modernist identity" that celebrates essentialized "others" and invented national histories (Friedman 1994:117). It encourages awareness that just about anywhere, past or present, culture is negotiable, symbols can be separated from things, and meaning systems are cognitively and strategically fashioned. Constructivists point out that contemporary ethnic movements and other identity struggles, in the face of global processes, often involve the "invention of tradition," the intentional creation of cultural identity, and the strategic manipulation of history to support new identities (Anderson 1983; Hobsbawm 1983).

Yet, I agree with Emberling that many anthropologists "tend to overestimate the potential for manipulation in past societies" (Emberling 1997:307). As Van den Berghe notes (1981:27) of ethnicity, it "can be manipulated but not manufactured." People forge their identities and create traditions "in a world already defined," both locally and globally, for "the past is always practiced in the present" (Friedman 1994:117, 141; Holland et al. 1998:46). Though often strategic, invented traditions and crafted identities involve significant historical and cultural continuity. Jing notes that "no tradition is invented overnight" (1996:45) for "whatever is invented must be adjusted to meet various social considerations and cultural conventions" (1996:68). Current emphasis on cultural evanescence reflects the peculiar corporate anonymity and cynical disjunction of symbol and reference in our current brand of capitalism (see Sennett 1998). Even if there is no coherent order that regulates all activities in a given community, activities are learned and "organized around sets of situated understandings and expectations" that have been, to a great extent, already established in the past (Holland et al. 1998:57).

In any society past or present, activities are learned in and organized by what Dorothy Holland and colleagues (1998:52) term "figured worlds." These are culturally configured realms in which "particular characters and actors are recognized, significance is assigned to certain acts, and particular outcomes are valued over others." This concept situates the actions of knowledgeable, empowered agents in enduring realms of shared experience, memory, and identity, and in "contexts of meaning and action." In figured worlds people develop statuses and roles, including positions of influence, prestige, and power, and most important, they "develop identities" (Holland et al. 1998:60). A figured world is a social domain that is, in part, collectively imagined and in part the product of concrete, regularized activity—as it is in the world of politics or academia, or among communities in a specific cultural context, whether totemic clans in aboriginal native Australia or nation states in the modern West. As individuals develop in specific instances of these worlds, in a particular family, gender, age group, ethnic group, and nation, for example, they bring creative ideas to them, authoring their own idiosyncratic narratives and actions. Through time, they become more familiar with their logics, more knowledgeable about their inner workings, and, via mimicry and creative appropriation, they change them just as they reproduce them.

Practice theory offers no coherent explanation of state development and collapse, but it establishes that complex societies consist of people whose actions involve dynamic relations between generative principles (webs of significance, generative schemes, or tacit knowledge) and practical activity (culturally situated but often creative and transformative actions). On such a foundation we can formulate models in which all individuals, and not just rulers and elites, continually transform culture and society (just as they reproduce them). We can also begin to understand how individuals participating in specific figured worlds come to hold different perspectives, interpretations, and political views of a given social order.

Still, archaeologists require models that, in applying these concepts, can account for the significance of cultural continuity in relation to profound, cumulative, and sometimes relatively rapid change. Since this is a primary aim of the book, it bears elaborating a few key concepts.

Continuity and Change

In all societies, certain key values, symbols, and elements of material culture demonstrate significant historical continuity. If we accept that humans actively create and recreate their worlds, continuity cannot be taken for granted; it must be explained as cultural production. Recently, anthropologists have begun paying serious attention to the continuities and even strategic essentialism that ground current indigenous movements. Fischer (1999, 2001), for example, finds that among contemporary Maya, certain ancient cosmological paradigms demonstrate great historical and regional continuity. This is in part because they serve to inform novel situations and impart meaning to new interpretations and actions. Enlisted in the volatile process of generating a pan-Maya identity, ancient paradigms manifest a fundamental cultural logic, or a web of generative principles, that provides cultural coherence even if conditioned by novel contingencies (Fischer 1999:474). Anchoring them are "authentic" artifacts, symbols, and gestures—glyphs, calendar systems, traditional dress, ritual practices, and monumental sites—that draw the past into the present, even if fragmentarily and creatively and their meanings radically transformed. In Maya identity politics, cultural "continuity is maintained by giving old forms new meaning and new forms old meaning" (Fischer 2001:13).

Historical consciousness or collective memory forms an essential part of a community's generative principles, linking the past and present with visions of the future. Among the contemporary Maya as elsewhere, it is inscribed in various nonwritten activities, objects, places, and social contexts as domains for expressing and reifying social memory (Chesson 2001; George 1996; Hendon 2000; Jing 1996; Rappaport 1990). In the Andes (as discussed in Chapter 2), woven clothing, ceramic decoration, oral narratives, songs, pilgrimages, landscapes, burial sites, political rituals, and even intricate libation sequences all evoke social memories particular to a group (Abercrombie 1998; Poole 1984). In emotional or politically charged contexts, including mortuary rituals or commemorative feasts, such memories vividly bring the past into the present, often recharging and reformulating a sense of group identity. History, forged in the present as shared memory, and evoked in charged activities or fantastical images, establishes a sense of temporal continuity and social coherence, legitimizing group interests and motivating political action. Group historical consciousness is not static, but rather "an ongoing process of interpretation whereby accounts are constantly assembled and reassembled" (Rappaport 1990:11). As native activists around the world demonstrate, the past has its uses: to some degree, it can be appropriated, fashioned, and redesigned to achieve practical ends in encompassing hegemonic worlds. Nevertheless, in no small part because such interests demand legitimacy, the things drawn upon are often images, monuments, and ideas rooted in the past.

Certain principles and practices may, therefore, endure dramatic sociopolitical changes. For example, Sahlins (1981, 1985, 2000) and Kirch (1984, 2000) interpret historical Polynesian chiefdoms as "performative" or "open" societies. For them such societies were "virtual," their hierarchical sociopolitical systems shifting continually, often dramatically, in relation to both local events and external circumstances (Sahlins 1985:153). These and similar societies pose problems for conventional cultural evolutionary thinking because, while they at once formed hierarchical "paramount chiefdoms," some appeared less than a century later as relatively egalitarian societies (Kirch 1984, 2000)—and others vice versa (Sahlins 1981). In addition, the more hierarchical these societies became, the more volatile were their sociopolitical structures. Social tensions in collaboration with demographic pressures and environmental conditions kept the formation of centralized states in check and the political life of the islands in flux. Still, certain mythical narratives, like that of the hero deity Lono, and widely shared religious ideals, such as *mana*, remained fundamental cultural principles, generating meaningful and traditional practices over the past two centuries.

Even relatively volatile societies, like those comprising Polynesian and recent Western civilizations, are characterized by certain principles of the long term, a continued vitality of certain images, master narratives, cosmic principles, historical genres, descent principles, and forms of social and economic relations. Specific meanings and practices change over the long run, in relation to shifting local, regional, interregional, even global conditions. Nevertheless, in many past societies, including many prehispanic civilizations, one's life ideally mimicked and "relived" those told in stories of past ancestors or culture heroes. We find this frequently: Moche rulers and priests dressing as archetypical mythical figures, or Maya elites invoking deceased lineage founders for advice and legitimacy. To the extent that traditions remain vibrant or their images present (e.g., Classic Maya temples), the past, even in entirely new domains of power relations and practical interests, is continually drawn into the present as certain elements are inevitably transformed—some, such as sociopolitical conditions, often more radically than others. In Western civilization, after two millennia of dramatic cultural changes and the rise and fall of countless civilizations, the cross is still a cross (despite profound changes and variations in meaning), an ancient sign of suffering, sacrifice, and redemption, and a symbol of common identity and shared memory for those who identify as Christians.

Nevertheless, entire ways of life and their attendant memories occasionally transform dramatically, as cumulative shifts and tensions intersect with a particular historical juncture. People and their material culture are always subject to unforeseen circumstances, and so society is transformed just as it is reproduced, if usually at a relatively slow pulse-rate. Everyday activities become significant events to the extent that they summon up and alter a society's deep cultural principles. In Fiji in 1841, for example, a fight over a pig incited a major war between two polities (Sahlins 2000). The event is understandable considering rising political tensions in Fiji in relation to the generative principles summoned up in the event—including those governing kin relations, marriage patterns, rights of royalty, and the symbolic value of pigs. For the most part people went about their lives, following their own projects and interests but not necessarily interested in changing the status quo. Yet over generations each action and each event, though informed by shared principles and ideals, was "burdened with the world," the volatile world of evershifting conditions (Sahlins 1985:138, 144). At particular historical junctures, such as occurred in 1841, everyday activities suddenly, and profoundly transformed society and its generative principles.

Such a perspective affords some understanding of the complexities involved in continuities and changes in history. Investigating Tiwanaku cities requires that we bring this type of historical approach down to earth, in the double sense of treating material culture and addressing the roles played by all of society, including those usually glossed as "commoners." To do this, we require dynamic approaches to power and identity that build on this perspective of practice and history.

Practice and Power

A practice approach to the relation of culture and action establishes a foundation for understanding social power in past states. Three points about power are important here; Power is pervasive; it inhabits culture; and it is productive. Typically, the apex of a political system, its leaders or government, are considered the principal locus of power in complex societies. For Service, state rulers serve, and for Fried, they appropriate, but for both they ultimately wield "the power." Ruling authority can be considered traditional, "shrouded in symbols" and legitimized by an ancient order (Weber 1947); it can be considered "naked," or openly secured by force of arms (Russell 1938); or it can be considered rational, and efficiently distributed among decisionmakers in a bureaucracy (Weber 1947). In all such views, leaders possess and exercise power, which is assumed to be a repressive force that descends from on high to inhibit social action. Power in this view is exerted *over* society, from a place above and to some extent outside of it. Faithful to enduring Western myths for the origins of inequality, "royalty is a foreigner" and power "a barbarian" (Dumézil 1973; Sahlins 1985:79).

Rather, power is an intrinsic condition of society. As Foucault observed (1980:142), power is made manifest in diverse cultural institutions and social relations and is "co-extensive with the social body;" no one is "outside of" power, for "there are no spaces of primal liberty between the meshes of its network." This is implicit in the mutual engagement of persons in figured worlds and hegemonic social orders. To the extent that they participate in such contexts, imbued with their generative logics and schemes, they are, however minimally, empowered. To the extent that they improvise, authoring their own ideas and actions in the face of novel circumstances, they actively, wittingly or not, transform those contexts and their attendant social relations (Joyce et al. 2001). In any social world, "power relations are always two-way . . . [for] however subordinate an actor may be in a social relationship, the very fact of involvement in that relationship gives him or her a certain amount of power over the other" (Giddens 1979:6).

Power is neither simply wielded as an object nor exchanged like a commodity. Rather it is a condition of social relations and their attendant cultural logics and ideological constructs. One way of discussing power is to distinguish its relatively subliminal and conscious manifestations as "two modalities" in a common cultural field (Comaroff and Comaroff 1991:28). We can speak on the one hand of what I term "practical hegemony," drawing on Gramsci's (1971:328) idea of a predominant "conception of the world that is implicitly manifest" in practical activity and "all manifestations of individual and collective life." Melding this idea to Bourdieu's habitus and Giddens' practical consciousness, the Comaroffs (1992:28) invoke such a concept in reference to the ideals and practices in a community that come to be "taken for granted as the natural, universal, and true shape of the social being." Practical hegemony, then, refers to the deep order of things, an underlying network of structures, symbols, and actions that are presumed to be natural—the way things are and always have been (also Bloch 1977; Kertzer 1988). It inhabits practical consciousness as "common sense," informing practices that are taken for granted and in most circumstances uncontested. Dimensions of practical hegemony in the United States include private property, the value of education, democratic political process, the nuclear family as primordial group, and the concept of a citizen's "inalienable rights."

Ideology in a specific sense refers to "a programmatic presentation of the world" that promotes "the legitimacy of an existing socio-political order" (Smith 2000:136). More broadly defined, ideology also encompasses the often articulated ideals and practices of a social group, and it inhabits the views, actions, and styles that are readily brought to consciousness. Ideology informs the "discursive penetration" of social worlds and the relative categorization of some people as "others" and some actions as abominable. For example, it underlies the idea that combatting communism or terrorism is fighting for freedom. Groups or subcultures in a common cultural or political field may hold different ideologies. It is often in the domain of ideology that people consciously distinguish themselves from others in actions, ritual practices, speech dialects, or material styles. It is often ideological that participants in subcultures, factions, interest groups, a gender, or any figured world, as subgroups within a broader social formation, consciously apprehend and identify one another.

The predominant ideology at any time is usually that of a dominant group. If leaders invariably seek to create anything, it is "truth," which is given popular expression in popular myths and master narratives. Yet probably in no system of inequality is a dominant ideology simply imposed (see Kertzer 1988). Custodians of an ideology, a particular rationalization of the world, must seek to "appropriate the consciousness of individuals" and groups (Pauketat 1994:15; also Kertzer 1988). They promote their view as a convincing, empowering, and perhaps ecumenical cosmology; one that effectively explains the world as it appears (or is becoming) and one that involves or promises some symbolic or practical benefit, whether now, in the future, or in an afterlife. Dominant groups may "seek to establish a universal diffusion of the acceptance" of the values associated with this worldview (Shils 1975:9), but in order to be "diffused" and internalized such values must have some redemptive value. A cosmology must offer its adherents "some advantageous ways of acting" (Bell 1997:81), some position of relative influence or prestige in the social and cosmic order, and it must tap nonrational domains of emotional or spiritual resonance.

To understand the dynamic relation of practical hegemony and ideology we must explore the idea that power is ultimately productive. Michel Foucault (1965, 1979) dedicated much of his career to discovering how emergent sociopolitical and cultural orders, through a multitude of institutions and characteristic social relations (as significant loci for power relations), construct specific types of individuals and entire bodies of knowledge. Many find his vision of the world, vacated by Enlightenment's "primal liberty" and in which "power is everywhere in society" (Sahlins 1996:407), a dark one. But for Foucault (1980:142) "there are no relations of power without resistances." From the French Revolution to the Punk movement, resistances are "real and effective because they are formed right at the point where relations of power are exercised" (ibid.). In this regard the Sex Pistols' impromptu concert on the Thames in 1977, in front of Buckingham Palace, was a strategic and effective event now submitted to the history it has helped create. Insofar as individuals can act, improvising on generative schemes in distinct figured worlds, domination and more subtle forms of subjugation implicate resistance. Resistance may be expressed in open reaction and violence, but most often it will be expressed in more subtle terms, as specific practices, ritual productions (including impromptu rock concerts), manners of dress, body decoration, and in the material styles one produces and uses—the things one's identity inhabits (Comaroff 1985; Hebdige 1979; Joyce et al. 2001). It may be expressed in what Scott (1990) calls "hidden transcripts," beyond the gaze or awareness of dominant groups, or more openly, as ethnicity, subculture, or panache. Further, because they are potent, meaningful, and readily available, images and materials associated with a pervasive, dominant worldview are the fairest game for expressing local identity and cultural resistance. Individuals may appropriate, reconstruct, invert, and combine them in novel ways—to simultaneously differentiate themselves from others, in some cases the dominant regime and its master narratives, and to express affiliation with an alternative, often more intimate identity or revolutionary cause (Comaroff 1985; Hebdige 1979).

In most situations, participation in systems of inequality, and the attendant marginality of most groups vis-à-vis a dominant ideology, produce some "contradictory consciousness" (Gramsci 1971:333) or "cognitive dissonance" (Kertzer 1988:97–98). Individuals will "hold contradictory attitudes, beliefs, or values," which because partly submerged in tacit knowledge and common sense, are often expressed unconsciously, inspiring local mannerisms (or dissimulation) that vary from context to context. Thus, the most effective ruling strategies will be the most intimate, effectively promoting cognitive resonance. The more successful they are, "the more of their ideology," the more of their truths, will have disappeared into the domain of practical hegemony (Comaroff and Comaroff 1991:26). A system that consistently insists on coercive strategies, like many totalitarian regimes, is ultimately unstable. Because humans in such a system are empowered with discursive knowledge, not to mention material resources, it is populated disproportionately by residents of a Hobbesian nightmare in which, "there is always within each . . . something that fights something else" (Foucault 1980:208). Each and all will seek some cognitive resonance, cultural coherence, and social resolution through a variety of subtle or, perhaps ultimately, not-so-subtle means.

Hegemonic power and ideological power are interdependent abstract modalities and their domains shift reciprocally through time, often gradually, but sometimes rapidly. As that part of a dominant worldview that is internalized and rendered natural, practical hegemony remains hidden away within accepted and even praised practices and institutions (e.g., educational systems, modern medicine, family planning, manners of socialization, legal procedures, and so on). Even so, it is threatened by cognitive dissonance, and "the vitality that remains in the forms of life it thwarts." If the hegemonic "is constantly being made," it can be unmade (Comaroff and Comaroff 1991:26), especially at volatile historical junctures, following sequences of particularly dynamic and transformative events. Critical here are the unresolved tensions expressed in hidden transcripts and other more or less subtle forms of resistance or difference. Such cumulative tensions occasionally produce tectonic transformations, as occurred in the waves of decolonization that swept South America in the early 1800s and Africa in the 1960s, and in the ethnic resurgence that disintegrated Yugoslavia in the 1990s. At such moments, that which is uncontested can again be brought to light, "reopened for debate," especially once "the contradictions between the world as represented and the world as experienced become ever more palpable, ever more insupportable" (Comaroff and Comaroff 1991:26). Perhaps in conjunction with profound environment, ideological, or political shifts, a social and cultural order may transform profoundly, violently, and rapidly. Such a volatile juncture, I argue, characterized Tiwanaku state collapse.

Identity and Power

Social identity and cultural affiliation figure prominently in the relation of power and culture. Hierarchical structures and historical events are perceived and engaged not necessarily as they are objectively or formally constituted, but subjectively, and in manners that reflect an idea of self in relation to others. Perspectives on a given society or cultural order, discursive knowledge of its workings, and interpretations of its dominant symbols, myths, and master narratives, vary considerably among constituent groups and individuals. Identity is a potent medium through which humans apprehend, navigate, and transform the social and cultural world. I define social identity in respect of the individual, as subjective affiliation with certain people in relation to (or in contrast with) others based on shared memory, place, ancestry, activities, gender, occupation, ritual practices, or cultural expressions. It is all of the characterizations of "us" that a person may use to identify oneself while moving from one social context and cultural domain to the next. As an active participant in many groups, any individual, especially those in urban societies, will juggle numerous nested, overlapping, and partially contradictory social identities at once (Holland et al. 1998; Sökefeld 1999). He or she, developing a tacit mastery in various social situations and figured worlds, will develop a relatively coherent sense of self that subjectively and strategically draws on these multiple identities. Self and situation are always reflexive, for "persons develop through and around the cultural forms by which they are identified, and identify themselves . . . with those associated with those forms and practices" (Holland et al. 1998:33). Through active participation in a variety of social situations, a person develops a sense of self; a relatively coherent identity that permits "at least a modicum of agency or control" in the world (ibid.:40).

Identities are forged in particular social conditions and historical realities that are shaped by power relations and prescriptive political structures. In any social universe, including states and world systems, we can expect to encounter multiple nested scales and overlapping dimensions of affiliation and identity (Cohen 1978). Each type of identification will correspond with a different range of people, memories, practices, places, symbols, and materials. Because a group occupies a unique place in the encompassing sociopolitical order, affiliation with it embodies a distinct network of power relations. At the local end of the continuum, any complex society consists of social groups that maintain corporate functions, or shared political, economic, and ritual activities. In some cases these will be individual households. In others, they are defined as extended families or clans comprising numerous households, as represented in Maya patio groups or Teotihuacan apartment compounds. Implicitly embedded in the activities of such groups, in fact in their existence as a group, is social production and reproduction (Friedman 1994). For constituent individuals and households, these groups, along with their activities and material culture, represent domains of identity and shared memory.

Ethnicity invokes a unique domain of social reproduction and identity. Even though anthropologists and archaeologists often conflate ethnicity and social identity (Cohen 1978; Emberling 1997; Jones 1997), ethnicity is one of its specific manifestations (Comaroff and Comaroff 1992; Royce 1982). Some, in fact, argue that ethnicity as we experience it, as a dynamic component of nationalism, essentially has been invented in contemporary Western nations, as a strategic and effective foundation for asserting claims against national governments (Glazer and Moynihan 1975; Roosens 1989). Certainly, in acknowledging the potency of indigenous movements, it is clear that many elements of ethnic identity can be fabricated relatively quickly, and to profound and widespread effect (De Vos 1995:23–24). Ethnic identity in the twenty-first century is a unique variant of the phenomenon. Nevertheless, broadly defined, ethnicity is a form and scale of identity with a long history in humanity, one that becomes salient in a network of interregional interaction or in a hierarchical political community.

Ethnicity is social identity that falls toward the "macro" end of the continuum. It like other social identities resides in common history or ancestry, a place or territorial landscape, and activities or cultural expressions. It is distinct from more intimate forms of identity in that, as a broad regional collectivity, it is an extensive "imagined community." It is imagined because members identify with persons they only occasionally and perhaps never see, "yet in the minds of each lives the image of their communion" (Anderson 1983:6). It is an encompassing but potentially potent figured world. More intimate communities and corporate groups are also imagined to the extent that activities are not always (or even mostly) collective, and face-to-face interaction is not continuous. But ethnic groups are usually not corporate groups, or at least corporate activity forms a relatively minimal part of their day-to-day coherence and reproduction.

Like other forms of identity, ethnicity is linked to relatively concrete events and phenomena. Ethnic groups may congregate and act together on specific occasions, perhaps periodically for major ceremonies or over a boundary dispute. It may lay dormant for a long time, perhaps barely perceived in practice, until facing a perceived common threat, or under a powerful or charismatic leader, it is recharged and to some extent fabricated. The coherence of such an identity may be tied to a common territory or ritual landscape, a distinct productive regime, land tenure, access to resources in a region, or rituals focused on common ancestors and shared memories. Its coherence also resides in distinctive styles of language and material culture—community spatial plans, architecture, ceramic vessels, body decoration, or dress. Giving expression to a latent sense of affiliation that lives "in the heart and mind," externalized material expressions are the body and soul, or the "symbolic capital" (Bourdieu 1997), of ethnic identity. As symbolic capital, such expressions can be strategically created, manipulated, and transformed at certain historical junctures. As an extensive group with potent symbolic dimensions and a strong (if periodic) sense of community and place, ethnicity is a powerful form of identity that often plays an influential political role.

Intrinsic to group identity in broad political communities is the designation of social status. The Comaroffs (1992:54) suggest that "ethnicity has its origins in the asymmetric incorporation of structurally dissimilar groupings into a single political economy." Ethnic identity is intensified as relations of dominance and inequality develop among social groups, as occurs in state formation. As status designations come to define and rationalize the unequal distribution of "material, political and social power by virtue of *group* membership," inequality is to some extent attributed to the "*intrinsic* nature of the groups concerned" (original emphasis) (Comaroff and Comaroff 1992:56). In state formation, identity, status, as well as productive roles and specialized occupations, may be collapsed and solidified as the ascriptive, natural characteristics of groups. Group differences may be expressed in ideas of purity, exclusive marriage patterns, distinct origin myths, material objects and symbols, body decoration and dress, or language. In mythical narratives, such differences may be explained as distinctions of class. Particular social, economic, and political differences become ontological boundaries. For example, Inca elites backed status and class distinctions with sumptuary rules that limited the right to wear elaborate clothing or use prestigious objects (Rowe 1946). Associated with such rules were cosmological ideas and myths differentiating groups by generational proximity to and ancestry from powerful deities and chthonic forces. Through life histories and across generations, relations of inequality sank into practical hegemony, becoming internalized as the natural order of things; the ancient, universal, and true shape of the world.

Yet, globally, individuals and groups participate in such systems for any of various practical or affective reasons, be they economic benefit, political advantage, religious prestige, or spiritual inspiration. Further, whatever public demeanors and gestures ("public transcripts") characterize relations between dominant and subordinate groups, both elites and nonelites will maintain more intimately shared hidden transcripts that challenge, question, or mock aspects of the hegemonic order (Scott 1990). Charging these more intimate actions and narratives is discursive knowledge in Giddens' sense, which remains vibrant even as a hierarchical order is internalized as practical hegemony. Groups will continue to forge and maintain their own ideologies and affiliations, and perhaps even more so in the face of increasing imperial or colonial hierarchy.

By participating in a hegemonic order, individuals and groups forge an identity that transcends constituent corporate and ethnic groups. As much as state formation involves the creation of a new sociopolitical organization, it also involves a new scale of social identity; a vast, politically centralized imagined community. Constituent individuals and groups, even those relatively subordinate, effectively promote the rise, reproduction, and intensification of state influence and authority through daily actions, gestures, and symbols. By affiliating with this vast system and identifying with its prestigious and potent objects, gestures, and narratives, individuals and groups are in some measure empowered. Thus, if the hegemonic system comes to be perceived as onerous or destructive, especially in relation to changing historical circumstances (e.g., environmental shift, a weak leader, political shift) or new political and economic opportunities, local ideologies can become charged just as previously unchallenged elements surface. At such historical junctures, individuals and groups can help undo such a system, whether by not participating or more dynamic, violent measures.

Urbanism and Heterarchy

Considering power and identity from a practice perspective encourages dynamic approaches to complexity and its fundamental social-spatial phenomenon, the city. Most archaeologists would concur that urbanism is the concrete expression of social complexity and state organization. Yet archaeologists have not articulated a comparative definition of the nonindustrial city that is much more systematic than those proposed in the early twentieth century. Most influential have been sociological definitions that emphasized a city's economic and political roles in society (e.g., Simmel 1950; Spengler 1934, Weber 1958). Like traditional approaches to complexity, these tended to treat cities as integrated, and integrative, systems. Weber (1958:65–120) argued that the true city, as a functioning system of social institutions, is by and large an autonomous and integrated community. He contrasts primitive and role-based domains of heterogeneity, dividing them along an abstract time scale. The emergence of urbanism, he argued, required the dissolution or submergence of kin, clan, ancestor cult, and other totemistic ties to new allegiances revolving around urban organizations. It required the disruption of intimate supra-household relations to more impersonal territorial and political relations. In fact, he speculates, true cities failed to develop where persistent kinship organizations blocked the coalescence of urban institutions. Cities were melting pots for distinctions other than those supporting an effective division of labor.

V. Gordon Childe's model of nonindustrial urbanism, among the most influential in archaeology, espouses key elements of this view. Central to Childe's vision is the idea that the city, though an extensive and densely populated focus of diversity, is a social community *sui generis.* The reasons behind urban development may be manifold, but urban societies are held together by two processes: first, by "organic solidarity" as Weber believed, through which "Peasants, craftsmen, priests and rulers form a community . . . because each performs mutually complementary functions, needed for the well-being of the whole"; second, by "ideological devices" which mask or render natural the appropriation of "social surplus" by a "tiny ruling class." (Childe 1950:16) As a diagnostic expression of complex society, the city incorporates varied specialists and social classes, but remains an integrated community with a shared sense of well-being. According to Childe (1950:16), in ancient cities there was simply "no room for skeptics and sectaries."

Understanding past cities as dynamic places for expressing diverse social identities and contesting power relations requires further attention to how they reify dominant cultural principles and yet incorporate local ideas and practices. Structural approaches have established that many past cities, in particular central or capital cities, were built landscapes that instantiated and expressed key elements of a dominant cultural order. Many were to some extent "exemplary centers," built cosmograms that in their layout mapped out ideal social-spatial relations of society and the cosmos, embodying social space as it always has been and should be (Kolata 1993, 1996a; Wheatley 1974). In Cuzco and Tenochtitlan, the political, cultural, and religious centers of the Inca and Aztec states, master urban plans of spatial and social organization reified many elements of their respective dominant ideologies, joining icons and narratives of a celebrated mythical past with patterns and symbols expressing the glorious destiny of an ambitious, imperial future (Van Zandwitjk 1985; Zuidema 1964, 1990).

Nevertheless most structural approaches downplay three dynamic aspects of such cities. First, as cultural and political orders changed, so did their central cities. The face of many enduring cities, such as the "eternal city" of Rome, changed dramatically over time, in line with changing political and religious ideologies, the idiosyncrasies of particular ruling dynasties, and shifting global conditions (Stambaugh 1988). Landmarks of different times and ideologies existed side by side at any time, with age-old temples and monuments shifting in significance and role as old forms were given new meaning and new forms old meaning. In any major city certain monuments, such as Rome's Hut of Romulus or Chicago's Water Tower, may remain by design, appropriated and refashioned in the present to serve as landmarks of a mytho-historical past and as symbols of a common identity and shared memory. Tiwanaku's early Sunken Temple, I argue, became such a place (see Chapter 4).

Second, more than they were "good to think," past cities were most patently "good to experience." More than abstract cosmograms, past central cities were by design phenomenological, and phenomenal, experiences. Cities like Rome were meant to be experienced, beheld in awe by citizens, diplomats, and pilgrims alike. Part of the experience, perceived as one wove through their dense landscapes, was a sense of grand urban order. Each city followed a spatial design that went far beyond the means, the power, and the knowledge of experiencing subjects, and in the Andes, they simultaneously reified the inviolable cycles of celestial bodies and approximated visual pathways with primordial sacred features in surrounding landscapes. Still, other aspects of the urban experience were as salient, including vast opportunities, prayer at a specific shrine or temple, the pomp of a state-sponsored ceremony, the intimate ebullience of a family festival, or an immediate sense of the city's bustling diversity.

Finally, many past cities were also, to one extent or another, cosmopolitan places. Just as Chicago has its distinct, often volatile ethnic barrios that are constantly in flux, so did Rome (and in particular, the nearby port of Ostia) and most other past central cities incorporate a significant measure of social diversity. Diversity inevitably included the distinction of locals and foreigners, but as saliently—and more subtly—it included social differences among populations, immigrants or not, who participated in the same far-reaching state culture and forged a common overarching identity. Ethnic segments, barrio communities, political factions, descent groups, age grades, and gender-based organizations formed vibrant figured worlds, claiming members and conscripts who simultaneously called themselves Roman, Inca, or Tiwanaku.

A paradigmatic example of such a city was Teotihuacan, arguably the most important political, economic, and ritual center in Classic Period Mesoamerica (AD 200–650). Extending over twenty square kilometers at its greatest extent, the city incorporated some two thousand walled residential compounds, collectively housing at least 125,000 people around massive monumental complexes that stretched along the city's primary axis, the "Avenue of the Dead." The city was a well-planned, highly ordered cosmogram; all structures followed a single alignment oriented to the pathways of celestial bodies and sacred terrestrial features such as mountains and caves (Manzanilla 1996; Millon 1994). Further, Teotihuacan ancestry was a powerful source of prestige for ruling dynasties in many Maya polities, far to the east. Nevertheless, Teotihuacan was not simply a royal or priestly city. Inhabiting compounds were semiautonomous kin groups who claimed distinct ancestors. Many compounds plied some specialized trade, and most differed in social status (Spence 1981; Storey 1992). It may well be that each group formed the segment of more encompassing lineages distributed around the city, whose head groups—those closest to spiritually powerful apical ancestors—enjoyed elite status (Headrick 1996). Be that as it may, some compounds were enclaves inhabited by "foreigners," some from Oaxaca and at least one from the Gulf Coast, and these groups maintained distinct identities as well as special ties with their homelands for many generations (Paddock 1983; Rattray 1990). Teotihuacan was a city and a ceremonial center, a representation of both state and society, in which distinct interests and multiple identities coexited in the same, densely populated place.

In dynamic and prestigious central cities such as Teotihuacan there was plenty of room for "skeptics and sectaries," and for the enduring vitality of primitive totemistic ties. As concentrations of social and material power, therefore, such cities were the places where predominant symbols and dominant ideologies were most saliently, often routinely, contested (Sennett 1998). Such cities were at once incredibly complex landscapes of monuments and meanings, some of the present and others the past, some of the dominant culture and others distant peoples and places. Past central cities were, like Mauss's "total social facts," total cultural phenomena.

Thus, hierarchy and specialization are not the only constituents of archaic states and their centers of power. Ethnicity, political factions, descent groups, and other figured worlds of identity may be endemic features of an entire social order and its political and ritual centers (Brumfiel 1994; Crumley 1995; Marcus 1993; McGuire 1983; Smith 1994; Stein 1994). In the Inca and Aztec states, much as in Polynesian polities, factionalism intensified with increasing political centralization, social hierarchy, and imperial expansion. The very centralizing institutions of such polities were rooted in kinship ties and factional competition. Ruling elites in Aztec and Inca cities maintained and even celebrated the kinship and lineage principles traditionally thought to be characteristic of primitive societies (Brumfiel 1994; Conrad and Demarest 1984; Zuidema 1990).

Responding to the implications of such interpretations, archaeologists have begun to develop alternative approaches to social complexity in built environments and anthropogenic landscapes. One is the simple concept of heterarchy. Crumley (1995; Crumley and Marquardt 1987) and others (Brumfiel 1994, 1995; Ehrenreich 1995; King and Potter 1994; White 1995) have embraced the concept to criticize the usual equation of order and complexity with hierarchy. Archaeologists often construct models of social complexity based on differences in the degree of hierarchy and political centralization. Nevertheless, complex societies always incorporate organizations that are unranked, or that "possess the *potential* for being ranked in a number of ways" (original emphasis) (Crumley and Marquardt 1987:163), and ranking itself is often just one among other elements of social differentiation. Heterarchy "reminds us that forms of order exist that are not exclusively hierarchical, and interactive elements in complex systems need not be permanently ranked relative to one another" (Crumley 1995:3). As King and Potter (1994:84) remark, the concept of "heterarchy does not negate hierarchy, it subsumes it."

Recent research has explored heterarchy in regional settlement patterns, focusing on functional differences between settlements and settlement clusters (e.g., Crumley and Marquardt 1987; King and Potter 1994; Wailes 1995). This work has investigated nonranked differentiation among economic, political, religious, and other nonkin institutions. As such, heterarchy "simply means that different functions can exist in a system without their arrangement being hierarchical" (Marcus and Feinman 1998:11). I expand the scope of the concept to include cultural affiliation and group identity in urban settings, dimensions of heterogeneity that are not always functional in a social system. Bringing the concept more closely in line with the archaeological concept of hierarchy, heterarchy here refers to the potential coexistence of multiple nodes of power; social, economic, ritual, or political. Domains of identity involved in expressions of heterarchy may include affiliations of occupation and role as much as affiliations of kinship, political faction, or class. Over time, groups may shift in relative status or power, or an entire social order may become hierarchical as an elite class crystallizes. Still, rifts of status or class may well follow or coexist with ethnic, clan, kin, and other such boundaries (e.g., Brumfiel 1994; Conrad and Demarest 1984; Fox 1987; Kirch 1984; Zuidema 1990). Thus, a hierarchical order may subsume, be grounded in, even celebrate a heterarchical social order. As power relations continually shift and as states rise and fall, social boundaries continue to form part of a society's basic organizing principles.

Identity and power are critical dimensions of social relations and cultural forms in complex societies, built into such constructed environments as the cities of Chicago, Rome, and Teotihuacan. So, they are potentially archaeologically detectable, in part, as expressions of hierarchy and heterarchy, conformity and heterogeneity. To approach Tiwanaku's two principal cities in this light, I embrace the practice perspective elaborated here, informed by attention to the relative significance of periods of continuity, gradual shift, and rapid change. Developing a nuanced approach to changing social and political relations in Tiwanaku requires, I believe, some understanding of documented cultural forms, those postdating European contact in the sixteenth century. Employing ethnohistorical and ethnographic analogy, rather than an excuse to interpret the past by the present, is an effective method for understanding the past by comparison and contrast. Later societies help flesh out the approach to identity and power developed in this chapter, and their patterns can be critically compared to those represented in archaeological contexts. In the following chapter, I outline in some detail major sociopolitical patterns, ritual expressions, urban forms, and interregional relations in the Hispanic south-central Andes, detailing the place of social identity and power relations in each of these dimension of Andean social life.

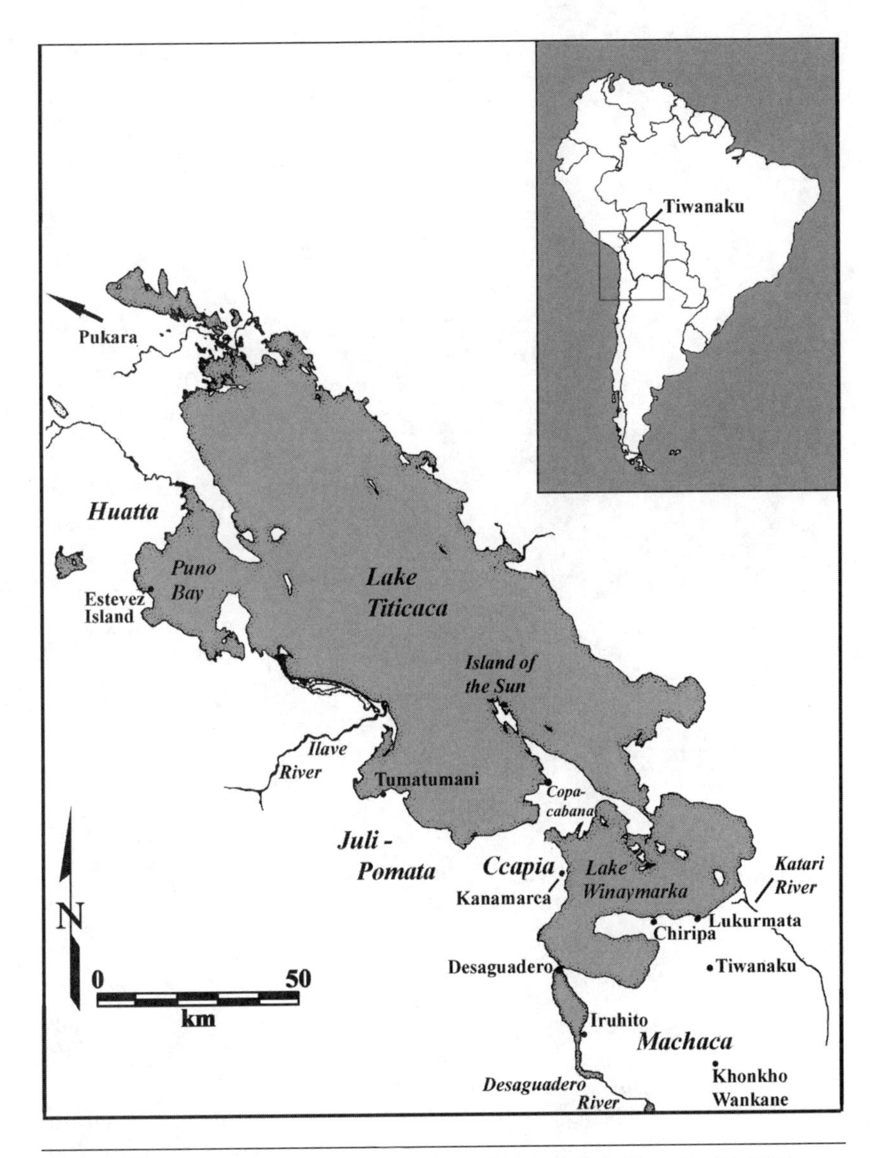

Figure 1.1 The Lake Titicaca Basin in the south-central Andes (adapted from Stanish 2003).

CHAPTER 2

Identity and Power in the Altiplano

Recent efforts in ethnohistory and historical ethnography in the south-central Andes have produced a rich corpus of data relating to the recent past, from the volatile phases following the Spanish conquest of the Inca state to the present. By scrutinizing written sources, including intricate fiscal and legal documents as well as narrative chronicles, ethnohistorians provide glimpses into the past that have truly exploded our understanding of the early Hispanic and late prehispanic Andes. Adding interpretive power to such research is a wealth of ongoing research in historical ethnography. It is helpful to draw on such documents and observations to outline aspects of social identity, power relations, and cosmic principles as they appeared in the sixteenth century. Patterns of life and society in documented periods also flesh out the theoretical ideas developed in Chapter 1 and outline general expectations for the more distant past.

In this chapter, I explore documented and recently observed relations, activities, and cultural principles in the south-central Andean altiplano. Synthesizing ethnohistorical and ethnographic research, I offer interpretations of such patterns to ground the practice perspective outlined in Chapter 1 in a specific cultural and historical context, with an eye toward understanding prehispanic patterns. I discuss social and political relations, cosmology and ritual practice, ceremony and urbanism, macroidentities and interregional relations as they appeared, as general domains of social life, from the sixteenth century onward. These domains were matrices for the daily expression and negotiation of power and identity. Particularly important in recent Andean sociopolitical organization were various forms of social grouping known as *ayllus*. Exploring their organizations, ceremonial practices, and political-ritual centers helps elucidate, as much through difference as through similarity, the more distant past.

Of course, Tiwanaku disappeared from the Andes some fifteen or sixteen generations before the Spanish arrived, swords and pens in hand. My motive is not to establish a determinate template for interpreting archaeological patterns. It is rather to contour specific documented and observed forms of cultural logic and practice to contrast and compare with earlier material patterns, with the aim of understanding long-term historical continuities *and* transformations in the region. A cautious perspective harnessing archaeological, ethnohistorical, and even ethnographic data helps establish a comprehensive understanding of long-term history in the Lake Titicaca Basin.

Ayllu as Identity and Polity

At the time of European contact, the altiplano supported loosely coalescing segmentary polities and political confederations in which productive organization and social power were distributed among constituent, mutually nested *ayllus* (Fig. 2.1) (e.g., Abercrombie 1986:24–101, 1998; Izko 1992: 75–80; Pärssinen 1992:351–362; Platt 1982:50, 1987; Rasnake 1988: 49–64; Rivera Cusicanqui 1992:102–22). *Ayllu* has been notoriously difficult to define, in part, as Rasnake points out (1988:51), because it was a complex and malleable concept "as inclusive as the English word group." Over the years it has been variously interpreted (see Rasnake 1988:50–51) as a tribe, a clan, a lineage, a kin group, a faction, an *estancia*, a territorial unit, "any group with a head" (Isbell 1978:108), and a group claiming descent from a founding ancestral mummy (Isbell 1997). Most are partially correct, but none seems complete. As I understand and employ it, *ayllu* was a flexible term for community that, to varying degrees, was partly imagined and partly the concrete product of kin-based relations, productive activities, access to common lands, ritual practices, claims to common ancestry, and political activity. It defined multiple embedded figured worlds and contexts of social identification and was, to varying degrees, an economic, ritual, and political group.

It is useful to discuss the concept in relation to the infra-*ayllu* group that invariably comprised them; the household. At the center of the contemporary household is the axial relation of a head couple, termed *chachawarmi* in Aymara (Abercrombie 1998:333; Harris 1985; Sillar 2000). The concept embraces the asymmetrical complementarity and potential antagonism of husband and wife, as well as their different domains of interaction and mutually supportive activities. However, households were (and still are)

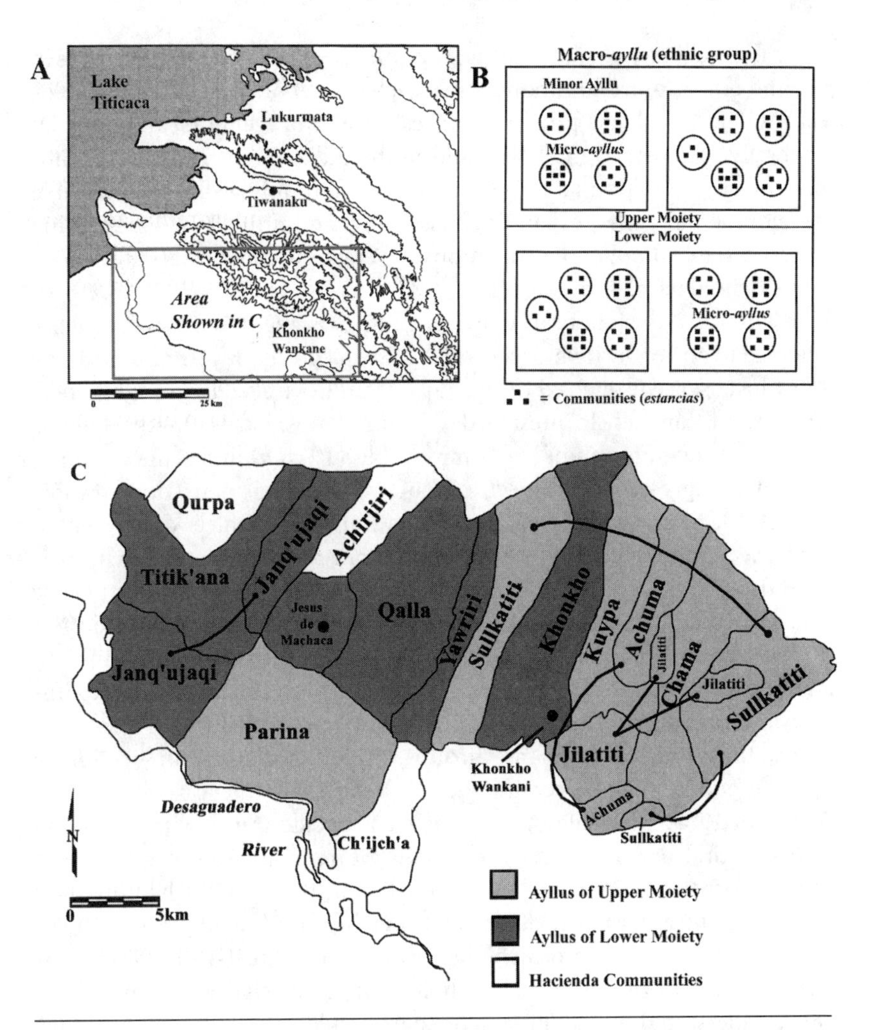

Figure 2.1 *Ayllu* organization in the Machaca Region of Bolivia, located south of the Tiwanaku Valley (A). Shown here is a schematic diagram of relations within a macro-*ayllu* (B) in relation to the current distribution of minor *ayllus* across the landscape of Machaca (C), focused around the central town or *marka*, Jesus de Machaca (black lines link segments of noncontiguous *ayllus*) (C adapted from Ticona and Albó 1997).

rarely nuclear families, they were ideally larger extended groups that formed the minimal corporate units of society. They often included several generations of people in a common descent group, which in some societies, such as K'ulta, were strongly patrililocal (see Abercrombie 1986, 1998) and in others, such as Kaata, were bilocal (see Bastien 1978). Households consisted of residential compounds or clusters of compounds incorporating several dwellings, corrals, storage buildings, and activity areas focused around one or more common patios. Each household centered on the oldest resident couple, its proximate ancestors and progenitors, and the man generally represented the household in the public arena of more encompassing groups. Upon its formation a household followed highly variable developmental cycles, expanding, fissioning, and ultimately disappearing over a variable number of generations. Several households together formed coresidential hamlets or *estancias.*

Ayllu was a flexible term that, depending on region or social context, referred to any of various larger scales of social group or community. In its most local sense it referred to a group of families linked by consanguineal or spiritual kin ties. In present-day K'ulta, Potosi, such a micro-*ayllu* is a "circulating connubium" of common blood (*wila*) and semen (*muju*), the vitalizing essences, respectively, of women and men (Abercrombie 1986:119). Micro-*ayllus* consisted of several local hamlets or residential *estancias,* each a cluster of several household compounds and their resident descent groups. Because many such *ayllus* were dispersed over diverse landscapes, a given region could include members of several *ayllus* just as an *ayllu* usually maintained *estancias* in regions far from its core territory. Members of a micro-*ayllu* revered a common ancestor, and through claims to common ancestry maintained rights to common lands and resources. Thus, they formed corporate groups. Some specialized in producing specific goods, such as ceramic vessels, textiles, or metals (Mercado de Peñaloza 1965:56), while others practiced specific trades within a broad agro-pastoral or agro-lacustrine productive regime (Abercrombie 1986; Wachtel 1994). A key role for micro-ayllus in the Andes, where markets were insignificant, was the collective ownership, production, and redistribution of resources. Micro-*ayllus* also differed in status, owing to the primacy of certain prestigious households (*casas principales*) among whom *ayllu* leadership responsibilities tended to circulate.

Nevertheless, *ayllu* also referred to more encompassing groups. Several micro-*ayllus* together formed larger minor *ayllus,* several of which formed more encompassing moieties. Moieties in some cases were also considered *ayllus,* two of which together formed a larger ethnic group, or macro-*ayllu.* While the number of scales varied, all documented regions consisted of such an embedded organization. In most cases, several such macro-*ayllus* formed encompassing polities or federations. In northern Potosi, Macha was the dominant of three macro-*ayllus* (or ethnic groups) that comprised the Qaraqara federation (Platt 1982:50; 1987). Macha consisted of two moieties (*Alasaya* and *Majasaya*) of five minor *ayllus* each, each of which in turn consisted of several micro-*ayllus. Ayllu* could refer to any of these embedded groups, and the precise scale of *ayllu* with which an individual identified varied according to social context (including the perceived identity of the person with whom an *ayllu* member is speaking). That many different types and scales of social groups were considered *ayllu* does not mean that they were homologous. Each scale had specific contexts for social identity as well unique roles and organizing principles. An encompassing macro-*ayllu* shared common ancestors and a landscape of sacred places, but much like an ethnic group, it formed a coherent group mostly during political confrontations or major rituals (Abercrombie 1986; Izko 1992:47–58). It was an imagined community more than a corporate group, but also a potentially powerful and encompassing polity more than an intimate descent group.

Each macro-*ayllu* consisted of an upper and lower half or moiety, termed Alasaya (or *arajja*, "above") and Majasaya (or *manqha*, "below"), Anansaya and Urinsaya, or Manansaya and Aransaya (Figure 2.1). As Wachtel (1994:13) notes of the Uru in Chipaya, west of Lake Poopo, "the principles of the [dual] order traditionally determined the distribution of land, the division of social groups, and the conception of the universe and of the sacred powers." In some macro-*ayllus*, including Chipaya, each moiety was a discrete, relatively independent *ayllu* with parallel political and economic functions. In most, however, the two groups of micro-*ayllus* together formed complementary parts of a more encompassing social, political, and economic whole, the macro-*ayllu*. The ultimate unity of complementary opposites was expressed in practical and symbolic terms. The various groups comprising a macro-*ayllu* gathered during major annual festivals and rallied when the *ayllu's* boundaries were threatened. Represented in the office and actions of a leader, or *mallku*, a macro-*ayllu* collectively formed a coherent political unit. Moiety division was one expression of fundamental dual principles that characterized society and nature at various scales, from the household to the macro-ecological division of Urkosuyu and Umasuyu (see below). Among moieties, the division was expressed in idealized terms that conjured human relations and, in some cases, the human body. The relation between two moieties was in some regions expressed as that between a procreative man and woman, or *chachawarmi*. The micro-ayllus of *alasaya* were categorically higher in status, collectively associated with the macro-*ayllu's* head and forming its "right side" (Bastien 1978, 1995; Rasnake 1988). The micro-ayllus of Majasaya comprised its "left side," and in some societies, such as the Kaata of Charazani, they were its legs and feet (Bastien 1978). On the landscape, the micro-*ayllus* of the upper moiety generally occupied the northern areas of a region, while those of the lower moiety occupied areas to the south. Nevertheless, the actual distribution of households and hamlets associated with particular moieties and micro-*ayllus* varied widely among societies and changed dramatically over time (see Albó 1972; Rasnake 1988; Wachtel 1994), giving rise to fascinating discrepancies between "ideal" and "lived" geographies of a macro-*ayllu's* settlement pattern. The symbolic unity of moieties as a relation of asymmetrical, opposed complementarity was given dramatic ritual expression in annual ritual *tinku* battles (Platt 1987; Rasnake 1988:56; Schüler 1988). At these times, during major feasts that involved the entire macro-*ayllu*, representative warriors from each moiety gathered on either side of the central town plaza to do battle with fists and slings, their battle-ready compatriots close behind. Blood spilled in battle, which fertilized the earth and nourished its generative powers, revitalized the macro-*ayllu's* vitality and integrity (Platt 1987; Schüler 1988).

Various characteristics of highland Andean life and society ensured that ayllus were anything but contiguous, static, or homogenous social organizations. Rather they were highly diversified and dynamic organizations of social relations, patterned practices, and novel activities. First of all, settlements pertaining to a given micro-*ayllu*, moiety, or macro-*ayllu* did not necessarily occupy the same territory or ecological zone. "Each ayllu was territorially fragmented into a kind of 'horizontal archipelago,'" formed of "islands in a sea filled in by the archipelagos of the remaining ayllus" (Abercrombie 1986:59; also Rasnake 1988:53). As Abercrombie (ibid.) goes on to describe K'ulta, "if each ayllu's segments were assigned a color on a map . . . the territory would resemble nothing more than a patch-work quilt." Platt (1987) points out that this spatial braiding of social groups and *ayllu* lands provided a formidable check against the centralization of power by ambitious leaders, and thus, state formation.

The historical reasons behind expressions of discontinuous territoriality are undoubtedly complex. On the one hand, it reflects in part a broadly shared ideal of zonal complementarity, or the desire to maintain direct control over lands and resources in other ecological zones (e.g., pasturage in the high puna, agricultural lands in lower, warmer valleys) (Murra 1972). Given relatively high cultivation risk (due to frost, hail, and drought) and limited resource diversity in the altiplano, many groups sought to colonize zones outside of the altiplano. Particularly significant in this regard was a desire to maintain access to warm valleys rich in herbs and hallucinogenic plants and amenable to the production of maize and coca, consumable goods critical to altiplano ceremonial practice. On the other hand, in K'ulta and Machaca (Abercrombie 1986, 1998; Choque and Ticona 1996), many *ayllus* occupied widely separated regions of ecologically similar zones. While access to diverse resources played a role here also, equally important in forging such patterns were past social alliances, political schisms, and years of repeated intermarriage among specific hamlets and *ayllu* segments (see Abercrombie 1998).

In line with predominant tendencies in residence patterns and land tenure, social affiliation often involved several overlapping *ayllus* at once. As Rasnake (1988:52–53) notes of contemporary Yura, "many people, by having landholdings in more than one *ayllu*, can potentially activate membership in several of them." Marriage establishes an alliance between two *ayllus*, and a couple will often seek to maintain active membership in both. Because each individual is his or herself the progeny of alliances established in preceding generations, the network of affiliations activated by a household at any time can be quite complex. In general, a household's primary obligations are to the *ayllu* nearest its primary residence, where it maintains its largest or most productive landholdings. Still, given the desire to maintain access to lands in multiple regions and zones, it is not uncommon for a household to maintain two or more residences at once, moving between them or visiting seasonally (Abercrombie 1986:73–74; Harris 1978:57; Murra 1972; Platt 1982:30–35). *Ayllu* identity and land tenure is kept active by participating in local feasts and ceremonies, whether as hosts or guests. Some such families are multiethnic, donning appropriate clothing styles in the local region, exchanging songs and dance routines, and in some cases speaking multiple languages. Even households without direct access to valley lands may seek affiliation with far groups, whether indirectly, through *ayllu* members who maintain such direct contacts, or directly, by establishing trading partners in distant regions (Abercrombie 1986:74). Through a diverse array of social relations and economic interactions, the *ayllu* affiliations maintained by a household at any time can be numerous, shifting with the specific projects and interests of a household's members.

Despite discontinuous territoriality and intricate identity politics, many macro-*ayllus* and multi-*ayllu* polities at the time of Spanish contact formed powerful political formations. They were "hierarchies of encompassment" in which power, identity, and rights to land and resources were distributed throughout mutually embedded groups (Abercrombie 1986). Political segmentation and local leadership were fundamental elements of the sociopolitical order, and a minimal ayllu's intimate ethic of kinship defined the principles and actions of social power at any social scale. Heading each level of *ayllu* was a representative leader, called *jilaqata* in micro-*ayllus* and *mallku* in macro-*ayllus.* While a lower moiety-*ayllu* usually had its own *mallku,* he was second to the *mallku* of the upper moiety, who also headed the macro-*ayllu.* At any level, a leader managed suprahousehold economic and political matters. While *jilaqatas* were elected, *mallku* leadership, at the head of entire polities and political federations, tended to become hereditary or to circulate among certain powerful households within prestigious micro-*ayllus.* Nevertheless, the power of the *mallku,* like that of the *jilaqata*, rested on the consent of his constituent *ayllus*. His legitimacy and prestige rested, in part, in assuring the well-being of his community, by overseeing the fair distribution of *ayllu* resources, settling internal disputes, and dealing effectively with external threats and boundary disputes (Abercrombie 1998; Izko 1992; Rasnake 1988). Rarely fixed or absolute, his position could be nullified if he failed to demonstrate sufficient leadership.

Thus, weaving together the social fabric that supported some degree of hierarchy was a profound egalitarian ethic. In principal, *ayllu* leadership was not about absolute power over others; it was a privileged obligation to serve the *ayllu*. Power was delegated to leaders in return for common benefits, and leaders were expected to follow a strict etiquette of reciprocity in words and deeds. At the center of this etiquette, an *ayllu* leader was expected to periodically host lively ceremonies and feasts to demonstrate his generosity (Abercrombie 1986, 1998; Murra 1980:135–136; Rasnake 1988). A leader and his household maintained privileged access to productive resources and sought surplus labor, in finished goods or work projects, to secure and extend his authority (Abercrombie 1986; Platt 1987). In the Qaraqara polity, for example, each *jilaqata* maintained plantations of peppers (*aji*) in temperate valleys to the east, while each *mallku* controlled his coca fields nearby (Platt 1987:75). Such material resources as well as extensive networks of social ties formed a fund of power that an astute leader cultivated to subsidize lively displays of generosity and to circulate relations of reciprocal obligation among other *ayllu* members.

Feasts were necessary in order to mobilize labor to complete a public project. An *ayllu* leader could not demand or even count on the support of his constituent *ayllus* and households, rather he had to formally *ask* them. As Platt (1987:75) puts it, "with the coca leaf and with vessels of chicha and food, the mallku would beg the Indians of their [moiety] so that they would come, dancing and singing, to work on their lands, guard their flocks, work their mines or their salt flats." Despite a half millennium of change, feasting remains a vibrant part of politics and social life in the altiplano. Astute community leaders and aspiring individuals spare no expense (and leave no potential debt relation untapped) in providing troops of bands and dancers, heaping plates of food, and truckloads of beer (*chicha*), and cane alcohol (*trago*). Their generosity demonstrates *cariño*, or affection and fairness, and justifies a limited degree of hierarchy and inequality in society. In the dominant ideology of the highland south-central Andes, enacted in lively rituals of consumption, privilege served (and serves) community and hierarchy fortified equality.

If hierarchy fortified equality, an ideal of equality simultaneously served political hierarchy. In the most influential polities of the south-central

Andes (Charcas, Qaraqara, Lupaca, Colla), *mallkus* were hereditary, powerful, and highly prestigious leaders. Like classic "aggrandizers" and networking chiefs in other world regions (Clarke and Blake 1994; Sahlins 1962), a *jilaqata* or *mallku* fortified his prestige and influence by amassing a fund of power, cultivating wide-ranging alliances, and promoting an egalitarian ethic that legitimized his position. *Ayllu* leaders were in some cases conceived in terms of intimate household relations, as the "elder-brothers" or "fathers" of the community (Abercrombie 1986:86; Bastien 1978; Platt 1987). In fact, the intimate relations within a household, with its inherent asymmetrical complementarity, were metaphorically attributed to the embedded and asymmetrical relations among the *ayllus* they represented. Macro-*ayllus*, associated with the most distant ancestors of the constituent groups, were conceived as the most ancient and encompassing progenitors. The two moieties composing it were considered male (Alasaya) and female (Majasaya) halves, like the man-and-woman focus of the household, with constituent minor and micro-*ayllus* and their respective, relatively proximal ancestors conceived as sons and daughters of the head pair. Hierarchical relations among *ayllus* in Andean polities were conceived, at least for certain contexts, as intimate relations among members of a household. *Ayllu* conjured an intricate sense of place and identity but it also condensed hierarchical sociopolitical relations spanning vast social landscapes. *Ayllu* was, in great part, political ideology.

The relations and ideals centered on *ayllu* expressed part of a deep but lived cultural logic that rendered sensible human relations and institutions that extended beyond the household. They manifested many of the generative principles that informed social, economic, political, and ritual activity. Because expressed in everyday rhythms, this cultural logic was, Sahlins would say, "burdened with the world." The early Colonial social landscape of the south-central Andes was not an unchanging, authentic native civilization that had petrified in place hundreds of years before its "discovery" in the early 1500s. It was a dynamic, changing landscape of polities, social relations, interaction networks, productive systems, cosmologies, ritual practices, and household activities that had emerged through prior events and historical conjunctures, including highly transformative phases of Inca and Spanish imperialism. Yet many generative principles, the habitus of everyday thought and action, have been tenacious despite more than five hundred years of relatively profound change on local, regional, and global fronts. While change has been real and profound in many domains of Andean life, so has cultural continuity. A question emerges: how and via what practices, ideas, and elements of material culture have these principles remained vibrant, even encompassing and appropriating to local rhythms the practices, ideas, and technologies of imperial regimes (e.g., Inca, Colonial, Republican)?

Ayllu as Cosmology, Landscape, and Ritual

The metaphorical intimacy attributed to *ayllu* relations and leaders had domains of significance that, while interwoven with group identity, rights to resources, and political ideology, went beyond these particular contexts of Andean thought and action. *Ayllu* relations formed part of a highly patterned (if variable) cosmology complex with dimensions straddling the domains of ideological and hegemonic power. In attributing intimate concepts of kinship to *ayllu* and other sociopolitical relations, grounded in relations with common ancestors, the various degrees of social distance between members of a macro-*ayllu* were collapsed. Perhaps better put, the entire ethnic group or polity formed, at least for certain interests and in specific contexts of action, a metaphorical macrohousehold or family. Social distance was rendered as geneological distance. Further, geneological relations were mapped onto the terrestrial landscapes associated with an *ayllu* or polity. Certain prominent features of the landscape, including springs, lakes, hills, mountains, and other natural features, were sacred to the groups who resided around and near them, and those who held them meaningful. To use the Quechua concept, they were *huacas* that incorporated powerful spiritual and animistic essences, and were places to witness and experience what Eliade (1959:20) terms the numinous. For members of particular *ayllus*, these were "interruptions" in physical space, "places qualitatively different from others" as loci for interaction and spiritual proximity between humans and ancestors, the present and the primordial, mythical past. Many were considered ancestral origin places.

In mapping embedded social and political relations across highland landscapes, distance across space became distance across generations, ultimately reaching deep into the mythical past. Each dwelling, household, hamlet, micro-*ayllu*, moiety-*ayllu*, macro-*ayllu*, and polity held certain local places sacred, as genius loci associated with the spirit of the shared ancestors of the respective embedded group (Abercrombie 1986, 1998; Arnold 1992; Martinez 1989). Each dwelling contained an altar or *misa* on its right-hand side, the half of the internal domestic domain associated with male activities. This was the locus of prayer, libations, and offerings by the resident nuclear family, which it spiritually represented and protected. Each central patio, in turn, contained an outdoor *misa* for offerings associated with the entire local descent group that *it* spiritually represented and protected. Hamlets of related and closely interacting households had other, more powerful sacred places. Among them were local hills (*uywiris*), or important spiritual protectors that embodied the spirits of the distant ancestors of these larger groups (Martinez 1989).

Iconic of an entire moiety or ethnic group, or even a region of interacting macro-*ayllus*, were prominent local mountains, the great ancestors (*achachilas*), and specifically their imposing peaks, or *mallku*. The snow-capped peaks of *achachilas* reached toward the heavens, mediating the terrestrial realm with its chthonic forces and the generative celestial bodies of the sky, including sun, *inti*, and moon, *paxi* (Abercrombie 1998:330–331). They embodied forces responsible for the primordial creation of entire societies and their constituent households- in them resided, or "palpitated" (Martinez 1989), the history, power, and identity of an *ayllu*. As the origins of storms and streams, mountains provided fertility and controlled the productivity of an *ayllu's* herds and fields; they were thought to protect the livelihood of entire ethnic groups and polities. In essence, the vitality of the social fabric and the identity of its constituent individuals were woven into the physical geography of its lands and territories by virtue of sacred places as ancestral progenitors and spiritual protectors. The past was present in the landscape, reflecting and shaping social interaction and identity.

In any region, the cosmic forces and sacred natural features that tied collectivities to meaningful, primordial landscapes were neither static nor abstract. Rather, they formed dynamic aspects of day to day social life that ayllu members sought to approximate or influence through proper activity and ritual practice. Social life thrived between the world of the heavens, or *alaxpacha*, and the dark and murky underworld, *manq'apacha* (Abercrombie 1998:346; van Kessel 1992; Kolata 1996b). Through proper ritual gestures and actions, *ayllu* members had variable agentive power to influence the cosmic forces that imbued these realms. Degree of human influence in the workings of the cosmos declined with distance from the local group and its primary sacred places. One can think of the concentric rings of cosmic forces (*misa*, *uywiri*, *mallku*, sky) as vertically oriented domains extending below and above social life and human settlement on the earth's surface. Deep inside the earth, personified by the female concept of *pachamama*, were the shadowy, little understood, but ultimately generative chthonic forces associated with the distant, vaguely remembered "great-dust" generations (Abercrombie 1998:358). Cycling above the earth were the celestial bodies of the sun, moon, Milky Way, and numerous constellations, which established the relentlessly predictable daily, monthly, and annual rhythms to which humans adjusted their daily personal and social activities. These bodies were associated with ancient heroic mythical figures (e.g., Tunupa, Viracocha), now often Christianized deities and forces who long ago, before the civilized world (*pacha*) of the present, established their cycles and gave rise to humanity (Abercrombie 1998; Albó and Layme 1992; Salles-Reese 1997). Humans ideally sought to live according to their cosmic rhythms, to follow their paths, continually seeking to replicate and harness their generative powers. Thus, important aspects of constructed space, everyday life, and periodic ritual are attuned to their cycles.

Throughout the south-central Andean highlands, moiety-*ayllus* were divided by the east-west axis of the sun's path, a cosmic-social division replicated in microcosm within the main plaza of the central town, or *marka*. In K'ulta, most houses were built with their doors facing east, to face the rising sun (Abercrombie 1986, 1998). Today, to inaugurate an important llama sacrifice (*wilancha*) for a festival, an offering of incense, llama fat (*untu*), and herbs is brought to a place east of the hamlet at dawn, where it is burnt, the rising smoke dedicated to the first rays of the sun. In the sacrifice the following day, the blood spurting from the animal's neck is directed eastward as a vitalizing life essence dedicated simultaneously to the earth, *pachamama*, and the rising sun.[1]

Just as the most ancient depths of *manq'apacha* were too abstract to be of direct relevance in most human affairs, so the celestial realm was beyond the pale of human intervention. Their cycles could be mimicked, their generative powers appropriated to human society and political systems, but they cannot be altered. Most amenable to human agency and influence were the cosmic forces associated with the ancestry and identity of local social groups. Whether resident in household altars or local peaks, these forces were most relevant for everyday social life and ritual activity. Principal means of engaging cosmic forces and summoning the past into the present included two linked practices at the center of Andean religion and society; sacrifice and pilgrimage. Sacrifices, or *ch'allas*, included burnt offerings known as *muxsa misas* that consisted of herbs, coca, first crops, candy, llama fat, llama fetuses, and other significant elements.[2] More important were sacrifices of live llamas, or *wilanchas*. In whatever form, *ch'allas* formed key moments in all major calendrical rituals, lifecycle ceremonies, and other major feasts, always accompanied by libations of fermented beverages (Saignes 1993). In the past, such beverages consisted of fermented grains, called *chicha* in Spanish, most commonly (and desirably) fermented corn beer, or *kusa*, but also fermented quinoa, or *ch'ua*. On ceremonial occasions beer was served in elaborate metal, ceramic, or wooden drinking chalices called *keros*, and small portions were poured onto the ground, usually around a specific place, before consuming the rest.

Libations were offered in repeating modular sequences, in some rituals forming complete cycles only after several hours. Libation sequences formed elements of longer ritual sequences, which in turn formed segments of regional ceremonies that took place over a sequence of several days. In K'ulta, for example, a local wilancha conducted during the annual macro-*ayllu* festival on September 14 took place over three consecutive days: animal vespers day, llama-cutting day, and the closing banquet (Abercrombie 1998:350–367). The most intricate libations occurred during the vespers that initiated the *wilancha*, in the local household of a feast sponsor. An elder lit two braziers or *sahumadors*, circling around to bring the domestic space into ritual time (Abercrombie 1998:347). Men and women conducted separate and parallel libations, the men seated around a raised altar and the women around a cloth spread out on the floor. The ritual unfolded as a sequence of dedications to local sacred places, beginning with closest and ending with most distant, forging a memory path leading from the most intimate to the most encompassing social groups. Libations were offered in strict order, first to the sponsor's household, then to his corrals, next to his wife's corrals, the sponsor's mother's corrals, his wife's mother's corrals, the sponsor's grandmother's corrals, his wife's grandmother's corrals, the animals themselves, and finally more distant spirits of crops and crop storage (see Abercrombie 1998:352–353). Within each of these segments, men first offered *ch'allas* to the local altar (*misa*), then to the protector (*uywiri*), and finally to the peak (*mallku*) of each place, while women simultaneously offered *ch'allas* in a parallel sequence of increasingly more encompassing house floors and valley plains (*t'alla*). Libations were then offered to the head couple's ancestors, beginning with the recently deceased, followed by deceased grandfathers, deceased grandmothers, and finally the distant apical ancestor.

Ch'allas proceeded in nested temporal sequences, moving outward in space and backward in time. Moving steplike through relations of asymmetrical complementarity (patrilineal and matrilineal corrals, altar and floor, hill and plain), they conjured the primordial power of ancestral spirits while reiterating the embedded character of society. Libations cognitively mapped relations among embedded social groups, along with their ancestors and productive resources, onto the landscape. Drinking in the altiplano was, and remains, about remembering and memorizing past events and ancestors, and in turn clarifying and redefining current social relations (Saignes 1993).

Further, through periodic pilgrimages to toasted sacred places the memory paths and social maps elaborated in *ch'allas, misas*, and *wilanchas* were immediately lived and experienced (see Randall 1982 and Sallnow 1987 for major ritual pilgrimages near Cuzco). Shrines abounded on the tops of local hills and mountains, ranging from simple cairns (which often serve also as boundary markers) to elaborate chapels fixed with internal altars. These were human-built, *in situ* places for *ch'allas* dedicated to the *uywiri* or *mallku* it embodied, and thus the social groups and ancestral spirits they invoked. Even today, these structures rise prominently on the landscape, visually marking the sacred places they signify. Coming across such a cairn, one will often see branches and bundles stuffed into the piled stones, and strewn around them burned areas, cigarette butts, and beer bottle caps. Entering a chapel, usually located either on a prominent hill just outside of a town or on a summit pass (*cumbre*) along a major road, one is immediately greeted with the pungent scent of coca and resinous incense. Most of the time cairns and chapels stand alone on the landscape, but periodically—and particularly during major annual feasts—they are visited by processions or small gatherings of people who come, sometimes climbing high above the town, to offer *ch'allas* to pertinent saints and spirits. Such *ch'allas* "express a communal prayer for abundance and fertility, a fervent plea for life, health, and good luck" for the *ayllu* and its constituent hamlets and households (Kolata 1996e:23).

Thus, *ayllu* inhabited cosmology and defined key dimensions of ritual practice, including libation, sacrifice, and pilgrimage. Such a ritual complex spanned ideology and practical hegemony. Cosmology was not simply "out there," statically hovering above and uniformly guiding everyday activity. Rather, it was lived, burdened with the world, and subject to change according to the humans who held it meaningful, and who reproduced and recreated it everyday according to their diverse interests and projects. For example, the number and location of sacred places in an *ayllu* changed according to circumstances and social cycles, such as the abandonment of a household or hamlet, or the establishment of a new household. Today, a household, hamlet, or micro-*ayllu* might even establish an *uywiri* to emphasize and legitimize a "social schism" within a community (Abercrombie 1998:502). Further, any major periodic feast with its constituent rituals is different from the last. Hosting a feast is one in a sequence of key events in the career of an aspiring *jilaqata* or *mallku*, and is by nature an affair of competitive generosity. Each host strives to outdo the sponsor of last year's feast, in part by introducing a modicum of novelty into the event. Thus, year after year and generation after generation, change in cosmology and ritual is inherent to its practice.

While many religious principles were routinely discursively penetrated, reflected upon, and talked about, others were self-evident and uncontested, forming, in a word, reality. Certain ideas of the sacred ran deep in the practical consciousness of altiplano inhabitants, forming axiomatic principles that informed human activities and careers. Symbolic linkages of society, space, and time have demonstrated great continuity. Practical hegemony in the altiplano has consisted of deep cultural logics and enduring practices that forge characteristic relations among humans, animals, spirits, and natural features. These relations, which may shift over time and differ from context to context, alternate in polarity between intimacy and distance, complementarity and opposition, and equality and hierarchy.

Ceremonial Convergence and Urbanism

Corresponding to highland Andean social organization and ritual practice was a distinct form of urbanism. At the time of Spanish contact major towns were, and to a great extent still are, important places of periodic social and ceremonial convergence (Abercrombie 1986, 1998; Albo 1972; Choque 1993; Vellard 1963:127–148). Prehispanic *ayllu* settlements in the altiplano consisted largely of hamlets and villages dispersed over immense areas, focused around larger settlements that served as political and ceremonial centers, or *markas.* Such settlements were conceptually divided in two along the east-west axis of the sun's path, forming a built microcosmic image representing the complementary opposition of a macro-*ayllu's* moieties. In the 1570's, through far-reaching reforms instituted by Viceroy Toledo in Lima, Spanish administrators created "a new politics of state, massing subjects to control them more efficiently" and "to guarantee proper deliveries of tribute and labor" (Abercrombie 1998:246). Among the most effective imperial strategies was the establishment of settlement reductions, (*reducciones),* which at least in Colonial theory involved the mass resettlement of native populations into Spanish-style towns, or pueblos, of some five hundred households each. The new nucleated pueblos were "places of amnesia," as Abercrombie puts it (1998:252). They followed new cosmic principles and cultural ideals, imposing spatial orders and daily practices that sought to erase native social memory, sever attachments to ancestors and landscape, and break up predominant aspects of Andean social organization. New pueblos incorporated new ritual places, they imposed new social boundaries to rend moiety and micro-*ayllu* loyalties, and they were the political centers of contiguous provinces (*repartamientos*) that separated *ayllus* from their far settlements and colonies. Reductions fostered considerable transformations, imposing new concepts of space, time, society, and human-landscape relations to configure a brave new world of European-style imperial domination.

Like many other aspects of Colonial life, however, new concepts of settlement were also in part appropriated to native social and cultural forms. To harmonize Colonial interests with indigenous settlement, Spanish administrators commonly built new pueblos on previous *markas,* simply redesigning previous settlements and giving them new names (Abercrombie 1986, 1998; Rasnake 1988). In the course of Colonial and Republican history, and particularly during the mestizo-led indigenous uprisings that peaked toward the end of the eighteenth century, many communities reverted to their prehispanic names as a form of cultural resistance and counteramnesia (Abercrombie 1998:239). Further, new ritual places were appropriated to old meanings. For example, church and plaza respectively came to represent masculine and feminine ritual places, mirroring the asymmetrical complementarity pervading native social life and ritual practice. More profoundly, households early on began to move back to their original hamlets and villages while maintaining houses and lands in the pueblo (Abercrombie 1986, 1998; Rasnake 1988:101). This was often done with the consent of local leaders and Colonial officials, since nucleated settlement ate into labor time by increasing the distance between a household and its scattered land holdings (Stern 1982:90).

Even more firmly, archaeological and ethnographic evidence complicitly demonstrates that from the beginning, resettlement was more effective on paper than it was on the ground. In the southern Lake Titicaca Basin, for example, archaeological survey demonstrates significant continuity between Early Colonial (pre-Toledan) and more recent settlement patterns (Albarracín-Jordan 1996a; Bandy and Janusek 2004). In the same region, many contemporary cantons and communities still have names and settlement distributions similar to those of *ayllu* settlements in the Early Colonial period. Surrounding the pueblo of Tiahuanaco (the head of a macro-canton within the Province of Ingavi, in the Department of La Paz, Bolivia) are numerous cantons that carry the same names as did the ayllus that surrounded the same *marka* in the sixteenth century (Choque 1993:22). Even to a greater extent, the same is true of the macro-canton of Jesus de Machaca to the south, which was less heavily influenced by the Spanish *hacienda* system (Ticona and Albó 1997). Thus, despite profound imperial transformation and the introduction of Western cultural ideals and practices, settlement in the Andean altiplano demonstrates great tenacity in settlement preference and patterning. New imperial forms have been appropriated to old meanings, and new patterns to old practices, creating considerable continuity despite hundreds of years of cultural and social transformation. Pueblos to a significant extent remain, in practice, *markas.*

As much as they were centers of permanent residence for certain households, past *markas* like contemporary Altiplano pueblos were magnet centers of political and ritual convergence for the *ayllus* residing in smaller villages and hamlets around them. They were incomplete communities inextricably tied to their surrounding hinterlands and far-off settlements and colonies. In part, pueblos were loci for Colonial or Republican state politics and practices, and thus stood apart symbolically and geographically from the more intimate domains of indigenous life. Yet they were also built icons collectively representing the *ayllus* inhabiting the smaller communities around them, with public ritual places focused in the central church and plaza while nearby barrios and streets were associated with specific micro-*ayllus* (Abercrombie 1998). *Markas* were where significant political reunions were called, when events and issues involving the entire macro-*ayllu* or polity were discussed. They were also where major festivals culminated. Through such concrete periodic activities, *markas* anchored the coherence and identity of widely distributed imagined communities.

On important ceremonial occasions *markas* became centers of ritual pilgrimage. Throughout the Andes, pilgrimage was a key element of prehispanic social and ritual life at least since the Initial Period (1800–500 BC). Pilgrimage to make ritual offerings, visit oracles, and experience the numinous was a primary motivation behind the growth of early Andean centers such as Chavin de Huantar in the Central Andean highlands (Burger 1992), Cahuachi on the south-central Coast (Silverman 1993, 1994), and Pachacamac on the Central Andean Coast (Shimada 1991; Uhle 1991 [1903]). Like Pachacamac, if on smaller scales, the most significant altiplano *markas* were inhabited ceremonial settlements rather than empty ceremonial and pilgrimage centers. Nevertheless, their population fluctuated significantly with the annual cycle. Throughout most of the year (except for market days), *markas* such as Tiahuanaco and Jesus de Machaca appeared all but abandoned. During major annual feasts, the most important lasting for several days, towns literally exploded in population. *Ayllu* members gathered from surrounding pueblos after conducting local *ch'allas* and libation sequences in their own households and hamlets. They followed well-worn paths that linked their hamlet to the central town, which for these occasions became pathways of ritual movement that tied together all of the dispersed hamlets and micro-*ayllus* into a common regional network of secular and ritual activity. Movement toward the *marka* was a ceremonial pilgrimage, often (especially for feast sponsors) conducted as a dance procession accompanied by music and *ch'allas*. Meanwhile, friends and relatives traveled from further away, from far settlements in the eastern valleys and, today, from major cities. Whether on foot or in automobiles, such groups stopped to offer libations at important places, including the summits of major mountain passes.

Such festivals were ritual eruptions in the practice of everyday life, times of reversal when the otherwise sparsely populated towns were encompassed in ritual time. People from all around converged on the *marka* that represented their *ayllu*. In a significant sense it was a ceremonial pilgrimage from private to public space, from the residential and ritual places of hamlets and *ayllu* segments to the residential and ritual places associated with the entire ethnic group and polity (Abercrombie 1998:384–388). A micro-*ayllu* had a representative house compound or group of compounds that it temporarily inhabited during these events, each hamlet occupying one or more constituent houses around a common patio. Larger *ayllus* and allied groups tended to cluster as contiguous town barrios. Otherwise sparsely occupied or empty, temporary urban residences, and especially those associated the feast sponsors' hamlets and *ayllus*, became lively centers of domestic activity and feasting.

Upon arriving in town, *ayllu* members began visiting and dedicating *ch'allas* to various houses and ritual places in sequence, beginning with those associated with their specific hamlet and successively to more public ritual places (the church, the plaza, local *uywiris*) associated with the entire macro-ayllu. *ch'allla* Sequences recapitulated in a public domain the memory paths enacted in the hamlet houses, moving from the most intimate to the most abstract deities and communities. They mapped each household's place within this more public, socially charged ceremonial context. During the course of festival the plaza, streets, and residential compounds were jammed with people, and everyday life was abandoned to music, dancing, *ch'allas*, and drinking. In *tinku* battle, the unity of a macro-*ayllu* was expressed in dynamic symbolic terms, through violent ritual practice that celebrated the complementary opposition of its principal components.

Feasts and ceremonies were imbued with power relations and "commensal politics" (Dietler 1996, 2001). For any male household head today, sponsoring local feasts is necessary for establishing respect within the hamlet and *ayllu*. As in many other past and contemporary societies (Hayden 1996, 2001; Hayden and Gargett 1990; Sahlins 1962, 1985; Vincent 1971), however, feast sponsorship was also a critical means of distributing relations of indebtedness and building social funds of power for aspiring and established political leaders. In the past, feast sponsorship was a prime strategy employed by ambitious political entrepreneurs to create a following and build prestige, and by established leaders (*jilaqata* and *mallku*) to organize corporate work projects while legitimizing and promoting their authority. Today, community feasting is part of a fiesta-cargo system formed of highly intricate, variegated sponsorship paths, each leading to a distinct chain of political offices, or a distinct political career path (Buechler and Buechler 1971). In K'ulta, the career path leading to the highest political positions takes at least twenty years to complete (Abercrombie 1998:370). Throughout the altiplano, feast sponsorship is a highly competitive affair, and it can be a highly effective strategy for building power and establishing consent.

In the past as in the present, the critical roles of reciprocity, generosity, and legitimacy emphasized the decisive role of society for any scale of leadership, whether in the domain of the household, hamlet, micro-*ayllu*, moiety, macro-*ayllu*, or multi-*ayllu* polity. Consent is given and enacted through ritual participation, in an ongoing contractual agreement that defines the terms of a group's hierarchical power relations. At whatever scale, a leader's legitimacy, prestige, and effective political power depend on the active consent of the many, without whom, through their willing participation in various ritual practices, libation sequences, and corporate projects, he is essentially powerless. Political power hinged on the ongoing consent of the people at least as much as people depended on the effective rituals and practical actions of a good leader. This reciprocal power relation could be created, recreated, or undone in major festivals centered on lively rituals of consumption, each of which also involved various sacrifices, offerings, and libation sequences on the part of participant households and groups. At all social scales, power was as thoroughly ritual as it was political, and it concentrated both in symbol and practice in the marka that represented the social group.

Interregional Dimensions of Identity and Power in the Altiplano

Groups in altiplano—whether corporate, ethnic, or polity—were not bounded entities but open domains of practice and identity, situated but dynamic figured worlds. Interregional affiliations and far-flung imagined communities formed an important part of life for most altiplano households and *ayllus*. The metaphors that shaped interregional relations mirrored those that gave meaning to more intimate figured worlds. They wove together predominant elements of society, nature, and the cosmos in frameworks of complementary opposition that paralleled human relations in more intimate domains and activities.

During the Colonial period, ethnic-like distinctions involving pan-regional affiliations, productive activities, and language differences co-existed alongside the ethnic-like distinctions just described. Although Aymara was predominant, Quechua, Pukina, and possibly less common languages such as Uruquilla all were spoken in the southern Lake Titicaca Basin (Bouysee-Cassagne 1987; Browman 1994; Torero 1987). Quechua was a language and ethnic affiliation introduced through the strategic of colonization policies of Inca imperialism during the Late Horizon (Stanish 2003). Pukina was spoken in small, relatively isolated pockets, and may represent an early lingua franca that became less common as Aymara and then Quechua filled that role (Stanish 2003). Less is known about Uruquilla (or Uru) which, if a distinct language at all, may have been spoken by groups distributed roughly along Rio Desaguadero, Lake Titicaca's primary drainage system (Bouysee-Cassagne 1975; Browman 1994).

Diverse theories abound regarding what past societies or groups spoke which languages, and when each language originated and declined. In light of documented language distributions, Torero (1970, 1987) argues that the Tiwanaku were Pukina speakers who succumbed to violent conquest by Aymara speakers around AD 1330. Developing this idea, others (e.g., Bouysee-Cassagne 1987; Espinoza 1980) link the origins of each spoken language to successive waves of migration and imperialism in the region. For them, the first inhabitants spoke Uruquilla, followed by the Puquina speakers of Tiwanaku, then the Aymara speakers of the Late Intermediate period polities (*señorios*), and finally the Quechua speakers associated with Inca conquest. What we can say with certainty is that multiple languages coexisted during the sixteenth century, and that Spanish soon replaced Quechua as an imperial lingua franca for the entire Andean region. The documented multilingual character of the region raises the likelihood that multiple languages coexisted in the more distant past.

The principal ethnic-like distinction in the region during the sixteenth century was that between Aymara and Uru, the latter referred to by Bertonio (1984 [1612], Bk. 2, 374) as *uma jak'i*, or "water people." Uru ayllus were counted as minority populations in *visitas*, or spanish regional inspections, and they concentrated along the edges of Lake Titicaca and on the Desaguadero River and its tributaries. In his *visita* of the southern basin in 1583, Mercado de Peñaloza (1965 [1583]:335–336) noted that some twelve to fourteen percent of the populations of the Machaca and Tiwanaku regions were Uru. While some claim that the Uru language was Uruquilla (Bouysee-Cassagne 1986:206; Julien 1983:62), others argue that it was a variant of Pukina (La Barre 1947; Mercado de Peñaloza 1965:336), and by the end of the sixteenth century many spoke Aymara. Whatever their principal or original language, more than likely many members of Uru *ayllus*, in part because they were largely subaltern groups, were multilingual. Today, people residing in remnant Uru enclaves claim to speak (or once to have spoken) Pukina, in addition to speaking Aymara and Spanish.

In the past as today, while Aymara tended to practice farming or pastoralism as predominant productive enterprises, the Uru tended to fish and harvest lacustrine and riverine resources. Social identification also invoked class distinction, for many Aymara referred to Uru communities as *chullpa puchu*, or rejects from the dark, primordial time of the *chullpas* (Wachtel 1994:31). Mercado de Peñalosa (1965 [1583]:336) states that the Uru "were people of little reputation, being capable of neither work nor cultivation, having neither towns in their domains nor harmony in their way of life, nor leaders to command them, but rather, each one lived of his own volition and they were sustained by what they fished and [*totora*] roots." As Bertonio (1984[1612], Bk. 2, 380) succinctly stated, Uru was "a nation of Indians despised by all." Apparently, Aymara and Colonial officials conferred this pejorative identity on groups whose daily routines emphasized fishing and hunting as much as, or more than, agrarian or pastoral pursuits (Julien 1983:55). Taking this idea further, some suggest that Uru was a recently fabricated category of role and status imposed by Spanish Colonial administrators to facilitate the imperial tax system (Stanish 2003). Nevertheless, the Aymara-Uru distinction undoubtedly had roots predating Spanish imperialism. If not necessarily an ethnic distinction, it was a native social categorization that crosscut others, melding social status and identity with specific productive practices, relative wealth or civility, and ecological associations. In its capacity as a class distinction, it associated relatively nonagrarian and nonpastoral (and thus, relatively impoverished and uncivilized) groups with the primordial savages who inhabited previous cosmic cycles.

Subsuming Aymara-Uru divisions and local ayllu segments, a major geopolitical division cut through the southern Lake Titicaca Basin in the sixteenth century. The Pacajes confederations that occupied the region were divided into two major geographical and political regions; Urkosuyu to the southwest and Umasuyu to the northeast (Bouysse-Cassagne 1986, 1987; Choque 1993; Izko 1986, 1992; Pärssinen 1992; Platt 1982, 1987; Rivera Cusiqanqui 1992). The central axis uniting them, or *taypi* in Aymara, traversed the altiplano in a southeasterly direction from Lake Titicaca. Urkosuyu included the major centers of Machaca and Caquiaviri, while Umasuyu included Achacachi, Pucarani, Chuquiapo (La Paz), and Viacha. Tiwanaku and Guaqui, both located in the Tiwanaku Valley and between the two regions demarcated by these towns, were considered part of Urkosuyu in most documents and Umasuyu in others (Choque 1993:18; Pärssinen 1992:353–354). Although the precise location of the central axis remains unclear, it most likely followed major features of the physical landscape. The area between towns clearly pertaining to either Urkosuyu or Umasuyu was comprised of the Tiwanaku and Katari Valleys, each the drainage basin of a major tributary to the lake. According to most accounts (see Pärssinen 1992:352–360), the boundary between Urkosuyu and Umasuyu passed somewhere through these valleys, and followed either the Katari River or the Taraco range that separates the valleys. Both natural features have formed important political divisions throughout recent history, and the Taraco range separates the province of Ingavi, which includes Tiwanaku, from Los Andes, which includes Lukurmata.

The relation between Urkosuyu and Umasuyu was one of asymmetrical and complementary opposition, and it invoked principals of social and spatial order characteristic of other social and cultural contexts. The terms *urku* and *uma* marked categorical distinctions in many aspects of life in the Lake Titicaca basin. *Urku* referred to male beings and activities and things associated with solidity, while *uma* referred to female beings and activities and things associated with liquidity, or lacking consistency. *Urku* referred to the high, dry, cold lands associated with pastoralism and the cultivation of highland crops (e.g., potatoes, oca, quinoa). *Uma* (literally, "water") referred to the lake and its adjacent lands, landscapes associated with Uru populations, as well as the lower, wetter, and warmer valleys of the Amazonian headwaters to the east. Valley lands were more amenable to the production of lowland crops such as maize and yielded mind-altering substances such as coca and hallucinogenic cacti and shrubs. As a regional designation, Urkosuyu included the warlike and centralized post-Tiwanaku polities of Colla, Lupaca, and Urkosuyu Pacajes, located west and south of the lake. As Capoche (1959, cited in Bouysee-Cassagne 1986:202) noted in 1585, "the urcosuyus [*sic*] have always had a higher reputation, and the Inka placed them at his right hand in public places." Umasuyu included the less centralized and poorly documented societies and polities east of the lake, such as Kallawaya and Umasuyu Pacajes (Bastien 1978, 1995; Saignes 1985). The *marka* of Tiahuanaco, ambivalent as Urkosuyu or Umasuyu, fell somewhere in between.

The Urkosuyu-Umasuyu distinction tends to be characterized in anthropological literature as a deep structural duality lingering in the cognitive realm of Lake Titicaca basin practical consciousness. In most accounts it is treated as a cosmic division hovering below society, an ancient cultural ideal with unclear practical significance. Nevertheless, the division thrived as a real political boundary throughout Spanish Colonial history, if with significant transformations (Choque 1993:20). This suggests the distinct possibility that the boundary, associated with characteristic cultural concepts, originated as a significant social, political, or ethnic boundary sometime in the more distant past. Following Kolata's lead (1993a, 1996b), I explore the possibility that the division originated or thrived during Tiwanaku political and cultural hegemony.

An important dimension of the Urkosuyu-Umasuyu division included distinct patterns of interregional interaction. Highland communities of Umasuyu, with productive systems emphasizing agricultural and lacustrine resources, tended to maintain strong ties to communities located in the lower valleys to the east. Because different altitude zones in this region are closely packed or compressed, interaction in many cases was intensive, characterized by discontinuous or continuous direct vertical control and constant movement between communities of different zones (Bastien 1978; Brush 1976, 1977; Flannery et al. 1989; Saignes 1985). Nevertheless, not all polities were centered in the highlands, and not all interaction involved highland colonization of, and direct control over, valley regions. The Umasuyu polity of Kallawaya, known for its itinerant religious and medical specialists, was centered in the upper valley zone, and it thrived from at least the Middle Horizon on interaction with highland and other valley societies (see Bastien 1978:22–23; Isbell 1983; Rendon 2000; Wassen 1972).

Communities and polities in Urkosuyu, while they maintained ties to eastern valley regions, nevertheless forged distinct ranges of interregional interaction networks. Titicaca basin polities such as Lupaca established and maintained colonies in western valley zones such as the Osmore drainage (Stanish 1989b; Van Buren 1996). Polities further south, such as Urkosuyu Pacajes, Killaka, and Qaraqara, centered in drier regions of the altiplano, balanced highland cultivation with intensive pastoral regimes. Pastoralism included circuits of long-distance exchange via llama caravans. Here, where direct ties to lower regions were impractical and costly, groups devised what Browman (1978, 1980) terms an "altiplano mode" of integration. Circuits of relatively horizontal interaction via trade caravans linked communities, many differentiated in occupation, into vast networks of interdependent societies. Many trade routes extended across the altiplano, over the high puna, and into lower valleys zones to the east and west (Lecoq 1987, 1999; Mendoza et al. 1994; Nielson 2001). Managed by specialized groups native to both highland and valley zones, they provided dependable distribution for a wide variety of products in a region where cultivation was risky, and established intimate connections among diverse societies in the altiplano and in lower valleys. Nuñez and Dillehay (1995) argue that a long-term emphasis on pastoral mobility and trade fostered loosely integrated polities in the south-central Andes, rather than the highly centralized states witnessed in the central Andean highland and coastal regions.

Categories such as Aymara and Uru and Urkosuyu and Umasuyu emphasize dimensions of social affiliation distinct from, though inevitably tied to, other domains of identity characteristic of the altiplano. If not an ethnic distinction, nor a strict language division, Aymara and Uru made broad reference to an interwoven interregional identity that linked status and livelihood with relative wealth and civility. Most Uru may have originally spoken Puquina or another language such as Uruquilla, but at least by the Early Colonial period many were multilingual. Urkosuyu and Umasuyu denoted inclusive regions linked to fundamental concepts of social and spatial order as well as broad interregional networks of interaction. They defined two ecologically and culturally distinct regions. By the Early Colonial period, at least, the boundary between them formed an important early political boundary in the south-central Andes. In following chapters, I examine whether or not such identities, concepts, and boundaries originated during the Tiwanaku Period, or at least if similar affiliations characterized Tiwanaku space and society.

Into the Prehispanic Past

Tiwanaku draws us deep into the prehispanic history of the south-central Andean highlands. Documented practices, organizations, and ideals provide a historically contingent and geographically specific framework for comparing and understanding patterns of life, society, and polity in Tiwanaku. Again, the purpose here is to inform and enrich our perspective of the distant past through comparative analogy (Stahl 1993; Wylie 1985), not to craft a timeless, "idealized conflation" of "Andean Culture" (Isbell 1995:7). Several aspects of more recent societies in the south-central Andes raise specific questions amenable to archaeological investigation. First, I investigate whether or not Tiwanaku was comprised of groups analogous to, perhaps even historically antecedent to, later *ayllus*. Were sociopolitical relations grounded in ritual, commensal politics, and an ideal of social reciprocity, as they were later? Was an ideal of domestic or community intimacy a significant element of Tiwanaku's political ideology, as it was later? Second, I investigate the roles of ritual and cosmology in the rise, consolidation, and collapse of Tiwanaku. Did Tiwanaku correspond with a dominant religious ideology, and to what extent did groups internalize this ideology as practical hegemony, as a naturalized worldview? What roles did ancestors, landscape features, and celestial phenomena play in Tiwanaku religion? In what manners were Tiwanaku cosmology and local ideologies expressed in built urban environments? Third, I investigate the roles of urban centers, specifically of Tiwanaku and Lukurmata, in their encompassing social and physical landscapes. Were such places centers of feasting, ceremonial convergence, and social coherence, as were later *markas*? From another perspective, did local communities appropriate state forms and institutions, as did *ayllus* during the Colonial Period? Fourth, I investigate the potential roles of broader identities and interregional interactions in Tiwanaku. Was there in Tiwanaku a boundary analogous or historically antecedent to the later Urkosuyu-Umasuyu division, and what was its significance? Were there in Tiwanaku ethnic-like divisions similar or historically antecedent to the Aymara-Uru distinction? Was Tiwanaku a cosmopolitan city, comprised of diverse groups as was Teotihuacan, or was it socially homogeneous, akin to an ethnic melting pot?

Sociopolitical relations in post-Tiwanaku polities of the Andean altiplano manifested a dynamic tension of egalitarianism and hierarchy (Platt 1987:98), interwoven and partially contradictory ideological tendencies with characteristic social, political, and ritual expressions. These polities, though they incorporated cultural principles that had arisen in the more distant past, also occupied very a specific environmental, cultural, and historical context. After Tiwanaku collapse, societies of the southern Lake Titicaca Basin had been incorporated into the Inca and Spanish empires, two imperial contexts involving significant social, political, and geographic reorganization. As documented in ethnohistorical sources, centralization was relatively weak overall, constrained by strong local forces and imposed imperial regimes. Heterarchy and a vibrant egalitarian ethic took the day, maintained by embedded organizations of asymmetrical but counterbalancing nodes of ritual, economic, and sociopolitical power. Of priority in the practical hegemony of individuals in polities such as Pacajes was a rigidly guarded etiquette emphasizing generosity and reciprocal obligation more than hierarchy and centralized integration. Based on what principles, symbols, or practices did Tiwanaku rulers manage to transcend the limits to centralization that characterized later polities of the region?

Tiwanaku was a convergence of sociopolitical realities quite different from those in Lupaca, Pacajes, or Qaraqara. Yet, just as it was recently, so it may have been before Spanish Conquest. In Tiwanaku, we may hypothesize, commoners and elites alike maintained some discursive penetration of the hegemonic social order, no matter how partial or incomplete their perspective or limited their potential for influential actions. As concrete expressions of local power, groups forged, reproduced, and maintained arrays of overlapping and nested identities through a variety of distinctive actions, gestures, and material symbols. State development and its ideologies of integration and hierarchy, and its overarching domains of cultural affiliation, undoubtedly infiltrated the most intimate domains of social life, transforming local groups and communities and their livelihoods, values, and identities. Nevertheless, state institutions, ideals, and practices would have been to some extent appropriated to local interests, ideals, and practices. In the following chapter I present three alternative perspectives of Tiwanaku and discuss the specific models and methods I employ to investigate the residential communities that inhabited its urban landscapes.

CHAPTER 3
Investigating and Interpreting Tiwanaku

In the past two decades Tiwanaku has become a major focus of investigation in archaeology. For years its influence in Andean cultural development was suspected, and it is now clear that it remained one of the most influential polities in the Andes for over six hundred years, by all measures a relatively long time. Interpretations of Tiwanaku's fundamental character have been remarkably divergent. Some of Tiwanaku's most dedicated researchers hold that it was the center of a highly centralized, tightly integrated state with imperial designs and far conquests. Others argue that Tiwanaku was a more loosely integrated polity organized by sociopolitical mechanisms similar to those characterizing later polities and federations, and integrated primarily by economic interaction or religious ideology. Meanwhile, there remains the question of Tiwanaku's ceremonial and symbolic significance, a long-standing inquiry with roots in the early assumption that Tiwanaku was primarily, if not entirely, an empty pilgrimage center. However, most ideas and models regarding Tiwanaku have lacked an intensive investigation of its urban populations.

This chapter consists of two sections. In the first, following a brief introduction to the Tiwanaku and Katari Valleys, I discuss three intellectual lines of thought regarding Tiwanaku's sociopolitical organization and historical trajectory. I then address major questions that arise out of these three views and develop several testable hypotheses. In the second section, I develop a theoretical and methodological foundation for an investigation of residential and ritual contexts at Tiwanaku and Lukurmata. I examine current debates regarding relations of style, ritual, and identity; issues of style, time, and chronology; and problems and prospects regarding household archaeology. Finally, I introduce the excavated urban areas that frame this investigation. Fundamentally, this book investigates Tiwanaku urban society and ritual over the long term, as viewed from the perspective of its diverse, largely nonelite urban populations. This extensive chapter establishes a "middle-range" theoretical framework for the investigation that follows in Parts 2 and 3.

Environment and Landscape in the Tiwanaku and Katari Valleys

The Andean altiplano is a high montane basin bounded by two mountain ranges, the rugged snow-capped Cordillera Real to the east and the older Cordillera Occidental to the west. In its heart, the drainage basins of the Tiwanaku and Katari Valleys, in the southeastern Lake Titicaca Basin, formed the cultural and political core of Tiwanaku civilization (Figure 3.1). Each consists of a valley plain that widens at its lower extreme. The region incorporates several mountain ranges; the highly folded Kimsachata and Chilla mountains south of Tiwanaku, the Cumana and Aygachi ranges north of Katari, and the low Taraco range, its westernmost extension a peninsula jutting into Lake Wiñaymarka, between the valleys. Each valley comprises several distinct microzones that were important for human settlement and land use. Most important are the valley plain or *pampa*, the low terraces and hill slopes of the lower colluvium or piedmont, and higher hilltops and terraces. The pampa and piedmont supported several wild faunal species that were hunted for consumption in the past, including various species of bird, *vizcacha* (*Lagidium peruvianum*, a rabbit-like rodent), rabbit, wild camelids, and deer (*Hippocamelus antisiensis* and others).

The Tiwanaku and Katari Valleys comprise distinct constellations of microenvironments. Most significant, the Katari Valley's floor forms a low, vast floodplain that is relatively flat for kilometers. In periods when the lake is high, water covers vast areas of this arable plain, known as the Koani Pampa. The slope of the pampa is so gradual that a rise in lake level of one meter will cause the lakeshore to migrate appoximately five kilometers inland (Binford et al. 1996). Further, unlike the Tiwanaku Valley, where numerous permanent and intermittent tributaries drain from the Taraco and Kimsachata ranges into the river, none of the intermittent streams in the Katari Valley actually reach a confluence with the Katari River (Argollo et al. 1996). During the rainy season streams carry water down to the plain, where it percolates into permeable deposits, producing a high water table that supports huge pools of standing water during rainy seasons.

The site of Tiwanaku sits on a low alluvial platform in the broad plain of the middle Tiwanaku Valley, some fifteen kilometers east of Lake Wiñaymarka. Most of the midvalley pampa supports hardy *ichu* and

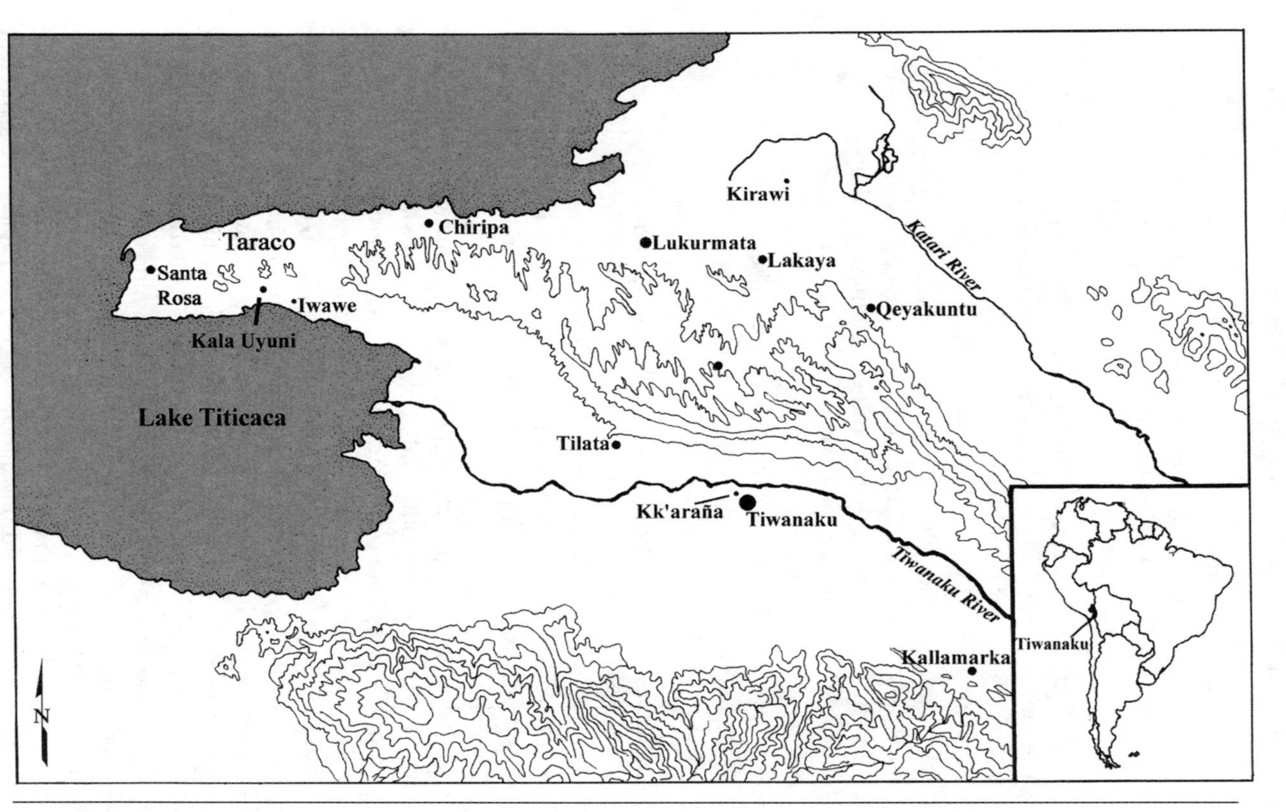

Figure 3.1 Map of the Tiwanaku and Katari Valleys with key sites mentioned in the text.

other grasses, marshy areas, and deep, clay-rich soils. The north edge of the Tiwanaku platform is bounded by the Tiwanaku River, and the west edge drops sharply into the marshy pampa, forming a slight ridge that overlooks the lower valley, and beyond it, the lake edge. Most of the Tiwanaku site is relatively unassuming, especially considering the extent of the prehispanic city it once supported. Kolata and Ponce portray the ruins in vivid terms:

> To the tourist, Tiwanaku appears as a city without an obvious plan. A few monumental stone structures loom isolated above the surface . . . as dramatic landmarks in an otherwise seemingly featureless plain covered by *ichu*, the tough bunchgrass of the high plateau. Yet the ground undulates; ancient public plazas and private courtyards persist in vague tracery. Weathered stone pillars project from the earth, marking the corners of ruined buildings now deeply buried under the fine-grained sediment of erosion from ancient adobe structures and from the surrounding mountainous landscape, deposited over centuries. Although much of what was once the internal order of Tiwanaku is obscure, sight lines remain along walls and between structures (Kolata and Ponce 1992:321).

Careful observation reveals subtle alignments, geometric features, and dense artifact scatters extending for kilometers around the more remarkable ruins now visited by hundreds of tourists every day. The contemporary town of Tiahuanaco, a pueblo at the head of an extensive canton, and a landmark to over two thousand years of continuous occupation, covers the northwest quadrant of the site.

The site of Lukurmata lies some thirteen kilometers northwest of Tiwanaku, a two-to-three-hour walk across the Taraco hills. Connecting the two sites is a clear, direct footpath formed over millennia of continuous travel. Lukurmata occupies the piedmont zone at the north edge of the Taraco range, dipping into a low marshy saddle and up onto a prominent natural crescent ridge to the north known as Wila Kollu, or Red Hill. In years when the lake is high, as it was when I began working there in 1987, Wila Kollu forms a peninsula jutting into the edge of Lake Wiñaymarka, and is visible for miles by land and by sea. Even more so than Tiwanaku—and for similar reasons—Lukurmata is unassuming save for Wila Kollu, which was sculpted to form a massive pyramidal temple complex. Lukurmata is currently a small community of some forty households, and like Tiwanaku it probably was never completely abandoned.

Abutting the ebbing and flowing lake edge, Lukurmata sits at the very southwest edge of the Koani Pampa. Thus, Lukurmata is ideally situated to exploit two major ecological domains: the lake and the nearby pampa. The marshy edge of Lake Titicaca provides a perfect environment for algae, submerged plants such as *lima*, and extensive beds of *totora* reed. Most served as fodder, and *totora* served a variety of additional uses, such as thatch for roofs, materials for reed boats, and hemp for rope. The lake edge and marshy stands in the nearby pampa are frequented by diverse species of indigenous bird (including ducks, geese, gulls, wrens, herons, ibises, and flamingos), and they support several species of fish of the genera *Orestias* and *Trichomycterus*. Covering the pampa are fossil raised field systems built in a variety of configurations. Residents of prehispanic Lukurmata and nearby sites played an important role in the construction and maintenance of these intensive agricultural systems.

Three Views of Tiwanaku

Tiwanaku's prehispanic character and history have remained an enigma for a number of reasons. First, the site of Tiwanaku has suffered centuries of looting and nonsystematic excavation. In 1605 the Spanish chronicler Lizárraga (1909:542) noticed that the impeccably carved ashlars of Tiwanaku were "used for the edifice of the church in this town." Between 1609 and 1653 Father Bernabe Cobo (1990:106) wrote that, "this place has been torn down in order to make use of the stones, the church of Tiaguanaco [*sic*] was built of them, and the citizens of Chuquiabo [La Paz] have carried away many of them in order to build their houses, and even the Indians of the town of Tiaguanaco make their graves with excellent slabs that they take from these ruins." Spanish secular and ecclesiastical leaders ordered that stones quarried from the Pumapunku complex, in the southwest quadrant of the site, be recarved and hauled to La Paz to furnish chocolate mills, and others sent to build the bridge of San Francisco and the church in Jesus de Machaca (Ponce et al. 1971:65–79; Squier 1878:274). The reuse of Tiwanaku carved stones continued until recently, as a visit to any public building or house compound in the contemporary town will attest (also Bandelier 1911; Posnansky 1945)

Nearly as problematic has been archaeological research at the site. In 1903, a French mission led by the geologist George de Crequi-Monfort (1904, 1906) conducted excavations in several of Tiwanaku's monumental complexes, including the Sunken Temple and the Putuni. Arthur Posnansky, an Austrian enthusiast of Tiwanaku who studied the site up through the 1930s, published photos that depicted the walls of the sunken temple deteriorating after years of intense rainy seasons and human activity (1945, Vol. 1: Plates VI–VII). Lack of proper supervision, Posnansky claims (1945, Vol. 2:106–113), caused the mission's damage to the temple and the monumental complex of Chunchukala located between the Putuni and the west balcony of the Kalasasaya. Compounding Tiwanaku's sad recent history is the fact that many later archaeological excavations remain unpublished. Some of the most significant include substantial excavations conducted by the Bolivian archaeologist Gregorio Cordero Miranda (see Ponce 1995).

This section outlines three broad theoretical scenarios regarding the character of Tiwanaku society. Instead of a comprehensive history of Tiwanaku study, which has been outlined elsewhere (Albarracín-Jordan 1992, 1999; Kolata 1993a; Kolata and Ponce 2003; Ponce 1995), I discuss three perspectives that have coalesced around the rise, expansion, and collapse of the polity. I outline the ideas that Tiwanaku was an ideological phenomenon, that it was an expansionist state, and that it was a segmentary polity. To some extent, each position emerged to counter the idea prevalent at the time. For example, Bolivian archaeologists promoted the state model to counter the ceremonial center idea, which was supported by some Peruvianists, and archaeologists have recently promoted models emphasizing local group autonomy in contrast to the state model. In this chapter I discuss the linkages among these perspectives in relation to their distinct emphases. Drawing on the theoretical focus developed in Chapter 1, I suggest that we require flexible perspectives that can account for a variety of cultural variables rather than rigid models that champion one or two.

Tiwanaku as Ceremonial Center and Religious Icon

Chroniclers, explorers, and archaeologists have been intrigued by Tiwanaku's religious significance. Among the earliest ideas is that Tiwanaku was an ancient Andean ceremonial or pilgrimage center. As succinctly put by the nineteenth century explorer Ephraim Squier (1878:300), "Tiwanaku may have been a sacred spot or shrine, the position of which was determined by accident, an augury, or a dream, but I can hardly believe that it was the seat of dominion." As noted elsewhere (Janusek 1994, 2003b; Kolata 1993a: 27–29), Squier was as struck by the utter lack of "any traces of habitations" near Tiwanaku's edifices as he was of the harsh local environment, which he considered "not a region for nurturing or sustaining a large population and certainly not one wherein we should expect to find a capital" (Squier 1878:300). He was apparently as surprised by the incongruous location of the magnificent ruins, with its "great number of beautifully cut stones," among the "wretched," "sullen," and "impoverished" Aymara (Squier 1878:269, 273, 300, 304). Though he believed "the civilization of ancient Peruvians was indigenous" (1878:569), Squier like Cieza (1959) before him had his doubts about the historical connection between the ruins and their current inhabitants.

Some of the first systematic archaeological research at Tiwanaku wound up supporting the assumption that Tiwanaku was little more than a ceremonial center. In the 1930s the archaeologist Wendell Bennett excavated ten four meter by four meter units at Tiwanaku using arbitrary 50 centimeter levels (Bennett 1934), with the explicit intent of defining Tiwanaku's chronology and locating ancient habitations. Although he located some features and wall foundations, Bennett's units mostly revealed superimposed layers of dense, seemingly unstructured midden. Because his units were narrow, and failed to reveal the full spatial context of those middens, Bennett was unable to draw definitive conclusions regarding habitation at the site. For "lack of definite information," Bennett (1934:480) decided that Tiwanaku was a "vacant ceremonial center," composed of little more than "an aggregation of temples." Later, in an influential book on Andean culture history, Bennett (Bennett and Bird 1964:138) repeated this interpretation, stating that the "site appears to have been a major ceremonial center, rather than a city or large village."

Bennett's conclusions had a resounding effect on Andeanists working in Peru, many of whom adopted his interpretation in their models of Andean culture history. John Rowe (1962), Dwight Wallace (1957), and Dorothy Menzel (1958, 1964) interpreted the Andean Middle Horizon as a long epoch dominated by two major cultural formations; Wari to the north, centered in the Ayacucho Basin of Peru, and Tiwanaku to the south, centered in the Lake Titicaca Basin of Bolivia. According to Menzel's model, Tiwanaku was the center of a popular religious cult that Wari zealots later spread by military force throughout much of the Andes. While Tiwanaku remained a ceremonial center, Wari developed into the center of a vast empire. Luis Lumbreras (1974:151, 1981) and others (Wallace 1980:143–144) adopted this position, arguing that the dispersion of "Tiahuanacoid" characteristics was the result of Wari imperialism, "since urbanism did not yet exist on the altiplano" during the Middle Horizon. Richard Schaedel (1988:772–773) more recently stated as much:

> The spacious and impressive, yet simple and elegant ceremonial center of Tiahuanaco, which can be likened to a "holy city," and its outlying shrines such as Lucurmata [*sic*] and Pajchiri, are in sharp contrast to the complex, space-intensive patterning of the multifunctional architecture of the Huari capital and the widely dispersed centers of Wirakochapampa and Pikillakta and the numerous administrative outliers (Schaedel 1988:772–773).

Summarizing an enduring idea, Schaedel (1988:773) concluded that although "the Tiahuanaco theocratic hegemony . . . was a long-lived tradition of holy places and pilgrimage centers . . . there was never a great concentration of power there."

Thus, a series of small test pits at the site, coupled with the apparent lack of surface habitations, have sustained some of the most influential models of Andean culture history. An unexpected assumption in these ideas is that Tiwanaku, as an important ceremonial or pilgrimage center, was of necessity vacant. Elsewhere in the Andes this was not the case. Pachacamac, center of the Ichma polity on the Central Peruvian Coast, provides a fascinating comparative model to the contrary. During the Late Horizon Pachacamac thrived as an important center of ritual pilgrimage, housing one of the most powerful oracles in the Inca realm (Albornoz 1967:83–84; Avila 1966:113–119; Cieza 1959:331–337; Cobo 1990:85–90, 169; Guaman Poma 1992:239–240; Menzel 1959; Patterson 1985:159, 1991:88–92; Pizarro 1965:183–184; Rostworowski 1992, 1999). Religious and political affiliation with its priests was highly desirable, attested by later Inca rulers' patronage of and consultations with the oracle before embarking on important campaigns. Pachacamac maintained numerous satellite settlements, each of which acquired a small branch oracle dedicated to Pachacamac in return for offerings made to the main shrine. Reminiscent of relations among embedded *ayllus* in the highlands, the Pachacamac network was described in intimate family terms. Branch oracles were brothers, wives, sons, and daughters of Pachacamac, depending on their relative prestige and influence. Nevertheless, Pachacamac was not simply a center of pilgrimage but a ceremonial city. It was a densely inhabited urban center that thrived on its religious prestige (Shimada 1991; Uhle 1991 [1903]). The city, moreover, had developed into a major ceremonial settlement by the Early Intermediate Period, and possibly earlier.

Parallel with the scenario of Andean ceremonial cities such as Pachacamac, most archaeologists now take account of mounting evidence for dense habitation at Tiwanaku in evaluating the significance of its cosmology and ritual. Some develop the structural idea that Tiwanaku's location and spatial order manifest an idealized cosmic representation of the sacred, elaborating Wallace's (1980:144) early suggestion that the site was "a physical expression of a symbolic system which played an . . . important integrative role in Tiwanaku society." Johan Reinhard (1985, 1990) emphasizes Tiwanaku's location in a sacred geography surrounded by significant ancestral peaks, or *achachilas*, most significantly Illimani to the east. As Reinhard and others point out (Kolata 1993a, Vranich 1999), the principal portals of major Tiwanaku monuments such as Kalasasaya, Akapana, and Pumapunku face eastward, toward Illimani's visible peak. They also face the rising sun (Cieza de León 1959:284; Kolata 1993a:97–98), thus facilitating visual connections with significant terrestrial and celestial features.

Kolata elaborates the idea of Tiwanaku as symbol. He suggests that the site was "conceived as the *axis mundi*" in the south-central Andes, forming "an icon of Tiwanaku rule and a cosmogram that displayed symbolically, in the spatial arrangement of public architecture and sculpture, the structure that framed the natural and social orders" (Kolata and Ponce 1992:318). Kolata (Kolata 1993a; Kolata and Ponce 1992:327) imagines the plan of Tiwanaku as two crosscutting conceptual schemes, "a circle within a square." On the one hand, Kolata hypothesizes (following Posnansky 1945, Vol. II:121) that an artificial moat surrounded most of Tiwanaku's monumental complex, forming an ontological barrier that physically separated the "sacred essence of the city" from the sprawling peripheries. The moat emphasized a conceptual "concentric cline" of sacredness that diminished toward the urban periphery, dividing the space and time of the sacred from "the space and time of ordinary life" (Kolata and Ponce 1992:318). On the other hand, Kolata imagines Tiwanaku divided simultaneously along an east-west axis according to the daily solar path, and along a north-south axis following a social division into moieties. Emphasizing these dual divisions in monumental terms were the "twin ceremonial centers" of Akapana, to the northeast (and inside of the bounded core), and Pumapunku to the southwest. Each is centered on a terraced platform mound, and the Akapana, the tallest construction in Tiwanaku, represented, Kolata infers (Kolata 1993a; Kolata and Ponce 1992), an artificial sacred mountain.

In subsequent chapters, I appraise the significance of pilgrimage and cosmology in Tiwanaku and Lukurmata during their histories as major settlements. Pilgrimage and cosmology were fundamental elements of ceremony and settlement in later altiplano *markas*, including Tiahuanaco. With these later centers in mind, I evaluate the potential role of ceremonial convergence in Tiwanaku and Lukurmata. I evaluate its significance by focusing on the activities of people residing in sectors outside of monumental complexes, and by investigating the role of cosmic symbolism in architectural patterns and visual alignments in the residential complexes they inhabited. Later towns in the Andes were integrated into larger settlement networks and ritual landscapes. They were incomplete settlements inextricably tied to the villages and hamlets that supported them, and which they collectively represented and periodically served as centers of ritual and social convergence. In this light, I examine Tiwanaku and Lukurmata in relation to their surrounding settlement networks and landscapes.

Tiwanaku as Autochthonous Political State

Visitors, Enthusiasts, and Early Archaeologists: Nearly as old as the pilgrimage idea is the idea that Tiwanaku was a densely inhabited settlement and the center of an influential civilization. Many proponents of this idea also considered the Aymara to be descendants of those who constructed and lived in the ancient settlement. Alfons Stuebel and Max Uhle, who visited the altiplano briefly in 1877, elaborated the first comprehensive description of the ruins in 1892. Uhle also was the first to document and photograph the ruins at Lukurmata in 1894 (Uhle 1912), followed in 1934 by Wendell Bennett (1936). A decade later Uhle (1902, 1903) outlined the first Andean chronology, in which the "Tiahuanaco chronological horizon," as well as the widespread distribution of the Aymara language, represented the diffusion of the first great Andean civilization.

More explicit about Tiwanaku as a densely inhabited settlement was Adolph Bandelier, an anthropologist who visited the ruins for nineteen days in 1894. He (1911:221) cogently noted that, until that time, "attention [had] only been paid to the striking remains of Tiahuanaco, and the more modest features neglected," even though they were "the most important, because illustrative of the mode of living of the people." Unlike other earlier visitors, whose attention focused on stone monuments, portals, and monoliths, Bandelier explicitly considered the likelihood that prehispanic dwellings had consisted largely of adobe, an impermanent material that had long since eroded onto the landscape. Local inhabitants, who told of ancient dwellings with stone floors and adobe walls, inspired this idea (Bandelier 1911:225). These local inhabitants he considered descendents of Tiwanaku's builders, for "the fact that Tiahuanaco was in ruins when the first Incas visited it does not necessarily militate against" such a possibility (Bandelier 1911:225).

Arthur Posnansky studied Tiwanaku throughout the early part of the twentieth century, though without systematically investigating the site. Years of meticulous measurement, analysis, and photographic documentation are published in his comprehensive four-volume opus, which remains a valuable reference for Tiwanaku monumental architecture, stone sculpture, and ceramic iconography. Posnansky considered Tiwanaku to be the first metropolis in the Americas, and an ancient and advanced center that fostered the development of all New World civilizations. Posnansky extrapolated the antiquity of Tiwanaku by examining the dimensions and alignment of the Kalasasaya temple in relation to hypothetical astronomical measurements (Posnansky 1945:Vol II, 87–105). Using these measurements, he divided the history of Tiwanaku into three legendary periods, the first of which commenced "somewhere beyond ten thousand years" ago (Posnansky 1945, Vol. II:90). Tiwanaku was built during a primordial "Second Period" by a superior Qolla race, the descendants of which he considered to be the contemporary Aymara.[1]

If Posnansky believed Tiwanaku was "The Cradle of American Man" and the center of a great civilization, his interpretations have ultimately fostered untenable and, to some extent racist, speculation. Aside from his farfetched chronology, for which Uhle took him to task (Albarracín-Jordan 1996a:35), Posnansky ignored Bandelier's suggestion that prehispanic houses were built largely of adobe. Instead, he posited that several small stone-lined subterranean chambers north of the Kalasasaya, now thought to be looted royal tombs, represented the cramped quarters of the ancient Qolla. As he explains:

> When one studies the marvelous ruins of Tihuanacu, he imagines that the great masters . . . must have had for their use dwellings no less sumptuous than the magnificent temples, palaces, observatories, and countless other constructions used both for holy worship and for defense in time of war. But the opposite is the case in this respect:the dwellings which were found are of a ridiculous size in comparison with other buildings (1945, Vol. II:113).

Implicit assumptions of a rupture between the past and the present are more explicit in Posnansky's consideration of the local Aymara. If the Aymara are descendents of the Qolla, he writes, they are a regressed, "unhappy people" who "are completely devoid of culture" and "lead a wretched existence in clay huts" (Posnansky 1945:Vol. 1, 33). In Posnansky's mind, the "great masters" could not have lived in the clay huts he saw around him. Posnansky's attention to monumental architecture and elaborate artifacts, coupled with his sensational ideas, continue to fire imaginations in Bolivia and abroad. Grounded in similar assumptions, popular New Age accounts of Tiwanaku, some of which draw on these ideas, consider Tiwanaku the work of enlightened Egyptians, Atlanteans, or even aliens from outer space (e.g., Hancock 1996 and von Däniken 1971).

Such speculation aside, North American archaeologists began to seriously consider Tiwanaku a major Andean urban center during the 1960s. John Rowe considered Tiwanaku a prehispanic city in an essay regarding early Andean urban settlements, in which he discussed the evidence for early occupation recovered by Wendell Bennett, Alfred Kidder II (1956), and Bolivian archaeologists (Rowe 1963:7–9). Shortly thereafter Edward Lanning (1967:116), in a popular book summarizing Andean culture history, explicitly took Bennett's idea to task. He noted that although Tiwanaku "is usually described as a ceremonial center . . . extensive refuse deposits have been reported there." He cogently added that, "its fame as a ceremonial center is probably due to the fact that all of the excavations . . . have been conducted in the nucleus of the city." In support of this idea, Jeffrey Parsons (1968:244), during a brief reconnaissance at Tiwanaku, noticed that the surface outside of Tiwanaku's visible monuments "is heavily littered with surface pottery" and "contains an abundance of large, low mounded areas." Parsons noted that such postdepositional patterns typify eroded adobe houses. Based on his observation, he considered Tiwanaku a past urban center with a minimum urban area of 2.4 square kilometers and a population between 5,200 and 10,500.

Carlos Ponce Sanginés and the Tiwanaku Military Empire: Meanwhile, Bolivian research and interpretation had been developing in reaction to Posnansky's speculations and the idea that the main site was simply a ceremonial center. In 1957, on the heels of the turbulent Bolivian agrarian reform, the die-hard positivist Carlos Ponce Sanginés and a group of dedicated colleagues, among them Gregorio Cordero Miranda and Maks Portugal, effectively institutionalized Bolivian archeology. Led by Ponce, they founded the Center of Archaeological Investigations in Tiwanaku (CIAT) in 1958 and the National Institute of Archaeology (INAR) in 1975 (Ponce 1995:262–263). The agrarian reform and the inauguration of Bolivian archaeology coincided with the rise to power of the Left-led National Revolutionary Movement (MNR). An integral part of the political party and the new national order, Ponce and his colleagues drew up itemized agendas for a staunchly nationalist, Marxist-inspired archaeology (Ponce 1961, 1978a, 1978b; 1980). Ponce's optimistic "National Archaeology," grounded in empirical research, state-of-the-art technology, and scientific methods, was diametrically opposed to the "Neocolonial Archaeology" of Europe and North America, which, he argued, "limited to university circles or the scope of museums, remains suffocated and without repercussion in national life" (Ponce 1978a:3). Putting this ideology in practice, Ponce and colleagues effectively impeded North American and European research at Tiwanaku until the late 1980s. Further, in line with MNR political ideology, in which indigenous leaders were enlisted as the bases of revolution, Ponce established direct cultural continuity between Tiwanaku and contemporary Aymara communities. Tiwanaku was now Bolivian cultural patrimony, and the Aymara were inheritors of the nation's glorious past (Ponce 1978a:6).

To support Tiwanaku's key role in the Bolivian nation, Ponce strove to demonstrate that Tiwanaku was the densely populated center of an imperial state that extended its control across much of the Andes via military conquest. He estimated that Tiwanaku reached a maximum extent of some 4.2 square kilometers, and housed a population of perhaps 100,000 people (Ponce 1981). He directed numerous state-funded research programs at Tiwanaku during the 1960s and 1970s, most of which focused on excavating and reconstructing some of the most impressive monumental complexes at the site (Alconini 1991). Among the most notable projects were the excavation and reconstruction of two early, adjacent structures, the

Kalasasaya Platform and "Semi-Subterranean Temple" (from here on, the Sunken Temple). The ambitious reconstruction of these complexes, in the process of bringing them to light, succeeded in aggrandizing them as monuments worthy of a proud and optimistic national spirit (Alconini 1991:63; see Chapter 4). Ironically though, as Lanning realized, this type of research largely served to strengthen the popular idea that Tiwanaku was primarily a ceremonial center.

Ponce sought to catalogue other major prehispanic sites in Bolivia. Based on years of travel and research, he hypothesized a broad area of Tiwanaku imperial control extending across Bolivia and into Peru, Chile, and Argentina. He also defined some of the prehispanic cultures that preceded Tiwanaku, most notably Chiripa and Wankarani (Ponce 1970), as well as the post-Tiwanaku culture of Mollo, ostensibly centered at Iskanwaya in the upper valleys east of Lake Titicaca (Arellano 1975; Ponce 1957).

Ultimately, Ponce sought to turn the table on Menzel's interpretation of the Andean Middle Horizon, by arguing that Tiwanaku was a dense urban center at the head of an imperial state. At the heart of his argument is a three-stage evolutionary narrative that begins with a small village and ends with an imperial state, roughly following Childe's (1936, 1957) Marxist-inspired evolutionary sequence for Near Eastern civilization. Ponce's evolutionary narrative, Like Childe's, founds Tiwanaku political evolution somewhat tautologically in increasing productive surplus and the rise of urban centers. According to Ponce (1980, 1981) Tiwanaku emerged in the "Village Stage" at around 1600 BC, and persisted as a self-sufficient hamlet of "modest proportions" until AD 1–100 (Tiwanaku I-II, Ponce 1980:27–30; 1981:71–75). At that point an unspecified "increment of agriculture" initiated a primary stage of "Urban Development" in which Tiwanaku began to experience increasing demographic growth, economic specialization and incipient socio-political hierarchy (Ponce 1980:30–38; Ponce 1981:75–78). Following a period of early urban development (Tiwanaku III), Tiwanaku experienced a period of "mature" development (Tiwanaku IV) characterized by "embellishment, modification, and perfection" in the city (Ponce 1981:78). According to Ponce, Tiwanaku now began to establish secondary urban centers in nearby regions, such as Khonkho Wankane in the Desaguadero Valley and Lukurmata in Katari (Ponce 1981:83).

During the subsequent "Imperial Stage," Tiwanaku reached the evolutionary pinnacle of its cultural achievement (Ponce 1980:38–41; 1981:85–88), expanding on a vast scale outside of the Lake Titicaca Basin. According to Ponce, Tiwanaku expansion was "distinctly warlike" and conducted "by military action" (Ponce 1981:85). Among Tiwanaku's most significant conquests was Wari. Beyond its clear chronological primacy in relation to Wari, Ponce argues, Tiwanaku's cultural and political superiority is obvious. As he explains (1981:84), the surface of Wari is "in reality. . . less than half of that covered by Tiwanaku, and with architecturally inferior temples." According to Ponce, Wari was a regional center of the expanding Tiwanaku empire; "those who suppose Wari was totally independent from Tiwanaku falls into lamentable confusion between decorative ceramic styles and the global and integral sphere of its culture" (1981:84–85).

Despite Ponce's hard-boiled nationalism, with its attendant interpretive biases, some of which have been disproved, and his overenthusiastic monumental reconstructions, many of which have been criticized, his contributions to Tiwanaku archaeology are abundant. Most significant, through tireless research, political activity, and voluminous publication, Ponce essentially jump-started Bolivian archaeology as a systematic enterprise. A major contribution of his was the employment of large-scale, stratigraphic excavations to understand the past. He was cautious about conflating ceramic style and cultural development, unlike many of his predecessors and more recent archaeologists. Ponce based his chronological sequence in the results of excavations under the Kalasasaya Platform (see below and Janusek 2003a). Based on structures recovered in these strata, Ponce took up Bandelier's prior suggestion, and recognized that around Tiwanaku's monumental complexes were hundreds of adobe dwellings and other "minor constructions." Although household archaeology was never a primary item on CIAT's agenda, in Ponce's model Tiwanaku was a vast city inhabited by elites, commoners, craft specialists, and traders (Ponce 1991). Ponce's vision and interpretations have had a profound effect on more recent archaeological projects, including those affiliated with Proyecto Wila Jawira.

Alan Kolata and the Tiwanaku Patrimonial State: Research directed by Kolata and INAR Director Oswaldo Rivera Sundt, a multidisciplinary effort entitled Proyecto Wila Jawira, not only resumed Ponce's emphasis on large scale excavations at Tiwanaku, it generated the first intensive regionwide analyses, including research into past productive systems and excavations at other sites in the Tiwanaku core. This was in keeping with Kolata's (2003a:3) comprehensive interest in "the relationship of Tiwanaku as a total cultural phenomenon to its surrounding environmental matrix." Kolata's research began as a relatively small-scale investigation of fossil raised field systems and settlement patterns in the Koani Pampa of the Katari Valley between 1978 and 1982. In 1986–87 Wila Jawira emerged as a major interdisciplinary project, in which ecologists, archaeologists, and graduate students conducted intensive research in the Koani Pampa and the nearby site of Lukurmata. Between 1988 and 1991 research efforts shifted to the site of Tiwanaku. Four years of continuous research included excavations on a vast scale and extensive regional surveys in the Tiwanaku Valley, while targeted research continued in the Katari Valley. In 1993–97 intensive archaeological research shifted once again to the Katari Valley, followed recently by specialized analyses and small-scale excavations in Tiwanaku.

Summarizing diverse bodies of Wila Jawira research, Kolata (1991, 1993a, 2003b), has developed a coherent interpretive portrait of Tiwanaku cities and the social, economic, and political relations that characterized the core region. Kolata interprets Tiwanaku as a highly centralized, autochthonous state with densely populated cities that thrived most critically on rural production of agricultural surplus. Kolata's interpretive vision follows three distinct research focuses, one centering on altiplano political economy and productive systems, one on spatial-symbolic relations and urban organization, and one on long-distance interaction and colonization. He interprets Tiwanaku political economy as a "troika" of productive systems grounded in lacustrine resources, extensive herds of llamas and alpacas, and most important, intensive farming. Central to his model is the argument, based on years of research (Kolata 1985, 1986, 1991, Kolata and Ortloff 1996, Ortloff and Kolata 1989; Seddon 1994), that the Koani Pampa was a key, centrally controlled proprietary agricultural estate of Tiwanaku ruling elites; "a constructed landscape of state production" (Kolata 1991:121). This argument is based on two interrelated bodies of evidence. First, raised field systems cover over seventy square kilometers of the pampa (Kolata 1986, 1991), and their management was organized as a regional system of production. For Kolata, centralized state action beyond the compass of local corporate groups is apparent in sophisticated systems of causeways, walls, dykes, canals, and other major hydrological features that extend from the piedmont out across the pampa. It is most salient in the artificial canalization of the Katari River itself, a massive undertaking that opened up hundreds of hectares of land to raised field production. Second, state action is apparent in a "hierarchical settlement network," the central purpose of which, Kolata argues, was the efficient administration of productive activities (Kolata 1986:760). For Kolata and others, such patterns manifest an integrated productive landscape built and maintained to generate consistent surpluses to support the regional requirements of an urban, centralized state.

A second focus is Kolata's interpretation of Tiwanaku cities as patrimonial centers of elite power and authority (Kolata 1993a, 1996b; Kolata and Ponce 1992). Grounding the power of ruling lineages beyond effective productive systems was an elegant and highly ordered cosmology (see above). According to Kolata, Tiwanaku's urban landscape followed a concentric gradient of social status. An artificial moat marked an ontological boundary that separated the sacred from the mundane, concentrating ritual power in the sanctified "island enceinte." Rising prominently over the sacred island was the Akapana, a human-wrought icon of a sacred *achachila.* Fixed with elaborate drainage systems that cycled water through its core and over its terraces, the Akapana represented the generative power of humans, crops, and herds. Living nearby, elite lineages linked themselves directly with its generative power. Thus, Tiwanaku's concentric symbolic order was simultaneously an inviolable social map that linked ruling elite lineages, along with their retainers and their residences, to this concentrated sacred power. According to Kolata, elites fashioned other major Tiwanaku cities, including Lukurmata and Khonkho Wankane, according to similar spatial and social orders. In the process, they "were appropriating images from the natural world and merging them with their concepts of hierarchical social order" (Kolata 1996b:233). Most potent among the generative natural forces mimicked in built monuments were those relating to agricultural production. "Tiwanaku elites intended their capitals and provincial cities to be seen and experienced as extensions, or reflections, of the natural structure of the cosmos" (Kolata 1996b:234).

These elements form the basis for Kolata's interpretation of Tiwanaku and its provincial centers as highly ordered and tightly controlled patrimonial settlements. Ponce (1981, 1991) and David Browman (1978, 1981) had hypothesized that Tiwanaku and other major settlement in the region were dynamic centers of economic production, in which certain groups specialized in creating a wide variety of valued and sumptuary goods. Kolata (1993a:173) counters that like other prehispanic Andean cities, Tiwanaku "had no markets." In vivid and disparaging terms he notes that:

> Western perceptions of ancient cities invariably conjure images of jostling crowds snaking through narrow cobbled lanes, spilling out of markets and bazaars, churning up clouds of dust in the frenzy to buy, sell, and barter. Bedraggled street vendors hawking cheap trinkets; sharp-eyed, tight-fisted merchants hunkered down over piles of precious rugs, spices, and other exotica newly arrived by caravan . . . porters, jugglers, clowns, prostitutes, and thieves plying their trade in workshops, public squares, and back alleys all are familiar characters in this perception of the archaic city." (Kolata 1993a:173).

Acknowledging the role of economic interaction in major Tiwanaku centers, Kolata concludes that "Tiwanaku's *raison d'être* had little to do with commercial, or mercantile activities. The social map of Tiwanaku was not a riotous mosaic of many peoples anonymously and independently pursuing their livelihoods" (Kolata 1993a:173–174). Rather for Kolata, Tiwanaku and its provincial settlements were pure, highly ordered symbolic icons, oddly reminiscent of the ideal cities envisioned by ruling elites in early dynastic China (Chang 1983; Wheatley 1971; Xu 2000). Tiwanaku, Kolata summarizes, "was an autocratic city, built for and dominated by a native aristocracy. In this sense, Tiwanaku was truly a patrician city; a place for symbolically concentrating the political and religious authority of the elite. Although not entirely absent . . . Tiwanaku boasted little in the way of pluralism and heterogeneity" (Kolata 1993a:173–174). For Kolata (1993a:241), "this was no idealized, American-style melting pot. Tiwanaku was a created, intensely hierarchical, culture of the state."

A third research focus of Kolata's, which builds on Ponce's idea of Tiwanaku imperialism, emphasizes Tiwanaku state control and influence outside of the altiplano. First, according to Kolata, Tiwanaku maintained wide-ranging influence across a vast region of the Andes through state-managed llama caravans (Kolata 1992, 1993a, 1993b). Through state sponsored caravan trade, Tiwanaku rulers established economic colonies in distant regions and clientage relations with local elites, who adopted emblems of status from their Tiwanaku patrons. Among the latter were exotic prestige items "associated with Tiwanaku cult and belief systems," including "a broad spectrum of elements associated with the ritual consumption of hallucinogenic drugs" (Kolata 1992:82).

Second, Kolata (1992, 1993a, 1993b) suggests that Tiwanaku established directly controlled colonies in closer peripheral regions, in particular warmer valleys east and west of the altiplano where a diverse range of crops could be grown. This hypothesis extends John Murra's model (1972) of direct verticality (or direct economic complementarity, see Mujica 1978, 1985 and Stanish 1992) to the coercive strategies of a centralized conquest state. Research in the south-central Andes confirms that in specific cases, Tiwanaku leaders practiced such strategies. It also vindicates Ponce's idea that Tiwanaku regional influence intensified during a late or Imperial Stage termed Tiwanaku V (see Chapter 8). Research on the Island of the Sun in Lake Titicaca indicates that Tiwanaku maintained regional centers, and that Tiwanaku cultural influence and control intensified after AD 800 (Bauer and Stanish 2001; Seddon 1998). Other major Tiwanaku regional centers in the Lake Titicaca Basin include Tumatumani, in the southwestern Lake Titicaca Basin (Stanish et al. 1997), and Estevez Island, in the Puno Bay, Peru (Figure 1.1) (Stanish 2003). In the warmer valleys further west, research conducted by Paul Goldstein (1989) and others (Bandy et al. 1996; Blom 1999; Blom et al. 1998) have established that after AD 800, Tiwanaku leaders established a colony dedicated to maize production and processing in Moquegua, Peru. In line with this evidence, Chilean archaeologists argue that Tiwanaku maintained firm control over valleys south of Moquegua, such as Azapa in northern Chile (Berenguer et al. 1980; Berenguer and Dauelsberg 1989). Drawing on such ideas and data, popular reconstructions often characterize the Tiwanaku polity as a contiguous block of control and influence covering much of what is today Bolivia, Peru, northern Chile and Argentina (see Morell 2002; Straughan 1991:41).

Local Autonomy and the Tiwanaku "Segmentary State"

In contrast to models of Tiwanaku as the political center of a highly centralized and tightly integrated imperial state, many researchers emphasize the apparent integrity of local groups and communities. Research on camelid pastoralism and trade caravans has emphasized the roles of relatively autonomous communities and loosely integrated sociopolitical networks in the past south-central Andes. Lautaro Nuñez and Tom Dillehay (1995; Dillehay and Nuñez 1988) argue that trade caravans served to distribute a wide variety of goods in a region where agricultural production was risky, fostering limited sociopolitical integration among autonomous polities and their agrarian hubs, or "axis settlements."

Tiwanaku developed in the midst of such economic interaction, David Browman argues (1981:415), "emerging as both the major power in trade and the political head of a loosely organized group of semi-independent trade centers." In the vast altiplano, he notes (1978, 1980, 1981), direct control over settlements in lower zones was impractical and costly. Rather than vertical archipelagos, most communities devised horizontal and indirect linkages through extensive trade caravans and specialized community occupations. Tiwanaku developed into an economically successful "industrial hub" that housed diverse "guilds of craftsmen" (Browman 1978, 1981). Key to Tiwanaku's rising economic power was the popular adoption of a "hallucinogenic complex," comprised of implements used to prepare and ingest mind-altering substances. The range of objects varied from region to region, following vibrant local interpretations of Tiwanaku religious ideas. Ritual participants ingested hallucinogenic substances in religious ceremonies, the importance of which is attested by elaborate temples and sculpted monoliths at secondary centers in the altiplano (Browman 1978). At least during the early phases of its development (through Tiwanaku IV), Browman concludes, Tiwanaku headed a loose federation of interdependent polities, and integration "was based on economic and theological ties rather than political expediency" (Browman 1978, 1981:416–417).

Recent evidence for Tiwanaku influence and interaction resonate with elements of this model. Extensive survey in the Potosi region of Bolivia, in the southern altiplano, has revealed very few sites with significant quantities of Tiwanaku-style artifacts and none with Tiwanaku-style monoliths or temple complexes (Lecoq 1999). This conclusion is supported by evidence from the valley regions of northern Chuquisaca, to the east, where a single Tiwanaku site has yet to be reported (Lima 2000). Overall, interaction between the altiplano and most eastern valley regions appears to have centered on trade rather than direct colonization or control (Janusek and Blom 2005). In Cochabamba, which was traditionally considered a Tiwanaku colony (Browman 1981; Caballero 1984; Kolata 1992, 1993b; Ponce 1980, 1981), direct Tiwanaku influence now appears limited to specific sites and regions (Cespedes 2000; Higueras-Hare 1996). West of the altiplano, Tiwanaku colonized the Moquegua middle valley, but it apparently had little or no influence on coastal areas nearby (Owen 1993). Similarly, extensive research in the Lake Titicaca Basin itself demonstrates that Tiwanaku control concentrated in specific areas (Stanish 2003). Thus, Tiwanaku influence was highly strategic, in many areas predicated on trade and influence rather than direct control. Most such regions were home to vibrant political and cultural developments that are just now coming to light, fostering inquiry regarding the influence these societies had on Tiwanaku development and integration.

In the Tiwanaku core itself, ongoing research indicates that groups at different scales maintained some degree of autonomy during periods of Tiwanaku hegemony. In a classic text on Tiwanaku, Ponce (1981) briefly considers the role of local communities in the formation of the Tiwanaku polity. Drawing directly on historical documentation relating to the town of Tiahuanaco, he suggests that Tiwanaku incorporated a dual division of moieties focused respectively on the Kalasasaya to the northeast and the Pumapunku to the southwest (Ponce 1981:86; 1991:19; Ponce et al. 1971:19–37). He speculates that the Tiwanaku valley housed "ayllus or ancient communities" that were similar to those currently surrounding Tiwanaku and that "came to be dominated by the city through state control" (Ponce 1991:19). In this view the state was an emergent formation distinct in essence from prior local communities, which were incorporated into rather than playing some dynamic role in the emerging system. More recently, and in response to current interpretations, Ponce (2001) has elaborated more dynamic roles for *ayllus*, moieties, and communities in Tiwanaku.

Kolata (1993a:241) suggests that while not an "ethnic melange" neither was Tiwanaku a single cultural identity. Although local groups do not figure prominently in Kolata's model, he argues that local consent was critical in establishing Tiwanaku authority and maintaining effective organization over its productive systems (1992, 1996a). He insists that control over the hinterland "demanded a measure of cooperation and collaboration with local leaders" (Kolata 1996a:17). Kolata turns to ethnohistorical and ethnographic analogy to identify the character of local groups, identifying "at least three distinct groups that appear to have intense, primary associations with particular ecological settings, socioeconomic structures, and ideologies" (Kolata 1993a:240–241). He speculates that Aymara, Pukina, and Uru were distinct ethnic groups that coexisted during the Tiwanaku Period, each corresponding with a distinct productive regime. While the Aymara tended herds of llamas and alpacas, the Pukina developed raised field systems, and the Uru, lower in status and at the base of the sociopolitical hierarchy, specialized in lacustrine resources. Aymara and Pukina, the dominant groups from which Tiwanaku rulers most likely were drawn, may have formed a cohesive state system via dynastic marriages.

Many archaeologists seriously consider the potential roles of local groups and communities in past productive enterprises such as farming. Clark Erickson (1988, 1992, 1993, 1999), based on research in the northwest Titicaca Basin near Huatta, Peru, argues that raised field agriculture developed out of the knowledge and skills of local lake-adapted populations, clusters of *ayllus* and communities that maintained their integrity and identities despite wave after wave of subjugation by Andean states. He (1993:413) concludes that "states of the region developed and collapsed with regularity, but the agricultural systems organized at lower levels continued relatively unaffected and perhaps thrived." According to Erickson, state rulers never "tampered with" ancient raised field systems (Erickson 1988:3481).

Some models stress the roles of *ayllus* to the near exclusion of centralizing forces and institutions, assuming a relatively static historical relation between state and *ayllu*. Building on Erickson's model, Gray Graffam makes such an argument for the Katari Valley. Based on sampled survey and test excavations in a segment of the Koani Pampa, he (1990:207–219; 1992) surmised that most (sixty-eight percent) of the raised fields in this region were built by *ayllus* "without bureaucracy" during the post-Tiwanaku period. More recent survey and excavation puts in question Graffam's chronology (Janusek and Kolata 2003; Kolata and Ortloff 1996; Seddon 1994). Like Ponce's early model, but emphasizing the *ayllu*, Graffam presumes a rigid temporal and social division between *ayllu* and State.

Potential for a more dynamic consideration of the play of central and local forces emerges from recent regional research in the Tiwanaku Valley and household research at Lukurmata. Treading cautiously between "centralized bureaucracy" and "local autonomy" models, Juan Albarracín-Jordan (1992, 1996a, 1996b, 2003) develops an interpretation of regional organization that considers the dynamic roles of local *ayllu*-like groups. Based on extensive regional survey in the Tiwanaku Valley, he hypothesizes that Tiwanaku formed a loosely centralized segmentary state similar to those historically documented. Evidence resides in the presence of discrete settlement clusters in the Tiwanaku Valley from the Middle Formative Period up until through the Early Spanish Colonial Period (McAndrews et al. 1997). By the Tiwanaku IV Period, Albarracín-Jordan suggests, distinct settlement clusters had formed around relatively large regional centers, and they were associated with different productive regimes—in the north part of the valley small-scale raised field systems, and in the south sunken water basins (*qochas*) and agricultural terraces. In Tiwanaku V (AD 800–1150), he argues, settlement density increased most significantly in the number of small hamlets, thereby weakening political centralization. Much like later polities in the south-central Andes, Albarracín-Jordan argues, Tiwanaku was a nested hierarchy of semiautonomous sociopolitical groupings, in which local leaders in regional centers enjoyed substantial political authority over the organization of local productive enterprises. The fundamental integrative mechanism in the region was not political centralization but religious ideology, which "provided a common 'language' among the different levels of authority" (Albarracin-Jordan 1996b:205).

In a similar vein Marc Bermann (1994, 1997, 2003), who conducted the first systematic household archaeology project in the Tiwanaku core, finds that changes in Lukurmata households did not correspond precisely with changes in the larger Tiwanaku polity. Bermann conducted excavations in a saddle on the ridge known as Wila Kollu, just below the prominent monumental complex at the site. Here, the greatest changes in household life and domestic economy occurred only late in Tiwanaku's political development (Late Tiwanaku IV, AD 600–800). These changes reflect the shifting roles of households in a changing political economy rather than changes initiated from above, and Bermann (1997:107–108) cites regional agricultural intensification and increasing local competition for land as likely primary causes. Balancing evidence for long-term shifts in the area, he (1997:106) notes that "it would be difficult to distinguish when Lukurmata became part of the Tiwanaku polity." Vertical integration involved complex relations between state leaders and local groups, and "incorporation into a larger political system [was] just a phase in the evolution of the smaller community" (Bermann 1994:11).

Research Questions and Hypotheses

These three broad scenarios provide a foundation for the questions, hypotheses, and objectives that guide this long-term study of Tiwanaku and Lukurmata.

Each of them emphasizes a unique perspective that is neither invalid nor erroneous. The line of thought exploring Tiwanaku as a prehispanic agrarian state emphasizes high urban densities, strong central political authority, and an autonomous political economy grounded in local agropastoral production. Ponce's and Kolata's models directly address the nature of Tiwanaku cities. According to Ponce's model, Tiwanaku urban centers, and especially Tiwanaku itself, incorporated substantial social differentiation along the lines emphasized by Childe (1950) and others, largely status (or wealth) and role. Tiwanaku housed an emergent middle class of artisans that manufactured elaborate goods and designed monumental buildings that directly supported the power and authority of ruling elites. Developing this idea, Kolata argues that Tiwanaku and its provincial centers revolved exclusively around elite power and activity, essentially forming extended elite households, or what he calls "hyper-oikoi" (1997, drawing on Weber's concept of *oikos*). Elites designed Tiwanaku and its outlying centers as rigidly ordered cosmic symbols tied to significant terrestrial and celestial features, linking the generative power of such features to the agentive power of rulers and priests. Beyond the requirements of occupations that served ruling elite lineages, Tiwanaku itself "boasted little in the way of pluralism and heterogeneity."

These models focus largely on sociopolitical hierarchy and direct elite control over social networks, specialized production, and productive resources. In them, at times, the state is essentialized as a static, omnipotent institution. In none is there significant discussion of the possible roles that social diversity, nested identities, or local leadership—like those prevalent in post-Tiwanaku societies—might have had state formation, constitution, or collapse. Following Kolata's model, the state was a ubiquitous character of Tiwanaku urban (and rural) society, "co-extensive with the social body" as Foucault might say, and inherent in the most private domestic ritual. Although Kolata argues that Tiwanaku was ethnically diverse, he does not develop its possible significance in relation to identity politics, power relations, or internal differences and tensions. Although he mentions the possibility of resistance, he (Kolata 1996a:17) suggests that Tiwanaku's benevolent and beneficial managerial policies were "sufficient incentive such that local communities readily contributed their labor to enhance the collective forces of production." Ultimately, it seems, resistance was unthinkable.

These ideas raise important questions: How was the state, with its integrative forces and institutions, apparent in urban residential life? How was it expressed in residential spatial organization and everyday practice? Was material culture highly standardized and homogeneous in Tiwanaku cities? Was specialized production directed by and for ruling elites (that is, was it attached to elite management and consumption)? Was status differentiation prevalent, and did it follow a concentric gradient in urban space? How did these patterns change throughout Tiwanaku's history?

Some of the recent models emphasizing the role and power of local groups lean toward an opposite extreme, accentuating the powerful local autonomy documented in more recent Andean political federations and contemporary Aymara communities. A key idea in all is that direct control over human activity or productive resources was in the hands of local groups, and was only indirectly controlled by state leaders. Not surprisingly, few of these models are based on research in Tiwanaku urban centers, and with the important exception of Bermann's model of vertical integration, none of them explicitly offers expectations for urban residential organization. Even in Albarracín-Jordan's model, any transformations attendant on Tiwanaku state formation wind up, in effect, as addenda accreted onto an *a priori*, loosely integrated network of nested *ayllu*-like groups. There is little discussion of the potential effects emergent state institutions had on preexisting segmentary systems, or of how and why those institutions developed in the first place. Thus, although Albarracín-Jordan is cautious about using the *ayllu* model to interpret the distant past, he essentially does so. The nested organization out of which Tiwanaku emerged, and through which it thrived, was essentially much like that of later polities such as Qaraqara or Pacajes. As archaeological patterns make clear, Tiwanaku was far different from such later federations.

These ideas also raise important questions: Was there significant local power and autonomy in Tiwanaku sociopolitical organization and political economy? How was it manifested in urban residential space and practice? Was there significant stylistic diversity in Tiwanaku urban centers? How was it manifested in relation to cultural standardization? Was specialized production the province of local groups, and if so at what social scale? How did these patterns change through time?

I also examine the cosmic and ritual dimensions of residential life in Tiwanaku. To do this I consider the possible symbolic and lived dimensions of urban spatial order, as well as the culturally informed activities that characterized that dynamic order, reproducing and transforming it over time. Further, I consider the ways in which a dominant cosmology may have been apprehended; not necessarily as a neat and impermeable system, but as a partially understood, in some respects contradictory, lived order that, because burdened by the world, was always in the process of creation, reproduction, or transformation. Examining the significance of ritual requires comparing activities between different residential areas, and between residential and monumental contexts. I address several key questions: If Tiwanaku was a ceremonial center, was it always the same kind of ceremonial center? How did the role of ritual or feasting change through time? How did public and private rituals vary, and what did they share? If Tiwanaku was a symbolic icon, in what ways did its spatial order and meaning change over the history of the site? How was its significance apprehended by different groups of people? How did local groups develop, adopt, or transform the predominant state culture, or perhaps appropriate it to local ideals and meanings?

Rather than attempt to set up a straw man from among the models described above, I sift out key elements in them to craft a historically dynamic perspective of Tiwanaku that emphasizes social affiliations and power relations in local practice. Following the theoretical approach outlined in Chapter 1, I adopt a practice perspective. This is critical to combat essentialism, a major weakness in many models regarding Tiwanaku's constitution and prehispanic history. Many interpretations treat the Tiwanaku polity as a single, static, unchanging essence. Tiwanaku was a "vacant pilgrimage center," an "intensely hierarchical state," or a "nested hierarchy" of *ayllu*-like groups. Some models that posit Tiwanaku was a religious center ignore the possibility for significant urban residence or political integration. Models that posit Tiwanaku was a highly integrated state tend to downplay the dynamic roles of local organizations, interactions, and identities, while models emphasizing local groups tend to posit weak or absent integrative institutions. The relations between state institutions, local groups, and ritual practices, as well as their historical trajectories, are rarely elaborated in depth.

To address the questions posed by past research and interpretations, I seek to elucidate the impact of local organizations and social practices on Tiwanaku state dynamics. Evidence for state-scale social complexity is sought in characteristic expressions of urban heterogeneity, particularly specialized craft production and status differences. In many models, valued goods in centralized societies are produced in great part by attached specialists, who "produce goods [for] or provide services to a patron, typically either a social elite or a governing institution" (Brumfiel and Earle 1987:5; also Earle 1981). Many archaeologists concur in addition that "archaic states were societies with (minimally) two class-endogamous strata (a professional ruling class and a commoner class)" (Marcus and Feinman 1998:4). Therefore, evidence for attached production and class divisions in Tiwanaku urban centers would indicate sociopolitical and economic relations typical of other archaic states. To attached production and class divisions, I add evidence for hierarchical organization in the regional settlement networks of which Tiwanaku and Lukurmata formed primary parts. Many archaeologists agree that regional settlement patterns are closely related to specific productive organizations and sociopolitical structures (Flannery 1976; Johnson 1977; Paynter 1983; Wright 1977; Wright and Johnson 1975).

Nevertheless, we can expect to find expressions of social diversity or heterarchy. Sociopolitical and productive organizations may have been grounded in nested *ayllu*-like groups and integrated hierarchies of encompassment. Interest in expressions of local power in archaic states and empires has focused on incorporated peripheral and rural regions, leaving us with the implicit assumption that their core cities were homogeneous in culture and practice (Bermann 1997:108). State cores, it is assumed, are *prima facie* not key areas for investigating identity formation and political resistance. Challenging this assumption, I assess the relation between a cohesive, hierarchical order and the expression of social boundaries and differences. I do this in part by examining the possibility that productive activities such as craft specialization and farming were locally organized and directed as "independent" (Brumfiel and Earle 1987) or "embedded" (Ames 1995; Janusek 1999) forms of production. Drawing on analogy with later societies, I examine potential correspondences among such variables as specialized production, social status, and social identity, comparing expressions of hierarchy and conventional aspects of complexity on the one hand, with expressions of local identity and sociopolitical heterarchy on the other.

Further, I compare contrasting patterns of conformity and diversity in various types of Tiwanaku material culture. These include ritual activities, spatial orientation, architectural design, diets, mortuary practices, cranial modification, and—most important here—stylistic characteristics of ceramic assemblages. Evidence for the creation of a coherent elite-focused ideology, and its expression as a naturalized practical hegemony, is sought by assessing the expression of uniformity in key patterns of material culture. I examine conformity in residential spatial organization and in the relative ubiquity of a definable state culture, or what I consider a suite of similar techniques, styles, practices, and values promoted by ruling elites. Evidence for the expression of social identity is sought by comparing ceramic assemblages and other categories of material culture from various excavated residential contexts at Tiwanaku and Lukurmata. Diverse lines of evidence allow us to refine our portrait of Tiwanaku sociopolitical organization and the role of social difference, identity, and ritual practices in the historical dynamics of this native state.

In relation to changing state institutions and ideologies, on the one hand, and shifting local identities and practices, on the other, I examine the significance of urban rituals and ceremonies. I examine ritual practices in relation to shifting balances among horizontal and vertical relations; that is, between groups relatively similar in status and between elite and nonelite groups. For example, I discuss the roles of cosmology and ritual in the rise of Tiwanaku as a major center. Terence Turner (1996) speculates that Andean complex societies arose out of specialized ceremonial centers, which succeeded in transcending early limits to centralization by appropriating the power (via ritual specialists) to intervene in extrasocial forces. Kolata suggests that Tiwanaku rulers sought to appropriate powerful generative forces by constructing built environments attuned to celestial movements and specific positions in a landscape. A primary concern also may have been to demonstrate power of cosmic mediation for a diverse audience, whether pilgrims or others seeking to be part of the Tiwanaku experience. Addressing these ideas, I appraise the extent to which cosmic meanings were built into early settlement organization, and how spatial orders changed over time.

In order to address these inquiries, I next outline the approaches to style, chronology, and residential archaeology that frame this study.

Style, Ritual, and Time in the Study of Tiwanaku Residences

Style and Identity

Specific problems in the Tiwanaku heartland prompt an explicit approach to style. In the Andes, as elsewhere, archaeologists conventionally employ style, in particular ceramic style, as a tool to fashion regional chronologies. While chronologies are important and stylistic change is useful, often implicit is the assumption that style is simply a passive reflection of social process. In this section I develop an approach to style and regional chronology that takes this assumption to task (also Janusek 1999, 2002, 2003a). First, drawing on ongoing research and interpretation I acknowledge that material style often plays an active role in history and social interaction. Second, I develop a chronology that addresses the relative significance of successive phases of slow and rapid change, and the significance of the materials employed to gauge those phases.

A great deal of research indicates that material style often plays an active role in social interaction, especially in expressing social status and identity (DeBoer 1990; Dietler and Herbich 1998; Hebdige 1979; Schortman 1989; Shennan 1989; Wiessner 1983, 1990; Upham 1990:103–107; Wobst 1977). As Holland et al. (1998:63) point out, in key social contexts, material culture can "play a pivotal role" in "its capacity to shift the perceptual, cognitive, affective, and practical frame" of human activity. It is the particular capacity of material culture, as concrete symbols, to condense and focus all of those frames that lend it particular power in human interaction.

As discussed in Chapters 1 and 2, identity indexes various types of groups in a given social and cultural universe. We can expect that different types of identity will be expressed in specific elements of material culture. The relation of identity and materials draws us into a familiar tension in contemporary studies, one linked to the clash of essentialist and constructivist visions of culture (Emberling 1997; Jones 1997). On the one hand, anthropologists have traditionally focused on identity as an essential, unquestioned quality of a particular society or culture. Identity is a given, a basic characteristic of human nature as defined and reproduced within a particular cultural order (Geertz 1973; Shils 1957). Ethnic and other identities are considered primordial characteristics of human behavior, and their corresponding symbols and objects relate more or less directly to their deep-seated meaning systems. A problem with this position is that it takes too literally the naturalized, hegemonic order of any cultural world as a primordial given (Jones 1997). The position ultimately denies individuals any active or constructive role in society, for they are too burdened by the immutable and determining attachments inscribed in cultural identity. Identity is abstracted as an ineffable characteristic of a person or society, with little if any attention to the fluidity of its boundaries, the social contexts of its expression, or the historical circumstances of its formulation.

Beginning with Barth (1969) and Cohen (1974), the anthropological tide has shifted toward an emphasis on the dynamic, situational aspects of ethnic and other identities. Following this instrumentalist perspective, what is important about ethnic identity is not any deep-seated significant meaning system, but the construction and maintenance of boundaries. Identities are defined not so much in reference to internal cultural coherence, but strategically, as "us" as opposed to "them." In this view, people design, employ, combine, even suppress or blur aspects of their identity to advance their political and economic interests. The problem with such positions is that, in drawing attention to the strategic foundations of identity, ethnic and other groups are reduced to interest groups in which individuals homogeneously seek political or economic advantage. The reduction of identity to strategy assumes that human action is universally rational, its intentions directed toward maximizing self-interest. Like many models of cultural evolution, this presupposes a highly abstract and one-dimensional concept of individuals. Further, it empties all social groupings and figured worlds of internal coherence and historical consistency (De Vos 1995; Royce 1982), and treats them as vessels into which any of an infinite variety of cultural attributes may be strategically poured (Jones 1997:77).

Addressing the relation of meaning and strategy, and identifying power relations and social affiliations in material culture, demand a critical approach to style. Many recent studies—in particular ethnoarchaeological studies—demonstrate that the relation between human action and material culture is never simple or straightforward (DeBoer 1984, 1990, Dietler and Herbich 1998; Hayden and Cannon 1983; Hodder 1982; Stark et al. 1998). Any approach to the relation between style and society must proceed cautiously and self-consciously, acknowledging that a particular material style may have meant any of many things, many things at once, or perhaps nothing at all. Minimally, a cautious approach to style must acknowledge a few key points. First, we need to move beyond aesthetic and object-based approaches to style. These approaches tend to conflate style with elaboration, or the "dressing" added to an object that connotes wealth or leisure time (see Sackett 1977, 1990; Wobst 1977), while isolating objects as bearers of style from the processes of their production, significance, and use. Second, material culture is not a text to be read, for it rarely forms a coherent string of signs "created expressly and exclusively as an instrument of communication" (Dietler and Herbich 1998:244). Material culture is rather a product of practical activity and may be employed as an instrument of social expression. More often than directly referring to something, a specific meaning or social group, material culture evokes significance.

Third, style is as much a particular way of creating something as it is the characteristic attributes of a material object (Janusek 1999). It is as much the way one harvests clay as it is the particular motifs one chooses to decorate a vessel (see DeBoer 1984), or as much the specific technique employed to modify a child's head shape as it is the final head shape itself (see Blom 1999). In pottery, style is not simply a set of decorative attributes as opposed to paste recipes but also the specific technical processes that guided its production. These techniques involve, like Bourdieu's *habitus*, characteristic dispositions and decisions that are negotiated at innumerable stages in a creative process (Lemonnier 1986, 1993). Style and technique are inseparable in that style is both the characteristic way of doing something (Hodder 1990; Wiessner 1990) and the objectified result of an entire process of production (Dietler and Herbich 1998). Nevertheless it bears distinguishing between the style of techniques and of things, or between "technological" and "material style" (Lechtman 1977). It is important to remain aware that the stylistic significance guiding the production of an object is distinct from the various meanings it may evoke in its use-life.

Finally, each society or group, in line with specific generative predispositions and historical circumstances, will produce and employ a unique repertoire of material and nonmaterial elements to express identity, and the elements so charged may change through time. These may include specific gestures and dialects, for the most part invisible to archaeologists, but also specific activities, life ways, and material objects more amenable to archaeological investigation. There is no reason to presume that any given category of materials necessarily marked social identity (Barth 1969:14), nor that another did not. One must determine which elements of material culture may have been significant, for which specific reasons, and in what social contexts. A first step is to isolate items of material culture that were typically on display (Smith 1987; Wobst 1977), but it is not enough to measure past expressions of identity according to an "abstract scale of visibility" (Dietler and Herbich 1998:241). Rather, the things that marked identity at a particular social scale are usually those considered significant or that maintained key roles in contexts of social interaction (see DeBoer 1990; DeBoer and Moore 1982). They are in many cases objects of particular symbolic import in vibrant social gatherings and ritual contexts.

As material symbols, crafted objects reify ideas and affiliations and in their use they enunciate explicit or hidden agendas. If archaeologists have determined that style plays an active role in social interaction, they have been less successful at linking particular types of material style to their specific meanings, agendas, and referents. Wiessner (1983, 1990) has taken great steps in this direction by distinguishing active style, a "way of doing" or material characteristic to which "great social and symbolic" significance is attached," from passive style, a way of doing or material characteristic that is "not subject to regular. . . social comparison" (Wiessner 1990:107). The concept of passive style resonates with Sackett's (1990) ways of doing something that play little or no active role in social interaction or identification. Wiessner further distinguishes active style according to the specificity of its referent. Emblemic style has a specific referent, just as U.S. Republican party members proudly wear their elephants or Chicago Cubs fans wear caps embroidered with a red "C." Assertive style has a relatively vague referent, in the sense that a woman wearing tattoos, piercings, and visible body hair may signal she is lesbian. Style may also mark differences in status or occupation (Janusek 1999; Upham 1990). As discussed in Chapters 1 and 2, status, occupation, and identity may be three dimensions of a single social boundary, and in such cases style, active or passive, may simultaneously signal all at once.

In past complex societies such as Tiwanaku we can expect that stylistic references were complex in these and other ways. The specific practices and objects that are apprehended as style, consciously or not, are part of an encompassing cultural logic. Thus, both style and the way it is apprehended and interpreted are subject to change. A goal here is to determine the extent to which shifts in dominant styles coincide with transformations in broader social arenas. It is an intriguing possibility that radical shifts in power relations, as when a naturalized order of things becomes open to ideological apprehension and perhaps political contest, will correspond with shifts in particular stylistic expressions.

Style and Ritual in the Andes

In the Andes, the things and practices that mark identity usually have one of several interrelated qualities. First, they are objects that embodied, carried, or displayed elements or motifs of significance to a group, even if the group does not consciously apprehend them as such in every social context. These are most often crafted items of relatively high value, including woven clothing and mantles, carved bone and wood implements, wrought metal adornments, and elaborately forged and decorated ceramic vessels. Second, they are ritual practices that linked a group to its past through sequences of activities, events, and offerings that conjure and reaffirm collective memory (Abercrombie 1998). These may include rituals of consumption, elaborate libation sequences, and mortuary rituals. Third, identity markers include manners of decorating and modifying human bodies. Clothing and crafted items of adornment fall into this category, as do manners of decorating and modifying the body itself, through painting, scarification, tattooing, and modifying the shape of the skull or other body parts.

The most significant events for a group, society, or polity are those that involve decorated human bodies and valued objects in lively contexts that stimulate group identity and conjure its historical consciousness. Such public events generate a charged emotional ambience, a rush of immediate sensual experience and a heightened sense of group coherence that Emile Durkheim (1915), writing almost a century ago, termed "collective effervescence." In the Andes it is in lively social gatherings, ritual contexts, and ceremonial feasts that style becomes particularly potent (Abercrombie 1998; Buechler 1980; Rasnake 1988). Feasting promotes a spontaneous sense of *communitas*, "a direct, immediate, and total confrontation of human identities," evoking a "concrete, if fleeting, experience of community" (Turner 1969:132). In feasts, the stylistic properties of specific objects or clothing may be overtly or unconsciously acknowledged. Some stylistic elements may be consciously acknowledged, while others remain unnoticed and unacknowledged. For example, a vessel shape tacitly accepted as normal and unremarkable, to some, may appear unusual to others, or a particular motif on a woven tunic, exotic or unpleasant. There is no accounting for taste, for taste can be strategically cultivated but it is embedded in the habitual generative schemes of specific social groups, each with unique histories, identities, and stylistic preferences. In dynamic social contexts, stylistically dense items and practices cue information about their producers or owners, including their affiliations, status, and "place" in the larger system, most effectively so in items created and activities conducted with display in mind (DeBoer and Moore 1982; Smith 1987).

The most stylistically important goods and practices will maintain both religious and social significance (DeBoer and Moore 1982; Hoshower et al. 1995; Smith 1987). In past Andean communities, ceramic vessels carried the food and beverages that were so critical to the formulation, reproduction, and transformation (even the negation) of relations among humans, and just as significant, between humans, ancestors, and deep cosmic forces (Abercrombie 1998). In part due to their roles as vehicles mediating multiple relations, they often embedded dense stylistic properties that were highly visible in rituals of consumption and other dynamic social contexts. Serving and ceremonial wares were among the most sensitive and effective markers of social and cultural affiliation.

Tiwanaku Style and Chronology

Acknowledging that style plays an active role in society and history raises important issues relating to chronology. A first step toward building a chronology is acknowledging that it is a specific interpretation of long-term history (Braudel 1980:95). Because different types of material culture vary in their roles and meanings, we can expect that they will change to varying degrees and at different rates, following distinct temporal rhythms (Braudel 1980; Smith 1992). In a varied range of materials such as ceramic vessels, certain types may change substantially and abruptly while others change very gradually and perhaps minimally. Further, given the varied logics and diverse strategies deployed by different groups in a society, we can expect that at any time, style may vary significantly according to social context. A full appreciation of the complex relations of style and society can be addressed only when change in various types of material culture are examined and compared.

Until very recently, knowledge of Bolivia's prehispanic history was limited to what little was understood of Tiwanaku civilization, and changes in style were linked to its presumed rise and fall. Following popular European ideas that likened the rise and fall of civilization to the life history of an individual (Spengler 1934), Max Uhle (1903:786) considered Andean civilizations to "develop, flourish, and decay the same as man." As "superorganic" phenomena that followed uniform cycles of growth, maturity, and degeneration, such civilizations were gauged by their cultural achievements in the arts and sciences. Tiwanaku in its prime was considered to have achieved greatness, as manifested in awesome monuments and an exquisite art style, and for this reason influenced a vast range of Andean cultural traditions. Cultural florescence was thought to be reflected in stylistic uniformity and elegance, and cultural disintegration in stylistic diversity or decadence.

Wendell Bennett, the first archaeologist to conduct systematic research at Tiwanaku, brought some of these ideas to his interpretation of Tiwanaku prehistory. Based on stratigraphic changes in his two best pits (Pits V and VIII), he (1934) distinguished Early, Classic, and Decadent Tiwanaku as relative chronological phases with distinct ceramic styles. Early Tiwanaku, represented in deep occupation middens 1.5 meters to 2 meters thick, consisted mostly of undecorated vessel sherds and "two sets" of decorated wares; what we now term the Kalasasaya and Qeya styles. Later occupation middens were characterized by much higher quantities of elaborate, decorated ceramics. Bennett divided these later strata into Classic and Decadent phases. Bennett distinguished the styles as "a division of color treatment into a rich, varied group and a drab, restricted group." The drab group manifested a degeneration of "pictorial" style and an increasing emphasis on "pure design," exhibiting "a general confusion of elements and combinations which would have been sacrilegious to the Classic designers" (Bennett 1934:403–406). Thus, Bennett made important observations about stylistic changes but interpreted them according to a highly subjective scheme.

The Swedish archaeologist Stig Rydén, adopting Bennett's sequence and general excavation methods, took the analysis of Tiwanaku style one step further. Unlike Bennett, Rydén (1947) closely examined Tiwanaku undecorated ceramics, those which Bennett himself had admitted comprised the majority of ceramic sherds in any excavated context. Rydén examined in minute detail what he termed "utility" ceramics, and in doing so pioneered the analysis and categorization of Tiwanaku vessels based on parameters of form and function. He defined three broad categories of Tiwanaku ceramic pots: cooking vessels, water and fermentation jars, and artistic pottery. Although Rydén made a superficial distinction between functional and artistic vessels, his approach encompassed all vessels, an approach not replicated until the Proyecto Wila Jawira initiated its research in the 1980s.

It was Dwight Wallace who in his doctoral dissertation produced the first systematic critique of the Tiahuanaco horizon as a unitary phenomenon. He concluded that the horizon was not a single aesthetic unit, but rather consisted of at least three distinct stylistic configurations; Tiwanaku, Pukara, and Wari. His analysis remains the most comprehensive seriation of highland Andean ceramics. Wallace (1957) analyzed 865 Tiwanaku-style pots from museums and various published sources, and compared them to sherds excavated at five sites in the altiplano. He was the first isolate to Qeya, Bennett's second set of Early Tiwanaku pottery, as an early stylistic complex. For later Tiwanaku he (1957:127–130) upheld Bennett's distinction between Classic and what he called "Post-Classic" phases, but like Bennett pointed out that Classic-style ceramics were often found mixed with post-Classic vessels. Taking a regional approach, Wallace pointed out that Classic-style ceramics were not commonly found outside of Tiwanaku, and suggested that more than successive phases, the Classic-Decadent distinction may represent contemporaneous styles.

On this foundation Ponce (1980, 1981) developed his well-known chronology of three stages and five epochs. In this scheme he correlated, but sought to avoid confusing, artistic style and political development. He considered Tiwanaku I to correspond with Bennett's first decorated set of ceramics (Ponce 1971, 1991), the Kalasasaya style, while Tiwanaku II was represented by little more than coarse undecorated wares (1981). Ponce never made a strong claim for a correspondence between Tiwanaku III and Qeya, apparently because the ceramics were rare in the Kalasasaya. Less ambiguously, Ponce has denied a strict correlation of Classic style with Tiwanaku IV and Decadent style with Tiwanaku V. He (1981:72–73) argues that the Classic-Decadent distinction "is not founded on absolute stratigraphic differentiation" for "in the CIAT excavations [the styles] are found together with frequency." More forcefully than Wallace, he distinguished "classic" from "provincial" as coexisting styles, and argued for contemporaneous stylistic diversity at Tiwanaku sites.

Despite Ponce's observations, it remains common to conflate Bennett's division of Classic and Decadent styles with Ponce's IV and V periods (Mature Urban and Imperial stages). It is generally assumed that Tiwanaku IV is represented by finely executed ceramics with naturalistic designs and Tiwanaku V by more crudely executed ceramics with geometric, repetitive designs. This conflation carries with it assumptions embedded in the aesthetic approach to style. One basic goal of my research was to distinguish between style and time, examining change in various elements of material culture and, following Wallace's and Ponce's suggestions, the significance of contemporaneous stylistic variation. Ceramic vessels are central in this analysis. I examine and describe them with an eye to their significance in Tiwanaku culture and social relations, and explore the significance of change in ceramic assemblages and styles through the course of state formation, consolidation, and fragmentation. I also consider the particular roles of specific types, such as those used for storage in relation to those for serving and ritual consumption. Because properties of role and style vary by type, so does their respective significance in given social domains. It follows that some ceramic types may change much more slowly than others, following variable social and historical rhythms.

A Chronological Outline

The chronology developed here employs seriation in relation to excavated stratigraphic sequences and a large suite of radiometric dates (see Janusek 2003a). Ceramic seriation centers principally on parameters of ceramic form, function, and iconography in relation to other properties (surface treatment, design, firing, paste composition). Style is an important dimension of each of these properties. I categorize vessels according to a scalar hierarchy of class, type, and variant (Figure 3.2). Each class consists of a range of types that differs in form and role, and each type consists of numerous variants similar in basic form but different in composition, treatment, decoration, or in minor qualities of form. Vessels for most periods are categorized as one of four basic classes: a) cooking vessels; b) storage vessels; c) serving-ceremonial vessels; and d) ritual vessels. For several reasons, these classes must be considered continual rather than fixed categories. For one thing, sherds of cooking and storage vessels are in many cases difficult to differentiate, in part because many such pots clearly changed roles throughout their use-lives, and in part because certain variants could serve both functions. Serving and ritual vessels also must remain loosely defined in part because, as in more recent Aymara communities (Tschopic 1950:209), many could serve either purpose depending on context.

Combined, stratigraphy, seriation, and radiocarbon dating reveal three major periods of regional social, political, and religious development between 200 BC and AD 1570, the span encompassed in this book (Janusek 2003a). The Late Formative Period dates from approximately 200 BC to about AD 500, and it encompasses two principal phases, Late Formative 1 (200 BC–AD 300) and Late Formative 2 (AD 300–500). Characterizing most Late Formative residential contexts were certain continuous material patterns and daily practices, a common "cultural tradition" as Mathews (1992:220) suggested. These included household ceramic inventories comprised of undecorated domestic wares, such as cooking *ollas*, annular bowls, storage jars, and smaller proportions of vessels dedicated to serving and consumption, mostly *vasijas* used as pitchers, and small bowls, or *cuencos*. Elaborate serving-ceremonial ceramic assemblages, on the other hand, changed markedly between the two phases. Late Formative 1 contexts yield Kalasasaya red-painted or incision-zoned wares, while Late Formative 2 contexts yield Qeya wares (cf. Mathews 1992, 1997). However, attempting to date occupations using decorated ceramics alone is problematic.

The Tiwanaku Period can be divided into four phases: Early Tiwanaku IV from AD 500 to 600, Late Tiwanaku IV to AD 800, Early Tiwanaku V to AD 1000, and Late Tiwanaku V to AD 1150. The beginning of the Tiwanaku Period corresponded with the abrupt appearance of Tiwanaku-style redware, and to a lesser extent blackware, ceramic vessels. These wares involved great innovations in technological style, which for the most part remained popular throughout the entire 650-year Tiwanaku Period. Thus, following Ponce's observation I emphatically repeat that there is no clear stylistic difference between successive Tiwanaku phases (Janusek 1994, 2003a). Although diverse in its range of types and variants, Tiwanaku style demonstrated a relatively high degree of standardization in certain canons of

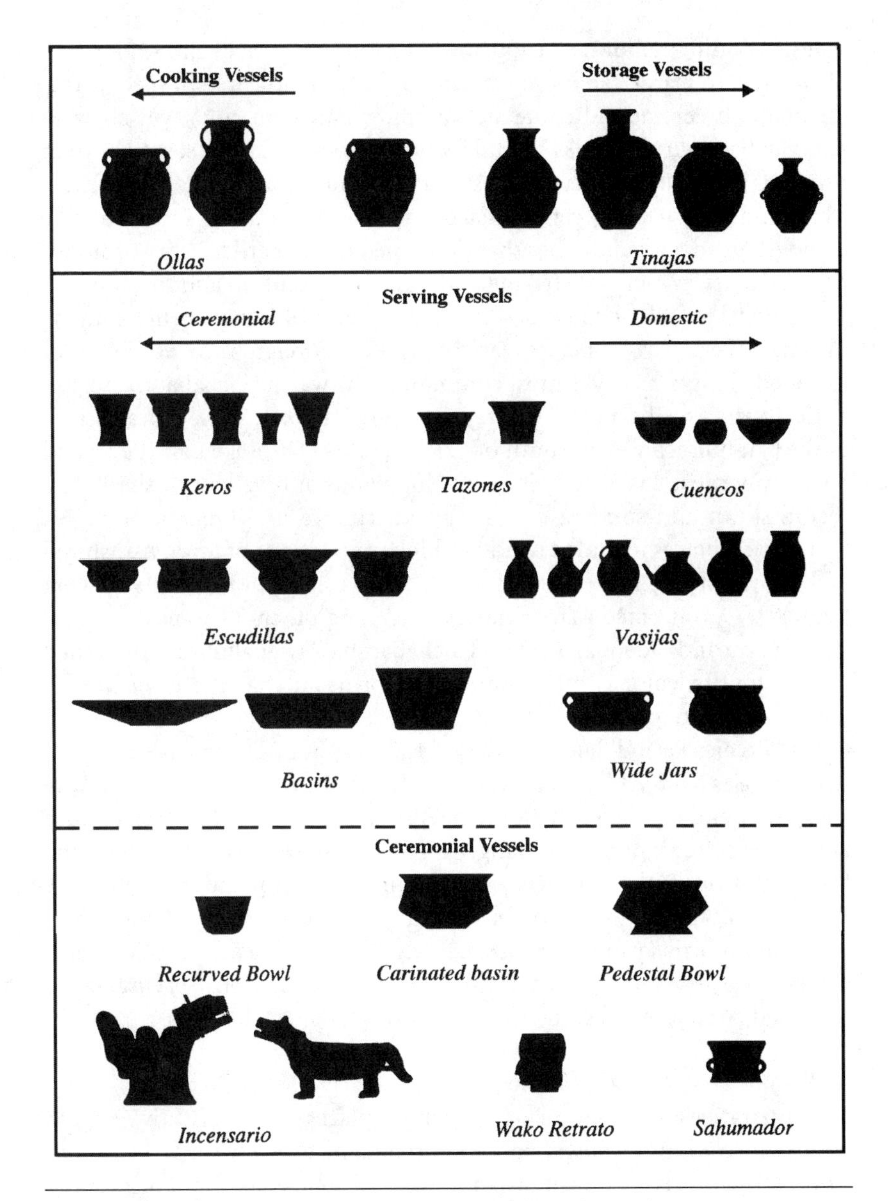

Figure 3.2 Major classes, types, and variants of Tiwanaku ceramic vessels.

form, treatment, and iconography. Large liquid storage and fermentation jars, or *tinajas*, became increasingly common throughout the Tiwanaku period. These accompanied a wide range of elegant serving-ceremonial vessels. Most common were drinking chalices, or *keros*, everted bowls, or *tazons*, and serving pitchers, or *vasijas*, but a number of special serving types, including elaborate flaring bowls, or *escudillas*, small ellipsoid bowls, or *cuencos*, and large ceremonial basins, or *fuentes*, appeared in specific residential and ceremonial contexts. The most common ritual vessels were annular-base burners, or *sahumadors*, which appear to have served both in rituals of purification and as domestic lamps, and in Lukurmata, large feline, llama, and condor-effigy ceremonial burners, or *incensarios*. Tiwanaku-style iconography depicted themes that developed out of earlier Late Formative decorative styles, but was strikingly different in execution and meaning.

Nonlocal vessels formed a small but significant component of many Tiwanaku Period assemblages (Janusek 2003a). Foreign wares at Tiwanaku included: Omereque style, most common in the warm Cochabamba region to the southeast (Ibarra and Querejazu 1986); Yampara style, characteristic of the Chuquisaca valleys south of Cochabamba (Janusek et al. 1997); and Yura style, most characteristic of the highlands and valleys of the Potosi region south and southeast of Tiwanaku (Ibarra and Querejazu 1986). Some assemblages included relatively high proportions of foreign-inspired and hybrid styles, most notably the Cochabamba-Tiwanaku style, what Bennett (1936) termed "Tiwanaku Derived" and others "Tiwanaku Expansive" (Ibarra and Querejazu 1986). Cochabamba-Tiwanaku wares included unique motifs, color combinations, and forms such as the *challador*, or narrow-based kero.

The Pacajes Period dated from AD 1150 to about AD 1450, divided into Early Pacajes from AD 1150 to AD 1475, Inca Pacajes to AD 1535, and Late Pacajes, essentially the Early Colonial Period, to AD 1570. Material culture and many cultural practices changed significantly after AD 1150, upon the fragmentation of the Tiwanaku polity and the depopulation of its large settlements. Among more notable changes were dispersed settlement patterns, new mortuary practices, and new serving-ceremonial ceramic assemblages. In a dramatic switch from the Tiwanaku Period, serving wares consisted largely, once again, of a limited variety of small bowls.

Household Archaeology: Problems and Prospects

A comparative investigation of residential places is one effective way to approach relations of power and identity in a historically sensitive framework. This book is a study in urban residential archaeology and principally of the nonelite populations residing in Tiwanaku's two primary cities. When initiated this project was conceived as an exploration in household archaeology, and one fundamental objective was to define the material constitution of the household unit (Janusek 1994:81; also Blanton 1994; Netting et al. 1984; Stanish 1989a; Wilk and Rathje 1982). Abundant research highlights the value of households for investigating social, economic, and ritual organizations and activities in past complex societies

(Alexander 1999; Ashmore and Wilk 1988; Bermann 1994, 1997; Flannery and Winter 1976; Hayden and Cannon 1983; Hendon 1996; Hirth 1993; Manzanilla 1993, 2002; Mehrer 1995; Palka 1997; Smith 1987; Spencer-Wood 1999; Stanish 1989a; Wilk 1983; Wilk and Rathje 1982; Wilk and Netting 1984). A focus on past household space and activities is an effective way to move beyond monumental grandeur and elegant cosmologies and to investigate the practical rhythms of daily life.

Archaeologists recently have offered important cautionary tales that are relevant for a comparative study of a complex society, such as this investigation of Tiwanaku. They point out, for example, that the household is an ethnographic concept with highly varied material correlates and crosscultural significance (Wilk 1991; Wilk and Netting 1984). Adapting the concept to archaeological study, most agree that archaeological households were minimal coresidential groups that shared corporate functions and common tasks, including production, consumption, distribution, and social reproduction (Stanish 1989a). Just about anywhere households were dynamic groups that experienced regular domestic cycles (Hirth 1993; Smith 1992; Tourtellot 1988), and so they varied greatly over time. Further, rather than being strictly domestic groups, in most complex societies many households were highly diverse, open systems of membership (vom Bruck 1997) that were variably linked to wider communities (Brumfiel 1991). Kinship ties may have been fundamental in defining such a group, but other aspects of group identity and activity, such as occupation or ritual affiliation, may also have been as prominent.

Many archaeologists now consider the past household as "a symbolic construct defined and contested through practice" (Hendon 1996:48; also Brumfiel 1991; Gillespie 2000; Joyce 1993; Tringham 1991, 1995 Wright 1991). Rather than an undifferentiated social entity with singular corporate goals, a household may consist "of social actors differentiated by age, gender, role, and power, whose agendas and interests do not always coincide" (Hendon 1996:46). A household is often where power relations and social differences are most consistently negotiated on a day-to-day basis. It is a privileged arena for the enculturation of those relations and differences in the context of a society's changing values, ideologies, and practical hegemonies (Bourdieu 1977). In nearly any society the household is where generative schemes are most intensively inculcated and played out. If households are in any sense fundamental units of social organization, they are highly diverse groupings inextricably tied to larger social, economic, and political organizations and activities. This view encourages us to consider households as more than simply domestic groups (Ames 1995; Feinman and Nicholas 1995; Hendon 1996; Janusek 1999, 2003b; Manzanilla 2002; Mills 1995). As research in Tiwanaku makes clear, domestic activities are often inextricably linked to activities not traditionally considered part of the household, such as craft production and mortuary ritual.

Bermann and I found that such considerations and complexities are pertinent to an undertaking of household archaeology in the Andes. Many interpret the contemporary native Andean household as the primary unit of economic activity (Bolton 1977; Custred 1977) or a nucleus of social organization (Collins 1986; Harris 1985). However, today's Andean households are indigenous responses to several hundred years of Western political systems, economic markets, and cultural values (Stanish 1992:19–20). They have become prominent throughout Hispanic Colonial and Republican history as primary corporate groups just as more inclusive social groupings, such as *ayllus*, have eroded.

Past Andean households often incorporated much more than what are typically considered domestic activities. In Tiwanaku, as in prehispanic centers such as Teotihuacan, conventional divisions between domestic, ritual, and specialized spaces and activities break down (Ames 1995; Feinman and Nicholas 1995; Janusek 1999, 2003b; Manzanilla 1996, 2002). Much of Tiwanaku was devoted to activities not explicitly domestic, and residential areas were places for important ritual practices and specialized economic activities. The places where people slept, ate, and raised children often were the same places where they conducted periodic ceremonies or plied a particular trade. This is in keeping with ethnohistoric and ethnographic research, which pinpoints households within *ayllu*-based organizations as the focus of much communal ritual and specialized production.

The nature of Tiwanaku, and to some extent of Lukurmata, as dynamic urban settlements also affected the results of this study in household archaeology. Excavations clearly demonstrated that in any residential sector, repeated cycles of building, disposal, abandonment, and renewal had continuously disturbed previous archaeological contexts. Tiwanaku in particular was an extraordinarily dynamic site. As Bennett first noted, at least forty percent of excavated occupations consisted of middens and refuse pits, many several meters in crosssection and several meters deep. The complexity of deposition patterns at Tiwanaku explains why isolated excavation units (e.g., Bennett 1934; Kidder 1956; Ryden 1947) have revealed little of its chronology and social character. On the positive side, the sheer volume of refuse and space devoted to refuse alludes to Tiwanaku's significance as a major center. The patterns indicate that through time, household life was increasingly linked to the site's role as a place of ceremonial convergence.

The theoretical and practical complications of doing household archaeology in Tiwanaku invited a broader research focus. Excavation strategy concentrated on broad exposure in several subjectively chosen areas of Tiwanaku and Lukurmata (see Janusek 1994:80–87). Much more often than repetitive household units, excavations consistently exposed segments of larger bounded compounds that incorporated the remains of a wide spectrum of life spanning domestic, specialized, and ritual activities. These, I argue, were the activity areas of larger suprahousehold groupings (see Smith 1993 for a similar study in Central Mexico). Consequently, I employ the general term "residences" instead of "households." Rather than attempting to elucidate a partial and arbitrarily defined group of domestic activities, I seek to illuminate the practical dimensions of daily life in Tiwanaku, and offer a perspective on the social composition of the two urban centers. By examining changes in residential life from the perspective of its encompassing urban settlements, we illuminate some of the historical dynamics of urban formation, growth, and depopulation. This perspective reveals some of the dynamics involved in the formation, consolidation, and collapse of the larger polity.

Residential Excavations in Tiwanaku and Lukurmata

As this is a study centered on but not entirely limited to residential areas, I seek to define the material constitution of coresidential groups. To this end, I employ Stanish's (1989a) working definition of the household as "the smallest artifactual and architectural assemblage that is repeated over a settlement." Two of the most fundamental questions are: Did domestic units at Tiwanaku and Lukurmata consist of single domestic structures, repeating patio groups, or residential compounds? Was there a standard principle of domestic organization that pervaded residential settlement, or was there substantial diversity in the configuration and use of domestic space?

To begin addressing these questions it is crucial to distinguish primary and secondary residential contexts (Schiffer 1996; LaMotta and Schiffer 1999). Primary contexts consisted of occupation surfaces, occupation zones, structural fill, and associated features. Some occupations consisted of prepared floors (*pisos*) or trampled surfaces (*apisonados*) associated with foundations, features, and artifact scatters. In other cases, daily refuse and adobe from eroding walls gradually accumulated over ephemeral surfaces, forming a thin primary midden or occupation zone. In cases where occupation surfaces were not clearly defined, we were generally able to define thicker occupation zones. Though occupation zones were usually associated with domestic structures and features, their excavation lacked the more precise control over stratigraphy provided by definable surfaces. For outdoor areas I found it useful to distinguish principal and ancillary activity zones. This distinction resonated with differences among activity areas in contemporary house compounds, where areas such as central patios are locations for a great diversity of activities, including everyday food preparation and periodic feasts. Other areas, generally smaller or more peripheral spaces between structures or at the corners of compounds, tend to be used as corrals or to store recently harvested crops, large ceramic vessels, refuse, or other domestic objects.

Secondary contexts include outdoor middens, refuse pits, ash and refuse deposits, and primary contexts turned into refuse deposits. In Tiwanaku, such secondary contexts are particularly abundant, a noteworthy pattern. In general, secondary contexts tend to be dense with refuse, contain larger artifact fragments, and yield a relatively wide diversity of botanical and artifactual remains. Along these lines, many primary residential contexts had been quarried after they were abandoned. Apparently, abandoned structures and activity areas were prime locations for mining adobe. The resulting amorphous pits, which were in many cases extensive, usually then served as convenient places to dispose refuse until the areas were ultimately reoccupied. This pattern, ubiquitous at Tiwanaku and Lukurmata, points to continual building, renewal, and the production of refuse.

Tiwanaku's monumental complexes are comprised of two areas that are presently hemmed in by chain link fences. The northeast area is dominated by the Akapana Platform complex, which measures over fifteen meters high (Figure 3.3A). On its north side and extending west are the reconstructed Sunken Temple and Kalasasaya Platform, which abuts the Putuni complex further west. Dominating the southwest area is the extensive Pumapunku Platform complex. Reconstruction projects and present site layout foster the impression that monumental complexes were built more or less at the same time, which was not the case. Complexes were initiated in different chronological phases and were built over long periods of time, during which their respective significance and role changed dramatically.

Excavations revealed residential complexes under the Kalasasaya, on the Akapana, and in Putuni. For the most part, however, the residential excavations most pertinent to this study occurred outside of these complexes. Methods consisted of extensive horizontal blocks placed in several strategically chosen areas (Janusek 1994; Kolata 2003a). The bulk of the research presented here focused on a sparsely inhabited, undulating plain that extends east of the Akapana. From the Akapana to the eastern edge of the site, this plain can be divided into four zones; Akapana East 1 (or AkE 1), Akapana East 2 (or AkE 2), Marcapata, and Ch'iji Jawira (Figure 3.3A). Akapana East 1 refers to an extensive area near the edge of the settlement core. Excavations here covered 624 square meters along the raised bank of an artificial channel known as "the moat," and exposed a long sequence of ritual and residential complexes. Excavations in two blocks approximately

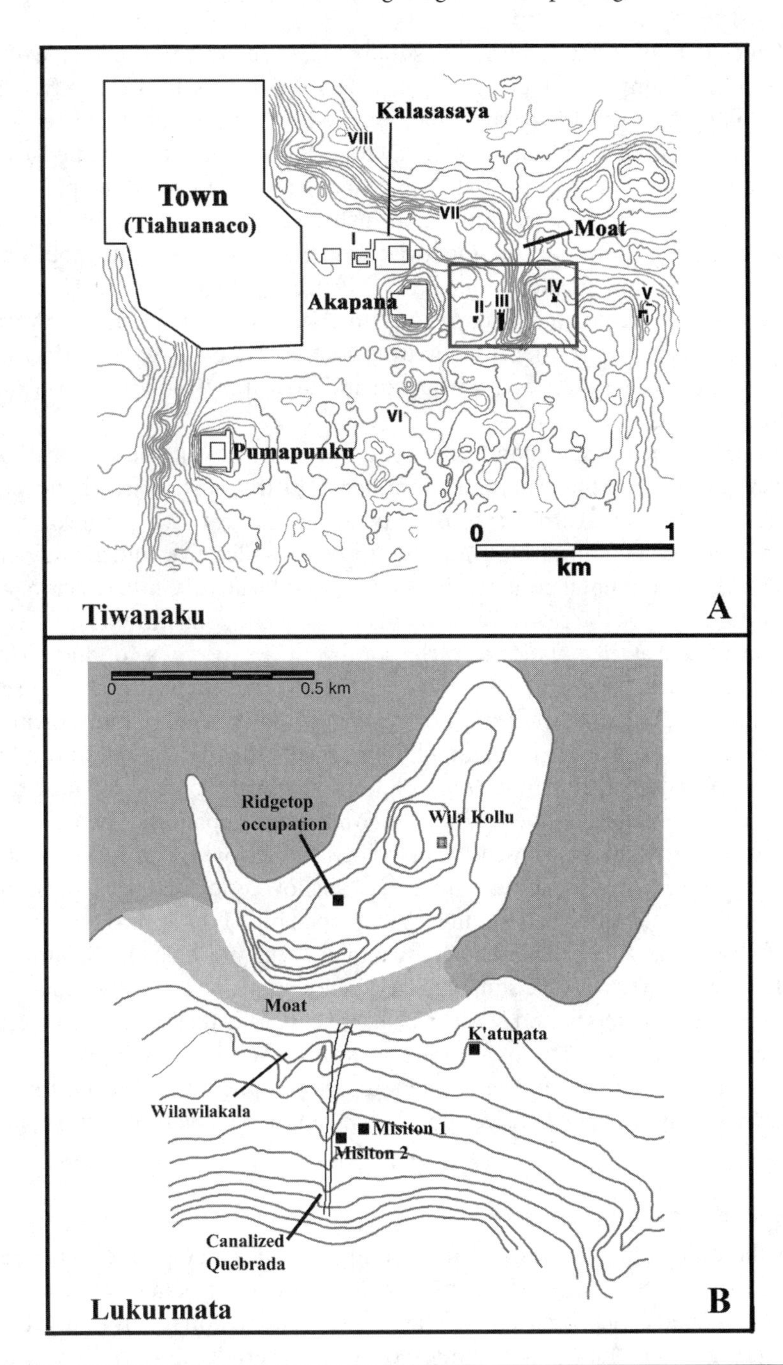

Figure 3.3 Contour maps of Tiwanaku (A) and Lukurmata (B) with major excavation areas. Numbered areas of Tiwanaku shown in A are Putuni (I), Akapana East 1M (II), Akapana East 1 (III), Akapana East 2 (IV), Ch'iji Jawira (V), Mollo Kontu (VI), La Karaña (VII), and Kk'araña (VIII).

70 meters to the west, totaling 170 square meters, exposed the east side of a residential compound (Akapana East 1M). Excavations in Akapana East 2, a knoll on the east side of the moat, exposed 176 square meters of yet another residential compound. Ch'iji Jawira, a low mound at the east edge of Tiwanaku, housed a residential group that specialized in ceramic production. Other pertinent residential areas include La K'arana, northeast of the Kalasasaya, Kk'araña to the northwest, and Mollo Kontu South, south of Akapana and the smaller Mollo Kontu Platform (Figure 3.3A) (Couture 1993, 2003). Sequential occupations in Akapana East, compared with those in other areas, offer a fascinating first portrait of a great variety of nonelite cultural practices in Tiwanaku and their transformations over the long term.

The principal monumental complex of Lukurmata sits on the peak of Wila Kollu, a modified natural prominence in the north part of the site (Figure 3.3B). The complex consists principally of a raised platform and sunken temple complex built into the top of a walled pyramidal platform mound. Monumental constructions have been located in other sectors as well, and include the early K'atupata platform to the south and the unexcavated Wila Waranka platform to the southwest. Excavations conducted by Marc Bermann (1989b, 1990, 1993, 1994, 1997, 2003) revealed a long sequence of residential occupation southwest of the Wila Kollu monumental complex, in a saddle of the natural hill known as "the ridge." Excavations by Karen Wise (1993) north of Wila Kollu, in the North Point sector near the lake edge, revealed a sequence of post-Tiwanaku occupations. The research most central to this study focused on the Misiton sector several hundred meters southwest of Wila Kollu, in an area of shallow residential terraces rising gradually up the slope of a modified flat-topped hill of the Taraco range. Research on a terrace here consisted of two major excavation blocks; Misiton 1, where excavations of 112 square meters revealed a small neighborhood of residential workshops, and Misiton 2, near a canalized *quebrada* to the west, where excavations of 272 square meters revealed a residential sector containing a circular structure and a bounded storage complex. One other pertinent area is Ch'iarkala, an extensive suburb community just west of Lukurmata.

Conclusions

In the following chapters I explore residential life, sociopolitical change, and ritual places and activities in Tiwanaku and Lukurmata by comparing the excavated areas noted above. The extended discussion forms a narrative covering more than fifteen hundred years of prehispanic history, and includes the Late Formative, Tiwanaku, and post-Tiwanaku Pacajes periods. I outline a particular interpretive perspective of urban development and change, one that highlights local social practices, affiliations, and ideologies, and emphasizes their dynamic roles in the rise, constitution, and collapse of this native Andean polity. The theoretical ideas and approaches outlined in the last three chapters inform critical junctures of this long-term narrative. Equally significant, evidence for shifting power relations, expressions of social identity and diversity, and long-term continuities in regional identities over the long run contribute creatively to the theory and practice of residential archaeology in complex societies on a comparative scale.

Tiwanaku was a formation in many ways unlike other archaic states. It was also in many critical respects unlike later societies in the region, although it was grounded in certain similar (and historically related) fundamental principles of ritual practice and sociopolitical organization. Tiwanaku was unique, and its particular environmental context, organizational characteristics, and historical circumstances, illuminated by the kind of approach advocated here, highlight the dynamic roles played by the humans who comprised it and their practical rhythms of daily life. Patterned practices, informed by generative cultural principles, have resounding effects on the constitution and historical trajectories of larger communities and polities. Local values and practices and their expressions as identity and role in power relations, I seek to demonstrate, are dynamic elements of complexity that conventional approaches often overlook.

PART 2

CHAPTER 4

Ritual, Society, and the Rise of Urbanism

Until very recently the Late Formative was virtually a cipher in the scheme of Lake Titicaca culture history, crippling attempts to understand Tiwanaku's early development. As Carlos Lemuz and Jose Luis Paz note (2001:105), it has been the "most obscure, complex, and lest understood" period in the southern basin. For years what little was known of this period came largely from Bolivian excavations in the Kalasasaya platform. At last, research over the past decade allows us to clearly discern two phases in the region, Late Formative 1 and 2 (200 BC–AD 300 and AD 300–500), and is taking great strides in ascertaining social, political, and ideological conditions of the time.

In this chapter I examine Tiwanaku and Lukurmata for the Middle and Late Formative periods, during which both settlements emerged as major centers in the southern Lake Titicaca Basin. I synthesize a host of recent research contingent on emerging patterns of domestic life and ritual activity, emphasizing the significance of distinct types of ritual environments and activities and the roles of local groups in the formation of the nascent Tiwanaku polity. First, I present evidence for Middle and Late Formative residential occupations at Tiwanaku and Lukurmata, followed by evidence for monumental construction and ritual activity at the two sites. Because this is the first venue in which much of this research is published, I elaborate in some detail key elements of excavated Late Formative occupations. Next, I compare and analyze Late Formative residential and ritual spaces, emphasizing the place of local groups in the coalescence of new attitudes attendant on emergent social complexity and urbanism.

Middle Formative in Tiwanaku and Lukurmata

At Tiwanaku and Lukurmata most excavated Tiwanaku Period occupations rest on precultural soil (Bermann 1994; Ponce 1993). However, at both sites recent research demonstrates clear evidence for relatively small-scale Middle Formative occupation, in both cases distant from later monumental complexes. At Tiwanaku, abundant Middle Formative ceramics were found in Late Formative 1 occupation contexts in the Kk'araña area (Figure 3.3A). Although excavations here located no well-defined Middle Formative occupation, they also had stopped short of precultural soil. Recent surface survey in Mollo Kontu also revealed Middle Formative ceramics, alluding to contemporaneous settlement approximately two kilometers to the south (Blom et al. 2003).

Although contingent on future research, we may hypothesize that these areas formed two different Middle Formative settlements. Regional survey in the Tiwanaku Valley revealed between ten and twelve groups of contemporaneous small settlements in the Middle valley (Albarracín-Jordan 1996a:90). The later Tiwanaku urban settlement covered two middle formative settlement groups, one north of the Tiwanaku River, not far from Kk'arana, and one further south, near the later Pumapunku complex (Mathews 1992, 1997). Quite possibly, Kk'araña and Mollo Kontu were small sites at this time, and the inhabitants of one affiliated with the north group and the inhabitants of other the south group.

Two Middle Formative occupations are also known from Lukurmata, though neither has yet been excavated. The first site, Wilawilakala, occupied a low ridge facing Wila Kollu, some 350 meters southwest of the earliest known Late Formative 1 occupation (Figure 3.3B). Artifacts covered an area of some 0.8 hectares, and like those of other Middle Formative sites they included large quartzite and basalt hoes (*chuntas*). Another Middle Formative site of approximately the same size occupied a low alluvial terrace overlooking the small valley east of Lukurmata. During the Middle Formative, these two small settlements were part of a larger network of seven widely distributed sites in the Katari Valley, located approximately ten kilometers from the major ritual center of Chiripa, on the Taraco Peninsula, and about the same distance from the center of Qeyakuntu, to the southeast (Figure 3.1).

Late Formative 1 in Tiwanaku and Lukurmata

Tiwanaku

At both sites Late Formative occupations were far more extensive. At Tiwanaku, early excavations revealed Late Formative 1 residential occupations located near and even under later monumental complexes such as Akapana and Kalasasaya. Early test units northeast and west of the Akapana (Bennett

1934; Kidder 1956) revealed Late Formative middens, domestic hearths (Bennett 1934), and structure foundations (Cordero 1955, cited in Kolata and Ponce 2003:26). In the Kalasasaya, strata two to four meters below the surface revealed large rectilinear wall foundations, a cobble pavement, ash and refuse deposits, and several hearths (Figure 4.1A and B). Associated with this occupation, what Ponce calls Tiwanaku I (here Late Formative 1A), were two offering pits and two human burials, which together contained 35 elaborate Kalasasaya ceremonial vessels, including rare incision-zoned wares (see Ponce 1993:Table 1). The sub-Kalasasaya occupation also included an incision-zoned ceramic trumpet and a small ceramic whistle representing a stylized dwelling or shrine with a nested door jamb (Ponce 1980: Figure 81). The substantial construction of the foundations, the presence of elaborate offering contexts, and the elaboration of associated crafted objects together suggest that this early occupation was unique. Above these strata was a superimposed occupation, Ponce's

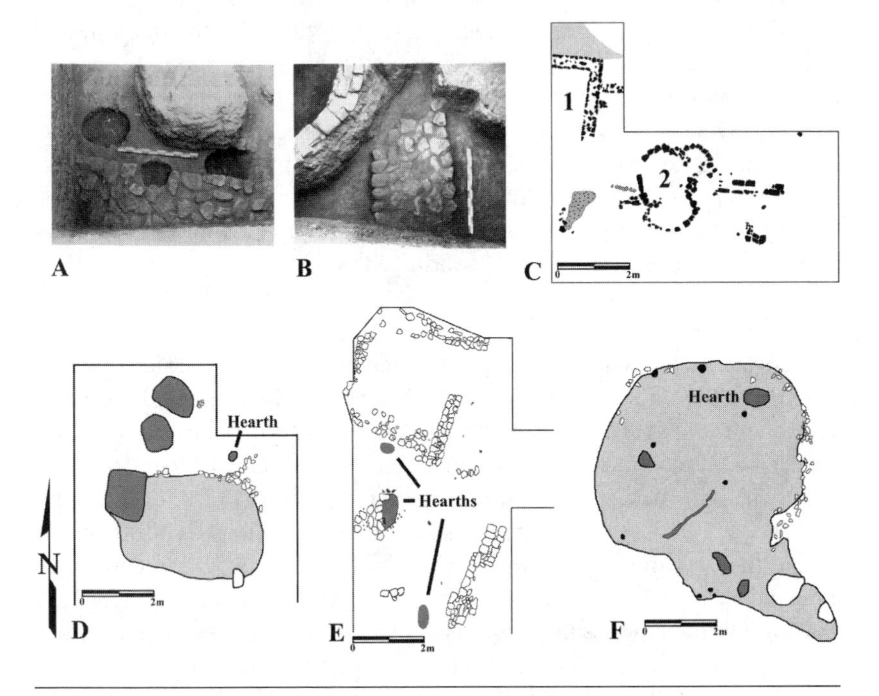

Figure 4.1 Excavated Late Formative 1 residential occupations in Tiwanaku and Lukurmata: sub-Kalasasaya (A and B) and Kk'araña (C), Tiwanaku, and the first (D), third (E), and sixth (F) sequential occupations on the ridgetop, Lukurmata (A from Ponce 1993, B from Ponce 1981, D-F adapted from Bermann 1994).

Tiwanaku II (here Late Formative 1B), which included a semicircular foundation associated with lenses of ash and carbon (Figure 4.1B).

More recent excavations conducted under the auspices of Proyecto Wila Jawira revealed a substantial Late Formative 1 occupation in Kk'araña, a hill some 500 meters northwest of the sub-Kalasasaya occupations (Figure 4.1C). Notable features include the corner of a rectangular structure associated with an outdoor surface and an ovoid building with attached semicircular bins. Distributed across the occupation were middens and ash deposits representing domestic activities. Associated deposits included numerous hemispherical terracotta beads, diagnostic adornments common at contemporaneous sites (Bermann 1994; Kolata and Janusek 2003; Mathews 1992), as well as bones of camelids, small mammals, birds, and fish. They also included worked bone tools such as weaving implements, adornments, and a small spoon to ingest mind-altering substances.

Occupations in Kalasasaya were highly elaborate in relation to those in Kk'araña, and it is not yet clear whether the two formed one contiguous settlement at this time. In particular, sub-Kalasasaya ceremonial ceramic vessels were highly distinctive. No other area in Tiwanaku and in fact no other site in the Lake Titicaca Basin has yielded similar caches of Kalasasaya incision-zoned wares. Tiwanaku, even if it formed a dispersed community of residential sites surrounding the sub-Kalasasaya complex, was already a significant settlement by the end of Late Formative 1. Most likely, sub-Kalasasaya was an elaborate residential complex inhabited by high status groups. In light of the likelihood that the nearby Sunken Temple was built in Late Formative 1, as discussed below, it is possible that such groups tended it and coordinated rituals conducted therein.

Lukurmata

Late Formative occupations also were substantial at Lukurmata. Here, excavations in the saddle of the north ridge just below Wila Kollu revealed a series of six superimposed Late Formative 1 residential occupations (Bermann 1994:59–96), each including residential structures or at least living surfaces and their associated refuse pits, hearths, activity areas, and burials (Figure 4.1D, E, and F). All of the occupations yielded hemispherical terracotta beads similar to those found at Tiwanaku. In each of the first two occupations was an ovoid surface similar in form to the structure in Kk'araña (Figure 4.1D). The third yielded more substantial remains, including two rectangular structures with cobble foundations that were associated with human burials (Figure 4.1E). An outdoor surface with a large, centrally located hearth occupied the place between the two buildings. This occupation produced a small bone spoon carved into a clenched fist and, as in the sub-Kalasasaya area of Tiwanaku, part of an incised ceramic trumpet (Bermann 1994:75).

The fifth and sixth occupations consisted once again of ovoid living surfaces, but they were larger than those in the earlier occupation (Figure 4.1F).

Changes in ceramic assemblages through the occupation sequence may reflect shifting networks of regional interaction. The first two occupations, each with a small ovoid surface, yielded a variety of utilitarian and local wares, such as "thin red" bowls, but no Kalasasaya-style decorated wares. Kalasasaya sherds in both red-painted and rarer incision-zoned varieties first appear in the third occupation, the one with rectangular structures, just as thin red and other local wares disappear (Bermann 1994:73–76). Nevertheless, Kalasasaya red-painted bowls appear only around the large hearth, a communal activity space. Characterizing the fifth and sixth occupations, both associated with ovoid living surfaces, was a return to more traditional ceramic patterns, including a significant drop-off in relative quantities of decorated Kalasasaya sherds and the reappearance of thin red bowls (Bermann 1994:86–88). A question arises from this sequence: Do such changes mark shifts in the life-history of a single residential group over several generations, as Bermann suggests, or do they represent a more dynamic history in which different residential groups occupied this area of Lukurmata sequentially?

Late Formative 2 in Tiwanaku and Lukurmata

Tiwanaku

Recent research at Tiwanaku points to significant developments during Late Formative 2, including a dramatic expansion in residential occupation and the creation of monumental ritual spaces. Ceramic assemblages recovered from Bennett's early test units around the Akapana, coupled with radiocarbon dates recovered from Kidder's adjacent units (Ponce 1981: Table 1; 1990:48), indicate that occupation continued in these areas. Occupation also continued in Kk'araña, where a new clay floor was packed over the old residential occupation (Figure 4.2A). Bounded by remnant adobe wall foundations, the new floor was associated with a hearth, refuse pits, ash deposits, and a posthole. Found here were hemispherical beads and several worked bone implements, including broken snuff tubes. Decorated Qeya sherds, though uncommon, were present. They included part of a large angular bowl depicting a crowned feline head, pieces of small pitchers depicting nested triangular motifs, and a small incense burner, or sahumador, with incised, nested step motifs (Janusek 2003a:Figure 3.23).

Pristine Late Formative 2 occupations appeared well beyond the area occupied during Late Formative 1. We encountered one in Akapana East 1, some 300 meters east of the Kalasasaya (Figure 4.2B). Here, resting on a prepared floor, was a small semicircular structure similar in construction and form to the early structures in sub-Kalasasaya and Kk'araña. More recent excavations some 280 meters south of the Kalasasaya revealed a later Late Formative 2 occupation in Mollo Kontu (Blom et al. 2003), consisting of thin midden lenses directly under early Tiwanaku IV occupation. In both areas ceramic assemblages consisted exclusively of nondiagnostic sherds of domestic wares; neither yielded decorated Qeya sherds. The Putuni area just west of the Kalasasaya was also first occupied toward the end of Late Formative 2. Features here included a prepared pit (feature 134) containing a cache of broken vessels diagnostic of the Late Formative-Tiwanaku transition (Couture and Sampeck 2003:229–232; Janusek 2003a: 49–50), and an enigmatic but substantial platform of clean red clay. The features yielded both Qeya and Tiwanaku-style sherds as well as sherds of diagnostic transitional variants, including tan *escudillas* with vertical black bands. Clearly, Tiwanaku was expanding precipitously toward the end of Late Formative 2.

Lukurmata

Excavations at Lukurmata reflect patterns of continuity more than expansion. Bermann's excavations on the ridge revealed at least three superimposed occupations dating to Late Formative 2 (Bermann 1994:103–148). All included occupation surfaces associated with hearths, activity areas, refuse pits, and in some cases special purpose buildings (Figures 4.2 C and D). The first Late Formative 2 occupation, defined as the earliest with Qeya-style sherds, included five rectangular clay floors, three of which clearly were dwellings (Figure 4.2C). A feature representing either a drainage canal or the foundation of a compound wall separated the structures into two groups (see Bermann 1994:107). Significantly, either side of the canal/wall yielded a specific range of local and exotic wares. The second and third occupations revealed floors associated with poorly preserved foundations and outdoor trampled floors, or *apisonados.* In the third, which was a transitional occupation with both Qeya and Tiwanaku sherds, was a specialized storage building (Figure 4.2D). Associated with these two occupations were several fragmented bone tubes and spoons, clear evidence in Lukurmata for the ingestion of mind-altering substances.

Ceramic patterns distinguish the ridge occupations from known Late Formative 2 occupations at Tiwanaku (Figure 4.7D) In particular, Qeya wares associated with the ridge occupations were stylistically distinct from those found at Tiwanaku (Bermann 1994, 2003; Janusek 2003a). As at Tiwanaku, Qeya sherds included polychrome sahumadors, bottles with triangular motifs, and tall flaring rim bowls, or *escudillas,* with painted nested triangles and mythical beings. Others, however, represented types not found at Tiwanaku, including tripod bowls, cups, and proto-*kero* forms. Tripod bowls displayed fitted triangular designs, while cups and proto-keros displayed unique undulating steps and bands. Also found in the ridge occupations were sherds of several nonlocal bowls associated with warmer valleys to the east (Bermann 1994:125).

Summary

During the Late Formative, in summary, Tiwanaku and Lukurmata incorporated populations practicing domestic and other activities. Residential activities, where we have sufficient data, appear more or less similar from one area to the next and continuous through time. Comparing Middle and Late Formative residential contexts, faunal analysis shows a decisive increase in the relative presence of domesticated camelids, or llamas and alpacas, marking an increasing consumption in camelid beef (Webster 1993;

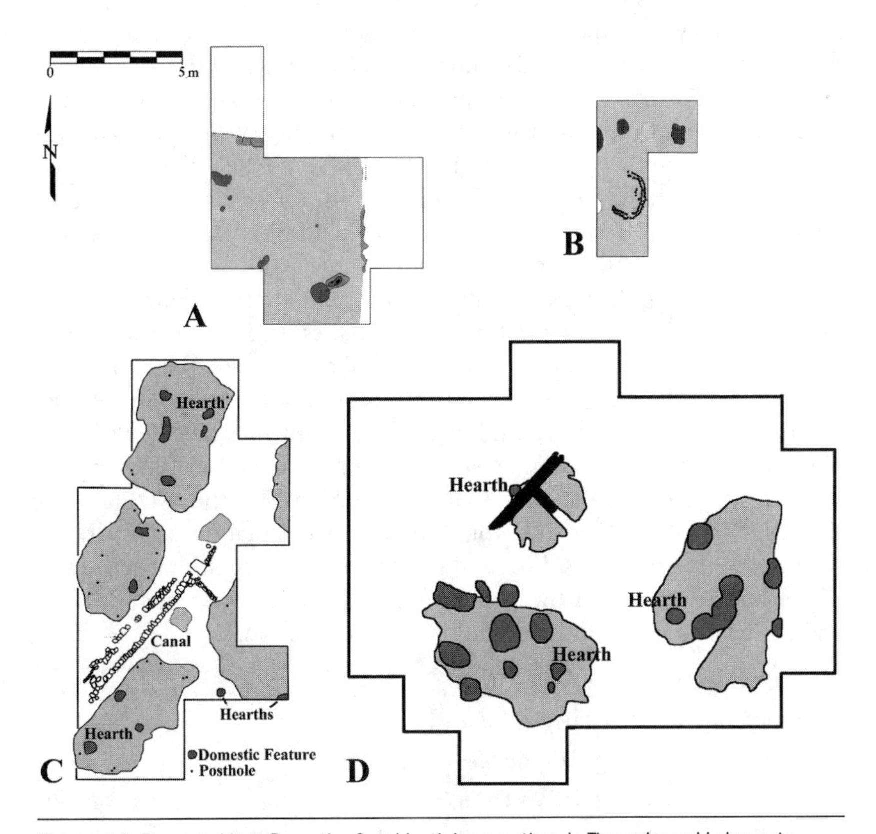

Figure. 4.2 Excavated Late Formative 2 residential occupations in Tiwanaku and Lukurmata: Kk'araña (A) and Akapana East 1 (B), Tiwanaku, and two sequential occupations (C and D) on the ridgetop, Lukurmata (C and D adapted from Bermann 1994).

Webster and Janusek 2003). Late Formative households cooked, stored, and consumed food and drink; they prepared and consumed camelids, smaller mammals (e.g., *cuy*, *vizcacha*) and birds; they crafted and used bone tools in activities such as spinning, weaving, and sewing; they knapped and used lithic scrapers, knives, and small arrow points; and they wore terracotta beads and carved bone ornaments. At the same time, no residential context at Tiwanaku or Lukurmata has yielded significant quantities of lithic hoes (Giesso 2000), agricultural tools common at smaller sites in the Tiwanaku (Mathews 1992, 1997) and Katari valleys (Janusek and Kolata 2003).

The relatively small areas exposed in most residential sectors discourage detailed examination of spatial organization in architecture and activities. Still, some of the data are provocative. Both Late Formative 1 and Late Formative 2 residential sectors included semicircular, ovoid, and rectangular structures and surfaces. In Late Formative 1, structural form correlated in some cases with a specific ceramic assemblage. At Lukurmata, only the occupation with rectangular dwellings yielded decorated Kalasasaya wares. During Late Formative 2 greater spatial complexity was apparent in some areas. For example, in Lukurmata a drain/compound wall separated residential space into two groups, and in Kk'araña an adobe wall bounded an extensive outdoor surface. In both areas significant architectural features separated well-defined activity spaces, most likely bounding the immediate activity areas of specific co-residential groups.

Of particular note are differences in overall patterns of architectural orientation and spatial organization at the two sites. All rectilinear structures dating to the Late Formative in Tiwanaku followed a directional orientation of five to eight degrees askew (to the east) of the cardinal directions. Contemporaneous structures in Lukurmata, meanwhile, diverged sharply in orientation from one another, varying from twenty to forty-five degrees askew of the cardinal directions. In the Tiwanaku period after AD 500, spatial order at both settlements would follow the orientation originally established at Tiwanaku. As discussed in Chapter 5, I suggest that this was a significant expression of the coalescence of a single hegemonic ideology and political system in the southern Lake Titicaca basin.

Ceremonial Space in Tiwanaku and Lukurmata

Tiwanaku: Kalasasaya and the Sunken Temple

Monumental structures dedicated to communal ritual activities at Tiwanaku and Lukurmata were constructed for the first time during the Late Formative. The first built at Tiwanaku was the trapezoidal semisubterranean or Sunken Temple (Figure 4.3). Measuring 21.5 by 28.5 meters, it suffered

Figure 4.3. View of Kalasasaya and Sunken Temple with the later (Tiwanaku V) Putuni Platform Complex in the foreground (photo courtesy of Johan Reinhard).

significant transformation during its reconstruction in 1961–64 (Ponce 1995:263). In particular, in the course of consolidating extant walls and fixing the structure with cement drains, CIAT archaeologists created a structure less vernacular and to some extent more rectangular in appearance than the original. Overall, most stones forming the Sunken Court were roughly worked. Interior walls consisted of rough sandstone pilasters supporting wall segments of smaller ashlar and fieldstone masonry. The walls were fitted with anthropomorphic heads, many carved of a rare light-colored volcanic tuff, of which no two are exactly like. Though many are eroded, most depicted angular, impassive deitylike heads with headbands, grimacing figures, and even skeletal and phantasmlike beings. An elaborate stairway descended from the south wall to a trampled surface, or *apisonado* (Ponce 1990:142–144). Inside of the temple stood a sandstone monolith depicting an anthropomorphic figure with a face mask, accompanied by smaller monoliths and two elaborate basalt receptacles that may have been offering pedestals or thrones. However, whether these objects stood in the original temple is not known.

Situated west of and facing the Sunken Temple, the Kalasasaya platform was first constructed in Late Formative 2 (Ponce 1961:19, 1981, 1993). The edifice visible today, a major reconstruction produced by CIAT archaeologists between 1965 and 1973 (Kolata and Ponce 2003:28), is a massive earthen platform (117.5 by 132.7 meters) bounded by an extensive revetment of monolithic stone pilasters and intervening sections of smaller ashlars (Figure 4.3). In plan, the edifice comprises a massive outer platform surrounding a walled inner temple, with an imposing, well-worn entrance to the east and a balcony extension to the west. A wide plaster wall foundation divided the inner temple from the west part of the platform. Although at present not obvious, the inner temple contained a smaller sunken court with a thick plaster floor (Ponce 1991:53). A variety of analyses indicate that the sandstone comprising many of Kalasasaya's stones had been procured from a *quebrada* in the Kimsachata range at the south edge of the Tiwanaku Valley, while carved andesite blocks, including the massive pilasters forming the so-called balcony, had been quarried as far away as Yunguyu near the Peruvian-Bolivian border (Ponce et al. 1971).

Yet, the monumental reconstruction now treaded by hundreds of tourists weekly varies significantly in form and details from the original Late Formative structure (see Ponce 1961:26–29). First, architectural features just outside of the platform, including an incomplete "stairway to nowhere," suggest that a lower terrace once surrounded at least the north and east sides of the edifice (also Bennett 1934:372; Posnansky 1914:108–109).

Second, metrical analyses of andesite blocks from later monumental buildings, including the Putuni just to the west, suggest that sections of the Kalasasaya were cannibalized to build or reconstruct them (Alexei Vranich 2001, personal communication).

It is also likely that the Kalasasaya was constructed in stages rather than at once. Browman (1980:114) alludes to an early temple beneath the Kalasasaya, and a simple walk on the outer platform after recent rains reveals undocumented wall foundations and features. In fact, the CIAT excavations that defined substantial sub-Kalasasaya occupations and Late Formative 2 construction fill were concentrated under the inner sunken court (Ponce 1961:16–19; 1990:155). Prior to CIAT research, one of Bennett's early test units (Pit II) outside of the court had yielded nothing predating Tiwanaku IV (Bennett 1934:374, 448, 453). Ponce (1981) concludes that in Tiwanaku IV, long after its initial construction, the Kalasasaya was the subject of modifications meant "to embellish" and "amplify" it, including the addition of the west balcony wall. It is likely that in Late Formative 2 the Kalasasaya platform consisted primarily of the structure now visible as the inner court. In this scenario, sometime toward the end of the phase or in Tiwanaku IV, much of the outer platform was first built and the inner temple was converted into its innermost sanctum.

A conjunction of data suggests that the Sunken Temple was first built before the Kalasasaya, as Ponce suggests (1990:156). The two structures follow slightly distinct architectural orientations. Excavations I directed at the site of Khonkho Wankane in the Machaca region south of the Kimsachata Range recovered a sunken temple of similar size and trapezoidal shape that was first built during Late Formative 1 (Janusek, Ohnstad, and Roddick 2003). The monoliths found around the site are carved in a distinctive style, as are many found in and around Tiwanaku's Sunken Temple (Ponce 1990:123), and the primary entrance to both courts is from the south, unlike any other known monumental construction at either site. According to Louis Girault's ceramic analysis, the earliest diagnostic ceramics from the Tiwanaku Sunken Temple were of Qeya style (Girault 1990:215; Ponce 1990:158). However, until very recently little was known about Late Formative 1 undecorated wares (Janusek 2003a), which by far form the bulk of such ceramics assemblages. In fact, in Khonkho's temple diagnostic Kalasasaya sherds were rare. I suggest that the Tiwanaku Sunken Temple was first built during Late Formative 1, at roughly the same time as the sunken temple at Khonkho Wankane. An early date would explain why its orientation varies markedly from that of the Kalasasaya. By the end Late Formative 2, the Sunken Temple and early

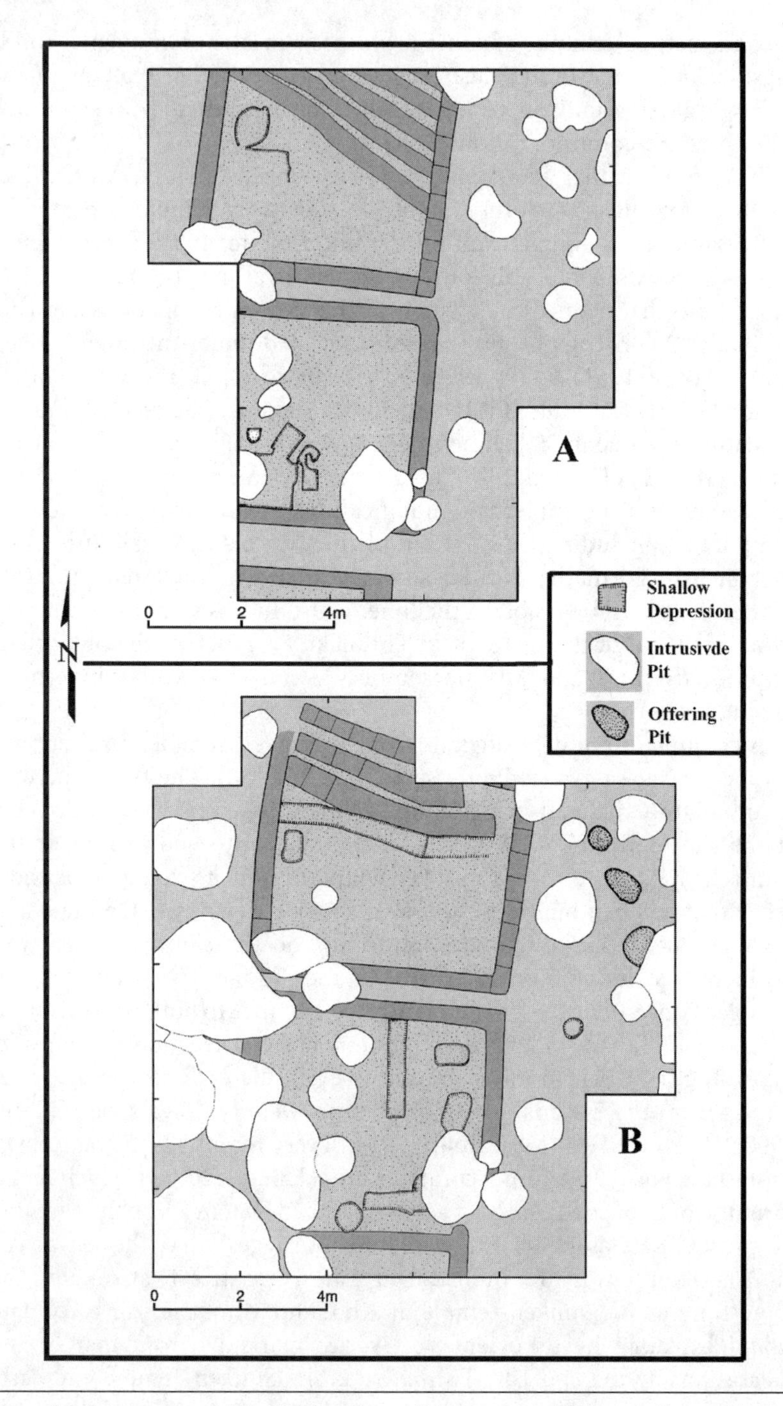

Figure 4.4 Two superimposed ritual surfaces (A and B) and associated features in Akapana East 1.

Kalasasaya formed a conjoined unit for complementary ceremonial activities (Kolata 1993).

Tiwanaku: Akapana East

Meanwhile, excavations in Akapana East 1 revealed an entirely different form of built ritual environment. They revealed two unusual occupations over the early residential occupation dated to Late Formative 2 and Early Tiwanaku IV (Figure 4.4). However, "occupation" is not the best term to describe the new floors and their associated features. Rather the floors appear to represent a new and unique form of ceremonial space in the region. Compared with the previous occupation, the first new floor marked a thorough about-face in the character of local activity (Figure 4.4A). It was elaborately prepared, and on it stood at least two adobe structures. Each structure measured about 4 meters by 5.5 meters, oriented six to eight degrees east of north, with foundations definable to the very adobe brick.

The floors presented an array of unique patterns. Interior and exterior spaces were sharply distinguished in soil color and texture. The floors inside of the buildings consisted of yellow sandy clay, while the outside floors consisted of red silty clay. The fine, homogeneous texture of the floors distinguished them from other residential surfaces in Tiwanaku and Lukurmata, indicating that the soils were specially selected and carefully mixed. Interior floors contained shallow depressions in ovoid and roughly rectangular shapes, and the northeast corner of the north structure was particularly elaborate. Here, a slightly raised section of the floor incorporated diagonal bands of alternating yellow sand, like the interior floors, and red clay, like the exterior floor.

Most striking, the floors were impeccably clean. Unlike other occupations at Tiwanaku, residential or ceremonial, the floors both inside and outside of the buildings were entirely free of ash, stains, artifacts, or any other domestic residue. In effect, they were sterile. However, just above the floor and a few meters east of the structures we located the rim of a scalloped Qeya sahumador. The vessel formed an effigy feline and showed internal burning, indicating it had been used to burn resin or incense.

At some point the occupation was renewed. The first surface was covered with clay and capped with a nearly identical floor with similar features (Figure 4.4B). The fill was relatively clean, but contained a few camelid bone splinters and small ceramic sherds, including a few sherds of Tiwanaku-style serving wares. On the floor the elaborate banded surface and the wall foundations were rebuilt. Indoor and outdoor floors were again distinct in color and texture, but interior surfaces incorporated a new configuration of shallow depressions, this time with long rectilinear pits that may have supported stone foundations long since removed.

Again, floor surfaces were impeccably clean except for a single, worn llama astragalus embedded into the floor of the south structure.

Several unique patterns distinguished the second floor from the first. First, the new buildings were covered in white plaster. Second, two shallow pits, apparently offering pits, were sealed below the surface of the floor outside of the north structure. Each was lined with a thin, even layer of finely pulverized bone. Much of the bone was discolored and encrusted in a light green precipitate, suggesting that the powdered remains were deposited with some liquid or vegetal substance.

Finally, a tumulus of clean clay covered the second surface. Not only was it highest (fifty centimeters thick) over the two buildings, its fill contained several chunks of adobe brick, indicating that it consisted of the collapsed walls. It is significant that the floor surface directly under the tumulus yielded no refuse whatsoever. Even though the buildings collapsed, or were purposefully destroyed, it appears to have been a single event during which the floors were kept free of outside impurities. The top of the tumulus comprised two superimposed surfaces. The earlier surface was covered with charcoal and yielded a calibrated radiocarbon date of A.D. 450–690 (see Janusek 1993a:Table 3.1), or Early Tiwanaku IV. Most likely, the charcoal represented a burnt offering dedicated to the area's final closing and ritual interment. The second surface then covered and sealed the burnt layer.

We located three human bodies in the southern part of the tumulus, just over the second floor (Blom et al. 2003). The remains of an infant and an incomplete, partially disarticulated adult were placed near one another. A few meters to the south, several bones of another incomplete adult were placed in a shallower area of the fill. Most unusual, Deborah Blom's analysis indicated that this body had been defleshed. None of the interments occupied a visible intrusive tomb, suggesting that the bodies were interred when the tumulus was formed, that is, during the ritual interment of the structures. Furthermore, the unusual patterns displayed by the buried adults suggest that they were deposited as secondary interments; as partially disarticulated, and in one case defleshed, mummy bundles. It appears that these individuals were placed in the mound as offerings dedicated to the area's closing and final interment.

Lukurmata: The K'atupata Platform

Although at Lukurmata it is likely that monumental construction on Wila Kollu preceded Tiwanaku IV (Bermann 1994:159; Rivera Sundt 1989), to date there is no clear evidence that it did. Excavations on an extensive alluvial prominence to the southeast of the hill, in an area termed K'atupata, revealed another clean ceremonial space dating to the Late Formative 2-Early Tiwanaku IV transition (Figures 3.3 and 4.5). Excavations in the

Figure 4.5 Views of the K'atupata platform (A) and its paved surface (B) in Lukurmata.

west half of K'atupata exposed an extensive stone pavement covering at least 700 square meters (Estevez 1990; Janusek & Earnest 1990a). It consisted of densely packed cobbles set into a compact matrix of clay and white lime precipitate, together forming a surface with plasterlike durability.

The surface of the pavement descended gradually to the south, toward the lake, and some of its edges were eroded or quarried. Perforations from later burials and a small test unit showed that the pavement rested on prepared strata of pebbly brown sand on pure clay, together forming a massive artificial platform.

Like the floors in Akapana East, both the pavement and the fill directly above and below it were completely clean. Covering the northern surface of the pavement was a tumulus of clean yellow sand and covering the southern surface was a clean stratum of brown silty clay. The distinct colors and textures are reminiscent of the distinct soils employed in Akapana East, in Tiwanaku. Several areas just above the north section of pavement revealed durable segments of what might have been rectangular building foundations like those in Akapana East (Estevez 1990), and near them were shallow ovoid depressions also reminiscent of those in Akapana East. It is likely that buildings constructed of clean and finely selected adobe were built on top of the pavement, but unfortunately those excavated were not well preserved.

Like the floors in Akapana East, the K'atupata pavement was kept impeccably clean until it was covered, suggesting that its closing also represented a ritual interment. Serving vessel sherds in the yellow and red tumuli directly above represented the Early Tiwanaku IV Period. Thus, the pavement complex was entombed no later than Early IV, contemporaneous with the floors in Akapana East. K'atupata later served as a mortuary sector, further alluding to the likelihood that the area originally had great ritual significance. Ultimately, however, the northern edge of the pavement was mined for its fine soil and perforated by refuse middens (Janusek & Earnest 1990a).

Society and Ritual in Tiwanaku and Lukurmata

Changing Settlement Networks

Tiwanaku and Lukurmata first emerged and changed dramatically during the Formative period (Figure 4.6). Both settlements were occupied at least as early as the Middle Formative as relatively small settlements. Associated ceramic wares and lithic tools link the sites to the far-reaching Chiripa cultural complex (Bandy 2001; Hastorf 1999). Chiripa consisted of interacting communities and small-scale polities in the southern Lake Titicaca basin, each of which centered on political-ritual centers such as Chiripa on the Taraco peninsula. Settlement networks on a regional scale were heterarchical rather than hierarchical, characterized on the Taraco peninsula itself by several clusters of local two-tier hierarchies (Bandy 2001). At some of the larger sites elegantly carved Yayamama style stone monoliths and

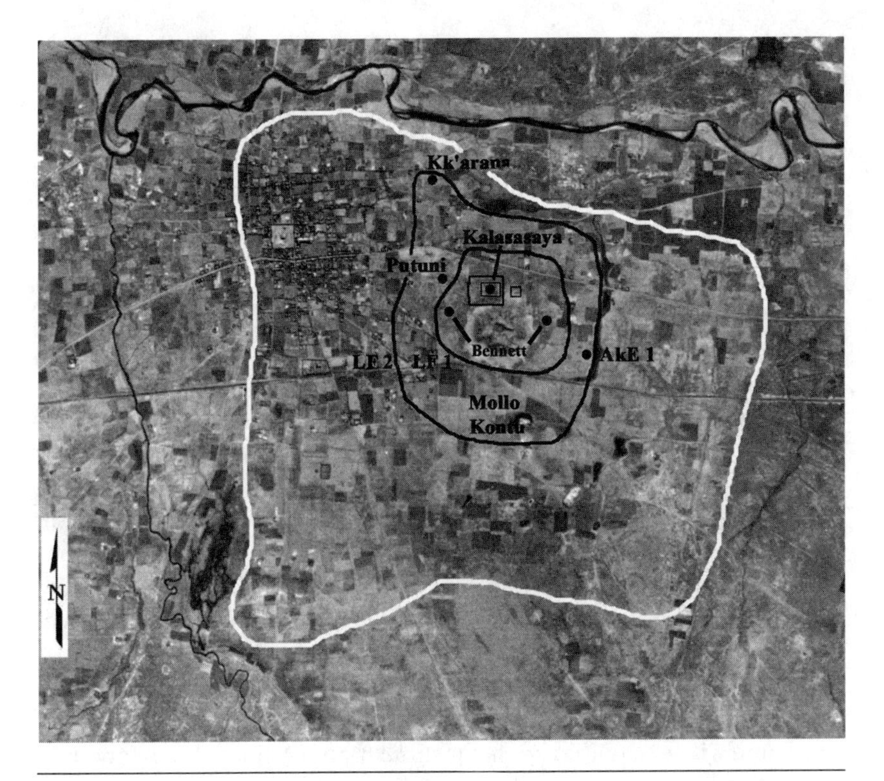

Figure 4.6 Proposed extent of Tiwanaku during Late Formative 1 and Late Formative 2 in relation to the site's maximum extent in the Tiwanaku Period (white line).

ceramic trumpets, as well as monumental platform and sunken court complexes, attest to shared basinwide religious principles (Mohr-Chavez 1988; Steadman 1997). Evidence to date suggests that settlements across the southern Lake Titicaca Basin were integrated through shared cultural conceptions, common ritual practices, and perhaps chiefly prestige and power (Stanish 1999, 2003). At this time, Tiwanaku and Lukurmata were small communities in these larger networks.

Regional settlement patterns changed considerably in Late Formative 1. Tiwanaku and Lukurmata became major settlements in their respective valleys. At Tiwanaku the trapezoidal Sunken Temple was most likely first constructed, and it remains for future research to determine if monumental construction characterized Lukurmata. Surveys in the Tiwanaku and Katari valleys indicate that both sites were major settlements surrounded by clusters of smaller sites (Albarracin-Jordan 1996a; Janusek and Kolata 2003; Mathews 1992, 1997). However, neither site was particularly unique on a panregional scale. On the Taraco peninsula, less than twenty kilometers from either site, Kala Uyuni expanded to perhaps twenty hectares during early Late Formative 1 (Figure 3.1) (Bandy 2001). Research in the Machaca region has identified Khonkho Wankane as another major Late Formative 1 ceremonial center (Janusek, Ohnstad, and Roddick 2003), and in the nearby Ccapia region Cackachipata and Kanamarka became major local centers (Figure 1.1) (Stanish et al. 1997).

Meanwhile, in Late Formative 1 a major polity centered at Pukara emerged in the northern Lake Titicaca Basin. Between 200 BC and AD 200 Pukara maintained considerable influence throughout the northern basin and established trade networks extending into lower valleys to the east and west (Goldstein 2000; Klarich 2002, Mohr-Chavez 1988; Mujica 1978, 1985; Stanish et al. 1997). Its leaders sought control over trade in obsidian and other valued goods (Bandy 2001; Burger et al. 2000). Significantly, Kalasasaya incision-zoned ceramic vessels and trumpets at Tiwanaku and Lukurmata, though uncommon, were strikingly similar to those in Pukara style.

Rather than Ponce's self-sufficient villages, Tiwanaku and Lukurmata were major autonomous centers linked to one another and other centers in the region via ceremonial activity, socio-economic interaction, and shifting political alliances. Each was the ceremonial and political center of a small-scale polity focused on emergent monumental constructions and communal ritual activities, with constituent populations residing both at the centers and in smaller villages and hamlets dispersed across their respective valleys. Tiwanaku and Lukurmata were centers of local multicommunity polities (Bandy 2001; Janusek 2004; Stanish 2001), each of which, though largely autonomous, may have temporarily come under the predominant influence or aegis of some other such center.

In Late Formative 2 Tiwanaku expanded dramatically (Figure 4.6). Occupations at both sites include two distinct phases, and several occupations date to a terminal transitional phase with both Qeya and Tiwanaku style ceramics. By the end of Late Formative 2 at Lukurmata, an extensive pavement in the previously uninhabited K'atupata sector formed an important platform for specific ritual activities. At Tiwanaku new monumental ceremonial places such as Kalasasaya covered early residential areas, and residence expanded precipitously, particularly during the terminal phases of Late Formative 2. Survey in the Tiwanaku and Katari valleys isolated few Late Formative 2 occupations due to a paucity of diagnostic artifacts, but excavations point to occupational continuity and the establishment of several new settlements (Albarracín-Jordan 1996b; Burkholder 1997; Janusek and Kolata 2003; Mathews 1992, 1997). We can hypothesize that Tiwanaku and Lukurmata were increasingly important centers in their respective regions, as centers in networks of interacting multicommunity polities that encompassed greater numbers of settlements and expanding populations.

Toward the end of Late Formative 2 Tiwanaku emerged as a major ritual and residential center on a panregional scale, approaching one square kilometer in area. Regional changes emphasize the increasing importance of Tiwanaku in the Lake Titicaca Basin. First, Pukara declined in importance in the northern basin at around AD 200 (Klarich 2003; Stanish 2003), precipitating significant shifts in trade networks and power relations across the basin. Second and perhaps precipitated by such shifts, Kala Uyuni was abandoned and settlement growth on the Taraco Peninsula declined "catastrophically" (Bandy 2001). It is at this point that Tiwanaku, in 200 years or less, expanded to over five times its size with new residential sectors and diverse monumental structures and ritual places. No other site in the two valleys or on the peninsula compared in occupational extent or monumental scale to Tiwanaku. Tiwanaku became the primary center in a settlement network consisting of smaller regional centers and their constituent communities, including Lukurmata in Katari, Santa Rosa on Taraco, Kallamarka in the upper Tiwanaku Valley (Figure 3.1) (Portugal and Portugal 1975), and Khonkho Wankane in Machaca (Janusek, Ohnstad, and Roddick 2003). As part of shifting regional networks of trade and power, Tiwanaku had emerged as the most important center in the entire basin.

Social Diversity in Late Formative 1

Understanding the trajectory of Tiwanaku's rise requires some explanation of emerging social differences in the southern basin. Excavated Late Formative 1 residential contexts at Tiwanaku and Lukurmata reveal significant patterns of similarity and variation in spatial organization, domestic activities, and material culture. In particular, comparisons on a regional scale reveal differential access to and use of valued crafted goods. Inhabitants of most residential areas acquired and used significant quantities of red-painted Kalasasaya serving wares, in addition to a variety of plainware ceramic vessels for cooking, storing, and consuming food and drink (Figure 4.7). Decorated red-painted bowls and pitchers were present not just at Tiwanaku and Lukurmata but at other major and minor sites in the two valleys and on the Taraco peninsula (Bandy 2001; Janusek and Kolata 2003). Nevertheless, the frequency of Kalasasaya red-painted wares varied significantly in relation to site type and activity area. Most Kalasasaya serving bowls were found in outdoor communal spaces and most ceremonial wares appeared in associated mortuary and offering contexts. Excavations at smaller sites in the Katari Valley revealed similar patterns. At the site of Kirawi more than ninety percent of recovered Kalasasaya sherds came from a single outdoor midden (Janusek and Kolata 2003). While present,

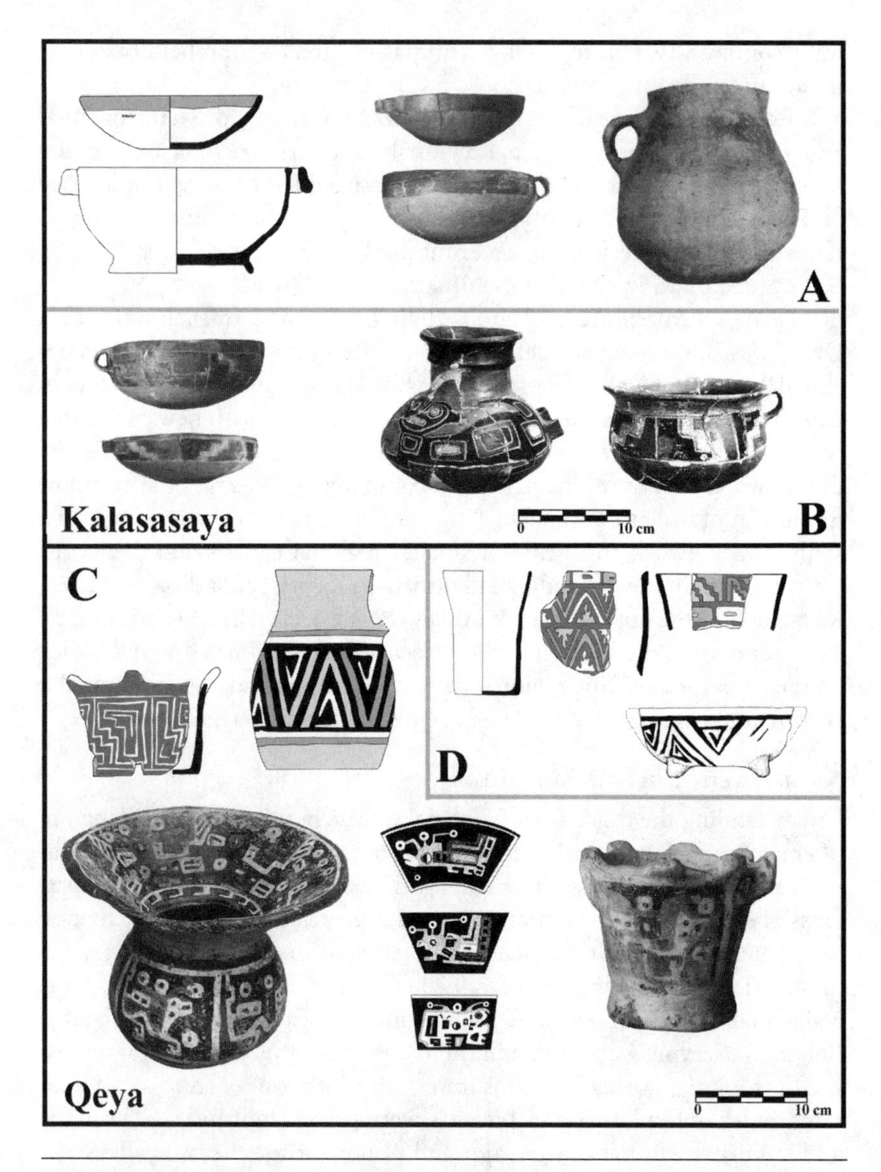

Figure 4.7 Selected Kalasasaya and Qeya wares, including redware (A) and incision-zoned Kalasasaya forms (B), as well as classic (C) and Lukurmata-styles types (D) of Qeya wares (D adapted from Bermann 1994).

they were far less common in dwellings and their associated activity areas. Thus, while Kalasasaya red-painted wares were popular and well distributed on a regional scale, they were most significant in relatively public contexts. Apparently, they were most significant in communal meals and feasts. The increasing consumption of camelids in the Late Formative may be tied to the rising importance of commensalism.

Further, not everyone used Kalasasaya red-painted wares at all times and places. For example, residential changes at Lukurmata included a shift from ovoid to rectangular structures, correlating with a shift from strictly local wares to the use of Kalasasaya red-painted and incision-zoned wares. It is likely that the changes reflect shifting interactions with Tiwanaku and other communities (Bermann 1994). By the same token, it is worth considering the scenario that a new group had moved into and occupied the area. In this case such a shift would imply a great deal of movement in and out of any particular residential sector, and by inference contemporaneous social diversity within the larger community. In either scenario, social diversity in Lukurmata, marked by differences in architectural form and in the use of elaborate serving-ceremonial wares, most likely involved status differences.

The use of serving and ceremonial wares also varied at a regional scale. At each site Kalasasaya wares coexisted with a range of unique, local ceramic types. At Tiwanaku such types included vessels of beige or orange paste, and at Lukurmata they included thin red bowls and orange wares. Thus, some ceramic types, including the most elaborate and popular wares, were obtained via regional interaction networks while others were crafted locally. The highly selective distribution of Kalasasaya incision-zoned wares and trumpets, in light of their conspicuous affinity to elaborate Pukara wares, alludes to emerging social differences in the region. While similar wares were also found at Lukurmata, they were rare or absent at smaller sites in the Tiwanaku and Katari valleys, where undecorated and coarse bowls were far more common (Janusek and Kolata 2003). Elaborate serving and ceremonial wares appear nearly exclusively in ritual or offering contexts associated with the high status residential areas of the major centers. They were limited to use by high status individuals or groups in specific, relatively intimate and exclusive ritual settings.

Thus, in Late Formative 1 only certain inhabitants of Tiwanaku and Lukurmata acquired and used the most elaborate serving and ceremonial wares. The selectivity correlates with evidence that inhabitants of specific settlements, and specific sectors of settlements, conducted particular types of activities. Groups residing in the sub-Kalasasaya area, for example, may well have presided over ceremonies conducted in the adjacent Sunken Temple, as did inhabitants of a similar residential compound at Khonkho Wankane (Janusek, Ohnstad, and Roddick 2003). At a broader scale, no residential context at Tiwanaku or Lukurmata revealed evidence for direct involvement in agricultural production. This contrasts sharply with excavated residential areas at smaller sites in both the Tiwanaku (Mathews

1992) and Katari Valleys (Janusek and Kolata 2003), which consistently reveal high quantities of stone hoes. Farming was the domain of small rural communities while most inhabitants of Tiwanaku and Lukurmata, it appears, were not directly engaged with agriculture. Lukurmata and in particular Tiwanaku were becoming important nonproductive centers in their respective valleys, housing groups with specific roles and relatively high status.

Social Diversity in Late Formative 2

The selective distribution of elaborate goods intensified in Late Formative 2. The gradual disappearance of red-painted Kalasasaya wares marks the disappearance of widely distributed decorated ceramics in the southern basin. Inhabitants of all residential areas continued to use plainware serving bowls along with pitchers, *ollas*, and storage jars, but decorated wares became uncommon. Small quantities of Qeya vessels appear in Kk'araña, in Putuni, and around Kalasasaya, and slightly higher quantities of such wares also appear in occupations at Lukurmata (Figure 4.7D). Outside of Tiwanaku and Lukurmata, however, Qeya wares were rare and at many sites absent (Burkholder 1997; Janusek and Kolata 2003; Mathews 1992). In light of the numerous vessels recovered in mortuary contexts on the Island of the Sun (Bandelier 1911; Wallace 1957), Qeya wares, like Kalasasaya incision-zoned wares, must have been used mostly in ritual settings. Continuing a pattern established in Late Formative 1, only certain residents of Tiwanaku and Lukurmata acquired and used the most elaborate ceremonial vessels. Overall we see increasing status differentiation within any region as relatively high status groups at Tiwanaku and Lukurmata consolidated their privileged positions in relation to other groups and communities, whose relative positions, in effect, declined.

The stylistic variability apparent in Qeya assemblages at Tiwanaku and Lukurmata alludes to a significant regional boundary (Figure 4.7). The unusual forms and motifs of Qeya assemblages from Lukurmata are strikingly similar to contemporaneous Tupuraya and Mojocoya style complexes popular in Cochabamba and northern Chuquisaca, far to the southeast, where similar forms (*keros*, cups, and tripod bowls) already had become popular (Céspedes 2000; Janusek and Blom 2004). Residents of Lukurmata's ridge acquired and used Tiwanaku Qeya, local Qeya, and nonlocal assemblages, demonstrating affiliations with diverse regions and maintaining serving-ceremonial assemblages that were more diverse than those recovered from Tiwanaku. Meanwhile, Qeya wares similar to those at Tiwanaku appear at small sites in the Tiwanaku Valley, suggesting that differences between Tiwanaku and Lukurmata had a broader regional dimension. Stylistic variation may well mark a social boundary between the Tiwanaku and

Katari valleys, one that, as discussed in later chapters, was re-established and redefined in the context of Tiwanaku hegemony.

Sacred Place and Ritual Proxemics

By the end of Late Formative 2, Tiwanaku incorporated numerous built environments dedicated to a variety of rituals. The presence and diversity of these places were elemental to the rise of Tiwanaku's regional power and influence. J. Z. Smith (1987:103) notes that, "Ritual is, first and foremost, a mode of paying attention. . . . It is this characteristic. . .that explains the role of place as a fundamental component of ritual:place directs attention." Each monumental structure or ritual complex at Tiwanaku incorporated a suite of features and treatments that distinguished it from other spaces and marked it as a site for unique, ritually charged practices. The Sunken Temple and the adjacent Kalasasaya were the first monumental structures built at the center, and they manifested elements of monumental construction that would reappear later.

The Sunken Temple formed a relatively small, subterranean space for community rituals dedicated to the chthonic and generative forces of the early Tiwanaku cosmos. Supporting this suggestion are key elements of the temple. Carved stone heads fixed into the walls represented the mythical apical ancestors of groups comprising the larger community. The use of light-colored volcanic tuff, rare in Tiwanaku sculpture, emphasizes the significance of the tenoned images. The temple also housed monolithic sandstone sculptures carved in the Khonkho style characteristic of the Late Formative (Browman 1997; Portugal 1998), each of which featured an anthropomorphic ancestral deity wearing elaborate accoutrements and ornaments and decorated with zoomorphic mythical beings. Overall the temple was a microcosmic representation of early Tiwanaku cosmology, in which mythical ancestors or beings surrounded, and together faced, monolithic representations of more primordial and powerful ancestral deities that represented the more inclusive community and polity.

Whereas the Sunken Temple was built into the earth, the Kalasasaya formed an elevated plane rising above the earth's surface and the world of daily life. In plan it consisted of two or three concentric spaces, the outer walls and terrace of which were most likely built or at least expanded during the Tiwanaku Period. Height, volume, and elegant megalithic walls also served to distinguish the practices conducted on the platform as activities invoking more distant and powerful times and places.

A different range of attributes distinguished the built ritual environments of Akapana East, in Tiwanaku, and K'atupata, in Lukurmata. They included elaborate construction techniques, such as banded surfaces in Tiwanaku and a plastered cobble floor in Lukurmata. Depressions inside of the ritual chambers in Akapana East may have supported iconic idols or statues that have long since been removed. Here local ritual involved cyclical interments and other unique practices, as represented in shallow pits with pulverized bone and defleshed human remains. Reminiscent of recent rituals in the tropical lowlands of western Brazil (Conklin 2001), the last features may be associated with "endocannibalism," or consuming the flesh of deceased relatives.[1] The rituals conducted in Akapana East may well have centered on the deceased ancestors of local groups, and idols standing in the chambers may have depicted more genealogically distant ancestors of the associated group.

Built environments in Akapana East and K'atupata were distinguished by their impeccable cleanliness. The floor of the Sunken Temple, like that of the sunken temple in Khonkho Wankane, was littered with refuse. By all accounts such community ritual spaces were the focus of ceremonies that involved abundant feasting and commensalism. Prepared floors in and around adobe buildings in Akapana East and K'atupata were entirely different. They were distinguished by an obsession with keeping them free of the slightest residues of everyday, domestic refuse. Similar patterns characterized the relatively small ritual chambers associated with the earlier "Kotosh Religious Tradition" of the north-central Peruvian highlands (Burger 1992; Terada and Onuki 1982:252). Here, as in Akapana East and K'atupata, "Concepts of purity appear to have been implemented by rules of cleanliness" (Burger and Salazar-Burger 1985:115).

Cleanliness cross-culturally is critical to the maintenance of ritual purity (Douglas 1966). Powerful rituals require an exceptional context, a reality considered ontologically distinct from everyday activity. Sacred places and the purified bodies of ritual participants help establish that temporary reality. As Eliade (1959:20) noted, in such contexts believers "experience . . . an opposition between the sacred- the only *really* and *real-ly* existing space- and all other space . . . surrounding it." Everyday refuse, produced and used in mundane activities, retains its quotidian identity, threatening to contaminate sacred places and ritual bodies (Bell 1992). In Akapana East and K'atupata, domestic refuse was "dirt" in a real sense, or "matter out of place" (Douglas 1966:36). The feline-effigy *sahumador* sherd encountered in Akapana East corroborates this point. Rare in excavated residential contexts but common in human burials at Qeya Qolla Chico (Wallace 1957), these were ritual objects used in powerful rituals. Recently, Aymara communities employed incense burners to purify households and repel illness (Tschopik 1950), a generalized role possibly served by Qeya *sahumadors*. Thus, though we cannot detail the ceremonies conducted in these areas, cleanliness and purity formed elements of a distinct ritual attitude associated with them.

Despite their diversity, the spatial semiotics of ritual buildings and spaces in Tiwanaku and Lukurmata shared a fundamental characteristic in that, overall, they emphasized intimacy and, perhaps for certain occasions, exclusivity (also Moore 1996). This is especially clear if one considers the places from a phenomenological perspective, as they were experienced, and as people moved around and through them toward increasingly more significant and sanctified loci. Sunken and inner courts themselves were not immense plazas for mass congregations, but were relatively small enclosed places for small groups and select activities. They were the setting for intimate and powerful rituals that often occurred within larger community rituals and feasts. In such contexts they became the focus of key ritual events orchestrated by sponsors, political leaders, or religious specialists, and witnessed by a larger audience of participants and community members from outside.

As one moved up and onto the Kalasasaya platform toward the inner sunken court, one entered increasingly smaller and more intimate domains. Moving through nested spaces was a movement through places increasingly removed from the mundane outside world and toward inner sancta of increasingly removed space, time, and activities. Like the Sunken Temple and smaller buildings in Akapana East, most significant in Kalasasaya was the small sunken court, where rituals, like those in the Sunken Temple, may have invoked ancestral, generative forces. By Tiwanaku IV, the nested plan of the Kalasasaya mimicked the carved, nested outlines on massive stone gates that facilitated movement in and out of ritual places. Judging from the effigy whistle recovered under the Kalasasaya, the symbolic potency of portals had originated prior to Late Formative 2. The Kalasasaya, a monumental symbolic portal rotated over Tiwanaku's settlement landscape, joined the ontologically distinct worlds of the everyday and the sacred. Such metaphorical significance became animate in rituals coordinated by specialized, high status groups.

Society and Ritual in the Emergence of Tiwanaku

While specialists and high status groups coordinated the construction of monuments and orchestrated many of the rituals conducted therein, many dimensions of residential and ritual life allude to the roles of local social groups in the ongoing intensification of social complexity. To some extent groups adopted elements of emergent religious attitudes in their daily lives. This is reflected in the use of valued goods such as decorated serving and ceremonial wares in residential areas of Tiwanaku and Lukurmata. In Late Formative 2, Qeya iconography emphasized beings with combined or ambiguous zoomorphic features hovering on a black background. These appear to have been *desconocidos* or powerful mythical beings unknown to this world but invoked in ritual practice through the intercession of specialists. The restricted distribution of such ceremonial wares, like that of elaborate Kalasasaya wares, alludes to the esoteric power of such specialists and the ritual aura of the specific contexts in which this power was invoked. It suggests that only certain groups, presumably relatively high status groups, were regularly participating in such ritual practices and fully acquainted with their associated esoteric religious knowledge.

The presence of mind-altering substances in residential contexts alludes to the local adoption of new ritual practices. Tubes and spoons were used for storing and consuming snuff, whether resin for coca or hallucinogenic substances for enhancing ritual travels, visions, and transformations. At a regional scale, the increasing importance of this "hallucinogenic complex" is corroborated by Bandelier (1911:173), who noted a "beautifully carved" bone spoon at the Late Formative 2 site of Qeya Qolla Chico. The increasing presence of snuff implements in residential areas corresponds with the construction of early monumental architecture at Tiwanaku, the maintenance of clean ritual environments at Tiwanaku and Lukurmata, and the increasingly common display of mythical and religious iconography on ceramic vessels. Local groups were involved with a diverse range of ritual practices, conducted in a wide range of spaces and settings, and even if to highly variable degrees, they were inculcating a new, prestigious, and elegant cosmology. To this extent local groups helped forge Tiwanaku's developing religious influence and political power and they ensured its early vitality.

The significance of small ritual places in monumental constructions is an important case in point. On the one hand, these domains were relatively intimate, and we can hypothesize, in particular for highly visible and centrally located complexes such as Kalasasaya, that their inner sancta were often restricted to ritual specialists or leaders and their kin. On the other hand, the emphasis on intimacy in ritual places parallels that of residential sectors, a form of symbolic replication that effectively transposed the closeness and proximity of domestic life to more esoteric and exceptional domains of life. In the Sunken Temple, the arrangement of diverse mythical ancestral figures around more ancestral monolithic deities may reflect the extension of family relations to the Tiwanaku cosmos and ancient past. Intimacy in public place and ritual formed part of an emerging ideology that grounded relations attendant on relatively public or communal ceremonies in the familial relations of domestic life. It was one facet of a religious attitude that naturalized social differences that were already apparent in life at Tiwanaku and Lukurmata by Late Formative 2.

More directly alluding to the role of local groups were ritual environments outside of the central areas of Tiwanaku and Lukurmata. In both

Akapana East and K'atupata, elaborate local ritual spaces appeared relatively late in Late Formative 2, at or just beyond contemporaneous settlement limits. At both settlements residential sectors occupied areas between these ritual spaces and the developing monumental cores. Amenable to future testing, the most likely scenario is one in which local social groups located in or near each of the centers conducted much of the ritual activity, maintenance, and periodic renewal in these sectors. They were private shrines attended by local *ayllu*-like groups. These were places for specific types of ritual practice, by all accounts relatively solemn and fastidious, that differed from and in some measure complemented and perhaps competed with rituals conducted in other places. They were built environments representative of a specific type of ritual cult. At both sites diverse types of ritual places and practices were distributed across space and society, many the domains of specific groups, but all part of a broader syncretism that may have involved overlapping participants at different times in ongoing ritual cycles. In this sense ritual place and practice, rather than becoming more exclusive, diversified and expanded. Ritual diversity and accommodation were elements in an emerging practical hegemony that naturalized emerging social conditions. Tiwanaku cosmology coalesced as a syncretistic cultural phenomenon, which in tandem with its emphasis on incorporation and communal intimacy rendered emerging sociopolitical conditions not just acceptable but highly attractive.

The practical consciousness and ideologies of diverse social groups were enmeshed with ritual constructions because it was they who helped build them. As Timothy Pauketat (2000:117) notes, "Unless we assume that [the common masses] were duped, were consciously coerced, or were without dispositions, then we must admit the possibility that their dispositions in some ways shaped monumental constructions." There was no clearly defined elite class nor yet the hegemonic productive, political, or ideological conditions that would facilitate coercive interactions with, or power over social groups. To the extent that leadership was consensual and leaders represented groups with unique interests and identities, people would have failed to cooperate in the creation of things openly divergent from traditional, accepted values and representations. Monuments such as the Sunken Temple and Kalasasaya not only had to "make sense" to be meaningful and effective ritual places, but they of necessity represented and aggrandized the shared values of the commons, even as they paradoxically aggrandized the leaders who planned and coordinated their construction.

Groups of diverse backgrounds and identities collectively identified with such projects. In this regard evidence for construction stages and ritual renewal is significant. Construction events in the Kalasasaya and in Akapana East mark significant periodic events in which groups gathered to recreate or enlarge significant monumental and communal places. Such moments of interaction, associated with sponsored ceremonies and feasts, involved the periodic affirmation of inclusive social identities (see Moseley 2001 for the Andes, Mendelssohn 1971 for Egypt, and Pauketat 2000 for Cahokia). In places such as Akapana East, ritual renewal fostered local group identities, whereas successive stages of work in the Kalasasaya fostered a more encompassing politico-religious community identity. Probably not clearly foreseen by leaders and commoners alike during the Late Formative, in particular after AD 300, the construction of such ritual places served, at various scales, to forge the emerging Tiwanaku polity in all of its developing complexity and inequality.

CHAPTER 5
Tiwanaku: Urbanism and Social Diversity

By AD 500 Tiwanaku was an extensive settlement centered on an elaborate platform and sunken court complex. During Late Formative 2, upon the decline of Pukara, it had emerged as the most important ritual and political center in the Lake Titicaca Basin. Over the next three hundred years, the Tiwanaku IV phase, the site would expand at least six-fold until approximately AD 800, the beginning of Tiwanaku V, when Tiwanaku would cover approximately six square kilometers. Overall, research corroborates Ponce's assertion that Tiwanaku IV was as a phase of mature urban development at home and initial expansion abroad (Ponce 1980, 1981).

In this chapter I seek to refine our understanding of Tiwanaku during this critical phase of state development by examining monumental and residential spaces at the site. Treating a variety of activities and key patterns of ritual, social, and spatial organization, I discuss material evidence for state development and local diversity across a broad swath of Tiwanaku's dynamic urban landscape. I seek to illuminate some of the processes involved in the rise of urbanism and the state, emphasizing the roles of ceremony, shifting power relations, and emerging social identities among Tiwanaku's new and diverse populations.

First, I summarize settlement patterns in the Tiwanaku Valley, setting Tiwanaku in a regional framework of demographic growth and social complexity. Next, I briefly discuss new monumental constructions and renewal projects, which indicate that Tiwanaku was by now one of the most important ritual centers in the Andes. Following, I elaborate in some detail patterns of residential life in Tiwanaku IV, and then synthesize those patterns in relation to various cultural elements and activities: spatial order, feasting, craft production, status, style, diet, and mortuary ritual. Tiwanaku was a cosmopolitan center incorporating diverse groups, all of which participated in Tiwanaku's political economy and ceremonies and inculcated Tiwanaku's cosmic vision, but many of which also forged distinct social networks, cultural affiliations, and social identities.

Settlement in the Tiwanaku Valley

Tiwanaku reached a peak extent of six square kilometers in Late Tiwanaku IV, though its permanent population appears lower than once thought. Based on a brief reconnaissance, Jeffrey Parsons (1968) originally estimated that the site covered 2.4 square kilometers and housed a population of 5,200 to 20,000. Parsons derived this estimate by drawing on demographic profiles in the central basin of Mexico, which estimated population based on surface scatter densities (Parsons 1968:245; Sanders et al. 1979). Tiwanaku would represent a high-density settlement with a population density as high as 10,000–12,000 people per square kilometer. Ponce (1981) later revised Tiwanaku's extent to 4.2 square kilometers, and simply plugged this new size into the old formula, coming up with a range of 9,750 to 46,800 people (Ponce 1981:62). Following this formula, at six square kilometers, the most recent estimate, Tiwanaku would have housed over 70,000 inhabitants. As Kolata notes, however, ceremonial spaces formed significant proportions of urban space, as did networks of channels, reservoirs, and agricultural features including *qochas*, or sunken basins (2003a:15). In addition, occupational density varied considerably among residential areas, and many areas were periodically abandoned over local group histories and household cycles. A blanket formula fails to apply to Tiwanaku, where perhaps fifty percent of the site was either nonresidential or unoccupied at any time.[1] I conservatively estimate that its permanent population by AD 800 was between 10,000 and 20,000 inhabitants.

Survey in the Middle and Lower Tiwanaku valley revealed some 100 sites dating to Tiwanaku IV, a dramatic increase in settlement density from the Late Formative (Figure 5.1) (Albarracín-Jordan and Mathews 1990:82; McAndrews et al. 1997:73).[2] Sites were well distributed across major ecological zones, and favored the pampa. Most sites were relatively small, ranging from 0.01 to 10 hectares, and together present a primo-convex rank-size distribution indicating that Tiwanaku was the primary center. Sites formed three broad tiers, including towns (3–10 hectares), villages (1–2.9 hectares), and a range of smaller hamlets (.01–0.9 hectares). On a logarithmic scale, settlement in the valley outside of Tiwanaku presents

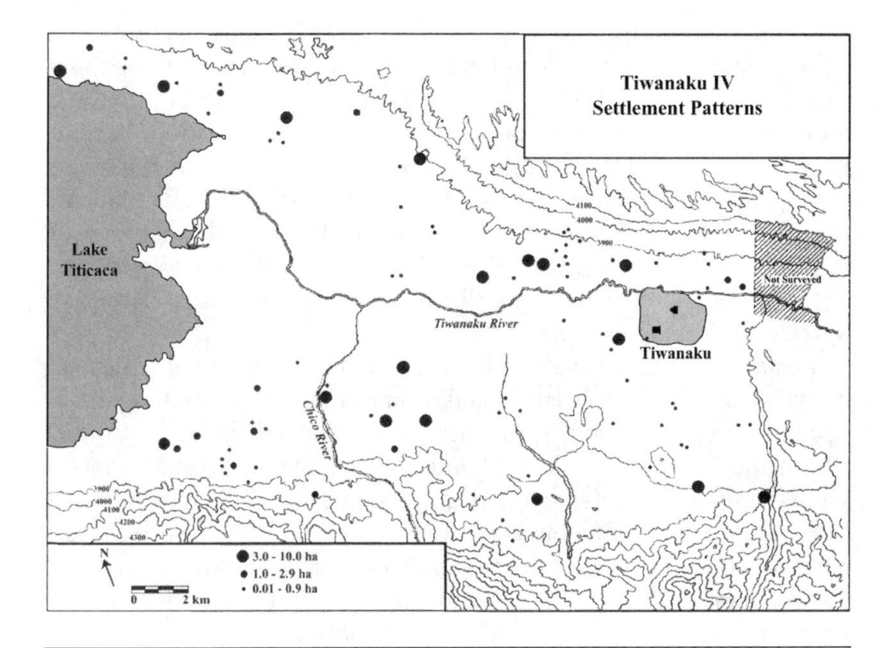

Figure 5.1 Settlement distribution in the Tiwanaku Valley during Tiwanaku IV (adapted from Albarracín-Jordan 2003).

striking rank-size convexity, alluding to heterarchical organizations and multiple networks rather than a unitary hierarchical system. Based on these patterns, Albarracín-Jordan (1992) argues that the Tiwanaku valley encompassed several semiautonomous communities.

Inhabitants of these settlements were involved in agricultural production and the distribution of goods to Tiwanaku (Mathews 2003). Agricultural features associated with Tiwanaku Valley settlements were relatively diverse. Unlike many low-lying floodplains on the lake edge, such has Huatta in Peru and the Koani Pampa in Katari, the Tiwanaku Valley floor is variable in altitude and local conditions (Albarracín-Jordan 1990, 1996a). Here most relict raised fields, which in some areas clearly dated to the Tiwanaku period, were largely limited to the northern part of valley, an area of some twenty square kilometers near the Tiwanaku River and the lake shore (Albarracín-Jordan 2003; Mathews 2003). Compared with raised field systems in the Koani Pampa, raised fields here were smaller, with a lower ratio of canal to field surfaces, and formed dispersed segments. Regional survey suggests that raised field production, while significant, was not nearly as extensive as it was in the Katari Valley. Complementing raised field production here were agricultural terraces and extensive sunken basins in the higher areas of the southern part of the valley.

Tiwanaku serving and ceremonial wares appear at sites of all sizes and types. Frequencies of decorated wares varied significantly, pointing to selective distribution or distinct site roles. At Tiwanaku, sherds of such wares comprised between nineteen percent and twenty-five percent of ceramic assemblages while at towns such as Tilata and Iwawe they varied between nine percent and thirty-five percent of assemblages (see Mathews 1992:303–304). At villages and hamlets such as Obsidiana they represented relatively small (less then ten percent) proportions of entire assemblages. Nevertheless, in relation to the distribution of Qeya wares, Tiwanaku wares were ubiquitous in the region.

Tiwanaku was the primary center at the head of networks of settlement stretching over a vast heartland. Unlike some pristine central cities, such as Uruk in Mesopotamia and Teotihuacan in Mexico's central basin (Cowgill 1997; Sanders et al. 1979; Wright and Johnson 1975), Tiwanaku's emergence did not create a demographic implosion or rural vacuum. Rather it fostered the creation of a local landscape densely populated with clusters of smaller towns, villages, and hamlets. It also correlated with the popular use of Tiwanaku-style serving-ceremonial wares and the adoption of common practices and dominant ideals at a regional scale.

Monumental Construction and Ritual Space

The Tiwanaku Moat

Monumental construction in Tiwanaku manifests a single master plan, elaborated in depth by Kolata, but also local ideological expressions and interpretations. With respect to a master plan, few proposals have stirred such debate as the idea that a massive artificial ditch or "moat . . . surrounds and separates like an island the most important and sacred part of Tihuanacu"; (Posnansky 1945:II, 121). The hypothesized moat is some twenty to forty meters wide and outlines a roughly rectangular area of 0.9 kilometers, following a clear orientation close to the cardinal directions (Kolata 1993a; 2003b). On the ground it is visible as a wide, swampy channel partially filled with sediment. It is still visible north, east, and south of the Kalasasaya and Sunken Temple, which are near the exact center of the space it bounds, while its west side has been obliterated by the more recent town of Tiahuanaco. The form and coherent orientation of the channel indicate that it is at least in part anthropogenic. A smaller ovoid channel surrounds the Mollo Kontu platform, a Tiwanaku IV-V ceremonial structure, suggesting that such features characteristically formed significant boundaries in Tiwanaku settlement landscapes.

It is likely that the Tiwanaku moat, a major planned construction project, had both religious and more practical significance. Posnansky suggested that it primarily served defensive purposes, and imagines that it may have facilitated travel on balsa boats. Kolata (1993a; 2003b) suggests that the moat maintained symbolic significance as a channel that physically marked and isolated the sacred site core as an "island enceinte." During its construction, it and others like it undoubtedly served as quarries or "borrow pits" to provide fill for the major edifices they encircled.

Precisely determining the moat's significance, however, requires some understanding of its timing. Unfortunately, to date no archaeologist has examined its chronology or construction techniques. Nevertheless, it is significant that the moat surrounds the area most densely inhabited in Late Formative 2, and that the Kalasasaya and Sunken Temple are at the center of the island enceinte it forms. Later constructions, and in particular the Pumapunku, disrupt the symmetry apparent in this arrangement. I hypothesize that the moat was first formed in Late Formative 2, perhaps in part to build the Kalasasaya platform, and that construction continued while building other monuments after AD 500. Assuming this was the case, the initial significance of the moat was to demarcate the early settlement itself, in part bounding ceremonial from more mundane spaces as Kolata suggests, but also distinguishing inhabited from largely uninhabited areas. Whatever its adjunct defensive or economic purpose, the moat was a planned and organized master project that defined the ordered and civilized space of Tiwanaku in relation to sparsely inhabited worlds just beyond it.

Monumental Complexes and Ritual Diversity in Tiwanaku

The scale of monumental construction at Tiwanaku increased extraordinarily in Tiwanaku IV, attesting the success of Tiwanaku's religious ideals and rituals. Though collectively constructions manifest elements of Tiwanaku's emerging master cosmology, a suite of elements indicates that these ideals and rituals were highly diverse. The Sunken Temple remained a center of ritual activity, as witnessed in a new floor, abundant Tiwanaku serving and ceremonial wares, and Tiwanaku-style stone sculpture, notably the immense Bennett stela. Kolata's (1993a) iconographic analysis of the sandstone sculpture, which depicts an impassive deity or ancestor in a new Classic style, draws out the significance of associated icons of fertility and regeneration. Through time the temple must have accrued great significance as an ancient ritual place, made conspicuous in the juxtaposed display of sculptures from the past (Late Formative) and present (Tiwanaku IV). The Sunken Temple remained a microcosm for Tiwanaku cosmic principles, but now with an emphasis on relics representing the past. It reified an interpretation of history as Tiwanaku cultural patrimony, curiously like the recent display of an aggrandized simulacrum of the temple in the heart of La Paz, Bolivia.[3]

The Kalasasaya, as discussed in Chapter 4, was enlarged and embellished during or just before Tiwanaku IV. In addition to an outer platform, a series of small above-ground structures (Ponce 1961:22), which Ponce dates to Tiwanaku IV, appeared around the periphery of the inner court. Under the patio itself CIAT excavators located the Ponce Monolith, lying on its side and etched with a Christian cross, which, as Vranich (1999:49) points out, indicates that its burial was the work of Spanish zealots. The Classic style iconography carved into the andesite sculpture depicted, like that of the Bennett sculpture, an impassive deity or primordial ancestor, indicating that Kalasasaya was now more than ever an awesome center of religious inspiration and ritual practice.

In Early Tiwanaku IV the immense Akapana was raised near the Kalasasaya and Sunken Temple (Kolata 1993a; Manzanilla 1992; Ponce 1981), approximating but slightly further askew of cardinal directions than the latter. Like the Kalasasaya, it is likely that the Akapana was built in stages. Kolata (1993a) interprets the final massive, terraced structure as a human-made "sacred mountain" and icon of abundance that mimicked nearby *achachilas* in its monumental form and intricate drainage system (Figures 5.2A). The basal revetment echoed that of the Kalasasaya in the use of massive pilasters and intermittent ashlars, but in the Akapana the architectural "ante" was raised in that pilasters were shorter and blocks were beveled and impeccably fitted. Six superimposed terraces rested atop of the first, forming a series of increasingly higher, smaller nested spaces that culminated, as one scaled the west stairway, in a high platform that presumably surrounded a deep sunken court that is now gutted. Supporting each outer wall was an intricate buttress system consisting of an interior retaining wall with recycled and (in many sections) roughly fitted ashlars, and between it and the outer wall, series of small walled chambers filled with earth, adobes, and fieldstones (Vranich 2001). Such complex engineering must have been tested and developed over many years, and most likely involved building the entire structure with only its retaining walls and adding the public outer wall only once the structure had settled and proven sound.

Covering the ground in front of Akapana's foundation and on its lowest platform, in the northwest sector of the monument, were the residues of complex offerings associated with rituals conducted over a long span. Along with camelid offerings, ten humans, apparently disposed as wrapped bundles (Blom et al. 2003), were strewn at the base of the first terrace wall (Manzanilla and Woodard 1990). Covering the top of the first terrace were hundreds of smashed serving and ceremonial vessels, many of which had been filled with food and drink (Wright et al. 2000). Two radiocarbon measurements date the feature to AD 600–650 (Janusek 2003a:Table 3.10). Four carbonized wood samples retrieved from nearby offering contexts, plus one retrieved from a camelid offering near the west stairway, produced divergent dates. The one-stigma ranges of two are AD 540–780, and may date rituals conducted during or just after Akapana's inauguration. Three others, including the camelid offering, date to Tiwanaku V. Apparently, rituals involving mummy bundles and sacrificial camelids were conducted over a long period of time, perhaps at key moments of construction or major Tiwanaku events. While early foundation rituals inaugurated the structure, ceramic smash may have dedicated a major event of reconstruction and renewal. Use of recycled stones in Akapana's retaining walls further suggest that Akapana was first built in Early Tiwanaku IV and, perhaps following partial collapse of its upper terraces, reconstructed employing a more intricate buttress system at around AD 800.

The Pumapunku, located several hundred meters southwest of the Akapana, was an independent ritual complex associated with an extensive plaza to the east (Figure 5.2). Although once thought to postdate the Akapana, a single radiocarbon measurement dates Pumapunku's initial construction to Early Tiwanaku IV, roughly contemporaneous with that of Akapana (Vranich 1999). Vranich's recent research documents at least two later construction phases, represented in superimposed revetments and elaborate colored floors. It further documents that the south side of the complex never was finished. Although considered "Akapana's twin" (Kolata 1993a; Ponce et al. 1971), the Pumapunku differed significantly in form, spatial configuration, and the character of ritual activities conducted therein. The main platform was extensive, measuring over a half-kilometer east-west, mimicking in plan the carved outline on the back of the Gate of the Sun (see Vranich 1999:Figure 10.2), which some suggest originally stood here (Conklin 1991). Built into its west face was the primary entrance, set on top of a natural escarpment modified as a massive esplanade that visually aggrandized the Pumapunku when approached from that direction. One moved up a stairway through stone gates, some covered with *totora* reed lintels, through a narrow, walled passage that led to a paved inner courtyard containing a deeply sunken patio. Just to the east, in front of the extensive east plaza was a portico of carved stone portals set on massive sandstone slabs (Cobo 1990:100–103; Protzen and Nair 2000). Weighing tons, these slabs are among the largest used in any New World monument.

Collectively, patterns of monumental construction and spatial organization allude to local cults and their associated religious orders. Each complex was built in successive stages, at times of organized group labor and ceremony when, on a much grander scale than before, Tiwanaku's increasingly influential politico-religious identity was breathed life in moments of *communitas*. Powerful rites of renewal during such events involved massive offerings of humans, camelids, food and drink, and ceremonial containers, as found on Akapana's foundation terrace. Like the Sunken Temple, each temple

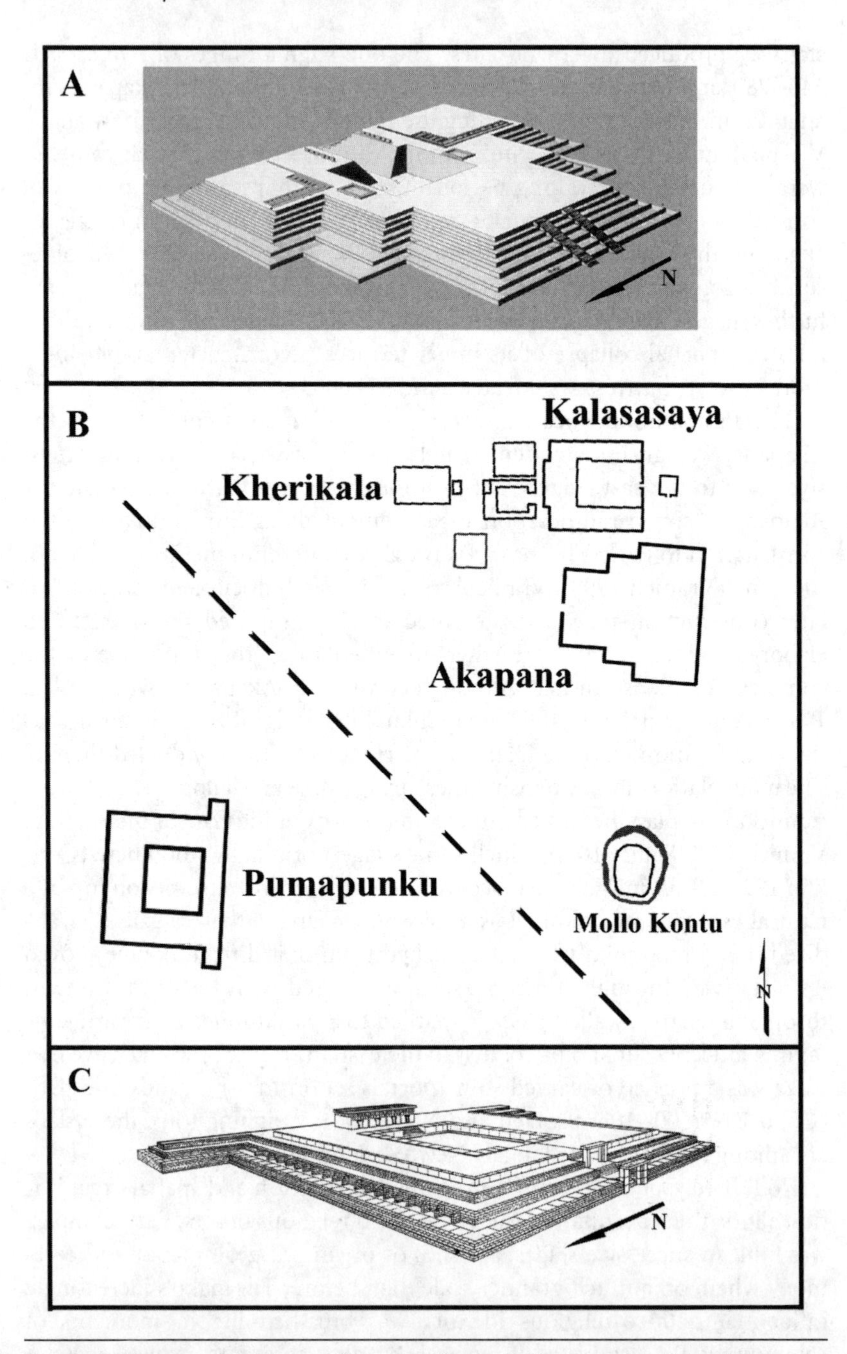

Figure 5.2 Monumental structures in Tiwanaku, with hypothetical reconstructions of the Akapana (B) and Pumapunku (B) complexes (A adapted from Manzanilla 1992; B adapted from Escalante 1997).

was a ceremonial complex and separate cult center in and of itself. Although recent dates suggests that the structures coexisted in Tiwanaku IV, each was established following a slightly different architectural orientation, and expressed a slightly different understanding of Tiwanaku ideology and a specific emphasis on some of its elements. In fact, ritual diversity was plainly expressed in the very different forms and associated elements of the complexes. The Sunken Temple presented an interpretation of Tiwanaku's primordial origins, and ceremonies conducted there may have invoked ancestral and chthonic forces to ensure or enhance social and cosmic regeneration. Later platform complexes and renewal projects in the Kalasasaya, Akapana, and Pumapunku increasingly emphasized mass, solidity, and grandeur. All shared certain characteristics, including an "obsession with the horizon" as Conklin suggests (1991:290), as well as a nested plan mimicking the double jamb of the stone portals associated with such structures (Protzen and Nair 2000, 2002). Each monument was a massive, coherently planned icon of passage between sacred and mundane dimensions of the Tiwanaku cosmos. Nevertheless, each complex was distinct from the others in form and ideological significance. While the Akapana emphasized height and visual dominance, the Pumapunku emphasized horizontal extent and ritual passage in its form and in the massive stone gates and decorative "blind portals" found in its east portico. Possibly, Vranich suggests (1999), the Pumapunku provided a point of entry into Tiwanaku to facilitate initial religious experience and indoctrination for visiting pilgrims.

Each platform structure drew subjects up onto raised platforms, through relatively small gates and passages, and into smaller inner temples and inevitably a sunken court. Despite the monumental scale of Tiwanaku ritual complexes, intimate spaces provided ideal environments for the most significant ritual practices (Moore 1996). Yet precisely who entered the innermost sancta is under debate. Drawing attention to the small scale of the innermost courts, Kolata (1993a:164) suggests only priests and elites were allowed as privileged "interlocutors with the divine." It bears questioning, however, whether small scale necessarily implies restricted elite access. Unlike many restricted access compounds in the coastal Andes (Moseley 1992), access to each of the principal Tiwanaku monuments was via a large, monumental stairway that led directly onto the platform and into the inner temple. In the Pumapunku and Kalasasaya these stairways show heavy wear. Such patterns may suggest long-term use by relatively large numbers of people. In this light, small size does not necessarily signify restricted access, though perhaps at times these areas were restricted to exclusive groups. Developing out of Late Formative monumental spatial arrangements, it instead gave concrete shape to a fundamental tenet of Tiwanaku religious ideology: social intimacy.

Finally, monumental complexes and ritual environments, though many cluster inside of the moated core, were dispersed across the urban landscape. Through Early Tiwanaku IV ritual activity of a relatively esoteric and fastidious character continued in Akapana East 1 at the far edge of the core, until the buildings were destroyed and the place ritually interred around AD 600. Set entirely outside of the bounded core, the Pumapunku was anomalous in respect to the concept of an exclusive sacred island. Nor was it the only monumental complex outside of the core. Due south of the Akapana, founded on a visual path between Akapana and Mount Kimsachata, a smaller terraced platform in Mollo Kontu was constructed sometime during Late Tiwanaku IV (Figure 5.2); (Couture 1993, 2003). Bounded by an outer revetment with a unique scallop at its northern tip, the platform included high quantities of quartz and obsidian fragments (Giesso 2003), which, Couture suggests (2003), were intentionally placed in the fill to accentuate the monument's sacred status as a miniature icon of a mountain. Further accentuating the significance of the Mollo Kontu platform, a small moat, undoubtedly the source of construction fill, completely surrounded the structure.

Thus, not only were monumental and ritual complexes structurally diverse, they were also distributed across the urban landscape, even outside of the area considered by some— perhaps traditional or orthodox Tiwanaku elites—the most sacred and significant part of the city. Each complex was the focus of a particular religious cult or order, a segment of Tiwanaku's emerging master cosmology, but each also was the focus of a separate ritual group or faction. Ritual environments like those in Akapana East and Mollo Kontu were surrounded by residential spaces, suggesting that they were tended by local residential groups. Diverse cults thrived alongside and to some extent formed constituent segments of an emerging dominant ideology. Tiwanaku religious ideas and practices clearly remained incorporative and syncretic, and the groups and ideologies associated with each cult remained coherent and vibrant. Tiwanaku was composed of multiple coexisting ideologies and distinct religious groups.

Residential Space and Domestic Activity in Tiwanaku

A comparative investigation of residential spaces and activities across Tiwanaku's urban landscape reveals a parallel tension between a uniform and highly prestigious state culture and local social networks, economic activities, and group affiliations. Most of my research in residential sectors focused on Akapana East, which includes Akapana East 1 (or AkE1) and Akapana East 2 (or AkE2) (Figure 5.3). Akapana East 1 refers to an extensive area inside of the moat, near the edge of the settlement core.

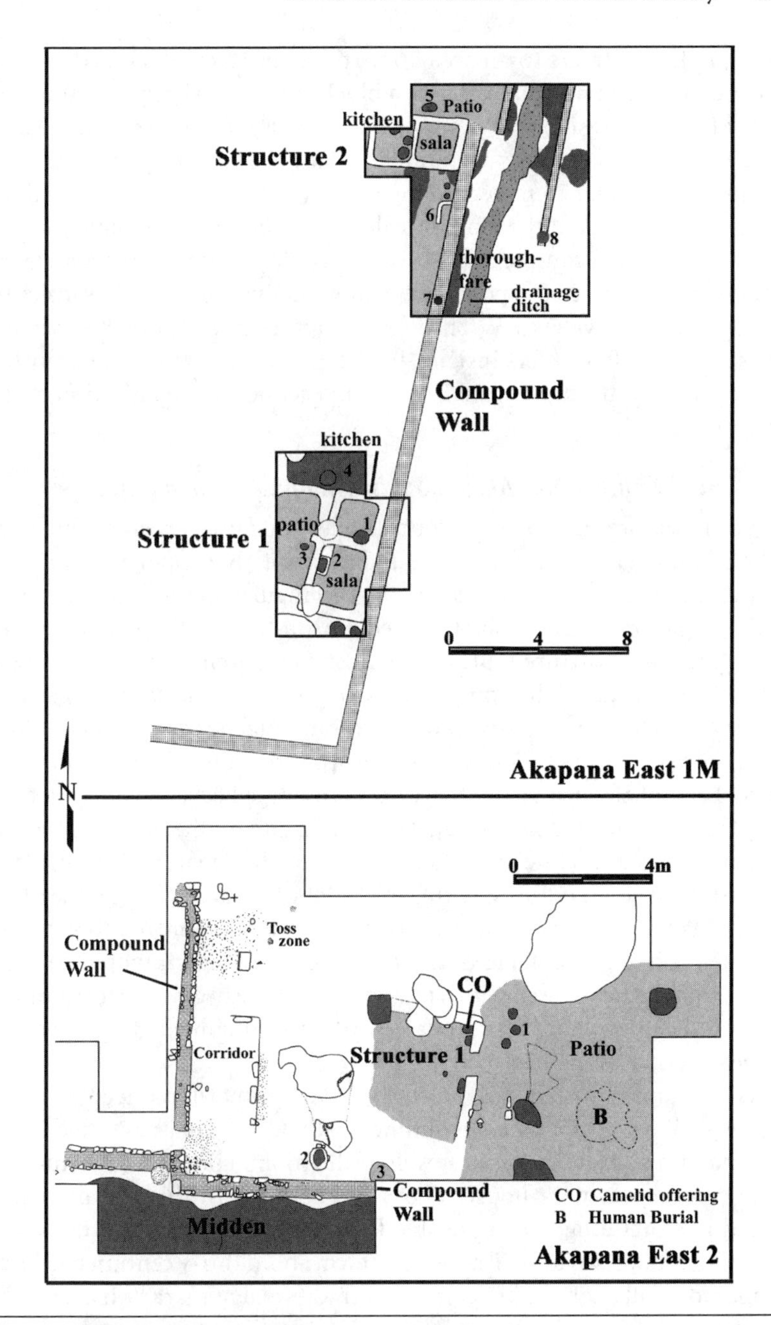

Figure 5.3 Plans of excavated structures and features in Akapana East 1M and Akapana East 2. Key for Akapana East 1M: 1-hearth; 2-fuel bin and seat; 3-storage chamber; 4-midden; 5-storage pit; 6-storage bin; 7-infant; 8-adult burial. Key for Akapana East 2: 1-storage bins; 2-hearth; 3-seat. See Janusek 1994 for detailed illustrations.

Akapana East 2 refers to an area approximately 120 meters farther east, outside of the moat. Two excavation blocks in AkE 1M revealed the west edge of a large residential compound with two small structures, each with activity areas and refuse middens dating from Early through Late Tiwanaku IV. Some 70 meters to the east, in Akapana East 1, excavations along the west bank of the moat revealed middens and refuse pits postdating the early ritual complex. In Akapana East 2, outside of the moat, excavations on a low mound exposed occupations dating from Late Tiwanaku IV through Early Tiwanaku V. Through comparison with other excavated areas, Akapana East offers insights into the practical rhythms of daily life as well as key patterns of spatial, social, and economic organization in the urban center.

Residential Compounds: Akapana East 1M and Akapana East 2

In AkE 1M, a large north-south cobblestone foundation crossed both excavation blocks (Figure 5.3). This foundation clearly supported a massive wall that bordered the east side of the rectangular mound. An east-west wall foundation of similar size followed the south edge of the mound, indicating that the structure represented a coherent, architecturally bounded compound. Inside of the compound, structure 1, to the south, measured 5.5 by 2.4 meters, and consisted of two rooms attached to a small outdoor patio. The structure's foundation and walls were built principally of earth brick. Each of the primary activity areas contained several superimposed surfaces of compacted sandy clay. The small room on the north side of the structure served as a kitchen with a corner hearth. The hearth consisted of a deep ash-filled pit outlined with baked adobe bricks and large vessel fragments. Like many Aymara hearths today, a small opening, reinforced with a broken cooking vessel, faced into the room. The superimposed surfaces of this room were covered with a thin lens of greenish-gray ash, carbonized camelid dung, cooking ware (olla) sherds, and fragmented camelid and guinea pig (*cuy*) bones.

The second room, or *sala*, probably served primarily as sleeping quarters. A shallow rectangular bin outlined with adobe bricks and filled with ash and dung bordered the west wall of the room. Like similar features in contemporary Aymara houses (Loza Balsa 1971:73), this bin may have served to store dung, a combustible fuel. Between the bin and the north wall of the room was a small adobe platform about thirty centimeters high, similar to small adobe seats (*patillas*) in traditional Aymara houses. On the earliest surface, two basalt nodules with pounding scars were found directly in front of the platform, indicating that generalized lithic production was one activity carried out here. Although the room contained no obvious sleeping platforms, its north quarter was compact and free of ash, suggesting that simple beds of textiles or *ichu* grass were laid along the warm wall next to the hearth.

An outdoor patio with ten superimposed surfaces occupied the west side of the structure. Charcoal from the second surface provided a calibrated radiocarbon date of AD 590±108 (Janusek 1993a:Table 3.1), which centers in the Early Tiwanaku IV phase. Changes in ceramic assemblages on the subsequent eight surfaces indicated that occupation continued through Late Tiwanaku IV without hiatus or major change. The surfaces revealed artifacts representing a wide range of activities, confirming that the patio was a key locus of domestic activity. The first three floors were associated with a deep pit, the restricted globular shape of which suggests that it served as a storage chamber. Like contemporary Aymara subterranean bins, this chamber most likely served to store dry consumable goods, such as tubers and quinoa. During the formation of the fourth occupation surface, the chamber was converted into a refuse pit.

An outdoor midden and refuse zone occupied the area north of structure 1. Layers of greenish-gray ash with dung and domestic refuse alternated with more compact layers of laminated silty clay, the latter derived from seasonally eroding adobe walls. The area along the north wall of the kitchen contained chunks of burnt adobe and broken *ollas*, where inhabitants discarded hearth cleanings. A great deal of the artifactual material has been burned, indicating that refuse was burned regularly for sanitation purposes.

The north excavation block in Akapana East 1M revealed a second domestic structure. The foundation wall of the compound continued through this area, broken by a staggered section that appears to have been an entrance structure 2 was not as well preserved as structure 1, and it lacked clear floor sequences. Like structure 1, its foundations consisted principally of adobe brick, reinforced in places with fieldstones. A kitchen with three hearths occupied the west end of the structure. A deep hearth or oven, similar to that in structure 1, occupied its southeast corner. The hearth consisted of a pit outlined with baked adobe bricks, and contained a small opening plugged with a cut sandstone block. As in the kitchen of structure 1, green ash, dung, *olla* sherds, and burnt camelid and rodent bone fragments were strewn over the surface of the room.

A room (*sala*) with a compact floor occupied the area between the kitchen and the compound wall. Here, a nearly complete cooking vessel sat upright in a small subterranean basin. North of the room was a poorly preserved patio containing a boot-shaped subterranean storage pit. Like the storage pit outside of structure 1, its chamber, once it fell into disuse, was converted into a refuse pit. South of the structure, a trampled surface served as an auxiliary outdoor activity zone and midden. Three shallow pits and an L-shaped stone feature along the west side of the compound wall served as storage bins.

About four meters east of the large compound wall was a parallel wall foundation that bounded the west edge of a second compound. The area in between the two compounds consisted of compact soil covered with superimposed lenses of refuse midden. Traversing this space was a long, irregular band of laminated sandy loam containing gravel and artifactual refuse. This feature clearly represented a drainage ditch that received waste and water from the domestic compounds, much like the ditches that run through the roads of altiplano towns today. Like the pre-Hispanic feature, these ditches gradually fill with laminated, gravely loam. The area between the compounds, I suggest, was an unpaved street facilitating circulation through residential sectors of the settlement. In Tiwanaku V, a small drainage canal carried waste water into the street from inside of the east compound (Chapter 7). The image of walled residential compounds separated by narrow streets, with water trickling into open drainage ditches, is strikingly reminiscent of contemporary Andean towns.

Excavations in Akapana East 1M revealed two mortuary contexts. One was a human infant buried in a small pit in the foundation of the easternmost compound wall in the north block excavations. The second burial was located at the south end of the parallel compound wall to the east, and may have been a later feature that intruded into the foundation. The poorly preserved remains represented a young adult female who was buried in a flexed position, facing east. Several of the bones (including many vertebrae, hands, and feet) were missing, suggesting that it was a secondary interment.

Excavations in Akapana East 2, outside of the moat, revealed substantial evidence for human occupation during the Late Tiwanaku IV and Early Tiwanaku V phases (Figure 5.3). One excavation unit here reached precultural red clay directly under Late Tiwanaku IV occupations, indicating that this area was first occupied later than the earliest occupations in AkE 1M. Much of the occupation was later disturbed by postabandonment quarrying, deflation, and plowing. What remained consisted of a single domestic structure surrounded by several features, occupation surfaces, and wall foundations.

Two large foundations, supporting compound walls similar to those in AkE 1M, surrounded a single structure. Only the northeast corner of a structure with three superimposed occupation surfaces remained intact. The foundations consisted of adobe blocks on cobblestone foundations. A preserved doorway opened to the east, facing a trampled outdoor surface. The earliest floor consisted of finely selected red clay, and it rested on a thick, thirty-centimeter layer of ash and refuse. The upper two surfaces consisted of sand, like those in AkE 1M. The final surface was covered with a thin lens of carbonized ichu grass, the remains of the collapsed roof. The structure measured at least four by five meters, but poor preservation prevents a more precise determination of its full dimensions.

East of the structure was an outdoor patio consisting of two superimposed, compact surfaces. As in the case of Akapana East 1M, this patio revealed residues of diverse activities. Associated with the patio was a deep cylindrical pit and a cluster of three small circular pits, what may have been subterranean storage bins. A cooking area littered with *olla* sherds occupied the space south of the structure. A nearby platform of red clay, similar to the *patilla* found in AKE 1M, may have served as a seat or bench. Further west, the west compound wall and a parallel foundation framed a narrow corridor. At its north end was a dense cluster of large artifact fragments, including high proportions of sherds from elaborate serving vessel, exhausted grinding stones, and lithic debitage. The cluster most likely represented an interior toss zone, where broken or obsolete implements were discarded from the principal activity zones. We exposed a small area south of the compound wall, which had high densities of ash and domestic refuse, indicating that this area had been an exterior midden.

Akapana East 2 yielded two clear ritual contexts: a camelid offering and a complex burial (Figure 5.3). The camelid offering consisted of a llama fetus placed under the northeast corner of the structure. Under the patio, and marked by a stone protruding above the patio surface, was a human burial consisting of three separate chambers, each containing a separate individual. The main chamber (burial 1) was an adobe-lined shaft 1.9 meters deep that contained the poorly preserved remains of an adult male thirty-five to forty-five years old. Buried with the individual were two complete ceramic vessels. A smaller, unlined chamber to the southeast (burial 2) contained the remains of a child interred with a wide assortment of goods: basketry and textiles, as represented in carbonized remains, and three elaborate vessels, including a duck-effigy *vasija* (see Janusek 2003a: Figure 3.55c). To the north, a small adobe-lined chamber (burial 3) contained another child buried with two vessels.

Household Activities in Akapana East 1 and 2

The two excavated Akapana East zones presented a wide range of domestic activities. As expected, outdoor areas yielded evidence for the widest range of activities, and patios, in particular, were the principal focus of day-today social and domestic life for household members. Domestic activities served both the material reproduction and social well-being of resident social groups. Not surprisingly, the acquisition, preparation, and consumption of foodstuffs were principal household activities. Food preparation was consistently represented in certain types of ground stone implements, including flat *batánes* with a concave working surface at one end. Accompanying *batánes* were convex *moleadores* for grinding grains such as maize and especially quinoa, and rounded pestle-like crushers for processing peppers, dried meat *(charqui)*, and seeds. Butchering also was conducted in residential compounds, as reflected in substantial quantities of *ad hoc*, unretouched or quickly retouched lithic scrapers and knives, and in butchering marks on the bones of camelids, guinea pig, *vizcacha*, and birds. Dry foods were stored in underground pits; and foods and liquid were stored in large jars (*tinajas*) of varied sizes. Low numbers of small obsidian and quartzite projectile points indicated that hunting and possibly warfare were important activities for Tiwanaku's inhabitants (Giesso 2003).

Cooking was represented in hearths, deep ovens, and enclosed kitchens of varied sizes, and also in great quantities of cooking vessel sherds, dung fuel, and ash. Other common domestic activities included the production of bone and stone tools, reflected in significant quantities of lithic debitage and cut and splintered bone in all excavated residences. Surprisingly, while spindle whorls were abundant, other evidence of weaving tools such as bone needles, awls, and *wichuñas* were uncommon in Akapana East. Either weaving left little trace, or it was the domain of specialized groups whose residences have not yet been excavated.

Domestic life in Tiwanaku also included a range of activities related to the ritual reproduction of the household. Ceramic *sahumadors* were used to burn some substance with high lipid content, whether a plant resin or camelid fat (Tschopik 1950:208). Most likely, *sahumadors* served both quotidian and ritual ends. Like similar vessels in contemporary Aymara communities, they probably served as domestic lamps to provide light and warmth, and as ceremonial burners in intimate domestic rituals.

Burying fetal camelids and humans under the floors and walls of residential areas also was a typical ritual practice. Contemporary Aymara speakers practice rituals in which the burial of a human placenta and fetal camelid are elements of a broader context of offerings conducted during the construction or renewal of a house compound (Arnold 1992:51). Fetal burials in Tiwanaku, like those today, were undoubtedly ritual offerings intended to ensure the well-being of a house's inhabitants. Placing a human infant under a compound wall (as in Akapana East 1M) and a llama under the corner of an individual house (as in Akapana East 2) accord well with the respective scales of the social group. While the fetal llama was likely dedicated to a house and its inhabitants, the human fetus, under the compound wall, may have been interred by and for the entire social group living in the compound.

Sherds of elaborate serving vessels appeared in all residential areas, but in especially high proportions on patios and in middens, indicating that social gatherings and life-cycle rituals were important events in each residential compound. The most common serving vessels were everted bowls, or *tazons*, drinking chalices, or *keros*, and a variety of small pitchers, known as *vasijas*. Rarer special wares included flaring bowls, or *escudillas*, and large basins, or *fuentes*. Serving vessel sherds comprised between sixteen and nineteen percent of total assemblages in each of the compounds (Janusak 2003b: Table 10.2). Most of these vessels were finely made, and most displayed key elements of Tiwanaku corporate style: red or black slip, hyperboloid form, and elaborate polychrome iconography. The vessels, alongside clothing and other valued crafted goods, I argue, became important vehicles for the affirmation and negotiation of social status and identity during periodic local feasts and other rituals of consumption.

Middens and Ash Pits: Akapana East 1 and Kk'araña

Complementing evidence for dense occupation, material refuse was becoming an ever-present element of Tiwanaku's expanding settlement landscape. Large ash pits and extensive middens were present in all excavated residential areas, and some sectors were dedicated nearly exclusively to mass secondary deposition. In Late Tiwanaku IV, the area of Akapana East 1 along the west bank of the moat, once a significant local ritual place, was converted into the backyard of nearby residential compounds. Excavations here revealed several ephemeral hearths, a deep well, and over twenty deep, amorphous pits filled with immense quantities of ash, dung, and refuse. These tore through huge sections of preceding contexts. Similarly, excavations in Kk'araña revealed, in addition to three human burials and a deep well, extensive midden lenses and at least twelve large pits with immense quantities of ash and refuse. The wells in each area, which descended below the current friatic zone, also were filled with ash and refuse. The energy that went into excavating the ash pits as well as their amorphous form suggest that they served as borrow pits that provided the clay loam for the construction of earth brick buildings. Once excavated, the pits were filled with waste and refuse.

The type and sheer quantity of refuse found in sectors converted into backyard middens clearly represented more than just domestic garbage. The amount of refuse recovered in such secondary contexts was simply enormous, and the range of activities represented was broad. The pits yielded immense quantities of *olla*, *tinaja*, and serving and ceremonial sherds; splintered and butchered bones of camelids, guinea pigs, and birds; broken bone and stone tools; food remains; camelid dung fuel; and of course, incredible volumes of ash. Further, ash and refuse deposits in wells and most ash pits presented less than three strata of deposition, and several only one, suggesting that they were filled in a few dumping events. Pieces of a single vessel in many cases were strewn about different levels of the same pit or stratum. Further, the range of ceramic types and serving variants found in many such deposits was far greater than that from any primary residential context. A wide range of evidence complicitly suggests that the pits contained the residues not just of domestic activity but also of periodic major events, local rituals of consumption and more public feasts for which people of various household compounds, sites, or perhaps regions would have gathered.

Other Residential Sectors

Excavations in other sectors of the site confirmed that many spatial and activity patterns apparent in Akapana East were characteristic of Tiwanaku residential life as a whole. Excavations in Mollo Kontu (Couture 1993, 2003), La K'araña (Escalante 1997:255–287, 2003), Putuni (Couture and Sampeck 2003; Sampeck 1991), and Ch'iji Jawira (Rivera 1994, 2003) demonstrated that minimal households, each represented by dwellings associated with patios, middens, and ancillary buildings, were incorporated into larger, architecturally bounded compounds. As in Akapana East, material reproduction, mortuary and ritual practice, and local feasting characterized these residential areas. All yielded substantial proportions of ceramic vessels and lower proportions of other crafted objects (e.g., engraved bone) that incorporated elements or designs executed in Tiwanaku style. However, residential patterns in the Putuni, Ch'iji Jawira, and La K'araña varied in certain key respects from those in Akapana East, demonstrating important elements of variability in Tiwanaku residential life and activity.

Sub-Putuni Structures and Residential Activity

West of the Kalasasaya (Couture and Sampeck 2003; Janusek and Earnest 1990b; Kolata 1993a:149–164; Sampeck 1991), a Late Tiwanaku IV sub-Putuni occupation covered the primary Late Formative 2—Early Tiwanaku IV occupation briefly described in Chapter 4. Excavations in the Late Tiwanaku IV occupation, outlined in detail in Couture and Sampeck (2003), revealed parts of two extensive residential compounds divided by a large east-west compound wall at least 40 meters long (Figure 5.4A). Following the alignment of the Kalasasaya, and diverging slightly from that of the Akapana, all architecture in the two compounds followed an orientation eight degrees east of the cardinal directions. One of the most extensively excavated structures in the compound to the north served as a specialized kitchen for preparing and cooking food (Figure 5.4B). In and around it were several hearths, refuse pits, and abundant artifactual

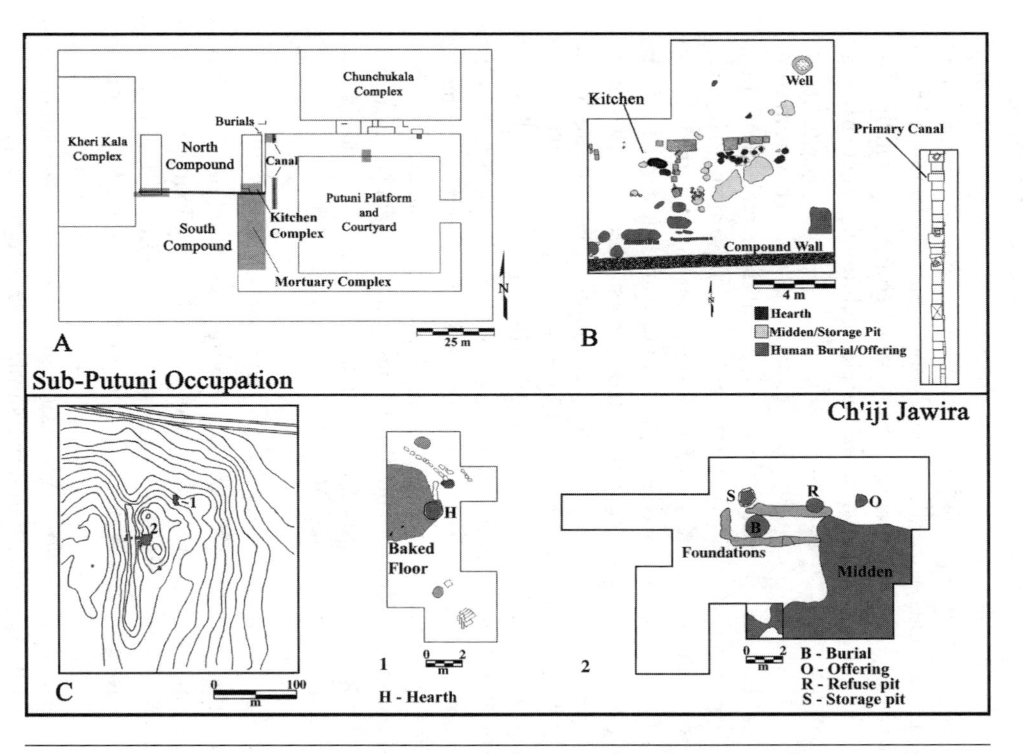

Figure 5.4 Plans of excavated structures and features in the Putuni area (A) and in Ch'iji Jawira (B). Note: sub-Putuni occupations in A are shown in gray in relation to later structures, such as the Putuni Platform and Courtyard (A adapted from Couture and Sampeck 2003; B adapted from Rivera 1994).

evidence for cooking and food preparation. The structure's walls rested on foundations composed of a combination of cut stone blocks and cobblestones (Sampeck 1991:47–47).

The Late Tiwanaku IV occupation in Putuni differed significantly from those in Akapana East in a number of ways, including the presence of a mortuary cluster of elaborate human burials located in the compound to the south (Couture and Sampeck 2003). Interments contained fine sumptuary offerings, including elaborate ceramic vessels, turquoise, sodalite, chrysacolla and bone beads, silver tubes, copper pins, and adornments of gold lamina, among other items. Some burials contained literally hundreds of sherds from broken serving vessels, including particularly high quantities of elaborately decorated *escudillas.*

The Late Tiwanaku IV sub-Putuni occupation also differed from those in Akapana East in its association with a monumental, stone-lined drainage network that drained runoff and waste toward the Tiwanaku River. First encountered by a French expedition around the turn of the century (Créqui-Monfort 1906), a primary canal of carved ashlars, measuring 1 meter high and 0.9 meters across, descended gently to the north about one meter below the occupation surface (Couture and Sampeck 2003; Janusek and Earnest 1990b; Ponce 1961:22). The canal followed an alignment six degrees east of north, similar to that of aboveground wall foundations, and it was sealed with hard clay. Nearby were several maintenance pits filled with muck and refuse. Numerous feeder canals, one of which originated in an *ad hoc* basin set into a Late Tiwanaku IV residential surface, drained into the primary canal. Judging from associated contexts and superimposed occupations, the canal was built in Late Formative 2 or Early Tiwanaku IV.

Residence and Ceramic Production in Ch'iji Jawirai

Located on the east edge of Tiwanaku (Figure 3.3A), well outside of the principal moat, Ch'iji Jawira differed from Akapana East in manners very distinct from those in Putuni. Here, on a low mound of about 1.2 hectares, Claudia Rivera (1994, 2003) and others (Alconini 1995; Franke 1995) located residential contexts and middens dating to the Late Tiwanaku IV and Tiwanaku V phases (Figure 5.4C). Many patterns of residence and domestic activity were similar to those found elsewhere. A ditch ten meters wide, most likely a natural stream bed modified to form an outer moatlike channel, separated Ch'iji Jawira from the rest of the site. Ch'iji Jawira's isolation was emphasized by a large compound wall on cobblestone foundations. The compound incorporated several incompletely preserved adobe building foundations associated with storage pits and refuse middens, as well as four human burials and an offering pit containing several elaborate serving-ceremonial vessels. Occupations and middens yielded cooking, storage, and serving vessel sherds, as well as weaving tools, lithic debitage, and ground stone *batanes* and *moleadores.*

Despite general similarities in spatial organization and domestic activities, Ch'iji Jawira differed from Akapana East in other respects. Dwelling foundations consisted purely of earth brick, and residential contexts were surrounded by superimposed ash lenses and immense quantities of refuse. *Sahumadors,* common in all other residential areas, were exceedingly rare at Ch'iji Jawira (0.01 percent of combined serving and ceremonial wares); (Janusek 2003b:Table 10.5). Also, small baked clay figurines, clearly made at Ch'iji Jawira and representing humans and animals, were common. These were relatively scarce in other residential areas. Drawing on the significance of miniature representations in contemporary *alasitas* festivals (La Barre 1948:195–196; Tschopik 1950:208), Rivera (1994) suggests that the figurines served local household rituals stressing abundance.

Further, the inhabitants of Ch'iji Jawira specialized in producing certain types of ceramic wares. The area was ideally located for ceramic production, adjacent to a semipermanent water supply and situated on the eastern periphery of the city, downwind from the prevailing northwest winds. Implements and by-products of ceramic manufacture, absent in other excavated sectors of the site, appeared throughout the mound. Implements included fragments of plaster molds, polishing implements, and yellow-, red-, and green-based pigments (Rivera 1994, 2003). By-products included misfired wasters, slumped vessels, and immense quantities of partially baked clay lumps, some with basketry impressions. Excavations indicated that firing procedures were relatively informal, consisting of open enclosures and small pit kilns (Franke 1995; Rivera 1994). Archaeobotanical analysis revealed that the plant fuels preferred by ceramic producers in Andean communities today were far denser in Ch'iji Jawira middens than anywhere else in Tiwanaku (Wright et al. 2003). Ch'iji Jawira was a large, bounded compound inhabited by people practicing both domestic and craft activities. Local specialists produced *tazons,* large jars, or *tinajas,* and *keros* with modelled zoomorphic heads (Figure 5.6G), most of which were not crafted for consumption by high status groups.

Residence and Storage in La K'araña

Likely evidence for specialized storage in a residential compound comes from La Karaña, within Tiwanaku's bounded core northeast of Kalasasaya (Figure 3.3a). Here Javier Escalante (1997:255–287, 2003) revealed sections of what appear to be two adjacent residential compounds dating from Late Tiwanaku IV to Early Tiwanaku V (Figure 5.5). Bordering both,

A

B

Figure 5.5 Views of rectangular structures (A) and the circular (B) structure associated with residential occupations in La K'araña (photos by Wolfgang Schüler, courtesy of Alan Kolata).

to the south, was a massive cobble-face terrace retaining wall that stood some 1.4 meters high. The west compound contained a rectangular structure of cobble and adobe foundations, comparable in size (3.8 x 2.4 meters) to structures in Akapana East 1M. The structure included a rectangular storage bin similar to that recovered in Akapana East 1M. Just to the east was an outdoor kitchen with a large hearth and a semicircular adobe foundation (Figure 5.5A). Between the structures, two subterranean drainage canals, consisting of an *ad hoc* combination of fieldstones and re-utilized *batanes* and ashlars, joined to form a single canal that descended to the north, toward the river. The east compound incorporated a large circular structure with a thick cobble foundation measuring almost seven meters in diameter (Figure 5.5B). The floor inside of the structure consisted of hardpacked clay, paved in places with flat sandstone slabs. In contrast to the heavily littered area outside, the surface inside was relatively clean and contained no domestic features, suggesting to Escalante that it served to store agricultural crops or other valued goods. Sweeping around the west side of the building was a covered vernacular drainage canal that, like the others, descended from the south terrace toward the river.

Urban Growth, State Culture, and Social Ranking

Residence and Urban Growth

Spatial organization in Akapana East and elsewhere reveals much about residential patterns in Tiwanaku and about the nature of Tiwanaku urban society. Tiwanaku was not settled in a disorganized way, through a random accretion of individual household units. Rather the city grew systematically, through the planned construction and occupation of large, uniformly aligned compounds. Each dwelling and its associated activities represented the smallest repetitive architectural element in the city: the coresidential household. Multiple superimposed floors in Akapana East point to long-term occupation by groups with long local histories spanning multiple generations. Households were encompassed within larger residential compounds, repetitive archaeological units that housed larger social groups. In Akapana East 1 and Ch'iji Jawira, multiple juxtaposed compounds may have formed entire barrios, or neighborhoods. Streets and canals ran between some of these planned compound providing arteries for the movement of people and water.

Settlement growth is demonstrated in two key manners. Most directly, it is represented in the chronology of residential occupation across the site. The settlement core was occupied during the Late Formative Period, but there is no evidence for substantial occupation outside of the moat before ca. AD 600, the beginning of Late Tiwanaku IV. Until this time, residential occupation in Tiwanaku concentrated mainly in and around the area bounded by the moat. Over the next two hundred years, settlement expanded well beyond this early boundary. Akapana East 2 and Ch'iji Jawira were first occupied in Late Tiwanaku IV, clearly indicating that the urban population of Tiwanaku increased dramatically during this phase. One residential sector after another was inhabited, until the moat, which may have bounded most of Tiwanaku during the Late Formative and Early Tiwanaku IV phases, was now well inside of the settlement. Thus, the moat's significance shifted through time (Kolata 1993a). If it originally bounded Tiwanaku, it now emphasized a roughly concentric gradient of social differences among the city's residential sectors and inhabitants.

Settlement growth is also demonstrated in the increasing importance of secondary deposition. Accompanying urban growth here as in any new city were immense volumes of refuse and waste, as the growing city began generating and consuming immense amounts of material. For Tiwanaku inhabitants, garbage was always nearby, so it was often burned to avoid scavengers. Some household waste was drained out of residential sectors via subterranean drainage canals, ultimately toward the Tiwanaku River to the north. Other refuse was discarded outside of houses, onto streets, and into old wells and extensive borrow pits. In some cases, entire abandoned sectors, including once significant ritual places, were converted into urban middens. Refuse pits and middens contained the waste generated in everyday domestic activities and in periodic rituals of consumption.

Conformity and Feasting in Residential Life

Parallel with predominant patterns among Tiwanaku's ritual complexes, a comparative analysis of space, practices, and material culture in its residential sectors reveals intersecting macro-patterns of conformity and heterogeneity. In all areas, certain material patterns emphasized conformity with broad urban patterns, which remained highly conservative throughout Tiwanaku IV. First, all residential architecture replicated a common directional orientation approximately six to eight degrees east of north. Compounds, dwellings, structures, streets, and terrace walls all replicated this ideal order within a few degrees, from which only vernacular drainage canals strayed. This orientation was reproduced both across the settlement and over time, in local cycles of construction, abandonment, and renewal.

The orientation, though slightly variable among Tiwanaku's monumental complexes, attests a formal urban design that reified a single, elegant spatial cosmology. It follows closest the orientations of the Akapana and Pumapunku complexes. This design was established in the Late Formative (see Chapter 4), and its proximity to the cardinal directions indicates that it simulated the movement of astronomical bodies, most saliently, perhaps, the daily east-west path of the sun (Kolata 1993a:96–98). In fact most entrances to compounds and residential structures faced east or west, as did primary stairways and portals to all major platform complexes. In addition, the urban orientation approximates visual pathways to major local peaks, including Mount Kimsachata to the south and Mount Illimani to the east (Posnansky 1945; Reinhard 1985, 1990). As in later Andean *markas*, the built environment approximated the cyclical movements of significant phenomena and established visual and ritual linkages with prominent features on the landscape. Tiwanaku instantiated principles that were timeless and sacred. Still, for most inhabitants, Tiwanaku was experienced rather than abstractly conceived, and people walked through it day after day more than they beheld it from some spatial or intellectual distance. Life in and pilgrimage to this built landscape instilled a grand sense of spatial order, an order that approximated the inviolable cycles and travels of mythical protagonists and that extended far beyond the power, knowledge, and life history of the experiencing subject.

The sudden appearance of Tiwanaku serving and ceremonial vessels was striking and significant. Ceramic assemblages during the preceding Late Formative had been far less diverse in form and role. The most elaborate Kalasasaya and Qeya vessels remained extremely limited in distribution, specialized storage jars were uncommon, and serving vessels consisted principally of small bowls. Abruptly, at approximately AD 500, a new repertoire of ceramic assemblages appeared throughout Tiwanaku and at all known related sites. Most remarkable were red-slipped serving and ceremonial wares that presented a range of formal variation. Assemblages now included a wide range of everted bowls (*tazons*), drinking chalices (*keros*), pitchers (*vasijas*), flaring bowls (*escudillas*), large basins (*fuentes*), and small bowls (*cuencos*), in addition to an array of vessels dedicated to ritual and other specialized activities (e.g., *sahumadors*, *wako retratos*) (Figures 3.2 and 5.6). Tall, high-volume cooking *ollas* and storage *tinajas* now became common. By Late Tiwanaku IV massive *tinajas* depicting sweeping water motifs comprised significant proportions of ceramic assemblages. Like large jars used recently in the Andes (Bertonio 1984; Tschopik 1950:206), Tiwanaku *tinajas* fermented and stored alcoholic beverages such as maize *kusa* and quinoa *ch'ua*.

As striking was the ubiquitous acquisition and use of Tiwanaku serving and ceremonial wares during the IV phase. Compared with simultaneous cultural developments in contemporaneous Andean regions, such as eastern valley polities, ceramic style in Tiwanaku now presented great uniformity (Janusek 2003a). Throughout Tiwanaku, most forms comprised a well-defined range of types. Most serving vessels had red-, orange-, or black-slipped surfaces, and iconography presented a notably standard range of mythical, anthropomorphic, and geometric designs. In any residential sector, most ceramic serving vessels displayed elements of Tiwanaku style. The pervasiveness of this style points to a thorough dissemination and overall acceptance of predominant Tiwanaku ideals and practices. The ubiquity of Tiwanaku-style vessels also implicates an operating system of redistribution in which goods were obtained as reciprocal compensation for participating in the emerging political economy. Some groups, such as the residents of Ch'iji Jawira, produced specialized goods, while others may have participated in public projects as court functionaries, camelid herders, farmers, or rotating laborers for monumental construction projects.

Elaborately crafted and visually stunning Tiwanaku serving and ceremonial wares were clearly desirable, in part a reflection of their stylistic and iconographic significance. Tiwanaku vessels were vehicles for the depiction of elaborate religious iconography, frozen and stylized images of Tiwanaku mythic narratives and ritual practices. Many motifs depicted on Tiwanaku vessels drew on themes with long histories and broad spatial distribution in the Andes, but their expression and synthetic combination were innovative and highly distinctive. At one end of the spectrum, iconography emphasized highly abstract motifs, including steps, undulating bands, and continuous volutes. At the other end of the spectrum were stylized anthropomorphic and zoomorphic motifs. Ceramic vessels for the first time became a medium for depicting humans, trophy heads, and deity masks, while zoomorphic images included felines (pumas, jaguars), predatory birds (condors, falcons, eagles), lake birds, and serpents. Early on, figures were typically represented as entire beings, but soon they were depicted more abstractly as isolated body elements and composite beings.

As patently, the appearance of new assemblages for preparing, storing, fermenting as well as consuming foods and liquids points to an increasing emphasis on rituals of consumption (Dietler 1996, 2001; Hayden 2001). As a diversified range of vehicles for Tiwanaku style and mythical icons, serving and ceremonial wares, in particular, formed a specialized repertoire that facilitated both domestic meals and communal consumption. *Keros* served as drinking vessels and *tazons* served either as common food bowls or more generalized consumption vessels, while *vasijas* were pitchers used to pour liquids held in large storage vessels into drinking *keros* (Betanzos 1996:67, 172; Janusek 2003a). In addition to these three basic forms were special ceremonial vessels such as *escudillas* and large basins that were less widely distributed. Decoration on each form followed a suite of rules regarding execution, combination, and adherence to specific design fields. *Kero* surfaces, for example, displayed four vertical zones, each with a particular range of designs. Tiwanaku serving assemblages, designed to disseminate a particular style and to facilitate private and public consumption, were guided by relatively strict canons of form and design. They would have been particularly significant and effective in social gatherings involving music, dancing, and drinking. As in the Andes today, feasts were critical for the negotiation of prestige and status.

Feasting is evident throughout Tiwanaku. The ceramic smash on Akapana's foundation terrace, with hundreds of broken vessels (Alconini 1995; Manzanilla 1992) containing food and drink (Wright et al. 2003), most likely was the residue generated during a particularly lively, significant feasting event. In the sub-Putuni sector, immense quantities of *escudillas* and other serving-ceremonial sherds in burials suggest that ritualized consumption accompanied local, elaborate mortuary rituals (Couture and Sampeck 2003; Janusek 2003b). Nevertheless, Tiwanaku serving-ceremonial wares and cooking, storage, and fermentation vessels appeared in every residential compound. Serving-ceremonial sherds were particularly abundant in outdoor areas and patios, and in secondary ash pits and middens. In conjunction with abundant evidence that much ritual and residential activity occurred in relatively intimate and bounded spaces, the ubiquitous distribution and acquisition of elaborate serving wares indicates that feasting was not entirely coopted or centralized but was common practice throughout Tiwanaku.

Status Differences in Tiwanaku Residences

Crosscutting material conformity in Tiwanaku's residential landscape was a roughly concentric gradient of status differentiation (Kolata 1993a:149–164). By AD 600, inhabitants of Late Tiwanaku IV compounds in the Putuni area distinguished themselves from other groups in several key ways. They incorporated ashlar masonry in their wall foundations and enjoyed access to an intricate subterranean drainage network with both practical and symbolic significance. Prestige goods and high-status objects of personal adornment were common in the mortuary complex. The range of ceramic serving wares found in sub-Putuni residential and mortuary areas was remarkably diverse. Serving wares included high proportions of elegantly wrought *escudillas* (thirty-five percent of serving ware sherds), a special form that was far less common in other residential areas (Janusek 2003b:Table 10.4) (Figure 5.6F). Other elaborate forms included basins, recurved *tazons*, and elaborate modelled figurines (Janusek 2003a, 2003b). *Kero* and *tazon* sherds, common serving wares in other residential areas and sites, comprised only fifteen percent of serving assemblages (Janusek 2003b:Table 10.4).

By contrast, in Akapana East 1M architectural foundations consisted purely of unmodified field stones and adobe, and residents had no access

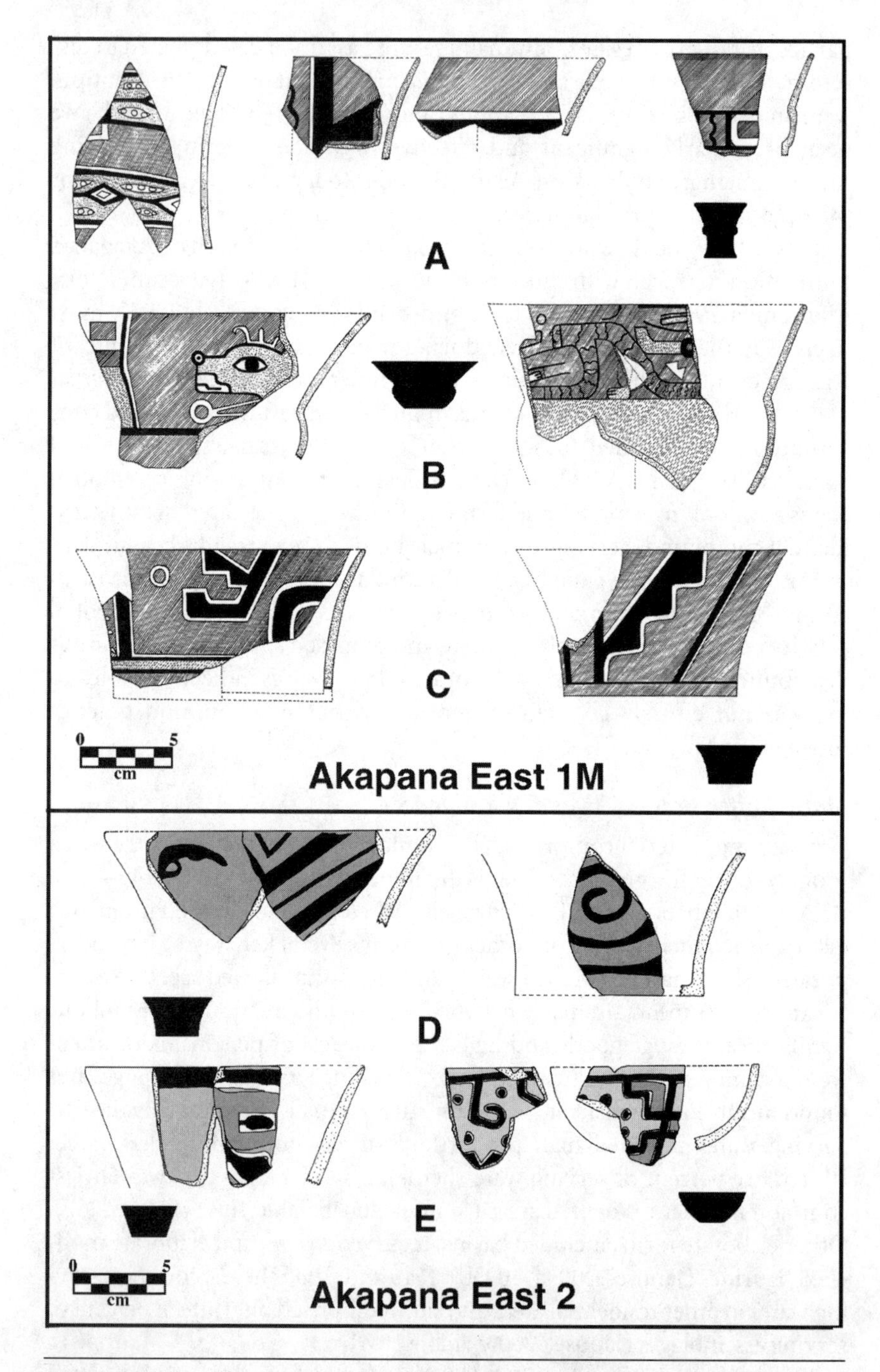

Figure 5.6 Serving ware fragments from Akapana East 1M (A-C), Akapana East 2 (D-E), sub-Putuni occupation (F), and Ch'iji Jawira (G-I), Tiwanaku. Shown are *keros* (A), *escudillas* (B),

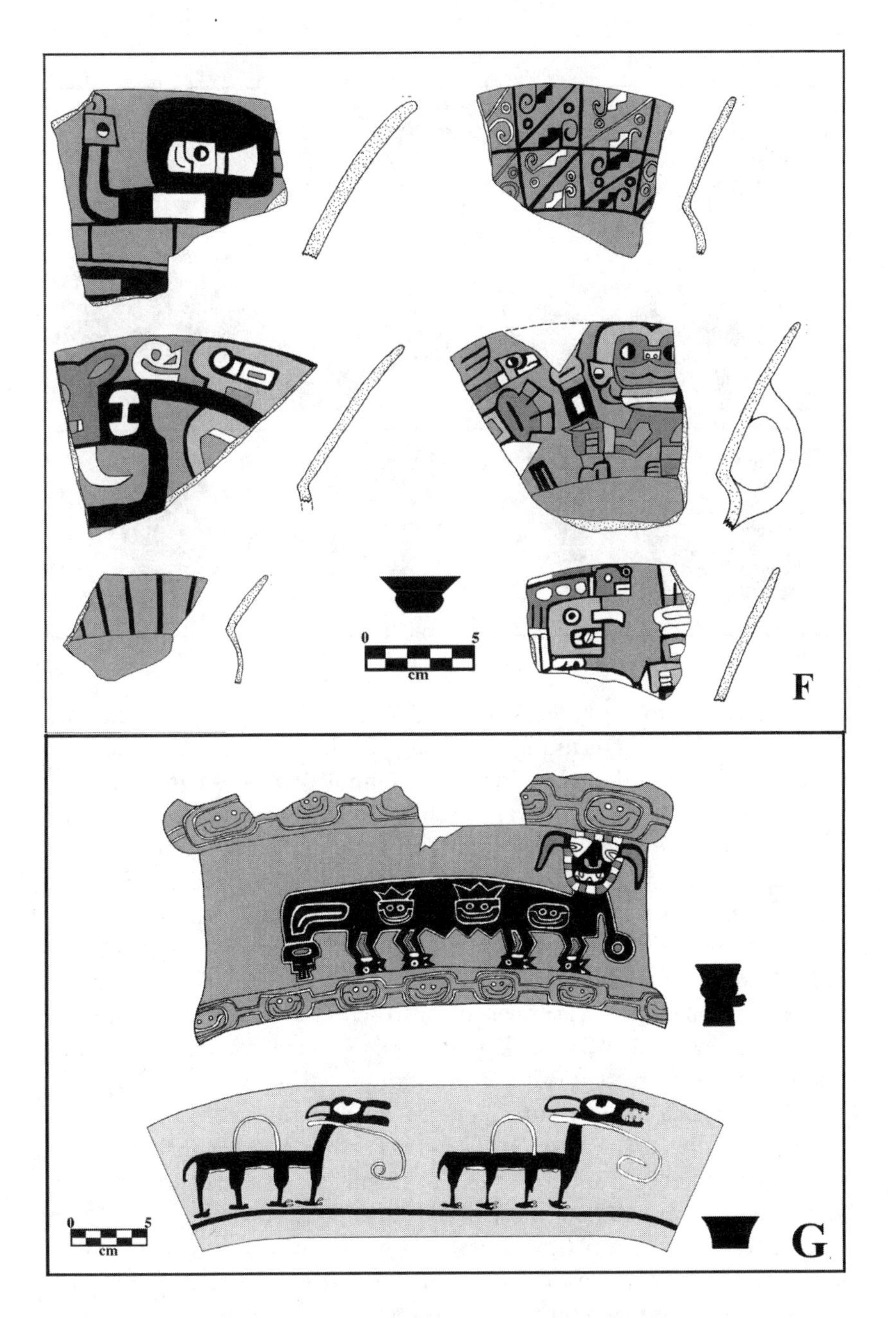

tazons (C-D), nonlocal bowls (E), *escudillas* (F), serving-ceremonial wares depicting camelids (G), and Cochabamba-style *keros/tazons* (H) compared with similar vessels recovered at Tupuraya, near Cochabamba (I) (G and H adapted from Alconini 1995 and Rivera 1994: Figures 12.1 and 12.2; adapted from Rydén 1959).

Figure 5.6 *(continued)*

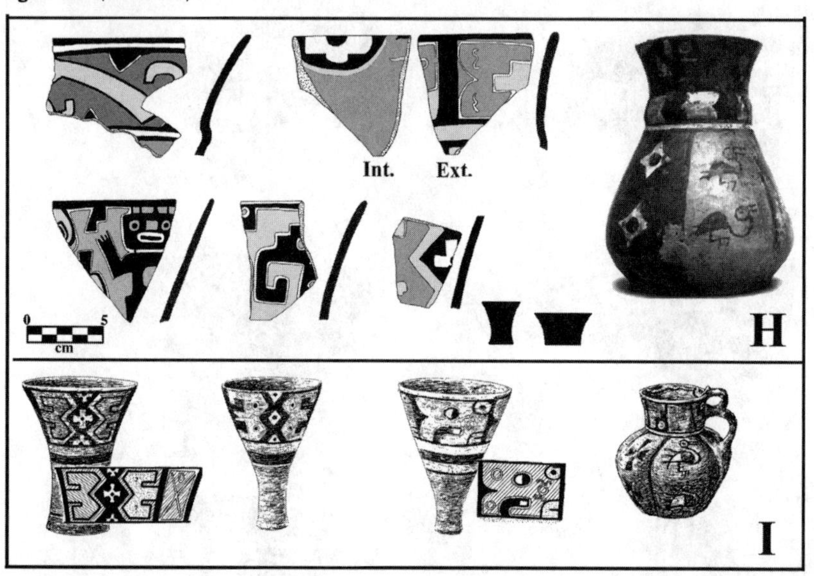

to formal sanitation systems. Waste and excess water were guided toward an open drainage ditch running down a street just outside of the residential compound. On the other hand, throughout Early and Late Tiwanaku IV all serving wares were in Tiwanaku style and most were finely formed and decorated. In striking contrast with the Putuni occupations, *tazons* and keros dominated assemblages here and elaborate *escudillas* were far less frequent (Figures 5.6A–C). Residential sectors beyond the moated core differed overall from those inside, increasingly so as one moved east across Tiwanaku's urban landscape. In Akapana East 2, as in Mollo Kontu South and La Karaña, domestic architecture was similar in construction and organization to that in Akapana East 1M. Waste and runoff drained into *ad hoc* canals leading toward outdoor streets. Most serving wares in Akapana East 2 displayed Tiwanaku-style elements, but 71 percent of them consisted of *keros* and *tazons*, while *escudillas* were uncommon. Further, in Akapana East 2 approximately twenty-five percent of the serving wares were more roughly formed and decorated than those in Akapana East I. Assemblages included a consistent proportion (seven percent) of nonlocal wares from valleys southeast of the altiplano (Figure 5.6E), which were absent in Akapana East 1M and in Akapana ceremonial contexts (Alconini 1995).

Material patterns in Ch'iji Jawira in Late Tiwanaku IV diverged most significantly from those inside of the urban core. Here, structures rested on pure adobe foundations, and domestic contexts were surrounded by dense refuse. More than eighty percent of serving wares were cruder in manufacture than those in Putuni or Akapana East I. *Keros* and *tazons* made up eighty-four percent of serving wares and *escudillas* were rare (Janusek 2003b:Table 10.4). Red slip, a hallmark of Tiwanaku ceramic style, was present on only a small portion (approximately twenty percent) of serving and ceremonial wares. Nonlocal vessels and vessels with nonlocal influence were common (Figure 5.6H) (Janusek 1999; Rivera 1994, 2003b).

Perhaps forming a material template for status differentiation in Tiwanaku was the material purity and elaboration characteristic of ceramic assemblages employed in significant ritual contexts. For example, the Akapana ceramic smash consisted almost purely of elaborately crafted serving-ceremonial wares, including ceremonial recurved *tazons*. Nonlocal wares and influences were absent, and iconography depicted repetitive icons of power such as felines, predatory birds, and stylized trophy heads. *Sahumadors* showed no evidence for burning, indicating they may have been crafted or acquired specifically for this ritual offering. Relative to wares from residential areas, these vessels were impeccably fired, polished, and decorated, and pastes were durable and forged from a limited range of clays (Alconini 1995). The ritual immolation of such crafted objects, together distinctive and pure in relation to objects employed by inhabitants of Tiwanaku's expanding urban periphery, involved conspicuous ritual consumption.

Differences in architecture, sanitation, and ceramic assemblages defined a concentric gradation of social status within the emerging city. High status residential groups concentrated around monumental complexes in the urban core (Kolata 1993a). If the moat was first built to demarcate the early settlement boundary, by Late Tiwanaku IV it came to demarcate the urban core with its dense concentration of ceremonial complexes from what was now a sprawling urban periphery. It simultaneously bounded groups with long histories and identities deeply rooted in Tiwanaku from newly established residential subdivisions. Newer inhabitants shared many elements of domestic activity and material style with those living near the center. However, they clearly formed the urban commons, a status expressed in the quality of crafted objects and in the types and proportions of elaborate goods they possessed and consumed.

Spatial Segmentation, Economic Specialization, and Social Diversity

Spatial and Architectural Segmentation

Alongside and in some respects interwoven with material expressions of conformity and status were notable material expressions of spatial segmentation, economic specialization, and material diversity. Such patterns implicate the diversified and segmentary foundations of Tiwanaku urban society. If architectural orientation reified a uniform spatial ideal, it also served as the principal means by which a group separated its daily living and work spaces from those of others. Bounded compounds or barrios formed the most salient units of social differentiation. Each compound consisted of a large perimeter wall enclosing one or more domestic structures and various activity areas. These bounded architectural units incorporated several minimal households, each represented by a dwelling and its associated activity zones. Though this pattern was repeated across the city, compounds differed greatly in size, internal spatial organization, residential density, and social activities, indicating that the nature of resident social groups also varied considerably.

Economic Specialization

A range of evidence for craft production in Tiwanaku indicates that it included both attached specialization, or production directed by and for elite consumption, and embedded specialization (Janusek 1999), production organized by coherent residential groups under the direction of local authorities. In a comprehensive analysis of lithic artifacts at Tiwanaku, Martin Giesso (2000, 2003) argues that many elaborate crafted objects consistently found at Tiwanaku, in particular small projectile points of chert and obsidian, were crafted by specific skilled groups as a state labor tax exacted from certain local urban populations. This was a form of attached specialization carried out by local groups under the aegis of state authorities and according to the central procurement and distribution of exotic or valued raw materials.

Some residential groups in Tiwanaku, however, practiced embedded craft production. Excavations in Ch'iji Jawira indicate that residents produced certain types of vessels, including large storage jars and serving *tazons* (Rivera 1994). A wide range of patterns, including the local character of most ceramic types produced and used here and the peripheral location of the barrio, indicates that production was not directly controlled by or conducted for ruling elites. Rather, it was conducted and managed in a local residential context, as the enterprise of a coresidential group. Although ceramic production in Ch'iji Jawira contributed to the overarching political economy, it was conducted and managed as the enterprise of a local group at the far edge of the city.

Significantly, no high-volume state storage structures have yet been found in Tiwanaku or anywhere else in the Tiwanaku heartland. Evidence for a nondomestic circular building in the east compound of La K'arana suggests that local storage characterized some residential sectors. Escalante (1997, 2003) identifies this as a formal state structure much like the *qollqas* used to store grains and valued goods earmarked for state distribution in the Inca imperial political economy (D'Altroy and Earle 1985; Levine 1992). In Inca centers, however, state *qollqas* were strategically located outside of local residential sectors and settlements, in places "not necessarily convenient for local populations" (Levine 1985:145; Morris 1982). The only known storage structure in Tiwanaku, however, if in the bounded urban core, was in a residential compound. The size and unique form of the structure suggest that it served the compound group rather than a minimal coresidential household, and quite possibly it indirectly served state interests in storing goods earmarked as taxes to central authorities. Overall, rather than state storage the structure represented a type of community storage directly associated with activities conducted by the resident social group (see Smyth 1989).

Ceramic Diversity

Spatial segmentation and local production and storage corresponded with significant distinctions among ceramic assemblages (see Janusek 1999, 2002, 2003b). Within compounds, ceramic assemblages maintained remarkable spatial and historical continuity. Between compounds, stylistic patterns varied significantly. For example, ceramic assemblages from Akapana East 1M and 2 revealed subtle but significant differences. All serving vessels from AKE 1M adhered to Tiwanaku canons of form and decoration similar to those in Akapana and Putuni assemblages (Figure 5.6A–C). Apparently, the inhabitants used only vessels with stylistic affinities to the Tiwanaku nuclear area. *Keros* and *tazons* displayed red, orange, reddish-brown, and less commonly black slip, and *escudillas* with elaborate mythical imagery were common on early patio surfaces. Designs on *keros* and *escudillas* became more stylized and abstract through time. Notable here, though, was the absence of *tazons* depicting continuous volutes.

Ceramic assemblages from AkE 2 differed in subtle ways (Figure 5.6D–E). Most contexts yielded Tiwanaku serving vessels (*keros, tazons, escudillas, vasijas*) decorated with mythical, anthropomorphic, or geometric figures, similar to those from Late Tiwanaku IV occupation surfaces in AkE 1M. Nevertheless, special serving wares like *escudillas* were much less common than they were in Putuni and Akapana East 1M. Nonlocal vessels, representing the eastern valley complexes of Omereque and Yampara (Janusek et al. 1995), composed five percent of serving wares and ten percent of combined *tazons, vasijas*, and *cuencos* (Janusek 2002). High frequencies of nonlocal *tinaja* sherds from these same valley regions also were significant relative to their frequencies in Putuni and Akapana East 1. Another distinctive stylistic pattern was the frequency of *tazons* decorated with continuous volute motifs (ten percent of *tazons*), a variant absent in Akapana East 1M but common in other areas of Tiwanaku. Other variants common here included *keros* with wide toruses or incised zoning and small carinated basins.

Ceramic assemblages in Ch'iji Jawira were by far most different from those in Putuni and Akapana East 1M in both technical and decorative style (Figure 5.6H). Although residents produced various types of vessels, most were clearly not crafted for groups residing in or near the monumental core. As mentioned above, *escudillas* were extremely rare, and red-slip decoration, the hallmark of Tiwanaku ceramic style, was present on less than twenty percent of serving and ceremonial wares. Llama motifs were common on *tazons* and ceremonial vessels from local offerings, and they even appear on slumped waster vessels (Figure 5.6G) (Rivera 1994:163, 2003; also Alconini 1995:198–199; Janusek 1999). These representations were extremely uncommon, far less than one percent of such vessels, in any other residential or ceremonial context. Nonlocal vessels and vessels with nonlocal influence were present at Ch'iji Jawira in even higher proportions than they were in Akapana East 2 (Rivera 2003). Most common were vessels in the Cochabamba-Tiwanaku style (Bennett 1936:402; Ponce 1981; Ryden 1959), a hybrid style typical of the temperate Cochabamba valleys, (Anderson 1996; Higueras-Hare 1996) approximately 200 kilometers southeast of Tiwanaku (Janusek 2002, 2003a). These included unique serving-ceremonial forms such as *challadors*, or *kero*-like vessels with narrow bases, large vasijas depicting birds, and small hand-molded bowls, or *cuencos*. Ch'iji Jawira's high percentages and great variety of forms in this hybrid style allude to close affiliations with groups in this region.

Thus, though all Tiwanaku residents obtained and used Tiwanaku-style vessels, each compound group simultaneously acquired and used a distinct array of serving and ceremonial wares. Key differences included the predominance of *escudillas* and a variety of other elaborate wares in Putuni, the prevalence of *tazons* with continuous volutes and nonlocal wares in Akapana East 2, and the popularity of camelid motifs and Cochabamba Tiwanaku vessels in Ch'iji Jawira. In addition, *sahumadors*, or ritual burners common in most Tiwanaku residential areas, were virtually absent in Ch'iji Jawira. In contrast, small figurines of humans and animals were exceptionally abundant in Ch'iji Jawira. Possibly, household rituals stressing abundance were performed to the near exclusion of an otherwise ubiquitous ritual complex involving *sahumadors*.

Archaeobotanical Diversity

Evidence for spatial segmentation, local production and storage, and ceramic diversity is supported by archaeobotanical analysis, which indicates that compound groups also maintained distinct diets. Wright et al. (2003) have determined that proportions of tubers, quinoa, and maize varied significantly among Tiwanaku sectors. Chenopodium, or quinoa seeds, were most frequent and best distributed throughout the site, followed by tubers and maize. The distribution of maize, however, was anomalous. Maize does not grow well in the altiplano and could be obtained in quantity only through long distance relations (Goldstein 1989; Kolata 1993b). By the fifteenth century, and undoubtedly earlier, maize was highly valued in the Andean altiplano (Murra 1980:8–14). We therefore expected greater quantities in high-status residential areas such as Putuni. In Tiwanaku, however, maize was most frequent in Akapana East 2 and best distributed among contexts in Ch'iji Jawira. These were compounds with consistent proportions of nonlocal wares associated with the more temperate eastern valleys where maize grows well. This suggests that social characteristics other than status fostered the acquisition of valued goods and the maintenance of long-distance ties. These characteristics, it appears, included social affiliations with groups in regions to which a compound group such as Ch'iji Jawira maintained kin-based or more widely cast ethnic-like social and economic relations.

Local Mortuary Practices

The presence of human burials and mortuary clusters inside residential compounds indicates that mortuary activity was not entirely relegated to discrete cemeteries. As in the Late Formative under the Kalasasaya, mortuary ritual in Tiwanaku IV was closely linked to daily residential life. To some extent, mortuary ritual was variable in practice. In Putuni, for example, scores of broken *escudillas* in burial chambers may represent a unique mortuary tradition common to this high status group. Overall, though, the desire to keep certain deceased individuals near living spaces shared by kindred implicates some shared type of ancestor veneration, in which, analogous to mortuary rituals practiced in the fifteenth century (Cobo 1956:163–165; Isbell 1997; Rowe 1946:286, 298; Zuidema 1978), groups periodically visited and made offerings to deceased individuals considered ancestral progenitors. The presence of burials under living spaces, fixed with a visible landmark in Akapana East 2, indicates that certain deceased, adults as well as children, were periodically remembered and bestowed offerings. The perceived relations among such deceased individuals and living families and compound groups remain unclear, but they appear to have played a significant role in the creation and periodic reanimation of group memory and identity. Evidence for local burials and mortuary rituals emphasizes the central place of shared memory for local groups and group identities in Tiwanaku.

Body Modification

In Tiwanaku and throughout much of the south-central Andes at this time, the human body itself was perhaps the most powerful and personal medium for inscribing and expressing social identity (Blom 1999; Blom et al. 1998; Hoshower et al. 1995; Janusek & Blom 2004; Torres-Rouf 2002). Deborah Blom's bioarchaeological analysis of human remains from various regions affiliated with Tiwanaku reveals different styles of cranial modification. Comparative analysis of human remains interred at Tiwanaku reveals two styles of cranial modification as well as unmodified normal skulls. Modified skulls consisted of a tapered or annular style and a flattened or tabular style. Distinct styles of head shape, like distinct styles of ceramic wares, involved distinct productive instruments and techniques. Annular style skulls were produced by tying tightly wound bands around a young child's skull, while the tabular skulls were formed by tying a contraption of flat boards to the front and back of a child's skull. Significantly, head shape styles crosscut differences in age, sex, and social status, and thus was associated with other forms of social identity. Different from other stylistic expressions, a particular head shape was a permanent marker of identity in that, imposed early on by parents or specialists, it could never be changed.

Various ethnohistorical references from the sixteenth century allude to the likelihood that a given head shape style corresponded with a particular style of headwear (Blom 1999; Janusek & Blom 2004). Although woven garments quickly deteriorate in the altiplano, woven hats from other regions and in museum collections vary in shape and style. Mary Frame's (1990) study of Tiwanaku-style hats includes both woven conical hats, or *chucos*, and short four-corner hats that were common in the coastal region of southern Peru, including the Moquegua Valley. Moquegua Valley burials dating to local phases of Tiwanaku hegemony exclusively demonstrate the tabular head style (Blom 1999), supporting the proposition that individuals with tabular head styles wore four-cornered hats and individuals with annular style heads wore conical *chucos*.

Bioarchaeology in Tiwanaku points to the fascinating conclusion that, alongside other expressions of identity, body shape expressed a form of identity with wide-ranging regional affiliations. While tapered, tabular, and normal rounded skulls were all represented in Tiwanaku, the tabular style, exclusively represented at Moquegua, predominated (at forty-eight percent of all observable skulls). The annular style, which predominated in the Katari Valley as discussed in Chapter 6, was found on just under a third (thirty-one percent) of the interred population. Each of the modified styles correlated with a distant regional population in which that style predominated, posing the possibility that unmodified skulls, comprising the smallest population at Tiwanaku, correlated with some other local or nonlocal group. Samples from any specific residential area are small and presently difficult to compare with any statistical significance, but in some cases individuals with skulls of different styles appeared in the same compound or neighborhood. Thus, distinct groups with social identities both inscribed on their bodies and woven into their clothing comingled and perhaps intermarried in Tiwanaku.

Conclusions

Tiwanaku had become the most important center in the Lake Titicaca Basin and among the most significant in the Andes. The new urban landscape was highly dynamic, comprising—among other things—a congeries of new ceremonial complexes that were long term, monumental projects in process. Built environments for a variety of ritual activities and religious cults increased substantially during Tiwanaku IV, attesting the significance and success of Tiwanaku's rising prestige and coalescing dominant ideology. The Sunken Temple remained a significant ritual center and axis mundi, but now coopted images and ideas from the past and reinterpreted them as Tiwanaku cultural patrimony, most likely under the authority of a new regime. The Kalasasaya was expanded, extended, and aggrandized and the massive Akapana and Pumapunku were initiated. Tiwanaku was an increasingly complex center with several immense, distinct ritual centers.

Although each monumental complex emphasized volume and grandeur, the innermost sanctum of each was a relatively small, intimate place. A number of features, including monumental stairs and massive stone gates, indicated that they were not always limited to high priests and esoteric rituals, but were visited and experienced by many. The ritual specialists directing ceremonies were divine interlocutors, but as in a Medieval Catholic Church, pilgrims and other nonelites entered these places, perhaps at specified times, to experience the specific brand of Tiwanaku religion it cultivated. Once inside, ritual experience was relatively intimate and personal, involving rituals witnessed firsthand in a sequence of increasingly smaller inner sancta (Kolata 1993a; Moore 1996). Intimate ritual environments, both fostered profound religious experience and naturalized Tiwanaku ritual power for pilgrims and priests alike, in part by mimicking the intimate domain characterizing domestic life. Religious experience and ritual participation were reasons for coming to Tiwanaku and in great part behind its prestige and residential growth.

The new urban landscape comprised vast residential sectors. Walled compounds represented the most salient units of social differentiation, as represented in multiple dimensions of local residential life. As the urban center expanded, many compound groups, in particular those settled outside of the core, maintained distinct socioeconomic networks, economic practices, shared memories, and identities. Most likely each compound group, composed of numerous households, represented a social group defined in an idiom of kinship who were related by common ancestry and perhaps ritually centered on individuals buried under living areas. It appears they were kin groups similar and perhaps ancestral to, though not identical with, the micro-*ayllus* so prevalent until recently in the Andes. Some of those groups, local expressions of identity suggest, were affiliated with broader groups and regions, and thus manifest ethnic-like forms of social identity. Some groups, like the inhabitants of Ch'iji Jawira and those with shared styles of body modification, may have had emigrated from far regions, maintaining interaction with their homelands for many generations (Janusek 1999, 2002). A predisposition for mobility would explain the prevalence of camelids in the iconography preferred by the ceramic specialists, and of nonlocal vessels and stylistic influences in many residential sectors of the urban periphery. As in the Andes more recently, local ritual practice, economic activity, and social identity were primary foundations of social power in Tiwanaku urban society. Ritual diversity and tenacious social identities, in particular as they related to broad ethnic and regional affiliations, index heterarchical dimensions of power in Tiwanaku. Tiwanaku was not a homogeneous melting pot, but perhaps, as critics of this American ideal noted of volatile U.S. industrial cities, more akin to a sizzling cauldron of social interests and tenacious, totemistic identities.

Nevertheless, urban growth simultaneously corresponded with increasing status differentiation and a concentration of power in the urban core. In part, status was defined by proximity to the various monumental complexes and ceremonial spaces as these became increasingly distant from the expanding urban boundary. At the edges of the settlement lived groups of lower status, in one case with strong local ties to a distant region. So, if social status was expressed as spatial order in a roughly concentric array, it was simultaneously defined by a complementary gradient of identity separating relatively pure groups or lineages, such as those inhabiting Putuni and Akapana East 1M, from groups with strong foreign ties. This status gradient was also tied to the history of settlement in the sense that those outside of the core were recently settled groups, essentially the new neighbors. Despite considerable heterarchy and local power, social, spatial, and temporal relations defined clear status differences in the city, ordered in a roughly concentric arrangement that concentrated power, though not exclusively, in the urban core.

Tiwanaku was ideologically and socially cosmopolitan, but it was also characterized by a dominant suite of practices, technologies, and material styles. It formed an emerging state culture that, to varying degrees, was employed by everyone, and its attendant ideologies were inculcated in practical consciousness as a naturalized cosmic and social order—an internalized practical hegemony. It is particularly significant that social identity was expressed in distinct configurations of serving-ceremonial wares, precisely those that both depicted Tiwanaku mythical icons and served as diacritical markers in social gatherings and feasts. On the one hand, feasts affirmed the emerging Tiwanaku order of things, as expressed in participation by guests and in the conspicuous display of a visually stunning and widely shared style. The influx of groups to Tiwanaku, and their participation in Tiwanaku's feasts as well as its political economy, enhanced the prestige and political legitimacy of the developing polity. On the other hand, many urban groups maintained vibrant identities and local means of production. Somewhat paradoxically, local identity and power were fortified by the acquisition and use of Tiwanaku style, and by participating in Tiwanaku's prestigious religious, economic, social and political spheres. In fact, local diversity was expressed in large part via Tiwanaku style and social practices. A simultaneous invigoration of central and local power was under way.

CHAPTER 6

Lukurmata: Urbanism and Community Identity

In AD 500 Lukurmata was already an important center in Tiwanaku's hegemonic sphere, and it remained throughout Tiwanaku IV the most important regional settlement in the emerging polity. Tiwanaku Period occupation was marked by the construction of a highly visible central monumental complex, apparent to the immediate eye as a scaled-down version of Tiwanaku public architecture (Rivera 1989). Research in surrounding areas has exposed ritual places, burial sites, and numerous residential areas, all overwhelmingly associated with Tiwanaku-style objects and activities. Lukurmata and its regional hinterland, evidence suggests, had a distinctive historical trajectory and maintained to a significant extent, throughout the course of and even after Tiwanaku hegemony, a separate regional identity. Grounded in a coherent historical consciousness and lucrative productive enterprises, the Katari Valley remained a semiautonomous region with considerable local social power. This chapter synthesizes abundant recent research at the site to explore the diverse activities that characterized Lukurmata throughout Tiwanaku IV. Focusing on residential areas and practices, I examine elements of life in Lukurmata that linked the settlement to Tiwanaku and its prestigious state culture, and those that distinguished it as a community with distinctive economic, social, and ideological foundations. I begin with a brief discussion of settlement patterns in the Katari Valley, which serves to locate Lukurmata in a regional framework of demographic growth, emerging settlement hierarchy, and intensifying productive enterprises. Next, I synthesize evidence for monumental construction and associated rituals in the central monumental complex known as Wila Kollu. Following, I present evidence for residential patterns and domestic shifts in the course of Tiwanaku IV, and then synthesize this data by comparing residential spatial organization and ceramic assemblages with a broad range of other patterns and activities. Interwoven patterns of continuity and change in Lukurmata have profound implications for understanding state development and collapse in Tiwanaku and the Andes at large.

Lukurmata and the Katari Valley

By the end of Tiwanaku IV Lukurmata had expanded from a community of about twenty hectares into a major ceremonial urban center of 120 hectares. Several nearby settlements were directly linked to the center, together forming a greater metropolitan community approaching two square kilometers. Following population estimates proposed for Tiwanaku, the core settlement alone could have housed a population of 2,500 people, and the greater urban community may have housed as many as 4,000. Although the ceremonial complex of Wila Kollu formed Lukurmata's civic-ceremonial core, a platform known as Wila Waranka in a gulley just to the west, covered with sherds of elaborate ceremonial vessels such as feline-effigy *incensarios*, also dated to Tiwanaku IV (Figure 6.1). Along with the K'atupata ceremonial platform, which continued in use in Early Tiwanaku IV, Wila Waranka indicates that communal ritual activity in

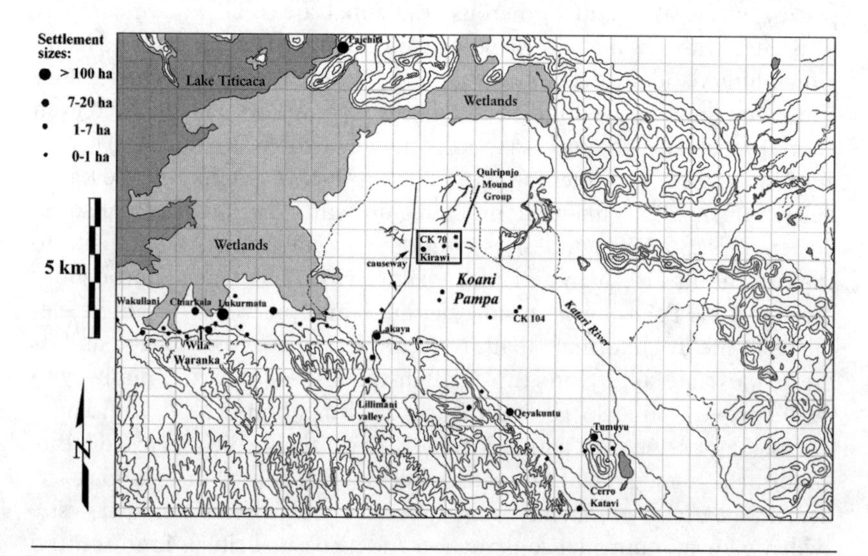

Figure 6.1 Settlement distribution in the Katari Valley during the Tiwanaku Period.

Lukurmata was distributed among several places in the larger metropolitan landscape, as it was in Tiwanaku.

Settlement survey in the southern Katari Valley revealed fifty-one sites with definitive evidence for Tiwanaku occupation, an increase of more than one hundred percent from the Late Formative Period (Figure 6.1). Settlements diverged greatly in size, collectively forming a multitiered settlement hierarchy. Settled along the lower piedmont zone were numerous small towns and villages, the larger of which were tertiary centers with monumental platforms. In Early Tiwanaku IV, Qeyakuntu became a major tertiary center with large artificial platforms facing the pampa (Janusek and Kolata 2003). Even more important was Lakaya, a major center with an extensive platform and the end point for a major "trans-pampa" causeway (Kolata 1986). Lakaya was strategically located at the mouth of the Lillimani valley, a drainage system that originated near Tiwanaku and apparently served as a transportation route between the valleys. Thirty-six smaller sites were distributed across the valley, all but eleven of them located in the lower piedmont zones surrounding the valley floodplain.

As in the Tiwanaku Valley, Tiwanaku vessels were by far more widely distributed than had been decorated Qeya wares among Katari Valley settlements. Differences in the relative proportions of elaborate serving and ceremonial wares implicate different roles among settlements and somewhat lower statuses for inhabitants of some smaller sites. At the important tertiary center of Qeyakuntu, roughly eleven percent of ceramic assemblages consisted of serving and ceremonial vessels (Janusek and Kolata 2003). In addition, some twenty percent of assemblages consisted of a unique Lukurmata-style, which included high frequencies of *incensarios* and tanwares, ceremonial and serving wares that were uncommon or absent at Tiwanaku and Tiwanaku Valley sites (see below). At CK-104, a small Tiwanaku mound in the Koani pampa, some eighteen percent of sherd assemblage represented Tiwanaku serving and ceremonial wares, fourteen percent of which were Lukurmata-style variants. Thus, while Tiwanaku-style wares were relatively well-distributed among sites of different sizes and scales, so also were wares in a distinct expression of Tiwanaku style.

During the Tiwanaku Period the lower piedmont remained the preferred areas of settlement. In total, seventy-three percent of Tiwanaku sites, and ninety-six percent of total settlement area, occupied the zone (Janusek and Kolata 2003). Such a settlement distribution differs markedly from that of the Tiwanaku Valley, where settlement was better distributed across ecological microzones. Clear settlement preference for the hill slopes reflects the distinct natural and anthropogenic conditions of the Tiwanaku and Katari valleys. Unlike vast portions of the Tiwanaku Valley, the Katari pampa is low, extensive, and prone to seasonal flooding, and in general maintains a high water table fed by percolating groundwater and intermittent streams. These conditions were optimal for raised field farming. Much of the visible surface of the pampa is covered with relict raised fields, and these are associated with sophisticated hydraulic structures designed both to divert runoff to major raised field sectors and to prevent flooding. Extensive excavations in the fields revealed that many field segments have been buried over centuries of sediment aggradation (Janusek and Kolata 2003; Kolata and Ortloff 1996; Seddon 1994). Of fourteen radiocarbon dates for raised field construction and use, only two date to the Tiwanaku IV period. Thus, it appears that in Tiwanaku IV, raised fields were cultivated on a relatively small scale in Katari, supplemented by less intensive farming practices on the floodplain and adjacent hill slopes.

Substantial regional evidence suggests that Tiwanaku authority over settlement and production in the Katari Valley was incorporative. That is, pre-existing social networks remained intact and control over production remained in the hands of local communities. Raised field production in the pampa correlated with a well-defined scalar hierarchy in which settlements of various sizes were distributed across the lower piedmont zone. Further, major towns such as Lakaya and Qeyakuntu were endpoints for one or more long causeways, features that facilitated transportation and production and linked each site with a specific section of the pampa. It is likely that the tasks of building and maintaining raised fields were distributed among the towns and villages settled in the piedmont zone. Each settlement planted, harvested, and directly controlled specific field segments located in nearby sections of the pampa, drawing upon the labor of constituent kin-based groups.

That state management was incorporative and the scale of raised field production relatively modest is manifested in other aspects of the regional settlement system. Because it was the most important local center by Late Formative 2, Lukurmata was a politically strategic and expedient place for a primary Tiwanaku regional center. However, at the far southwest edge of the valley it was not optimally located to control production across the pampa but rather to oversee a regional economy that balanced lake resources and local agriculture. The strategic position of Lakaya at the terminus of both a transpampa causeway and a route to Tiwanaku indicates that it played a more central role in managing production in the Koani Pampa. Overall, settlement patterns between AD 600 and 900 point to a regional political economy combining the lake, as a source of resources and as a means of effective transportation across the basin, and local farming, including segments of raised fields managed by authorities at local towns and villages.

Monumentality and Ritual

The Moat

A major strength of the moat hypothesis is that similar features are found at major settlements incorporated into Tiwanaku's sphere of control and influence. Kolata (1993a; Kolata and Ponce 1992) points out that a moat physically similar to that at Tiwanaku surrounded the monumental cores of several other sites, most notably Khonkho Wankane and Lukurmata. At these sites as at Tiwanaku, the channels were natural features augmented by human activity. At Lukurmata, a swampy channel forms an arc around the Wila Kollu ridge that connects with the inundated floodplain to the north (Figure 3.3b). Raised fields line the edges of the channel. Perhaps even more feasibly than at Tiwanaku, the channel, by essentially bringing the lake into Lukurmata, may have facilitated travel into the site via balsa rafts and boats, serving trade as well as monumental construction on the platform it surrounds. Like the smaller moat around the Mollo Kontu platform in Tiwanaku, a small moat surrounds a similar platform at the site of Chojasivi, a few kilometers east of Lukurmata. Thus, whatever one argues regarding the specific function and meaning of the channels, they clearly were a repeating pattern in Tiwanaku sites. This suggests that, as Kolata argues, they formed an important element of Tiwanaku's emerging cosmology. They isolated significant ceremonial constructions, including iconic mountains, as physically bounded, ontologically distinct sacred islands.

Wila Kollu

Monumental construction at Lukurmata intensified in Early Tiwanaku IV. The K'atupata platform thrived until perhaps AD 600, while in the moat-bounded core, the entire upper portion of Wila Kollu was modified to form a massive pyramidal platform with several superimposed terraces (Figure 6.2); (Bennett 1936). The terraces consisted of alternating sloped and tabular faces, and some were faced with cobble walls built over multiple construction events. In years of high water the platform towered over a peninsula jutting into the lake.

Although monumental construction on Wila Kollu manifests many characteristic elements of Tiwanaku monumental construction and form, it differs markedly in details. Capping the hill were two contiguous platforms faced with fieldstone revetments, both of which rested on a substratum of clean yellow clay (Bennett 1936:482, 489) and followed an orientation of eight degrees askew of north.[1] Facing the higher west platform was a revetment of andesite blocks with three stairways leading up and onto the

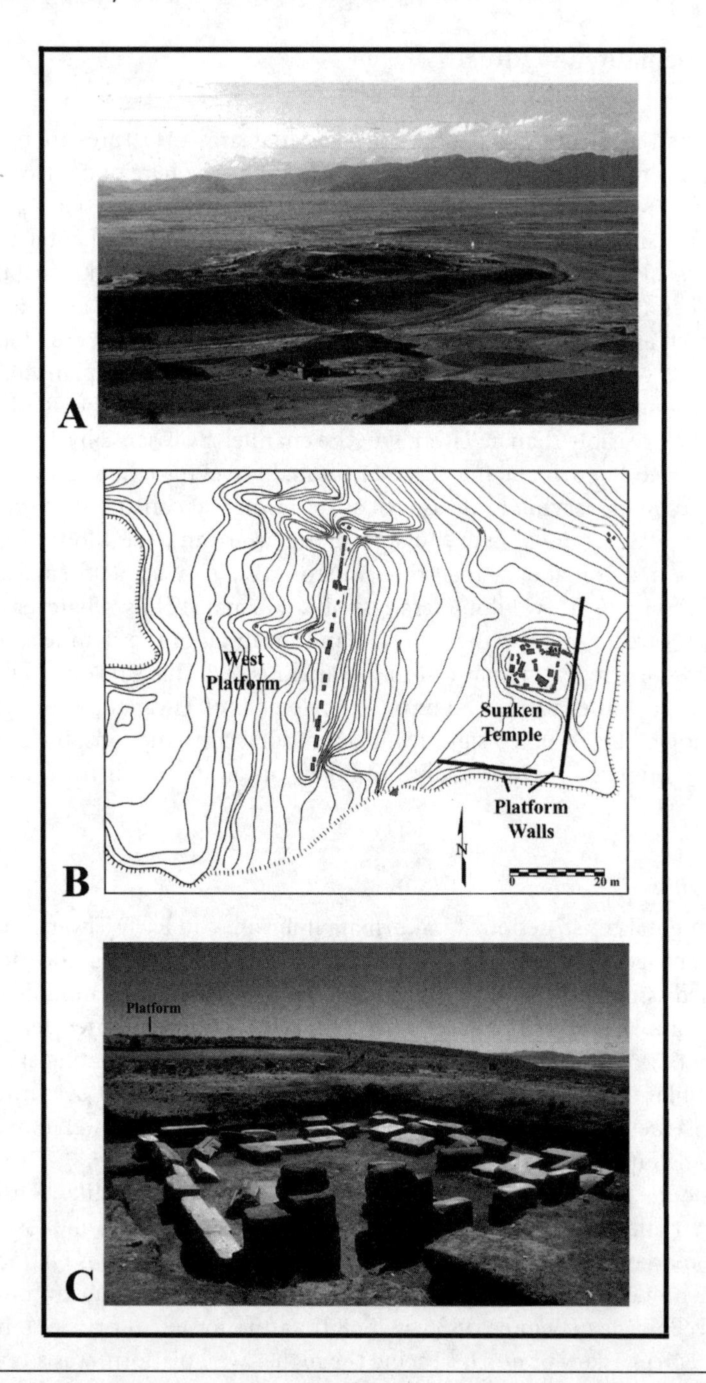

Figure 6.2 The Wila Kollu Complex in Lukurmata, including a view of the modified natural platform from the south (A), a contour map of the west platform and sunken temple (B), and a view of the sunken temple, facing northwest (C).

platform behind it (Bennett 1936:481–485). Much as in the Kalasasaya, two parallel retaining walls and a stone pavement further west rose above the andesite wall, defining smaller, higher areas within the larger terrace structure (ibid.).

Built into the lower platform to the east was a small sunken temple that was less than half the extent of the Tiwanaku temple. Like the Tiwanaku temple it incorporated an elaborate drainage canal. However, the Lukurmata temple was square rather than trapezoidal and it rested on a foundation of large, finely cut andesite ashlars (Bennett 1936:481). Rather than a large south entrance, entry into the court was via a narrow portal of elaborately carved blocks nestled into the temple's southeast corner. In architectural and spatial details, this small ritual enclosure differed significantly from the older Tiwanaku temple.

Emphasizing the distinctive character of Wila Kollu were associated ritual offerings with Lukurmata-style ceremonial vessels. In both platforms, outside of the sunken temple (Rivera 1989:69) and near the west platform wall (Bennett 1936:484), ceramic vessels were buried in small cists. In each case, the pit included an intact or broken feline effigy *incensario* containing burnt remains. Outside of the sunken temple, each offering included smaller *vasijas*, and near the platform wall, one included a blackware *kero*. Three similar subterranean offerings with intact feline *incensarios* were buried beneath a compact surface about 200 meters southwest of the higher platform, on a walled terrace on the north edge of the ridge (Bermann 1994:195–199). Nearby, on the terrace surface and in similar subterranean pits were fragments of *incensarios* and yet another local ceremonial vessel type; a flat-bottomed *escudilla* depicting feline/condor imagery. Also present were pits containing buried fetal camelids. Offering pits with *escudillas* and feline effigy *incensarios* have not been reported elsewhere, suggesting that they formed elements of ritual practice unique to Lukurmata's monumental core.

In some respects, Wila Kollu manifested Tiwanaku ideals of monumental architecture and sacred space on a relatively small scale. Other patterns, including architectural details and associated ritual patterns, distinguished the complex. Some details, such as the use of andesite blocks for the sunken temple, can be attributed to its relatively late date. Yet the configuration of ceremonial space and associated offering contexts allude to more profound differences in ritual practices. Unlike the entrances and gateways in Tiwanaku, the portal in the sunken temple at Lukurmata was small, providing entry for a limited group of people at a time. Unlike Akapana terrace offerings, offerings in and around Wila Kollu were relatively private and small-scale affairs. Thus, the significance of monumental architecture and associated rituals differed at Tiwanaku and Lukurmata. Activities associated with Wila Kollu were far more intimate and possibly more exclusive than comparable activities conducted in monumental complexes at Tiwanaku during this time.

Residential Diversity, Local Production, and Mortuary Practice

Ridgetop Occupations

Lukurmata expanded precipitously in Early Tiwanaku IV and its expansion included new residential sectors, craft areas, and mortuary clusters. Two superimposed occupations in the saddle below Wila Kollu dated to Tiwanaku IV, the first to the early and the second to late phase (Figure 6.3). A massive compound/terrace wall foundation bounded the north edge of the ridge. The early occupation consisted of four prepared living surfaces associated with refuse pits, a hearth, and outdoor patios (Bermann 1994:Figure 11.14). The late occupation consisted of seven clay-floor structures that formed two groups, each clustered around a common patio. Most of the structures contained large postholes, one or two hearths, and subterranean storage pits. Two of the buildings, one in each of the patio groups, contained high quantities of broken basins (Bermann 1994:184), suggesting the possibility that they had some specific role related to local storage or consumption. Each of the outdoor patios contained a hearth and included evidence for a variety of activities, including food preparation and the production of lithic and camelid mandible tools.

Mortuary rites were important elements of residential life in Lukurmata as they were in Tiwanaku, yet burial patterns varied between the settlements. On the ridge, ten human burials—eight cist tombs and two double-chamber tombs—were associated with the Late IV occupation (Bermann 1994:199–203). Double-chamber tombs, to date not found anywhere else, consisted of two stone-lined cists set one on top of the other (Figure 6.3b). The upper cist of each, which rose over the occupation surface around it, contained adult human remains while the bottom cist contained an intact feline-effigy *incensario*. Cist tombs on the ridge differed from those at Tiwanaku. First, the adult human in each was interred resting on his or her side. Second, some were lined and covered with stone slabs, which included exhausted *batanes*.

K'atupata: Mortuary Ritual and Residential Middens

Early in Tiwanaku IV the K'atupata pavement was covered and the area from now on was dedicated to mortuary and residential activity (Janusek and Earnest 1990a). Excavations exposed fourteen human burials grouped into three discreet clusters, two of which included both adult and child interments. Many burials incorporated elaborate offerings, suggesting that they represented high status interments. Like burials elsewhere in Lukurmata these exhibited patterns not found in Tiwanaku.

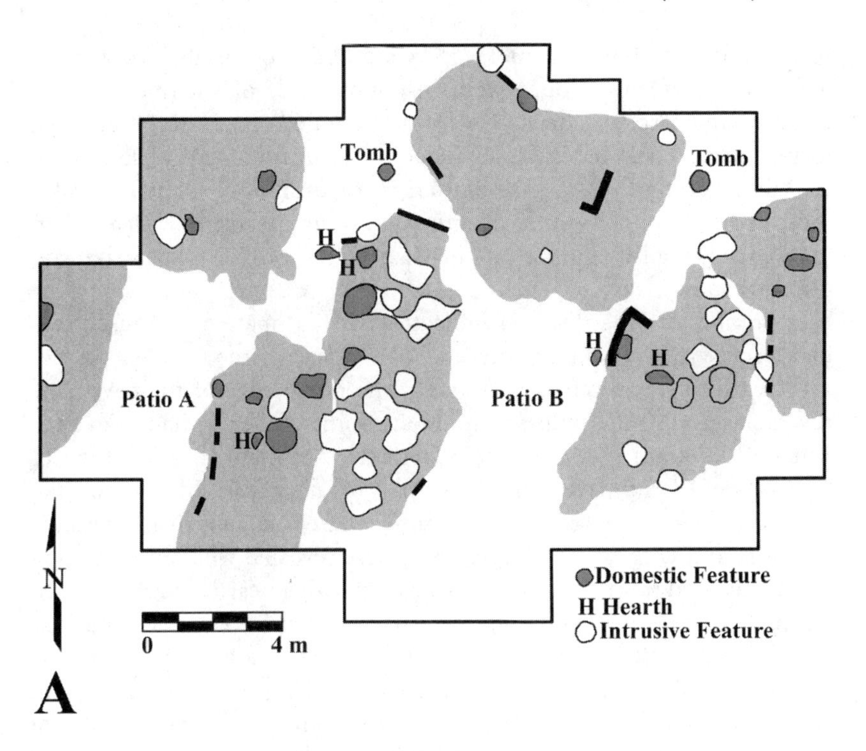

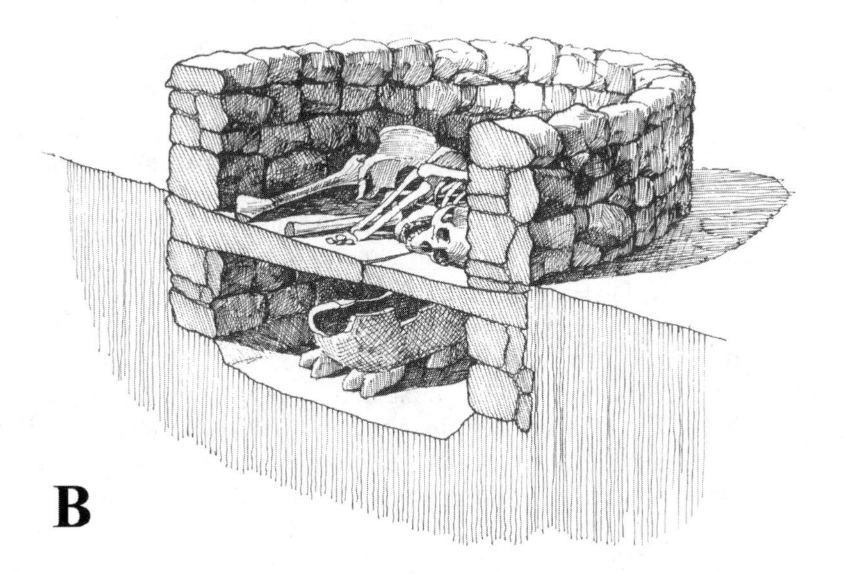

Figure 6.3 Plan of excavated Late Tiwanaku residential structures and features on the ridgetop at Lukurmata (A), with an idealized reconstruction of an associated double-chamber tomb (B) (adapted from Bermann 1994).

First, similar to offering contexts in Wila Kollu two burials incorporated feline *incensarios* with burnt remains, and sherds of such vessels were common in nearby middens. Burials also included other Lukurmata-style forms. Second, seven burials included small unfired clay vessels, many containing carbonized organic matter. Third, unlike burials at Tiwanaku, most here were either double chamber tombs or cist tombs with an offering bench. Finally, capping roughly half of the burials, were exhausted grinding stones.

A number of other features indicates that K'atupata now housed residential activity. Relevant features included one clay-lined storage pit, two cylindrical pits, two refuse pits, and at the north edge of the pavement, several large ash/refuse pits and middens. Some of the pits had been excavated into the north edge of the pavement, presumably to mine the rich dark clay of the subpavement platform. A primary residential sector may have occupied the area to the south, where the platform levels off (Janusek and Earnest 1990a). A profile here revealed what appears to be an ash-covered trampled surface associated with a hearth or ash lens. The chronology of mortuary and residential features remains somewhat unclear, but while the storage pit had intruded into an earlier tomb, at least one tomb had intruded into the trampled surface. Thus, it appears that both residential and mortuary activities continued side by side on the platform, and the burial clusters may represent families or other kin groups.

Ch'iarkala

Residential areas extended far outside of the urban core. A single unit in Ch'iarkala, some 700 meters west of Wila Kollu, revealed part of an elaborate Tiwanaku IV residential context (Figure 6.1). The context included a multiroom structure and hearth on a prepared floor consisting of red clay covered with plaster. Associated with these features were ceramic assemblages with high frequencies of Lukurmata serving-ceremonial wares, in particular large carinated basins (Janusek 2003a). Reconnaissance in nearby modern wells and adobe pits in the area revealed abundant structural remains, some with ashlar foundations. Together, archaeological patterns indicate that Ch'iarkala formed an important local neighborhood or "suburb" of greater Lukurmata, and may have maintained some special occupation or status in the expanding urban community.

Residence and Specialized Production in Misiton 1

Substantial research in the south sector of Lukurmata revealed fascinating evidence of residential groups practicing craft production. This part of Lukurmata's urban landscape consisted of broad terraces scaling the shallow slope of Cerro Kallinka, part of the Lakaya range that separates Katari from the Tiwanaku valley. Some 600 meters south and slightly west of Wila Kollu was Misiton (Figure 3.3B), a sector of residential activity near the upper end of an artificially canalized gulley or *quebrada* that guided rainwater down toward the swampy moat and its associated raised fields (Ortloff and Kolata 1989). A contemporary route from Tiwanaku leads the traveler to this *quebrada*, past Misiton, and down a footpath toward the lower portion of Lukurmata. Excavations nearby revealed sections of two compounds, termed Misiton 1 and Misiton 2, which occupy the same shallow terrace. Misiton 1, I have argued (Janusek 1993, 1994, 1999), housed groups who specialized in producing musical instruments.

A deep excavation unit in Misiton 1 revealed Early Tiwanaku IV occupation directly over precultural yellow sand and cobbles. Associated with a floor of dark red clay was the corner of a cobble foundation associated with a deep ash-filled hearth. Covering the floor was a thin lens of ashy midden. Alongside artifacts representing common domestic and ritual activities, which included a small snuff tube, were several larger cut and polished camelid bone tubes, numerous basalt pebbles with wear facets, and a burnished camelid rib tool; evidence, collectively, for specialized activity.

Four superimposed surfaces covered the first occupation, and the next two also yielded artifacts and features representing both common domestic activities and evidence for specialized production. The fourth occupation demonstrated increasing spatial complexity and yielded high quantities of elaborately decorated serving-ceremonial wares (Janusek 1994:196), patterns that continued in the last two occupations.

Extensive excavations in the final occupations revealed a residential complex comprising structures and activity areas and that exhibited increasing spatial segregation through time (Figure 6.4). The complex was oriented about twelve degrees east of the cardinal directions, slightly steeper than the orientation of other architectural complexes in Lukurmata. It consisted of a thin trampled surface of compact sandy clay on an aggregate base, with cobble and yellow clay foundations supporting adobe structures. Large outer wall foundations, in some areas three to four courses high, defined the north and west sides of a compound.

The penultimate occupation consisted of two patios and three structures (Figure 6.4A). The wall dividing patios 1 and 2 had been recently built, indicating that the division was relatively late. The dwelling included a hearth surrounded by ashy lenses and domestic artifacts. The two patios, and in particular patio 1, supported a wide variety of activities, including food preparation, consumption, weaving, the preparation and use of lithic tools, and again, specialized production. Frequencies of elaborate serving-ceremonial wares were higher than ever before (Janusek 1999).

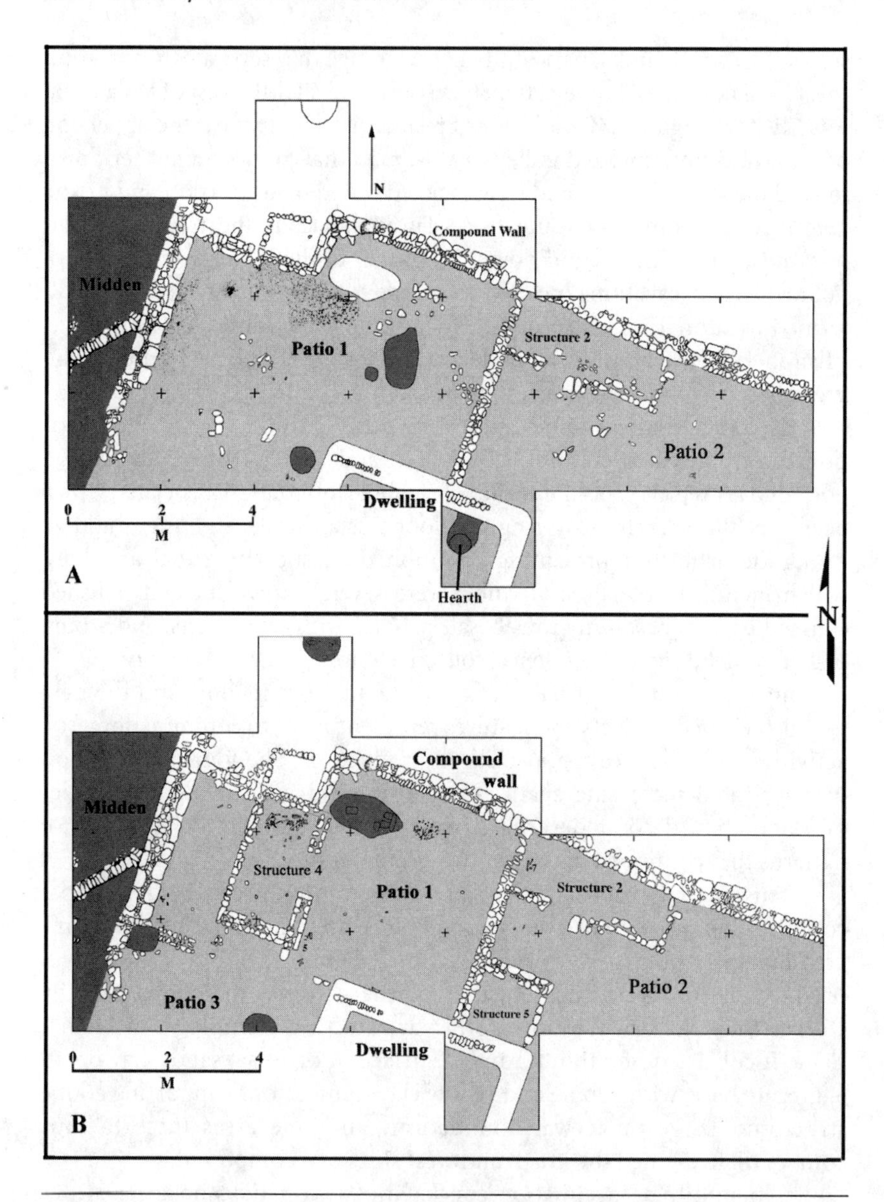

Figure 6.4. Plans of the two final superimposed occupations in Misiton 1, illustrating key structures and features.

The final occupation consisted of new surfaces and increasingly divided internal spaces (Figure 6.4B). Ceramic assemblages dated to Late Tiwanaku IV and Early Tiwanaku V. The construction of wall segments and a new rectangular structure (structure 4) divided patio 1 into four distinct spaces, creating a new patio (patio 3) with an outdoor hearth to the south.

Abutting the dwelling in patio 2 was a small bin (structure 5) that served either storage or, judging by several guinea pig bones, a small *cuy* pen. Among refuse associated with domestic activities in the patios were a small bone snuff spoon, fragments of pyroengraved bone tubes, and as before, elaborately decorated serving wares. Also distributed across the compound were abundant severed long bone tubes and ends, camelid rib scrapers, pebble and ceramic burnishers, and retouched quartzite flakes. More notable were several caches of cut camelid bone tubes, including a cache of seven in patio 1, another cache of seven in structure 2, and a cache of twenty-five in structure 4, in each case associated with by-products and artifacts related to specialized production (Figure 6.5). Between structure 4 and the west compound wall, a camelid pelvis crafted into a cutting platform lay next to a severed bone tube (Figure 6.5D).

Internal living and activity space in the Misiton 1 compound was increasingly segmented, and most notably so in the addition of a wall that divided one open patio into two separate patio groups. Possibly, the new wall represented the fissioning of an early group into two separate household groups. Each patio group incorporated a rectangular structure (structures and 2 and 4) that most likely served as a storage building and for the periodic production of bone tubes.

Excavations several meters to the west revealed the northeast corner of a contemporaneous structure that had been built over an extensive ash and midden deposit. The interior surface, outdoor refuse pits, and even the midden under the structure contained artifacts associated with both common domestic activities and, once again, the production of bone tubes. Between the two walled structures was an extensive stratified outdoor midden with more abundant artifactual residues of such activities, and under which ran an ad hoc cobble drainage canal caulked with greenish-gray clay (Figure 6.4). Thus, in Late Tiwanaku IV craft production was an important enterprise in Misiton 1, and not just for an isolated household but for a small neighborhood of households in Lukurmata's expanding periphery.

Panpipe Specialists in Misiton 1

The coresidential groups in Misiton engaged in the production of Andean panpipes (Janusek 1993, 1994, 1999), as revealed in a conjunction of consistent patterns. First, each of the bone tube clusters included flutes of various lengths. A cache in structure 4 alone ranged from 7.75 to 19.5 centimeters in length, and like others caches it was associated with severed long bone ends and segments (Figure 6.5). Each group of tubes was characterized by a graded variation of length that corresponded to tone variation, in each case emphasizing the notes of E, A, B, and C-sharp (see Janusek 1993:Table 1). When the tube ends were polished, as they

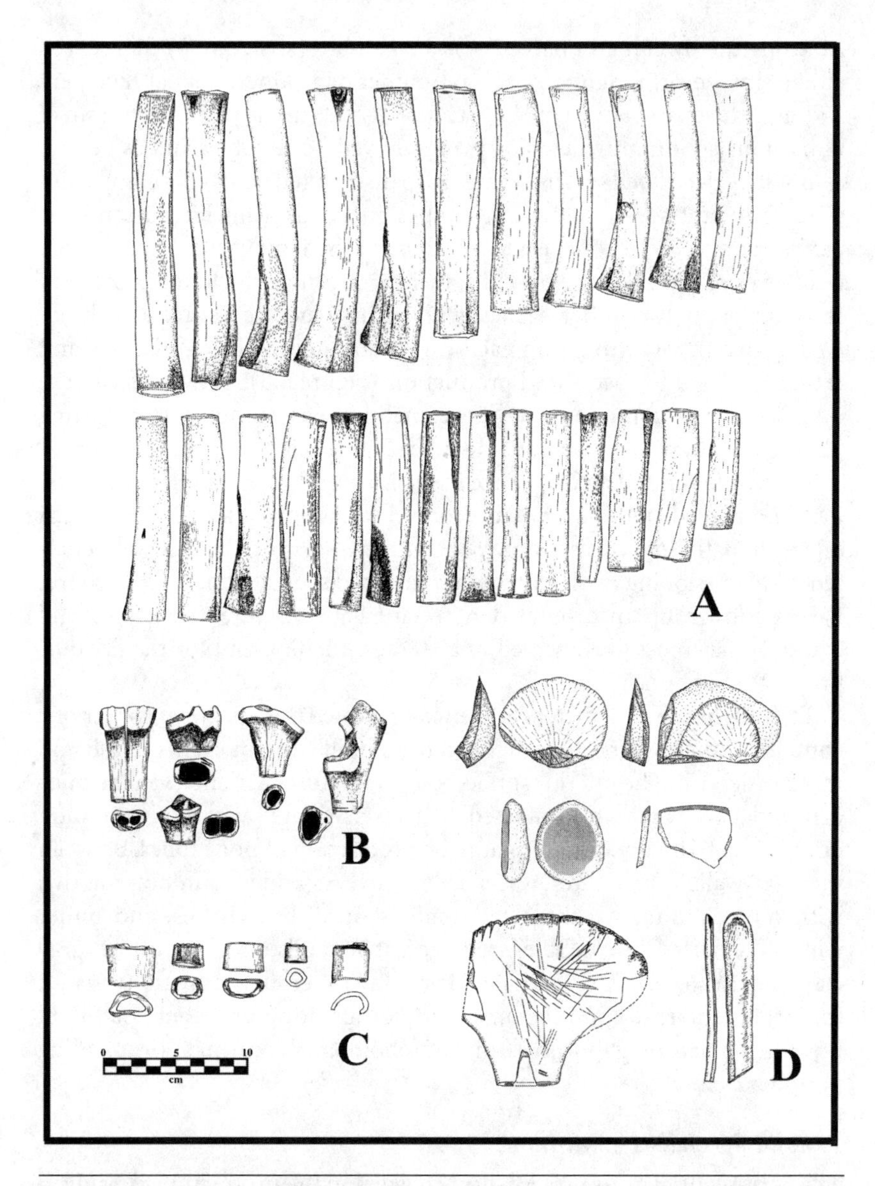

Figure 6.5 Cache of bone panpipe flutes (A) from the final occupation in Misiton 1, shown with production by-products (long bone ends, B, and tuning fragments, C), and various lithic, bone, and ceramic tools (D) used for crafting the instruments.

were in many cases, the polished end was always the smaller opening. The smaller end always produced the best tone and was easiest to play. In other types of bone tubes, such as pyroengraved snuff tubes (see Chapter 7), the larger end was polished. Further, as opposed to snuff tubes, the tubes from Misiton 1 were all within the playable size range of known contemporary and prehispanic panpipes, and all intact tubes produced a clear musical tone.

The tubes, along with their severed ends and segments, often displayed straight, deep cut marks near their ends that were oriented perpendicular to the lengths of the bones. These highly patterned marks differed from the hatched butchering marks commonly found on faunal remains (Webster 1993:226–336). These marks were made in the effort to achieve a particular length and tone via trial and error, indicating that the creation of a particular tube length was not a simple process. Similar notches are cut on cane and wood tubes by instrument specialists in the contemporary Aymara community of Walata, located in the Omasuyos highlands on the east side of Lake Titicaca (Gutierrez 1991:150). The notches, based on set measurements, mark where orifices will be placed in a *quena* or *pinkillu* flute, or where lengths of cane will be cut to form panpipes.

Production by-products constituted a substantial proportion of the artifacts found in and around the compounds. Severed long bone ends from all classes of camelid limb bones were most common, followed by broken sections of the flutes themselves. A particularly significant type of by-product consisted of short segments of bone severed at both ends (Figure 6.5C). The ubiquity of these artifacts inside of the compound and in nearby middens illustrates how important it was to achieve specific tube lengths. Like the patterned cut marks on tubes themselves, these short tuning lengths, absent in other residential areas, are difficult to explain if the craftspeople were making snuff tubes, containers, handles, or any other type of tube in which exact lengths are not required. They are most parsimoniously explained as the material consequence of creating, through trial and error, specific desired tones.

Various tools consistently accompanied the flute clusters (Figure 6.5D). Worn camelid ribs, uncommon in other residential contexts, probably served to clean the interiors of the tubes. Quickly retouched cobble flakes, generally of quartzite or chert, served as knives to perform the actual cutting, and pebbles and ceramic sherds were employed as implements to burnish the mouthpieces of the instruments. The proportion of chipped stone cutting and polishing tools relative to other stone artifacts in Misiton 1 was highly significant relative to the same proportion in Akapana East (see Janusek 1999). Further, the proportion of total worked bone related to flute production, relative to other types of worked bone, was highly significant when compared to the worked bone found at Tiwanaku.

Andean panpipes, or *sikus*, are known from prehispanic contexts throughout the south-central Andes, but they are generally made of ceramic, stone, or cane (e.g., Bolaños 1988; Grebe 1974:41; Haeberli 1979; Iribarren 1969). Cane panpipes are especially common in roughly contemporaneous burials in the dry regions of northern Chile and in northwestern Argentina, and their distribution correlates with that of the ritually charged hallucinogenic complex (e.g., Grebe 1974:43–44; Nuñez 1963:155–156). Yet bone flutes with orifices, including *quenas*, *pinkillus*, and *silbatos*, were common in Tiwanaku residential contexts dating to the Tiwanaku IV and V Periods (Janusek 1993). One from the Mollo Kontu sector displayed horizontal cut marks at each of its four orifices as did the panpipes from Misiton 1, but in this case marking the place where a flute was to be perforated rather than severed. Another from a late context in Akapana East was crafted out of a human ulna. Documented across the Andes in the sixteenth century, the use of human skin and bones to craft flutes and drums for ceremonies was a macabre expression of group power. The use of camelid bone to craft *sikus* and other musical instruments reflects the abundance and significance of this material resource in the altiplano. Further, it ties the ritual significance of llamas and alpacas to music and Tiwanaku ceremony.

The flutes in the Misiton 1 compound were left in the midst of production, for we recovered no completed sikus. The Misiton instruments were not stopped (see Olsen 2002), which would have restricted the sound chamber of the flute produce a tone. Yet preserved cane panpipes from Tiwanaku-related contexts in northern Chile were stopped with materials that would not have preserved in the altiplano.[2] Historical and ethnographic references suggest that four or five flutes would have been fastened together in one or two rows. Early references intimate that a complete *siku* consisted of a pair of bundled flutes (Garcilaso 1869:191; Walle 1914:149), and Bertonio (1984, II, 28, 3–6-317) notes that the harmony produced by playing the instruments had a distinct term (*ayarichi*). Historically, as today, there are various types and sizes of single and double-row flutes, corresponding to a complex system of classification and terms, but *sikus* are nearly always played in pairs. Musical troops incorporated pairs of panpipe players, and in most cases each pair consisted of a single size range complemented by pairs of larger (deeper toned) and smaller (higher toned) instruments. Each player therefore had his counterpart, each *ira* has *arca*, and their instruments often differed in number of pipes or specific tones in a pentatonic scale (Langevin 1991). The players complemented one another in counterpoint, rapidly alternating individual notes in a manner that demanded impeccable rhythm and timing. Parallel to Andean duality in other aspects of life (see Bouysee-Cassagne 1986, Harris 1985; Platt 1987), *ira* and *arca* were asymmetrical. *Ira* was dominant and the player started the melody and led the ongoing counterpoint, while *arca* followed. Through an alternating dialogue, or *kuti*, the two produced a single melody that harmonized with the other *siku* pairs in the troop, forming an intricate and nested set of complementary relations.[3]

Residential Activity and Domestic Architecture in Misiton 2

Excavations less than fifty meters to the west, nearest to the canalized quebrada, exposed another residential neighborhood (Bermann and Graffam 1989; Janusek 1994). As in Misiton 1, the first occupation here dated to Early Tiwanaku IV. Set on the same precultural loam found in Misiton 1, it consisted of a compact sandy floor covered by a thin lens of ash and refuse and the west edge of a rectangular structure. Covering this early occupation was a thick layer of midden with artifacts representing domestic activities, including food preparation and storage, the consumption of camelids, lake fowl, and fish, generalized lithic production, and weaving.

Covering the midden was an extensive architectural complex dating to Late Tiwanaku IV (Figure 6.6). Bounding the north side of the complex was a massive wall that served both as a compound wall and terrace face. Buried in its foundation was an offering pit with an elaborate *escudilla.* Built into the compound wall was an elaborate entrance, demarcated on either side by two buttresses, and consisting of steps and a paved walkway that led up from the lower terrace to the north. The excavated part of the Misiton 2 compound yielded three different areas. Behind the east section of the compound wall was a walled corridor. The south wall of the corridor connected with a massive north-south foundation that supported a substantial internal compound wall. The area east of the large foundation yielded several intriguing features, including structure foundations, adobe pits filled with cobbles, and a short stack of adobe bricks. Excavations here also revealed a severed long bone, a ceramic burnisher, and several quartzite knives, alluding to an association with Misiton 1.

To the west of the large internal wall was a circular structure associated with an outdoor activity zone. To enter the structure a person entering the compound would have had to pass through the corridor to the doorway, which opened to the west. Associated features and artifacts indicate that the structure was a dwelling, and that it was occupied for a long time. Inside was a primary floor of prepared red clay that had been resurfaced twice. In the structure were postholes, a storage pit (Bermann 1994:206), and nestled along its east wall, three hearths. A charcoal sample from the latest hearth yielded a calibrated date of AD 680–900 (Janusek 2003a:Table 3.2). Behind the dwelling were several outdoor features, including a large outdoor oven from which one charcoal sample, calibrated at AD 890–1000, indicated use in Early Tiwanaku V (Figure 6.6A). Near the oven were two features that served both as drains for seasonal runoff and as maintenance

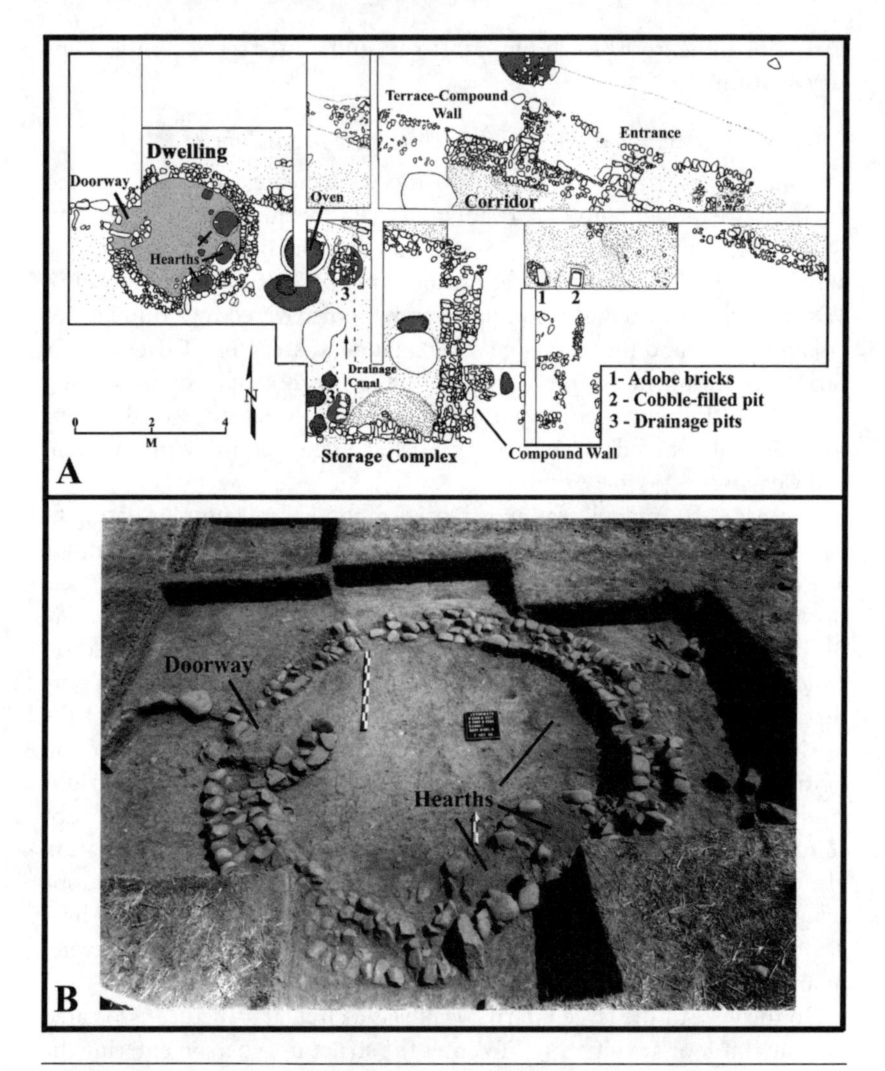

Figure 6.6 Plan (A) and view (B) of the Tiwanaku IV residential occupation in Misiton 2, highlighting the circular dwelling in the west section of the compound.

pits. The pits were loosely filled with cobbles and broken adobe blocks, and each descended from the living surface to a small subterranean drainage canal that passed underneath the complex.

Summary

Only excavations on the saddle below Wila Kollu provided a coherent glimpse of household space and domestic activities in Tiwanaku IV. Here, residential organization consisted of roughly rectangular buildings organized around central outdoor patios, a pattern that originated in the Late Formative. Buildings included dwellings and special purpose structures, and outdoor communal patios and hearths were loci for communal household activities. Similar to activities conducted in Akapana East, Tiwanaku, residential activities in Lukurmata included food preparation and cooking; the consumption of camelids, small mammals, tubers, quinoa, maize, and legumes (Wright et al. 2003); the production and repair of clothing as revealed in spinning and weaving implements; and the generalized production, retouching, and use of lithic tools.

As in Tiwanaku, residential life across Lukurmata included the ritual reproduction and well-being of the household. Ceramic *sahumadors* were used as lamps and ceremonial burners, and effigy *incensarios*, uncommon at Tiwanaku, served local mortuary rituals and offerings. Small bone tubes and spoons, though not exceedingly common, were found in all Tiwanaku IV occupations. Ridge inhabitants also buried fetal camelids under their living spaces, as offerings to ensure the good health or well-being of the resident groups. In some areas, human burials and mortuary rituals were an important component of local residential life. On the ridge, humans were interred between dwellings and below living surfaces, and in K'atupata, burial clusters were intermingled with domestic features. As at Tiwanaku, some deceased relatives were kept close to home, most likely as local ancestral progenitors considered to have some purchase on everyday affairs.

Urban Growth, State Culture, and Social Ranking

Residence and Urban Growth

Like Tiwanaku, Lukurmata expanded considerably after AD 500. During the early part of the Late Formative Period the moat, if already built, may have marked the settlement boundary. In Late Formative 2, settlement activity began expanding beyond the moat, attested most clearly in the K'atupata platform to the southeast. Many other areas were first occupied in Early or Late Tiwanaku IV, when the sloping piedmont south of Wila Kollu was reclaimed as a series of shallow terraces. Meanwhile, the ritual platform in K'atupata was ritually interred and the mounded area put to uses more closely tied to urban residential life.

Like Tiwanaku, Lukurmata incorporated spatially and architecturally bounded residential compounds, as exemplified most clearly on the ridge and in Misiton 1 and 2. Lukurmata grew systematically, through the planned construction and occupation of such compounds. Although spatial organization varied substantially, each compound incorporated one or more dwellings, outdoor areas and patios, and nearby ancillary structures. On the ridge and in Misiton 1, living areas pertaining to the coresidential household were organized into several adjacent, discreet patio groups. Two or more of these groups comprised a residential compound, a more encompassing coresidential social group. In Misiton 1 and 2 it appears that two or more compounds formed larger, bounded barrios or residential neighborhoods. Although no thoroughfares were uncovered in Lukurmata, canalized *quebradas* running through residential sectors, like the one adjacent to Misiton 2, probably formed important arteries of travel and communication into and through the settlement.

Settlement growth is clearly outlined in the chronology of occupation across the site. Until Tiwanaku IV, residential and ritual activity was limited principally to areas within and near the moat, and by the end of Late Formative 2, Lukurmata covered approximately thirty hectares. Over the next 200 years, urban residence and activity expanded well beyond this early physical boundary, eventually forming an urban community of some two square kilometers. Misiton 1 and 2, to the south, and Ch'iarkala, to the west, were first occupied in Early Tiwanaku IV, somewhat earlier than many residential sectors in Tiwanaku's urban periphery. As at Tiwanaku, one residential sector after another was inhabited until the moat was well inside of the settlement. If the moat originally encompassed most of the early settlement, by AD 600 it divided the growing city into different sectors. It remained an important physical boundary, but like the moat in Tiwanaku, its conceptual significance shifted to one of distinguishing social groups and activities in the settlement.

Settlement growth generated increasing quantities of refuse and waste, though to nowhere near the volumes witnessed at Tiwanaku. As at Tiwanaku, residential compounds maintained subterranean drainage canals to guide waste and runoff away from living areas. These connected with large artificial aqueducts, which cut through the terraces at various points to carry runoff down toward the moat. Subterranean storage pits now were far more common than they had been in Late Formative occupations, and most were eventually filled with ash and refuse. At Tiwanaku, however, various urban areas were dedicated to refuse disposal, and in interim phases between occupations in residential compounds, abandoned houses and their patios were mined for adobe and turned into local middens. At Lukurmata, only the K'atupata sector, and specifically the north edge of the mound covering the platform, formed an urban midden comparable to those characteristic of Tiwanaku. The smaller overall scale of refuse disposal at Lukurmata undoubtedly reflects, in part, the smaller population here and a corresponding lower density of residential and ritual activity. In combination with other patterns, however, it also indicates that Lukurmata was a very different type of center and urban community.

Conformity, Ceramic Style, and Feasting in Residential Life

Residential life in Lukurmata reveals crosscutting patterns of cultural conformity and local diversity, as it does at Tiwanaku. First, all residential architecture followed an orientation several degrees east of north. Orientation was somewhat more variable than it was at Tiwanaku, ranging from eight degrees in the Wila Kollu monumental complex to twelve degrees in Misiton 1 and Misiton 2. Nevertheless, it clearly manifested a spatial order that was reproduced in local cycles of construction, abandonment, and renewal. As at Tiwanaku it was a formal urban design keyed to a spatial cosmology that instantiated sacred celestial cycles and established visual paths with major sacred peaks. More visually impressive here than Illimani, though part of the same Cordillera Oriental, was the *achachila* of Illampu, almost directly north of Wila Kollu. Most likely, Lukurmata's orientation defined a visual path between Wila Kollu and Illampu. The common orientation is particularly striking in relation to the variability present during the Late Formative. Establishing a single spatial order that expressed significant cosmological principles and made visual and conceptual links to primordial sacred features on the landscape was elemental to Tiwanaku cultural hegemony at Lukurmata.

The relatively abrupt acquisition and use of Tiwanaku style was striking and significant. Ceramic forms comprised a well-defined range of types, serving vessels had red- or black-slipped surfaces, and iconography included a strikingly standard range of mythical, anthropomorphic, and stylized geometric designs. In any residential area, most ceramic serving wares displayed elements of Tiwanaku style. However, as discussed in detail below, Lukurmata ceramic assemblages were distinct. Residential assemblages included a greater variety of Tiwanaku serving and ceremonial forms than were present in most Tiwanaku residential assemblages. One is tempted to consider Lukurmata more "Tiwanaku" than Tiwanaku itself. Also, ceramic assemblages included a distinct complex of Lukurmata-style wares that incorporated unique elements of paste, form, treatment, decoration, and iconography (Janusek 1999:Table 3). In addition, at least thirty-five percent of ceramic vessels included unique paste recipes, indicating that much production was local.

Tiwanaku-affiliated serving and ceramic wares were clearly desirable, in part a function of their elaboration and stylistic significance. Vessels formed a discernable Tiwanaku style in characteristic expressions of form—such as the everted forms of *keros*, *tazons*, and *escudillas*—and in overall patterns of surface treatment and decoration. The vessels also were vehicles for the depiction of elaborate mythical and religious iconography. Yet the makers of Lukurmata-style vessels, while incorporating many elements of Tiwanaku style and new firing practices, employed novel techniques to create a range of innovative vessels. These techniques defined a range of distinctive vessels that, like other Tiwanaku-style wares, were obtained and used by groups throughout Lukurmata.

As at Tiwanaku, the appearance of new assemblages for preparing, storing, fermenting as well as consuming foods and liquids points to an increasing emphasis on rituals of consumption. As a diversified range of vehicles for Tiwanaku style and mythical icons, serving-ceremonial wares formed a specialized complex that facilitated both domestic meals and communal feasts. They would have been particularly significant and effective in social gatherings involving music, dancing, and drinking. Potent rituals of reversal, public feasts also were critical for the negotiation of status and identity.

Feasting is evident at Lukurmata in the sudden popularity of voluminous *ollas*, large storage *tinajas*, and a new range of serving-ceremonial wares. Together, these formed an entire technology designed to facilitate ritual consumption. As at Tiwanaku, such vessels were most common in outdoor patios and middens. Lack of evidence for extensive public plazas, such as those characteristic of major Inca regional centers, indicates that residential compounds were precisely where many feasts were hosted. Ritual feasting was not entirely centralized or coopted by state or local leaders, but was a common local practice. Direct residues of feasting events in Lukurmata, however, were less common than they were in Tiwanaku. No ceramic smashes were located in the monumental complex, and most burials and offerings incorporated ceremonial vessels for types of ritual activity not directly related to commensalism. Further, extensive middens filled with the residues of major feasts, a pattern so common at Tiwanaku, were far less common at Lukurmata. At the scale of the urban community, commensalism played a far greater role at Tiwanaku than it did at Lukurmata.

Social Ranking in Residential Life

Social ranking assuredly was an important part of Lukurmata urban society, but going on current evidence, its dimensions remain unclear. We would expect compounds near Wila Kollu to have housed relatively high status residents. However, spatial, architectural, and artifactual attributes in this area, as well as patterns of drainage and sanitation, suggest that the area was inhabited by a group of moderate status. In fact, in Late Tiwanaku IV the frequency of serving-ceremonial wares on the ridge dropped from twenty-three percent to eight percent of total assemblages (Bermann 1994:208). This drop may reflect many possible shifts, but a decline in relative status is a distinct possibility.

Further, status in the Misiton sectors is somewhat paradoxical. Here, far from the urban core, both Early and Late Tiwanaku IV occupations yielded relatively high quantities of serving-ceremonial wares. While domestic architecture on the ridge consisted of simple clay floors and earthen wall foundations, architecture in the Misiton compounds was far more elaborate, consisting of large cobble foundations several courses high. If the status of Late Tiwanaku IV groups in the Misiton sector was relatively high, it was undoubtedly related, in part, to a couple of related variables. First, for centuries inhabitants of Misiton 1 had crafted panpipes, which not only may have been a somewhat lucrative enterprise, but also identified the artisans a group with specialized knowledge and skills (see Helms 1993).

Second, Misiton 1 and in particular Misiton 2 were located near a route leading directly to Tiwanaku. Of course, whether or not the path was a major route of communication and travel in the Tiwanaku Period is unclear. In favor of the possibility is the fact that the path follows a prehispanic canalized quebrada that forms a convenient route into and through the site. Given this possibility, Misiton 2 may have been a place for people and goods en route to disembark. Supporting this idea was the construction of storage structures in Misiton 2 in Early Tiwanaku V, where goods coming into or leaving Lukurmata may have been temporarily stored (see Chapter 8). The presence of bone flutes in and around the Misiton 2 storage complex suggests that its inhabitants remained in some way involved in the production or distribution of goods produced in Misiton 1.

Urban Segmentation and Social Diversity

Spatial and Architectural Diversity

Alongside material patterns of conformity with Tiwanaku state culture and with Lukurmata as an urban community were patterns of spatial segmentation and material diversity. As at Tiwanaku, bounded compounds and barrios formed the most salient units of social differentiation. More patently than in Tiwanaku, however, compounds differed in internal spatial layout and in construction, implying that social role and identity varied considerably. On the ridge and in Misiton 1, dwellings and other structures formed small groups focused around communal patios and hearths. In Misiton 1, outdoor patios were in some cases separated by wall foundations. On the ridge, many dwellings and other structures were visible simply as clay floors with domestic features and artifacts, with walls on poorly preserved adobe and partial cobble foundations. Dwellings were difficult to distinguish from other structures. Misiton buildings were far better preserved, in part because of the greater effort and energy expended in their construction.

Dwellings also differed in form, and most clearly so in Misiton 2. Here, inside of a residential compound with rectilinear walls was a circular structure. Unlike the circular structure in La K'araña, Tiwanaku, which by all accounts served to store crops or other goods (see Chapter 5), multiple superimposed living surfaces and domestic features and artifacts unambiguously indicate that the Misiton 2 structure was a dwelling. Residents performed a wide range of common domestic activities and appear comparable in status to those of other sectors, but they inhabited a circular rather than a rectangular building. To date, no other circular dwellings are known from the Tiwanaku period in the two valleys, where the only comparable structures date to the post-Tiwanaku Early Pacajes Period (Wise 1993; see Chapter 9). It appears that here, as elsewhere in the New World (Bawden 1993:50–51; Rattray 1990; Stanish 1989a; Stanish et al.1993), house form and layout in some cases marked local social identities.

Ceramic Diversity

In relation to spatial segmentation, ceramic patterns were highly significant. Some stylistic patterns distinguished Lukurmata and the Katari Valley from Tiwanaku and the Tiwanaku Valley, while others distinguished residential sectors within Lukurmata. All residences and middens yielded a wide range of local serving and ceremonial wares, what I collectively term Lukurmata style, that were also common in contemporaneous occupations in the Katari Valley (Figure 6.7); (Janusek 2002; Janusek and Kolata 2003). These vessels, with unique paste recipes, forms, and decorative canons, appeared alongside stylistic assemblages common at Tiwanaku. In fact, many assemblages from Lukurmata were more diverse than were assemblages from Tiwanaku. Overall, variants of Lukurmata style incorporated technical and decorative twists on Tiwanaku style.

As at Tiwanaku, large jars or *tinajas* burgeoned in frequency across the site, attesting the increasing importance of fermenting and storing liquids and alcoholic beverages. Unlike *tinajas* at Tiwanaku, most Lukurmata *tinajas* displayed brown, beige, pale, or cream surfaces. Also unlike Tiwanaku, most storage and serving vessels incorporated beige to pale orange paste and were clearly crafted in unique production centers. Lukurmata assemblages also included tanware vessels, elaborate serving-ceremonial wares decorated with abstract curvilinear or rectilinear motifs on a highly polished, unslipped beige paste. They also included incredibly high frequencies of serving wares decorated with continuous volutes, and smaller quantities of vessels with short annular bases. Assemblages included elaborate ceremonial forms, including feline- or llama-effigy *incensarios* used in offerings and mortuary rituals, as well as special serving wares such as thin-walled *cuencos* and thick carinated or *tazon* basins.

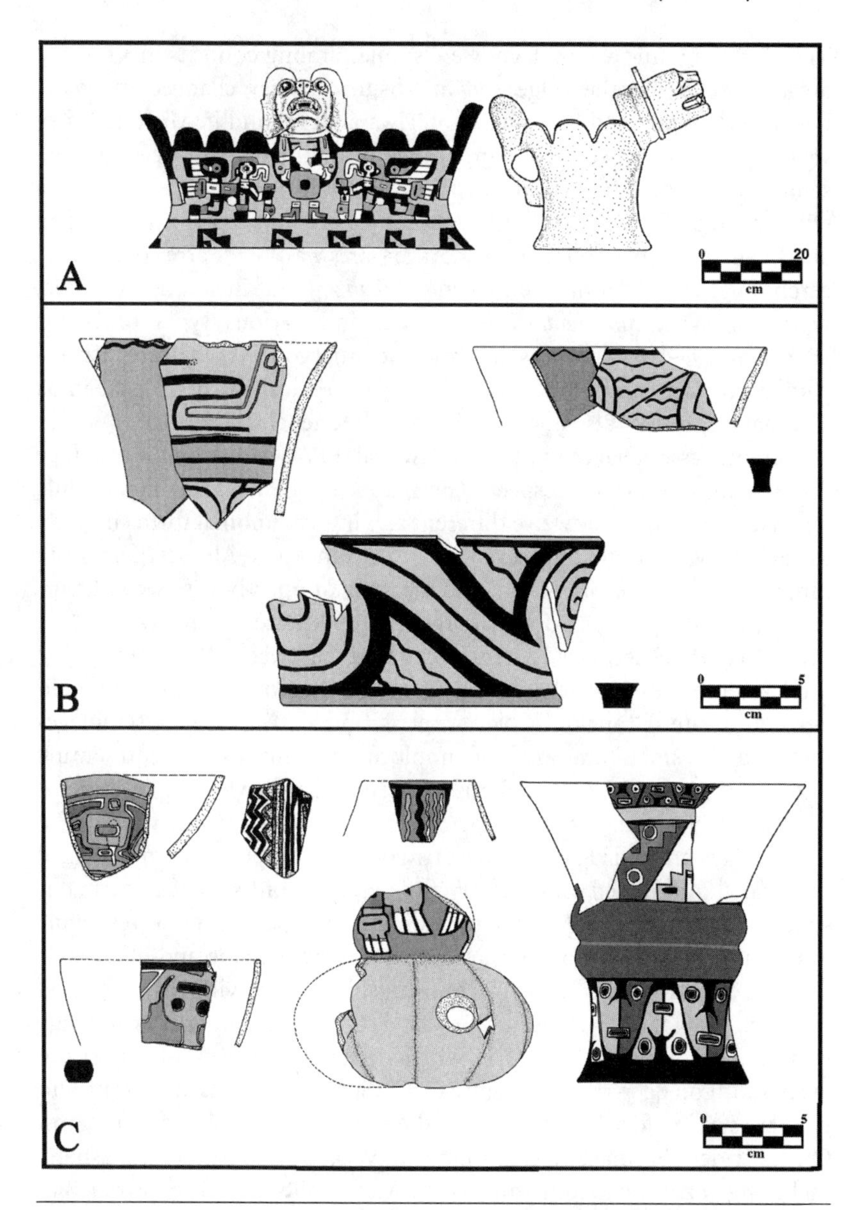

Figure 6.7 Lukurmata-style ceramic vessels: feline effigy incensario (A), tanware keros and tazons (B), and decorated nonlocal vessels and vessels showing nonlocal influence (C).

Most such serving-ceremonial wares and roughly fifty percent of others maintained paste recipes unique to Lukurmata and the Katari Valley.

Each excavated residential compound or midden in Lukurmata yielded a distinct constellation of ceramic assemblages. For the most part, as at

Tiwanaku, ceramic assemblages were similar among contexts in a specific area. However, on the ridge and in Misiton 2, they changed markedly between the Early and Late phases of Tiwanaku IV, and in Misiton 2 they varied markedly between contemporaneous bounded sectors. Ceramic assemblages in the Early Tiwanaku IV occupation on the ridge included a wide range of Tiwanaku variants. Accompanying new types of red-slipped and Lukurmata-style cooking and storage wares was a wide array of serving-ceremonial wares dominated by *keros* and *tazons* but including *escudillas*, *vasijas*, *cuencos*, *sahumadors*, *incensarios*, and various types of basins (Bermann 1994:168–171). As in other residential contexts, tanwares accompanied redwares and blackwares. *Challadors*, typical of the Cochabamba Tiwanaku complex, also appeared in small frequencies.

Ceramic assemblages in the Late Tiwanaku IV occupation on the ridge differed in several key respects (Bermann 1994:208–211). First, while Bermann documented twelve different serving-ceremonial forms in Early Tiwanaku IV, he found only seven in Late Tiwanaku IV. Almost their entire range consisted of *keros*, *tazons*, and a variety of open bowls. Second, tanware vessels dropped in popularity relative to redware serving wares. More dramatic, while decorated wares accounted for twenty-three percent of total assemblages in Early Tiwanaku IV, they accounted for only eight percent in Late Tiwanaku IV. Nevertheless, both early and late assemblages included "a small amount" of nonlocal serving wares representing Omereque, Yampara, Yura, and other poorly defined style complexes.

Misiton 1 ceramic assemblages were similar to Early Tiwanaku IV assemblages on the ridge. In the last two occupations, more than one third of Tiwanaku-affiliated wares (thirty-five percent) consisted of Lukurmata-style serving-ceremonial wares, including eleven percent tanwares, while nonlocal serving and storage wares, including Omereque and other style complexes, also were present (four percent of serving assemblages) (Janusek 1999:Table 3). One unique vessel combined a gourd or fruit effigy body, typical of the Yampara style, with a neck depicting a classic Tiwanaku avian motif on deep red slip (Figure 6.7C). Specific variants of tanware and redware serving forms distinguished the ridge and Misiton 1 occupations. On the ridge, Bermann located tanware variants not located elsewhere, including *tazons* with dots and stars. Meanwhile, a type of *tazon* that depicted a particular mythical feline was popular in the last two occupations of Misiton 1.

The early residential context in Ch'iarkala, far to the northwest, revealed a distinct ceramic assemblage of which fifty-six percent were Lukurmata-style wares and nonlocal wares were absent. However, fifty percent of all serving and ceremonial sherds consisted of a unique type of ceremonial basin in red, black, and tanware variants. The high frequency of this ceramic type suggests that the area served a specific ceremonial role in the larger community, and in relation to other patterns, its associated group may have enjoyed relatively high status.

Residential contexts and refuse middens in K'atupata yielded the highest proportions of Lukurmata-style wares (approximately eighty percent of serving assemblages). In general, this pattern continued throughout the Early and Late Tiwanaku IV phases. Assemblages included high proportions of elegant tanware serving vessels (twenty-six percent of serving assemblages) and other Lukurmata-style variants, including *cuencos* (fourteen percent), carinated and *tazon* basins (seventeen percent), serving-ceremonial forms with continuous volutes or a short annular base (together, twenty-one percent), and *incensario* fragments (two percent). Nonlocal vessels were notably absent, but many tazons depicted a straight linear band around the interior rim, a design common only on nonlocal Omereque bowls and *keros.* Storage *tinajas* slipped in tan, brown, cream, or buff comprised eighty-seven percent of all storage wares.

In Misiton 2, stylistic patterns of ceramic assemblages differed on either side of the internal north-south compound wall. In the east compound, as on the ridge and in Misiton 1, ceramic assemblages incorporated significant proportions of Lukurmata-style vessels (thirty percent of assemblages) and nonlocal wares were present. In the west compound, which included the circular dwelling, Lukurmata-style wares were far less common (approximately eighteen percent of serving wares) and sherds representing nonlocal wares absent. The location of the west compound near a footpath leading to Tiwanaku, possibly alluding to a close affiliation with the center, may help explain this pattern (see Chapter 8).

Ceramic assemblages were highly diverse in Lukurmata, most notably so in varying proportions of Lukurmata-style wares, in particular expressions of this style, and in the presence or absence of nonlocal vessels. The ridge, Misiton 1, and the east compound of Misiton 2 included high frequencies of Lukurmata-style wares, other Tiwanaku wares, and nonlocal wares associated with valley regions to the southeast. Inhabitants of these areas may have maintained some interaction, however indirect, with populations in far areas such as Cochabamba or Chuquisaca. Ceramic assemblages in other areas were different. Nonlocal wares were rare or absent in K'atupata, Ch'iarkala, and the west compound of Misiton 2. K'atupata middens, burials, and domestic features yielded high concentrations of Lukurmata-style wares, in fact the highest yet documented at Lukurmata. In Ch'iarkala, high quantities of elaborate basins suggest that local inhabitants maintained a specific occupation and status within the larger urban community. The west compound of Misiton 2, with its high proportions of Tiwanaku wares, was in some respects most unique in Lukurmata.

It is undoubtedly significant that distinction in Lukurmata was manifested in part in low frequencies of local wares, or conversely, in high frequencies of wares more typical of Tiwanaku. This may suggest that inhabitants of Misiton 2, near a path linking Tiwanaku and Lukurmata, had an important role and status in facilitating movement and interaction between the centers.

Specialized Production

Inhabitants of residential compounds engaged in various types of productive activities. As in Tiwanaku, coresidential households made a variety of general lithic tools and bone implements, which were used in common activities of food preparation, scraping, burnishing, cleaning, hunting, and storing substances. Among these were mandible tools, which as at Tiwanaku were ubiquitous in Lukurmata residential areas (Bermann 1994, 2003; Janusek 1994, 2003b; Webster 1993). Bermann located direct evidence for the production of mandible tools in a Late Tiwanaku IV residential patio on the ridge, and similar production by-product was located in secondary outdoor middens throughout Lukurmata. By all accounts, the production of mandible tools, like many other domestic tools, was a generalized household activity.

As in Tiwanaku, some residential groups in Lukurmata engaged in specialized production. Inhabitants of Misiton 1 produced musical instruments, and specifically bone panpipes, suggesting that groups living elsewhere made other types of instruments. As in Ch'iji Jawira, the relatively informal character of production in Misiton 1, in relation to the peripheral location of the neighborhood as well as its unique ceramic assemblages, strongly suggest that production was not directly controlled by or conducted for ruling elites. Like ceramic production in Ch'iji Jawira, craft production in Misiton 1 was not conducted in large-scale, nondomestic workshop industries. Bone panpipes like nonelite ceramics were crafted in residential workshops organized as suprahousehold compounds and barrios. Whether full or part time, production was organized and executed by corporate groups composed of households whose members, or some of whose members, also went about day to day domestic activities. Specialized producers were simultaneously semiautonomous coresidential groups that maintained unique ceramic assemblages and distinct networks of social interaction and affiliation.

Mortuary Practices

In Lukurmata, burials near dwellings and living areas indicate that, as in Tiwanaku, human remains and mortuary activities were not entirely relegated to discrete cemeteries. This was most clear on the ridge, where during Late Tiwanaku IV humans were buried under the patios and outdoor areas associated with local residential activity. Two of these were double-cist tombs in which an upper cist containing the remains rose above outdoor surfaces. Even more prominently than the mortuary complex in Akapana East 2, these burials were visible and accessible to local residential inhabitants and formed an integral part of everyday residential life. The desire to keep certain deceased individuals near the spaces shared by living kindred suggests some type of local ancestor cult enacted in rituals at the grave sites of deceased relatives and ancestors. Further, burials with visible above-ground interment chambers anticipate the emergence of specific types of mortuary rituals that would become common in post-Tiwanaku societies. Given their access to the human remains, the living may have periodically removed the bones during important ceremonies celebrating group ancestors, a common practice in some Andean regions in the fifteenth century.

Like spatial patterns and stylistic assemblages, mortuary practices varied significantly among residential areas. On one level, mortuary patterns differed among distinct compounds and neighborhoods. Burials on the ridge included double-cist chambers, a type not yet found elsewhere, as well as single-cist tombs, many lined with stone slabs and with the interred individuals on their sides. These patterns did not occur in K'atupata, which revealed a range of distinct mortuary patterns not found on the ridge. Here, tombs included unlined, horizontally arranged double-cist tombs as well as bench-cist tombs, while burial offerings included varieties of unfired clay pots. However, both areas shared patterns not found at Tiwanaku, including a double-cist arrangement, whether vertical or horizontal, the use of exhausted *batanes* as tomb lids, and the common inclusion of Lukurmata-style vessels, including effigy *incensarios*, as burial offerings. Thus, certain burial and mortuary patterns were particular to different groups within Lukurmata, while certain patterns distinguished mortuary patterns at Lukurmata from those at Tiwanaku. In tandem with significant diversity among an array of other practices and elements of material culture, these patterns allude to important social boundaries within and between the urban settlements. Their expression in mortuary practices indicates that such boundaries were intimately woven with emotionally charged expressions of group memory and identity.

Body Modification

Convincing evidence for social diversity and the significance of local and regional social boundaries comes, once again, from Blom's analysis of human remains from Lukurmata and the Katari Valley (Blom 1999).

Specifically, humans interred at Lukurmata and other excavated Katari sites (e.g., Qeyakuntu, Kirawi) presented patterns of cranial modification that were collectively distinct from those recovered at Tiwanaku. Of all interred individuals from Katari (n = 78), sixty-nine percent of those with reasonably intact crania who died during the Tiwanaku Period had some type of cranial modification. Of individuals with modified crania, eighty-nine percent maintained an annular style of modification, presumably associated with conical *chuco* hats, and eleven percent (only one individual) a tabular style of modification (Blom 1999:159). This pattern had a long history in the region, for one hundred percent of individuals interred during the Late Formative had skulls with crania modified in the annular style. This stands in stark contrast to evidence from Tiwanaku and other sites in the Tiwanaku Valley, where the tabular style predominated among individuals with modified crania.

Conclusions

Between AD 500 and 800, Lukurmata was a dynamic urban settlement and an important regional political and ritual center in the Katari Valley. After Tiwanaku, it was the most important center in the Tiwanaku polity. The social groups comprising Lukurmata, as well as their residential spaces and ritual places, manifest close affiliation with Tiwanaku's hegemonic state culture as well as a congeries of other nested and overlapping expressions of social identification. The new monumental complex on Wila Kollu, constructed following certain Tiwanaku canons of ceremonial space and architecture and serving as a major ritual place for populations throughout the valley, presents a local interpretation of the ideology and ritual practices characteristic of Tiwanaku hegemony. The presence of other built ceremonial places in Lukurmata, as well as monumental platforms at other settlements in Katari, indicate that monumentality and ritual practice were not completely coopted by Lukurmata religious specialists or entirely focused on Wila Kollu, but rather were dispersed as local nodes of ritual power across the urban and regional landscape. If anything, Wila Kollu, like Kalasasaya or Akapana, was a place for specific types of local rituals, perhaps associated with relatively exclusive groups or conducted at specific, particularly auspicious times.

Residential space and urban population expanded dramatically after AD 500. As at Tiwanaku, walled compounds and barrios, or small neighborhoods of compounds, formed the most salient units of social differentiation at Lukurmata. Relative to one another, these groups maintained unique socioeconomic networks and practices, as well as distinct social identities. In some areas, such as on the ridge and in Misiton 1, superimposed occupation surfaces and middens point to great continuity in local activities. In Misiton 1, residents of a local neighborhood practiced the same specialized, successful trade for several hundred years. It involved specialized knowledge and a dimension of group identity that was transmitted over several successive generations. Groups such as this maintained enduring local resource networks and practiced local domestic and mortuary rituals. As at Tiwanaku, each compound housed a social group that was most likely grounded in kin-based relations, and possibly related by real or fabricated ancestry focused on individuals buried under living areas. These groups appear similar to later micro-*ayllus.* Like some compound groups in Tiwanaku, many in Lukurmata maintained interaction networks and perhaps cultural affiliations with groups in far regions, in particular temperate valleys southeast of the Lake Titicaca Basin. The prevalence of nonlocal assemblages is especially significant in light of the nonlocal influence on local Qeya style wares in Late Formative Period 2. Local interaction or affiliation with the eastern valleys apparently spanned many centuries, beginning long before Tiwanaku solidified its hegemony over the Katari Valley.

Status differentiation in Lukurmata was not nearly as prominently expressed or characteristically patterned as it was in Tiwanaku. In part our evidence may be a product of excavation sampling at Lukurmata, but patterns of status differentiation among the several areas excavated to date allude to very different spatial and social arrangements of social hierarchy at the two centers. Lukurmata does not reveal a clear concentric status gradient as does Tiwanaku. Some groups living near the monumental complex, inside of the area encompassed by the moat, appear of comparable if not lower status than many groups residing in the far periphery. Particularly salient is evidence that this group experienced decreasing access to elaborate goods, and very likely social status, throughout Tiwanaku IV. Inhabitants of Misiton 1, meanwhile, enjoyed relatively great access to elaborate local and exotic resources even as social boundaries became more complex over successive generations, in part no doubt a function of their specialized knowledge and distinctive interaction networks. Inhabitants of Misiton 2 by Late Tiwanaku IV maintained elaborately built structures and used assemblages more characteristic of assemblages at Tiwanaku. They, like specialists in Misiton 1, may have held a particular occupation, possibly involving, I hypothesize, the movement of traffic, communication, or goods to and from Tiwanaku. Status in Lukurmata was not overtly associated with proximity to ancient temples or monumental complexes. Rather, or in addition, it was tied to other specialized activities and important locations, ritual and otherwise, that were widely dispersed across the urban landscape.

Urban expansion correlated with the abrupt, widespread distribution and popular acceptance of a dominant suite of overarching ideologies and technologies, boldly expressed in new material styles. It amounted to the expansion of an emerging state culture that, by the end of Early Tiwanaku IV, had been inculcated and internalized as practical hegemony, if to varying degrees, by everyone. Monumental and residential architecture now followed the ideal directional orientation that had for centuries characterized Tiwanaku ritual and domestic spaces. This uniform spatial order, which both instantiated timeless cycles and ritual pathways and appropriated Lukurmata's spatial order to an overarching cosmic vision, was a key element in the consolidation of Tiwanaku hegemony at Lukurmata. After AD 500, all residential groups used significant quantities of Tiwanaku-style serving and ceremonial vessels, alongside a range of large vessels for preparing, storing, and fermenting beverages such as *chicha*. Crystallizing a complex process initiated during the Late Formative, Lukurmata had transformed from an autonomous center to a prestigious regional settlement in Tiwanaku's coalescing political and ritual hierarchy. Sweet or sour, and most likely both, Lukurmata became Tiwanaku's second city. Fundamental to the process of regional incorporation was the local desire to accept, mimic, and appropriate the objects, practices, and ideals attendant on this highly prestigious, brave new order; an order that, if elegant in its visions and promises, was hegemonic in its scope and aims. The popular internalization of Tiwanaku state ideology and its sedimentation as practical consciousness and hegemony was the success of the nascent state and key to its power.

As at Tiwanaku, social identity in Lukurmata was expressed, in part, in distinct configurations of serving-ceremonial and storage wares, precisely those that became diacritical markers in periodic ceremonies and charged rituals of consumption. On the one hand, festivals affirmed the emerging Tiwanaku order of things, as expressed in the conspicuous display of a distinctive, broadly shared style and icons of ritual power. The influx of groups to Lukurmata, and their participation in emerging social hierarchies and an expanding state political economy, enhanced the demographic strength and effective power of high status groups and ruling elites. On the other hand, these same groups maintained or created distinct social identities and local means of production, fortified by their access to Tiwanaku-style goods and their participation in broader religious, economic, and social spheres. Paradoxically, Tiwanaku hegemony fostered local identity and social power, just as local groups fostered the increasing power of the state. The ever-increasing subordination of local groups, through their partly voluntary calculated participation in centrally coordinated rituals and events, Pauketat (2000) calls the "tragedy of the commoners." As discussed in Chapter 8, such a tragedy soon would have a particularly poignant resonance for the inhabitants of Lukurmata.

Nevertheless, Lukurmata was not created in Tiwanaku's image, nor could it be. Lukurmata had a long and established history as an autonomous regional center, and as multiple interwoven local practices and material patterns suggest, its history was periodically reanimated (and undoubtedly reinterpreted and fabricated) as a vibrant historical consciousness; a coherent collective memory antedating Tiwanaku hegemony. If Lukurmata was coopted and transformed into a major Tiwanaku regional center for the Katari region, it remained a distinct urban community, and in some respects a distinct *type* of city. For one thing, the monumental complex of Wila Kollu was unique in scale, configuration, and associated ritual practice. In relation to this, ambiguous evidence for status differentiation indicates that proximity to the complex, and residence within the bounded area around it, was not the predominant variable in establishing an urban geography of social ranking, which was far more salient at Tiwanaku. Though the moat formed a significant boundary, at Lukurmata we see no clear concentric cline of social status. If anything, and coupled with evidence for other ritual complexes, social status was tied to a range of other considerations, including specialized production and proximity to a variety of important places. In addition, large-scale ceremonial feasting apparently did not play the same central role in Lukurmata that it did in Tiwanaku. Ceramic smashes, ash pits, and extensive middens were far less common than they were at Tiwanaku. Tiwanaku and Lukurmata had become distinct types of urban centers, with different roles and statuses in the emerging hegemonic system, but also with different collective memories and tenacious, if ever-shifting, social identities and interregional affiliations.

In this vein, certain ritual and mortuary practices as well as clear patterns of stylistic variation distinguished Lukurmata and Tiwanaku, collectively marking a social boundary between the two urban communities and their entire sustaining regions. Inhabitants of Lukurmata formed a coherent community tied to a broader regional identity expressed in, from the perspective of an individual, permanent (head shape) and temporary (vessel assemblages) practices and styles. Social identity at this regional scale, undoubtedly expressed in major periodic celebrations as well as everyday activities, would have been more like that characteristic of later macro-*ayllus*, with dimensions of activity and social power more characteristic of ethnicity. Further, regional identity in Katari was inextricably tied to local productive enterprise, which included acquiring and harvesting lake oriented resources, such as fish, *totora* reeds, and birds, and cultivating raised field segments in the expansive Koani Pampa. In Tiwanaku IV, raised field cultivation was conducted on a relatively small scale, with specific sectors directly managed by local towns and villages and Lukurmata strategically located to balance lacustrine and agricultural production.

Lukurmata and the Katari region, if incorporated into a centralized state and to some degree subordinated to an emergent political, economic, and cultural system, remained at least in Tiwanaku IV a semiautonomous political unit within the ambit of Tiwanaku hegemony. It bears speculating that it was considered as something like a moiety in complement to the Tiwanaku Valley and its inhabitants, similar to analogous complementary divisions in society and landscape in the more recent Andes. In this scenario Lukurmata was a twin political and ceremonial center. Analogous with later communities, as state power developed, sociopolitical differences between the regions were subsumed within a dual order, ascribing to potentially conflictive differences an idealized relation of complementary opposition (Abercrombie 1998; Bastien 1978). Local social identity and expressions of local power in Lukurmata undoubtedly thrived on some memory or mythical fabrication of its prehegemonic history. More archaeologically clear, the Katari Valley, with its abundant lake resources and high water table, had great productive potential, greater in some measures than the drier Tiwanaku Valley. Based in common myths, respective territory, and rich local resources, and emphasized in characteristic styles of highly visible material culture and body modification, inhabitants of the Katari Valley formed a coherent social and political unit with tremendous power and influence. Even clearer than in Tiwanaku, in Lukurmata a simultaneous and potentially volatile invigoration of state and local power was well underway by AD 800.

PART 3

CHAPTER 7
Urban Transformation in Tiwanaku

Radical changes characterized Tiwanaku cultural development in Early Tiwanaku V. Ponce (1981) has characterized Tiwanaku V as a time of state expansion and imperial consolidation, a time when Tiwanaku military forces charged abroad to conquer and incorporate vast regions and polities, including Wari in the Ayacucho Basin of southern Peru. Yet ongoing research indicates that Tiwanaku never conquered Wari. In fact, the relationship between the two polities, most likely one of tense coexistence, remains enigmatic to this day. Further, many regions once thought to be under Tiwanaku political control and colonization, it turns out, were rather inhabited by local polities engaged in intense interaction with Tiwanaku. On a map, Tiwanaku would appear as so many modes and branches of influence and power rather than a contiguous territory of state expansion. Key areas of direct control included the southern Lake Titicaca Basin, focused on the contiguous valleys of Tiwanaku and Katari, the Cochabamba Valley to the southeast, and the Moquegua Valley, Peru, to the west.

In this chapter, I discuss evidence for transformations in the city of Tiwanaku, focusing on changes in its urban core after AD 800. Major changes included the crystallization of an urban elite class and their increasing presence and influence throughout the city. Changes also included the destruction of old residential compounds, most notably those in Akapana East, and their reconstruction as bounded areas more directly tied to elite activities and state interests. Accompanying spatial reorganization in such sectors was—across Tiwanaku and throughout the southern basin—an increasing role for rituals of consumption and increasing homogeneity in the material styles that defined Tiwanaku state culture.

First, I discuss transformations in monumentality and high status residence in the urban core, focusing on Akapana and Putuni. Following, I detail patterns of change and continuity in the residential sectors of Akapana East. Next, I compare ceramic patterns between the areas and discuss emerging settlement patterns in the Tiwanaku Valley, and then synthesize various strands of comparative research that point to a range of intriguing conclusions. Research at Tiwanaku reveals momentous urban transformations that involved and impacted social groups living in the city and throughout its hinterland. Changes generated after AD 800 fomented powerful social transformations that, I argue, ultimately wrought state disintegration.

Transformation in the Tiwanaku Valley

Although Tiwanaku V regional settlement in the Tiwanaku Valley was broadly continuous with patterns in Tiwanaku IV, it was marked by a virtual explosion in the number of relatively small settlements around larger sites (Albarracín-Jordan and Mathews 1990:129–135; McAndrews et al. 1997:74–75). From a total of one hundred sites in the lower and middle Tiwanaku valley, general surface survey revealed 339 dating to Tiwanaku V (Figure 7.1).[1] Many of the well-distributed larger sites, as secondary centers in the local valley network, expanded in size. Patterns collectively point to increasing demographic density, with increasing residential occupation and activity at major towns and, even more notably, at the smaller villages and hamlets around them. Continuing patterns noted in Tiwanaku IV, urban expansion did not produce a demographic vacuum in its rural sustaining area, but rather was part of a more encompassing pattern of demographic increase that included the entire valley.

As did prior regional settlement, Tiwanaku V settlement consisted of multiple nested and overlapping networks rather than a unitary hierarchical system. K-means cluster analysis revealed that settlement in the valley consisted of at least six extensive clusters, each including one to five small towns or villages (McAndrews et al. 1997). While there appears to have been an inner sphere of sites in close interaction with Tiwanaku, settlement clusters farther away demonstrate evidence for greater social and economic autonomy. Based on combined patterns, Albarracín-Jordan (1992) and others (McAndrews et al. 1997) argue that many local communities remained semiautonomous. Some go even further (Albarracín-Jordan and Mathews 1990a:133), suggesting that demographic shift toward local settlement may mark a gradual decentralization of productive management and ultimately political authority.

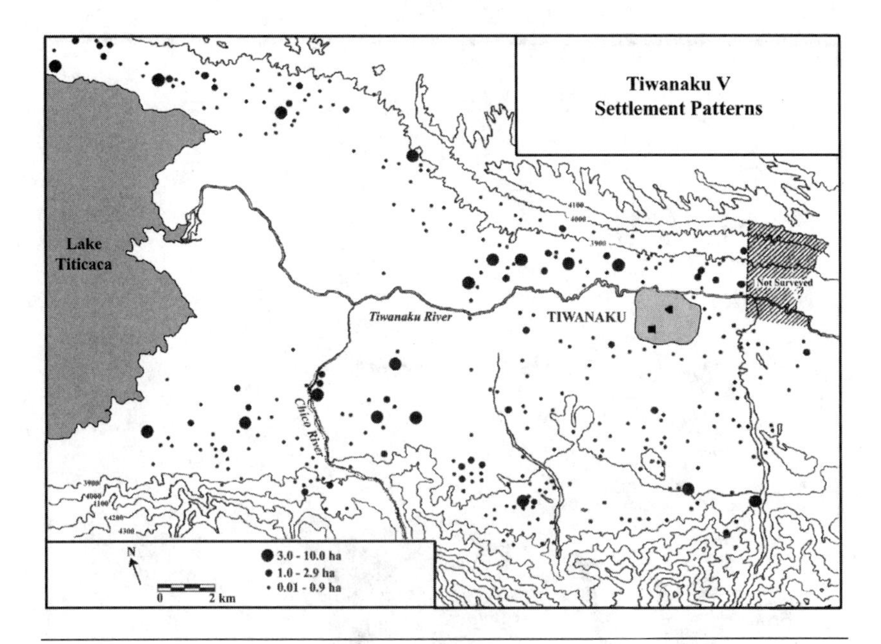

Figure 7.1 Settlement distribution in the Tiwanaku Valley during Tiwanaku V (adapted from Albarracín-Jordan 2003).

Settlements were evenly distributed across major ecological microzones, as they were in Tiwanaku IV, and with a moderate preference for the pampa. Some fifty-one percent of sites occupied the pampa while forty percent occupied piedmont hill slopes and nine percent nearby hilltops. The relative importance of raised fields and other productive regimes in the valley (terraces, *qochas*) cannot be precisely determined, but settlement distribution suggests that most systems continued to be farmed in Tiwanaku V. Intensified production in the Katari Valley (see Chapter 8) raises the possibility that raised field production was intensified in the Tiwanaku Valley as well, but this hypothesis awaits further research.

Ceramic assemblages associated with settlements outside of Tiwanaku now manifest a greater emphasis on mass production. Serving-ceremonial assemblages included high proportions of crudely wrought variants, including vessels slipped in less striking orange or brown slips, demonstrating decreasing control over their firing and treatment. Most depicted quickly executed, repetitive stylized imagery. Storage vessels and especially large *tinajas* increased in relative proportion to total assemblages (Figure 7.2A). Although Mathews (1992:343–344) counted them as only six percent of Tiwanaku V assemblages at small sites, this was an increase

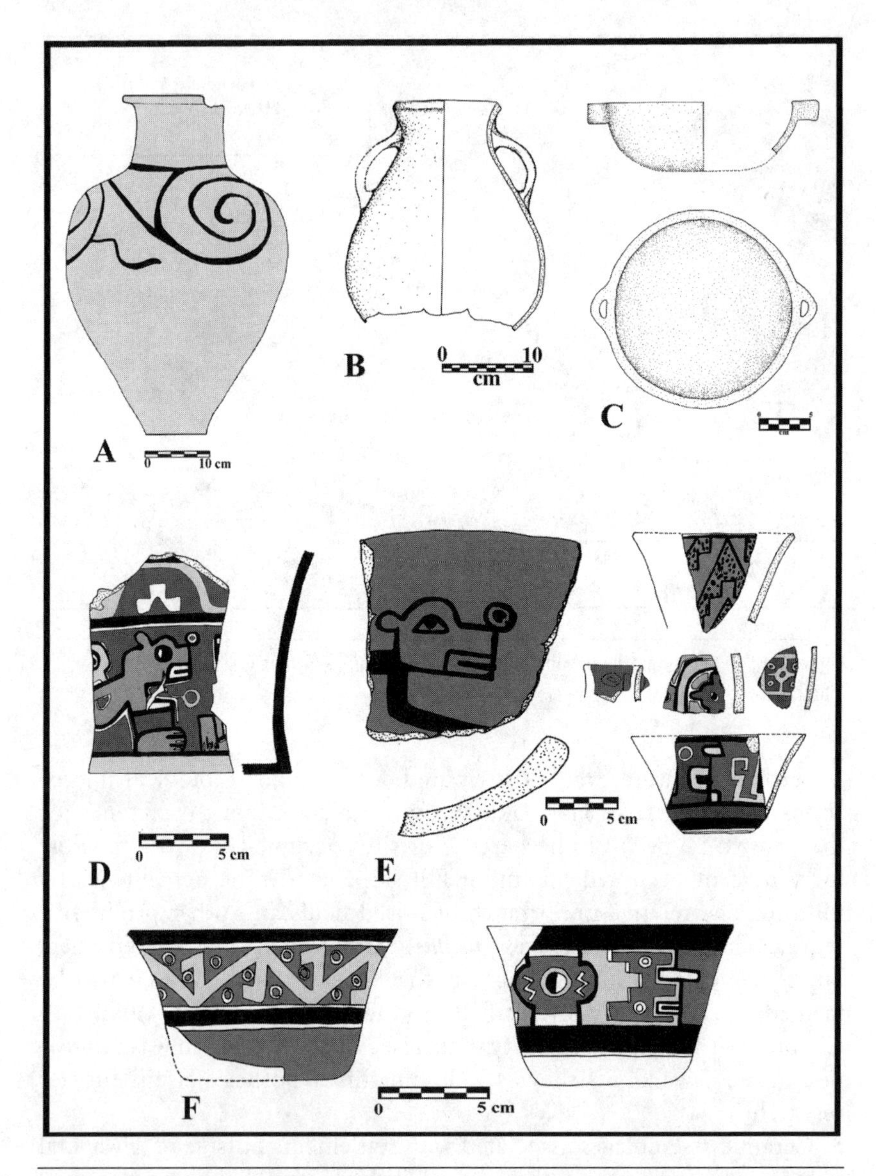

Figure 7.2 Representative Tiwanaku V ceramics vessels: a large tinaja with volutes (A), a relatively high-volume cooking *olla* (B) and roasting bowl (C) from the kitchen in Akapana East 1, a *kero* with feline motif from the south compound of Akapana East 1 (D), elaborate and nonlocal vessel sherds from the north compound of Akapana East 1 (E), and recurved *tazons* from the Putuni East Palace (F).

of almost three times earlier percentages. Thus, as the scale of settlement and density of population increased throughout the region, life in the valley involved an increased intensity in the production and storage of goods used in rituals of consumption.

Changes in Monumentality and Elite Residence

Monumental Architecture and Residential Activity

Many monumental complexes in the Tiwanaku urban core also witnessed significant transformation. It is not entirely clear what changes occurred in the Kalasasaya and Sunken Temple, but both most likely remained important places for ritual activity as sacred spaces with increasingly ancient histories. In Pumapunku, though many late features have been since heavily quarried, certain areas reveal important changes. The main platform was raised and resurfaced and new structures were built on top, while the stone-lined drainage system was elaborated and, perhaps most significant, the main passage from the principal stairway to the inner sunken court was filled in (Vranich 1999:231–232). The courtyard remained central to ritual activity in the complex; in fact its west edge was embellished with an elegant stairway, facilitating entry from the now higher platform. However, it appears likely that access to it was now more restricted. The platform's south edge, meanwhile, was never finished. As Vranich (1999:232) notes, "The Pumapunku complex remains . . . a monumental contradiction: over-engineered yet unfinished, monumental in appearance, yet façade-like in reality."

Clearer are changes in the Akapana in Tiwanaku V. Radiocarbon dates from camelid and human remains at the base of the structure suggest that such offering rituals continued throughout Early Tiwanaku V (Alconini 1995:102; Blom et al. 2003). These included an offering consisting of a decapitated carnivore placed in front of an elaborate drainage outlet, which effectively rendered it obsolete (Alconini 1995:102; Kolata 1993a:Figure 5.28; Manzanilla 1992:83). Excavations atop the Akapana, north of a massive pit that gutted the center of the monument, revealed an elaborate structure complex that, although built in Late Tiwanaku IV, was used most intensively in Tiwanaku V (Alconini 1995:115–142; Manzanilla 1992:54–70; Kolata 1993a:114–118). The complex consisted of a series of connected rooms surrounding a large paved patio, all consisting of impeccably cut ashlar masonry. Ceramic assemblages associated with the complex contained relatively high proportions of cooking *ollas* (four to eight percent of assemblages) and large *tinajas* (ten to twenty-six percent of assemblages), pointing to abundant food preparation and liquid storage as in other residential areas (Alconini 1995:Figures 66–67). It is likely that the complex housed Tiwanaku ritual specialists (Kolata 1993a:118; Manzanilla and Woodard 1990) or their associated attendants, who prepared food and drink for the extravagant Akapana rituals they directed.

As in other residential sectors, some of these specialists were buried under the patio inside the complex. Here, excavations revealed six burials with several intriguing features (Kolata 1993a:117–118; Manzanilla 1992:61–62). The burials were flexed like others in Tiwanaku and they all faced north, but five of them were aligned east-west in back of, and facing, the first. The principal burial included ritual offerings, including a miniature *vasija* and a bone snuff spoon, and most striking, the individual held in his/her lap a shattered feline effigy *incensario*. Several fragments of other incensarios, including a ceramic feline head, were located in other areas of the complex. In sum the burial arrangement clearly expressed social differences among the individuals, most likely including differences of role and status. Associated with the principal individual, who perhaps had been a ritual specialist, was an elaborate ceremonial vessel characteristic of the Katari region. The presence of *incensarios* in such a distinctive residential context alludes to some special link or affiliation between the specialists inhabiting or using the complex and ritual activities characteristic of Lukurmata. It raises the possibility, at least, that some of Tiwanaku's high priests were from the Katari Valley, and perhaps from Lukurmata.

The Putuni: Elite Residence in the Urban Core

Even more profound and abrupt changes characterized the Putuni area west of the Kalasasaya. At some point close to AD 800, the Late Tiwanaku residential complex was razed to the ground, leveled, and then ritually interred (Couture and Sampeck 2003; Sampeck 1991). Associated with the event were numerous dedications of disarticulated humans and camelids, which were placed in canals, on floors, and under new foundations (Couture and Sampeck 2003; Janusek and Earnest 1990b). Similar offerings were associated with major ceremonies or renewal events in the Akapana and Mollo Kontu platform. As Couture and Sampeck point out (2003), the Putuni offerings "were part of a broader pattern of ritual behavior associated with major episodes of architectural transformation shared by various groups across Tiwanaku's urban landscape."

An aggregate pebble layer capped with compact, finely selected red clay was packed over the entire razed occupation (Janusek and Earnest 1990b; Sampeck 1991:24). This formed a substrate to support the construction of the Putuni complex, an elaborate architectural ensemble consisting of a platform and courtyard structure attached to an area of elite residence and paved corridors and plazas (Figures 4.3 and 5.4a); (Couture and Sampeck 2003; Kolata 1993a). The main structure measured approximately fifty meters north-south by seventy meters east-west, and consisted of a shallow ashlar-faced earth platform some 1.2 meters high around a large open courtyard. Several small stairways provided entry onto the platform, but the primary entrance into the courtyard had been a polychrome staircase that was later dismantled early in the twentieth century (Posnansky 1945). Each stairway connected the Putuni with plazas or corridors paved with ashlars, including a paved corridor to the north between it and the Chunchukala complex that supported a series of rooms. Couture suggests that these rooms visually blocked and restricted access to the Putuni, "emphasizing the Putuni's aura of exclusivity" (Couture and Sampeck 2003).

Architectural patterns indicate that the Putuni platform visible today was a relatively late structure, and like other monumental constructions was built in stages. Many of the andesite and sandstone blocks comprising Putuni's platform faces had been recycled from older structures. Vranich (personal communication, 2001) suggests that some of the larger ashlars were refaced segments cut from massive Kalasasaya-like pilasters, and perhaps from an early section of the Kalasasaya itself. Nevertheless, features within the platform suggest that some blocks were cannibalized from an earlier version of the Putuni itself. Excavations in the earth fill of the platform revealed an early ashlar-faced revetment that was less substantial than those forming later platform faces (Janusek and Earnest 1990b:239). This early elaborate revetment indicates that the platform had been constructed and embellished in at least two different construction events.

Surrounding the courtyard, and set into the platform, was a series of paneled niches, each of a different configuration, most with small covered openings, and one with a sliding door construction (Janusek and Earnest 1990b:239). Although the niches were empty and their function remains unclear, Kolata and I have suggested they served a *chullpa*-like function, housing and providing periodic access to the mummified bundles of local ancestors or other ritual paraphernalia (ibid.; Kolata 1993a). Couture (Couture and Sampeck 2003) further speculates that they held the ancestral bundles of high-status individuals previously buried in the now-defunct Late Tiwanaku IV mortuary complex, much of which clearly had been disturbed at some point in the prehispanic past. In plan the Putuni complex simulated and aggrandized the conceptual arrangement of a residential patio group, metaphorically embodying intimate domestic space in a context of monumental ritual space and high status residence (Janusek 1994:294). Thus it is not inconceivable that, as in many Tiwanaku residential compounds, deceased ancestors formed an important part of the residential spaces of the living.

Associated with and in part built into the Putuni platform, to the west, were at least two large residential structures organized around a flagstone plaza (Couture and Sampeck 2003). The East Palace, set into a recessed section of the platform, was a rectangular structure set on ashlar foundations, consisting of at least five smaller rooms and an associated private patio (Figure 7.3). At twenty-two meters by six meters, or some 132 square meters, it was a large edifice, and it was associated with numerous residential features, including a hearth, four refuse pits, and three private wells. The walls consisted of adobe bricks made from clean, finely selected sandy clay, and they were elaborately painted in brilliant hues of red, yellow, orange, green, and blue (Créqui Montfort & de la Grange 1904; Kolata 1993a:153–154; Posnansky 1945; Sampeck 1991:35). Built into the floor was a perforated stone basin that diverted runoff into a subterranean tertiary canal, then into a larger ashlar-lined secondary canal and finally into the massive primary canal. For the most part the floor was relatively clean, free of the domestic refuse that characterized many residential structures. However, among artifacts associated with common domestic activities, including fragmented bones and sherds of *ollas* and *tinajas* (respectively, twenty-five and twenty-three percent of assemblages), were abundant sumptuary goods (Couture and Sampeck 2003; Giesso 2003). These included chert and obsidian projectile points and elaborate items of adornment, including beads of lapis lazuli, bone, sodalite, and obsidian, copper pins and labrettes, carved shell, gold lamina, and a wrought silver tube filled with blue pigment. The abundance of exotic prestige goods mirrored the remarkable array of elaborate goods included as offerings in six human dedications placed under the edifice upon its construction. One of them (Feature 38), an adult female, yielded a necklace of bone, shell, and a variety of exotic minerals, a copper disc mirror, a lead flask, abundant obsidian flakes, and a hammered gold pectoral depicting an impassive deity face.

Facing the structure across the plaza was a second residential structure, the West Palace (Figure 5.4); (Couture and Sampeck 2003). This structure, most likely built sometime later, mimicked the East Palace in several ways. It maintained double-course cut stone foundations, some recycled from earlier edifices such as the neighboring Kherikala, which Couture suggests was by now abandoned. It also maintained its own subterranean drainage system, including a primary canal that descended to the north, running parallel to the ancient primary canal under the Putuni. However, neither the foundations nor the primary canal was as well constructed as those in the West Palace, and there was no evidence that the adobe walls were similarly painted. Nevertheless, ceramic assemblages associated with the structure and its associated plaza areas were distinctive, suggesting that it served a specific role for resident groups. Among relatively low percentages of *olla* sherds were relatively abundant serving-ceremonial vessels and, most notably, large quantities of storage vessels, including abundant large vessel fragments (thirty-seven percent of assemblages). Most of these were large tinajas with long cylindrical necks, suggesting that a primary

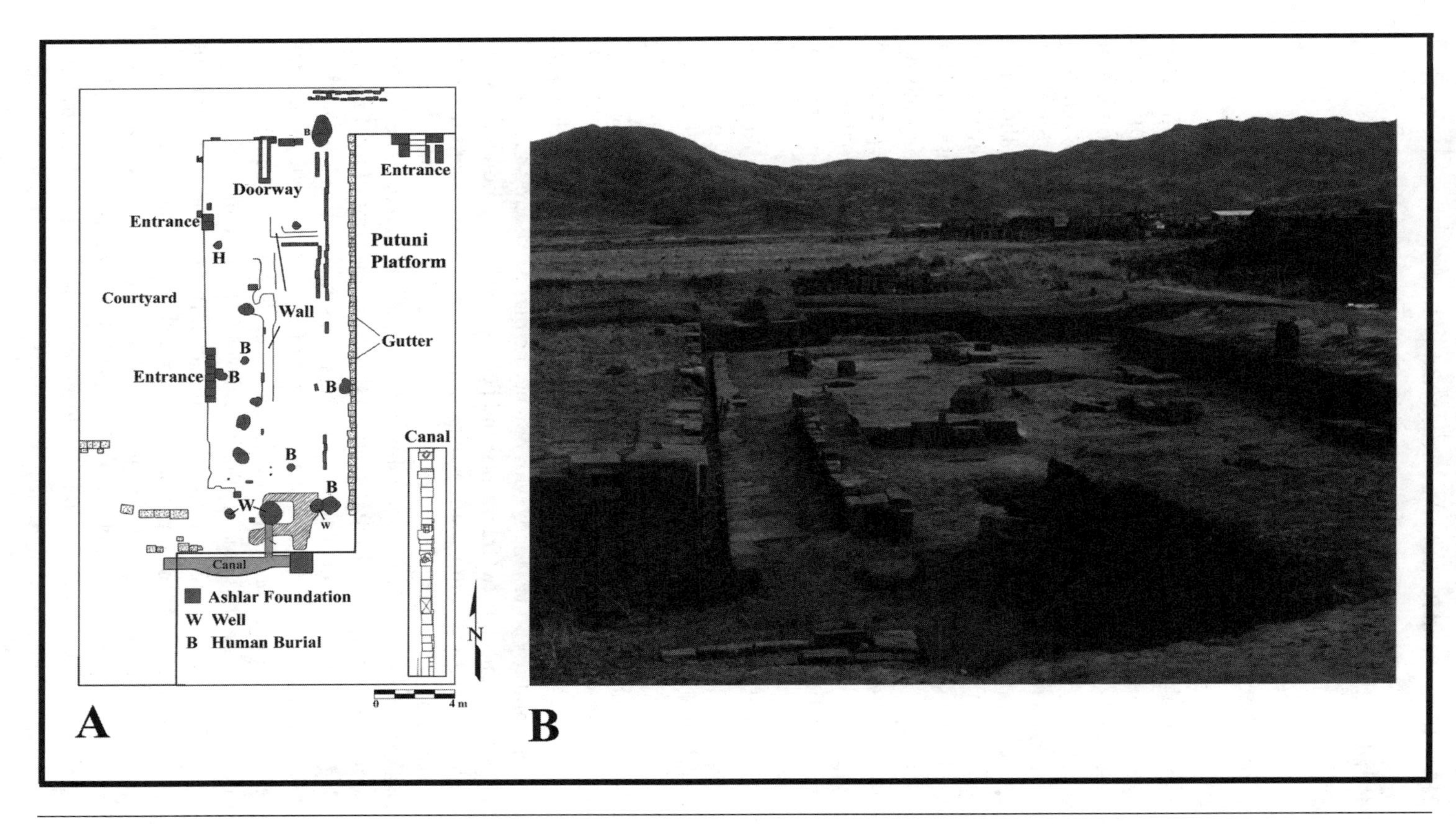

Figure 7.3 Plan (A) and view (B) of remnant structure foundations and features associated with the Putuni East Palace (A adapted from Couture and Sampeck 2003).

activity in the West Palace was brewing and storing, as well as consuming, fermented drinks.

New Urban Sectors

Akapana East IM and La Karaña

Substantial renewal characterized other residential sectors in the urban core at roughly the same time. In Akapana East 1M, a new compound wall was built almost directly over the foundations of the old compound (Figure 7.4A). Excavations here revealed a structure (structure 3) consisting of a series of rooms and a large outdoor patio or activity area to the east. The excavated rooms were much larger than any exposed in the earlier compound, and it is not clear that these served as dwellings. Nevertheless, the features and activities represented here were similar to those found in most Tiwanaku IV residential contexts. Several short foundation walls occupied the area near the external compound wall, most likely representing fragments of small storage structures. A long, vernacular cobble-lined drain carried runoff from inside of the compound and out into the drainage ditch running through the street.

Inside of the structure were relatively high proportions of cooking vessel sherds and a few areas where cinnabar was ground into red pigment. Meanwhile, food, liquids, and other goods critical to domestic reproduction were stored in small bins located in the outdoor activity areas. Here we also located a subterranean pit and exceedingly high proportions of storage and serving ware sherds. Other domestic activities included: food preparation, evident in two exhausted grinders; food consumption, represented in discarded camelid and *cuy* bones, many with butchering marks; weaving, identified in several wichuña and awl fragments; and generalized lithic production, as revealed in multiple hammerstones, expended cores, and abundant debitage.

Ceramic assemblages in the complex were different from those in earlier occupations in several important respects. *Tinaja* sherds had increased from twenty-nine percent to thirty-five percent of total assemblages, and up to almost forty percent of assemblages in the outdoor zone (Janusek 2003b:Table 10.11). *Tazons* (fifty-six percent of serving vessels) became more important just as *escudillas* (five percent) became much less frequent (Janusek 2003b:Table 10.12). More immediately noticeable was a redundancy in form and decoration relative to serving wares from previous occupations, and a much lower frequency of *keros* and *escudillas* depicting elaborate polychrome images. Now, more than seventy-five percent of such wares displayed abstract geometric motifs—step motifs, wavy bands, squared volutes, interlocking patterns, and circles—that traditionally had been limited to *tazons* and *vasijas.*

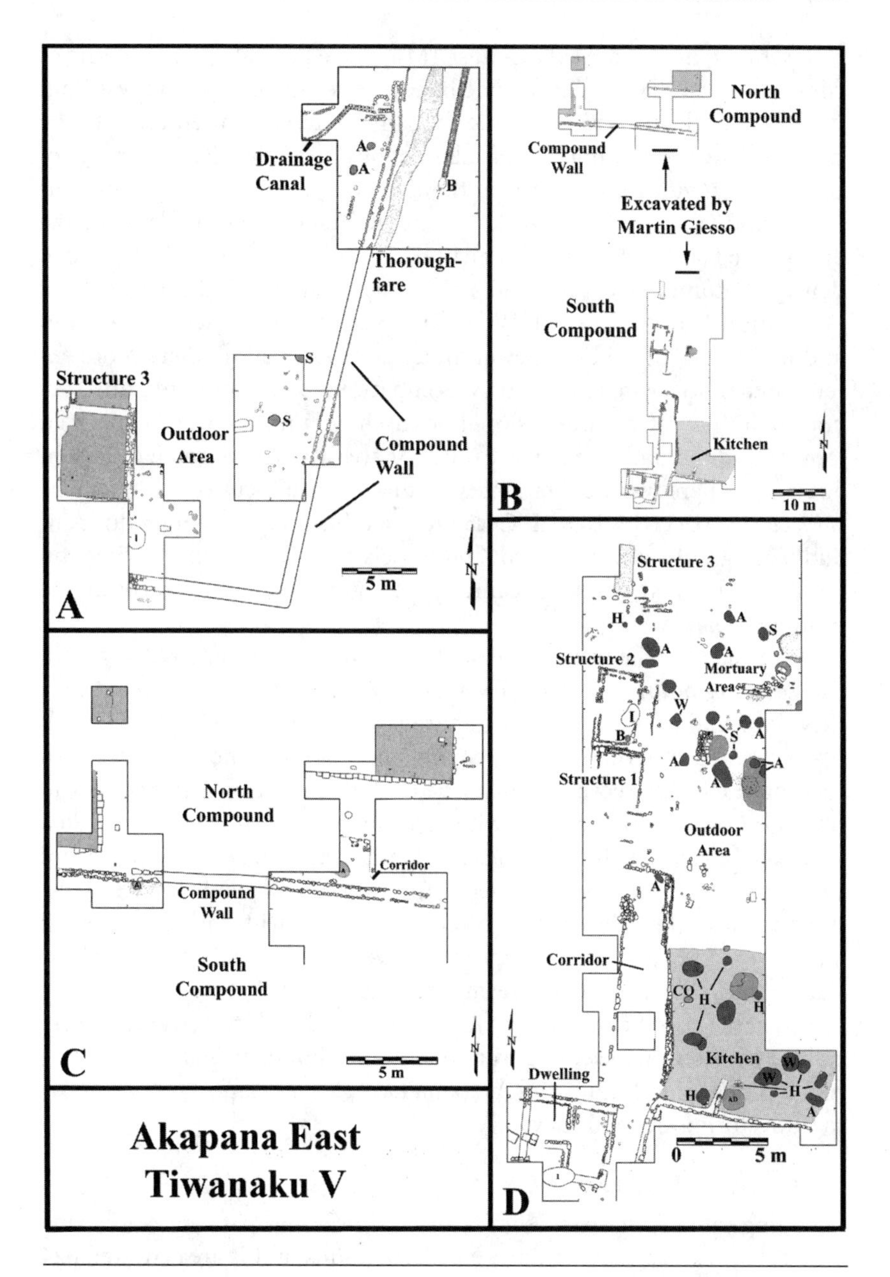

Figure 7.4 Excavated structures and features associated with residential occupations in Akapana East 1M and Akapana East 1: plan of Akapana East 1M (A), general plan of Akapana East 1 (B), plan of Akapana East 1, north compound (C), and plan of Akapana East 1, south compound (D). Key: A – ash pit; B – human burial; CO – camelid offering; H – hearth; I – intrusive pit; S – storage pit; W – well. See Janusek 2003b for detailed illustrations.

Overall, renewal in Akapana East 1M involved an intriguing mosaic of continuity and change. On the one hand, the second compound was built directly over the first, reproducing the same systematic orientation to the cardinal directions, similar vernacular architecture, and a familiar range of domestic activities. It appears as though the groups who built the new compound, and lived and worked there, represented descendents of the group who had occupied the Tiwanaku IV compound. However, the spatial density of domestic features and artifacts associated with the Tiwanaku V occupation had diminished. We located very few clear activity features and no hearths or middens, even though our excavations were more extensive than those in Tiwanaku IV occupations. The compound once occupied by two structurally similar household units now incorporated larger buildings and an extensive outdoor area, but also a smaller range of activities. There was neither a clear "house" nor a locus of complementary, closely packed activities. Ceramic assemblages were more redundant and iconography more stylized, and vessels associated with brewing and storing fermented drinks became more significant, particularly in the outdoor area.

At the edge of the urban core, La Karaña witnessed similar changes. In the west compound, the Late Tiwanaku IV occupation was covered by a new floor and a much larger structure (Escalante 1997:273, 2003). Built like other such structures on cobble foundations, the structure also incorporated a few recycled ashlars, had a doorway facing east, and had an outdoor drainage gutter lined with sandstone slabs. In it were pits filled with ash, burned earth, and other residential refuse. Like many structures in Akapana East 1M and 1, however, the structure contained none of the other features (hearths or storage bins) associated with earlier residential structures, and so does not appear to have served strictly as a dwelling. Rather, like the large structure in Akapana East 1M it appears to have served some specific set of functions. Associated with the structure were elaborately decorated serving wares alongside abundant shattered *tinajas*, highlighting, as in Putuni and Akapana East 1M, the importance of brewing and storing alcoholic beverages.

Akapana East 1: The South Compound

Shedding some light on the significance of these new patterns is Akapana East 1. Our exposure of Tiwanaku V occupations in this area covered 624 square meters, and revealed sections of two compounds separated by a large compound wall (Figure 7.4B). The south compound rested directly on ash-filled quarry pits and dense residential middens associated with Late Tiwanaku IV. This complex incorporated a number of structures and outdoor activity zones, and rested on ephemeral, unprepared *apisonados*

(Figure 7.4D). In many areas earlier features had not been leveled, so that, for instance, floors followed the contours of the mound covering the early, interred ceremonial complex. All architectural features were of cobblestone and earth foundations, and they consistently followed Tiwanaku's standardized spatial orientation. Unlike most Tiwanaku IV residential structures, however, structures in this complex employed a distinct type of mud brick—a more organic sod, or *tepe*—still employed in contemporary house compounds.

The south compound incorporated a series of small structures associated with one large specialized kitchen, a spacious corridor, and a dwelling. structures 1 and 2 were relatively intact, and partial foundations to the north defined the remnants of at least two similar structures. These structures contained few clear features or activity areas, and associated artifacts suggested that weaving, the production of lithic tools, and food consumption took place inside. They included only ephemeral, unprepared, and minimally trampled interior surfaces, indicating that they were not intensively used or occupied. The dwelling, by contrast, maintained a substantial *apisonado.* It consisted of three rooms and incorporated several carved stone blocks in its foundations. Unlike other structures, this one supported walls of fine yellow adobe, and was similar in both spatial organization and activities to Tiwanaku IV dwellings. Ground stone crushers, *batanes*, and *moleadores* to prepare food were found in and around the structure, as were other types of typical domestic tools.

Most cooking activities were concentrated in the kitchen. This extensive building measured 8.4 by 8.6 meters in area, and included two superimposed apisonados separated by some ten centimeters of accumulated soil and detritus, forming a thick, undifferentiated occupation zone. It contained a well, several refuse pits, and twelve hearths. Around the hearths, and scattered over two superimposed occupation zones, were thousands of carbon-encrusted cooking vessel sherds. In the kitchen, cooking vessels made up seventy-one percent of recovered sherds. Most were globular *ollas*, but at least eleven percent of these sherds represented a unique type of roasting bowl with opposing horizontal handles (Figures 7.2B and C). These bowls, undecorated and caked with soot, were reminiscent of Late Formative bowls and have not been found in other Tiwanaku V contexts. The structure also contained hundreds of camelid bone fragments, a relatively high proportion with butchering marks, and ad hoc scrapers and knives used to prepare the carcasses. Tools for weaving and spinning were also common. In short, the kitchen formed a large communal space for food preparation, cooking, weaving, and other domestic activities.

Most structures bordered an extensive outdoor area encompassing a remarkable variety of activities. Fresh water was obtained from a deep well outside of structure 2, while the ash and detritus of everyday life were deposited in several nearby pits. Four large globular pits, all clustered around a subterranean stone-lined feature, served as subterranean storage chambers. Two areas with high proportions of *tinaja* sherds appear to have been places where the large vessels were kept: one just east of structures 1 and 2, and the other in the corridor, where they comprised sixty percent of total sherds. Some thirty-five percent of *tinajas* represented large variants with a long cylindrical neck and opposing strap handles. Other activities represented in the complex included food preparation, cloth production (spinning and weaving), generalized lithic production and use, crushing minerals into ground pigment, and the consumption of camelids, *cuy*, and some fish. Serving and ceremonial wares, however, comprised only fifteen percent of assemblages, a relatively low frequency compared to assemblages from prior residential contexts.

Overall, serving assemblages in Akapana East 1 were stylistically similar to those in Akapana East 1M, and their greater diversity most likely reflects the greater sample size from the extensive excavated area (Janusek 2003b:Tables 10.11 and 10.12). *Tazons* (thirty-seven percent of serving wares) were decorated with stylized designs, and most were more poorly made and quickly decorated than they those manufactured in Tiwanaku IV. *Keros* (thirty-three percent of serving wares) were more common here than they were in Akapana East 1M, and though most displayed stylized designs common to *tazons*, a small proportion (approximately ten percent) displayed elaborate feline or avian motifs (Figure 7.2D). *Tazons* and *keros* with Cochabamba style elements, most common in Ch'iji Jawira, composed a relatively small, but appreciable (approximately nine percent) percentage of such forms in Akapana East 1. *Escudillas* were slightly more common than they were in Akapana East 1M, but fifty-four percent were undecorated, a rare pattern in Tiwanaku IV. We recovered only four nonlocal sherds, one representing Yura, from the southern altiplano, and three others a unique style possibly related to the San Miguel complex in northern Chile.

Residential rituals displayed striking temporal continuity. *Sahumadors* formed substantial components of all assemblages, and two fetal camelids were buried under the kitchen as a form of domestic offering, one inside of a decorated *cuenco*. Toward the east edge of the excavated portion of the compound was a mortuary sector. Here, near another partial structure foundation, were two burials containing adult males, and the disarticulated remains of a third mixed with a partial camelid skeleton.

One other notable pattern in the residential complex was the presence of exotic and sumptuary crafted goods for ceremonial practices, some alluding to intriguing affiliations with cultures known from eastern valleys and the lowland regions beyond (Figure 7.5). They included a small basalt bowl

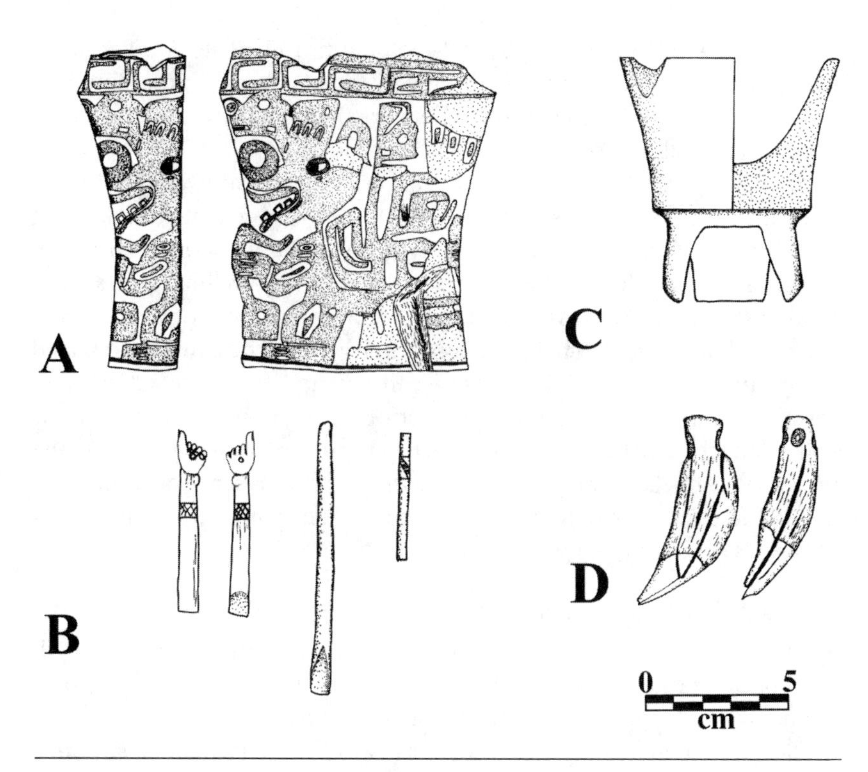

Figure 7.5 Elaborate and exotic objects found in Akapana East 1: bone snuff tube (A) and bone snuff spoons from the South Compound, and basalt tripod bowl (C) and two of for pendant jaguar canines (D) from in and near the North Compound.

and a camelid bone flute, or quena, buried near the north wall of structure 1. In the outdoor area, we located numerous bone and sodalite beads, and a few copper rings and pins. More remarkable were two pyroengraved bone containers found near structure 2, one of which displayed an elaborate mythical llama or masked shaman or warrior holding a trophy head in one hand and an axe in the other (Figure 7.5A). Nearby were three bone spatulas, one with a modelled human fist clenched in a gesture of power that is still carved on amulets used by Kallawaya healers from the warm valleys, of *yungas* east of Lake Titicaca (Figure 7.5B) (Girault 1987). The iconography and proximity of the implements suggest that they were used to store and consume hallucinogenic substances. Most extraordinary, in a domestic midden near the edge of the north compound we located a necklace of four large jaguar canines, each six to seven centimeters long and with perforated roots (Figure 7.5D). More recently, Kogi religious specialists in Colombia wore such necklaces, which as in Tiwanaku comprised the four canines of a single jaguar (Reichel-Dolmatoff 1971:Plate 5). The teeth must have been obtained through long distance networks extending into the Amazon basin and the person who wore them may have been a person of notable ritual status.

Spatial organization in the south complex was similar overall to that in Akapana East 1M. Domestic life was not ordered as repetitive clusters of similarly structured dwellings and activity areas. Rather, residential spatial organization was functionally differentiated. One dwelling and several smaller structures were associated with a communal outdoor zone, a storage corridor, a large kitchen, and a mortuary area. The complex revealed several unusual patterns. Patterns of construction and architecture were vernacular, and both interior and exterior occupation zones were dense with artifactual debris. Still, the occasional use of ashlar masonry, the prominence of elaborately decorated *keros*, and the presence of sumptuary goods and exotic ritual items indicate that the residents enjoyed preferential access to crafted wealth.

Akapana East 1: The North Compound

Spatial order and material patterns were entirely different in the north compound of Akapana East 1 (Figure 7.4C). Occupying much of the compound was an extensive edifice measuring approximately thirty meters north-south by at least twenty meters east-west and resting on ashlar foundations. It incorporated one or more extensive, slightly sunken courtyards, and was stepped in plan like the Pumapunku and Akapana. The structure was visible on the site's surface as an extensive depression surrounded by shallow linear mounds where its walls had collapsed. In many respects it was similar to structures in the Putuni Complex, and very distinct from those in the south compound of Akapana East 1. The soil around the courtyard revealed that the structure walls themselves consisted of clean adobe made of selected red earth. Also, the walls rested on ashlar foundations, consisting of blocks recycled from earlier buildings. However, the ashlars were fitted so that their aligned edges faced the interior coutryard, indicating that the most significant activities took place within. The coutryard floor rested fifteen to twenty centimeters below the outside surface, and it consisted of a clean, prepared clay resting on a gravel aggregate base.

The artifacts associated with the floor presented a variety of domestic activities, but a number of exotic and sumptuary goods confirmed that at least some of the people who used the structure enjoyed a distinct social status. We recovered typical domestic artifacts, as well as evidence for the consumption of butchered camelids and the use of sharp, expedient lithic flakes to cut and prepare camelid meat. But we also located a great variety of exotic vessels in the small area of the courtyard that we exposed. Alongside

Tiwanaku-style serving wares were fragments of a blackware effigy vessel, nonlocal sherds from the eastern Andean valleys and southern altiplano, and part of a small anthropomorphic jar with stylistic ties to the lowlands far to the east (Figure 7.2E).

Also associated with the structure were sumptuary goods. These included a copper band formed into an S-shaped design, most likely for adornment, and an exquisitely carved basalt tripod bowl (Figure 7.5C). It was just south of the edifice, at the north edge of the south compound, that we located the jaguar-tooth necklace. Between the edifice and the compound wall was a corridor, where we located part of an elaborate basin with a stylized feline design, and part of a recurved *tazon*, a ceremonial ceramic type common in the Akapana and Putuni residential areas (Figure 7.2E). The floor near the compound wall was littered with domestic refuse, including deposits of ash and burned soil. Around these deposits were artifacts associated with food preparation, including high proportions of *olla* and *tinaja* sherds, cut and splintered camelid bone, and some fish bone.

The north compound revealed an urban context and suite of activities very different from those to its south. Excavation units some thirty meters to the north of the north compound revealed a contemporaneous partial cobblestone foundation, large refuse pits, and ashy middens. Thus, the north compound and its unique edifice appear to have been circumscribed by more vernacular, residential compounds and middens. The north compound structure's focus around a sunken courtyard, along with its elaborate form and construction, imply that it was for activities of a relatively public, ceremonial nature. Further, the presence of exotic and sumptuary goods in and around the prepared floor suggests associations with individuals of relatively high status. The edifice apparently was the setting for social gatherings, feasts, or ceremonies that, whether exclusively or in part, involved Tiwanaku elites.

Continuity in the Residential Periphery

While massive renewal projects were radically transforming major sectors of the Tiwanaku core, residential patterns in most investigated areas of the urban periphery continued much as they had developed in Late Tiwanaku IV. Consequently, the distinction between occupation surfaces and features dating to Late Tiwanaku IV and Early Tiwanaku V is not always clear. In Akapana East 2, the final interior surface—the last of three—and the upper patio surface dated to Early Tiwanaku V. Both were prepared surfaces, and certain areas of the patio included a pebble aggregate base. Activities and artifact patterns associated with the surfaces and their associated features were continuous with earlier patterns. Continuity characterized other residential areas as well, including Mollo Kontu South

(Couture 1993, 2002). Here, as in Akapana East 2 residential activities continued much as they had developed in Late Tiwanaku IV, and a compound wall was renovated and rebuilt directly over its earlier foundations.

In Ch'iji Jawira, Rivera (1994) found that distinguishing Tiwanaku V from earlier surfaces and middens was more difficult, in part because the area witnessed significant postdepositional disturbance. Apparently, in one area after the other, the mound was gradually converted into an urban midden, covered with extensive sheet lenses and perforated with large adobe quarry/ash and refuse pits. Midden contexts revealed artifact patterns similar to patterns from primary residential and production contexts, indicating that they contained the refuse generated by local inhabitants. They further indicated that craft production remained an important activity throughout Early Tiwanaku V.

Ceramic Conformity and Diversity

In considering Tiwanaku V ceramic assemblages, it is helpful to categorize residential areas as three roughly concentric groups; those associated with monumental architecture in the urban core (Akapana, Putuni), those associated with new structures and activity areas toward the edges of the core (Akapana East 1M and 1), and those associated with more continuous occupations in the urban periphery (Akapana East 2, Ch'iji Jawira). In each residential compound of the urban periphery for which ceramic analysis has been conducted, ceramic assemblages demonstrated remarkable continuity from Late Tiwanaku IV through Early Tiwanaku V. In the other two areas, they revealed substantial changes. In the Akapana, Tiwanaku V ceramic assemblages were substantially different from Late Tiwanaku IV assemblages (Alconini 1995:Figures 66 and 67). New patterns included smaller proportions of *escudillas*, *keros*, and *vasijas* in relation to higher proportions of recurved *tazons*, higher quantities of large cooking *ollas* (though low relative to other residential areas), and much higher frequencies of large *tinajas* (twenty-six percent of all sherds) for brewing and storing beverages.

Changes in ceramic assemblages associated with the Putuni complex were similar to those in Akapana in several ways. Recurved *tazons* became popular (nine percent of serving ware sherds) along with large serving basins (seventeen percent) relative to lower proportions of *escudillas* (from thirty-four percent in Late Tiwanaku IV to seventeen percent of serving ware sherds) (Figure 7.2F). Meanwhile, the proportions of storage vessel sherds jumped from twenty-eight to thirty-two percent of total assemblages, more than half now consisting of large *tinajas*, pointing again to an increased role for brewing and storing beverages. Serving-ceremonial assemblages in the Putuni differed from those in the Akapana in certain respects. For example, only Putuni assemblages included *keros* and vasijas with Cochabamba style elements. However, relative to other residential areas, serving-ceremonial wares in both complexes comprised high proportions of entire assemblages, and large proportions of these were finely crafted and elaborately decorated.

As a whole, ceramic assemblages in new occupation complexes of Akapana East were significantly different from those in Putuni and especially Akapana. First, as in these areas, large *ollas* and *tinajas* comprised higher proportions of ceramic assemblages, and *escudillas*, while present, had declined in proportion to other serving wares. However, much higher proportions of serving-ceremonial types consisted of more crudely made and quickly treated or decorated variants. Some new forms, such as hand-molded *cuencos*, and the stylized decoration on others manifest the increasing popularity and stylistic synchretism of Cochabamba and standard Tiwanaku styles. Further, in Akapana East and in the urban periphery, as in smaller sites of the Tiwanaku Valley, most serving wares now displayed a more diluted orange to brown rather than red slip, and surfaces on most serving wares were more roughly burnished than they were on vessels associated with monumental complexes. A combination of new patterns, including the increasing rarity of polychrome redwares and the increasing synchretism of Cochabamba with more standard Tiwanaku elements, amounted to greater overall homogeneity among ceramic assemblages outside of the monumental core.

Transformation and Continuity in Tiwanaku: A Synthesis

Continuity in Urban Residential Patterns

Some aspects of residential life in Tiwanaku continued much as they had appeared in Tiwanaku IV. For example, despite significant changes in the constitution of ceramic assemblages, Tiwanaku ceramic style was highly conservative overall. Most assemblages displayed a similar technical style, they included a similar range of forms, and they depicted similar iconographic themes. Any stylistic changes were gradual rather than abrupt, and varied in expression from one residential sector to another.

Parallel with the conservative character of Tiwanaku ceramic style, all monumental and residential structures were built and reconstructed following the same orientation established centuries earlier. Ideological and visual linkages with celestial and terrestrial features remained a fundamental pillar of urban order, and tied the entire center into an encompassing sacred landscape framed by key cosmological features. Continuity in style and urban order highlights the conservative character of Tiwanaku culture and ideology. Although undoubtedly shifting in specific meanings and associations across generations of inhabitants, many characteristic principles of Tiwanaku's prestigious and apparently conservative worldview remained as they had been formulated centuries earlier. By now, after many successive generations, most of these principles had been internalized as practical hegemony; as a coherent and naturalized vision of the social and cosmological world.

Complementary patterns in any residential sector emphasized continuity in the local expressions of Tiwanaku culture, and in the local practices and values that linked each social group with the broader, more intensely hierarchical society. Groups continued to live in bounded compounds, distinguishing themselves from others as kin-based groups with unique social networks and identities, and often with specialized occupations. The continued vigor of the urban social boundaries established during or even before Tiwanaku IV is vividly expressed in the maintenance of local compound rituals. Groups continued to store and ingest mind-altering snuff, as well as host and participate in local ceremonies involving commensalism. They continued to bury fetal camelids under the floors and walls of residential buildings and activity areas, practicing rituals dedicated to the health, abundance, or well-being of the resident group. Many continued to bury deceased relatives under living areas, sometimes in discrete mortuary clusters. This was vividly represented under the patio of the new residential complex on top of the Akapana, with its distinctive arrangement of human interments. People desired to keep certain relatives and relict bundles close to home, within the bounded area that was home for the living. Each coresidential group, in essence, spanned multiple spiritual and corporal generations. Through mortuary practices and offerings, which emphasize the significance of emotional bonds and collective memory among local groups, group members sought social coherence and well-being for the present.

Change in Urban Residential Patterns

Nevertheless, by AD 800, the beginning of Early Tiwanaku V, Tiwanaku was changing significantly. What were the causes and trajectories of these changes? An elaborate residential complex was built on top of the Akapana sometime toward the end of Late Tiwanaku IV. It incorporated elaborate architectural elements and was associated with distinctive ceramic assemblages that included an array of elaborate vessels, such as recurved bowls. The configuration of subfloor burials expressed differences of status or role among the people who perhaps once inhabited the complex, by all accounts some of the prestigious religious practitioners and their attendants who directed major Tiwanaku ceremonies. Intriguingly, associated effigy *incensarios* allude to an affiliation with Katari, offering the possibility that some Tiwanaku high priests came from, or identified with, the priests and specific rituals conducted in that region.

In Putuni, a high status residential complex was razed and restructured as a monumental complex, a momentous process accompanied by complex dedication rites. In addition to elaborate architectural elements and abundant sumptuary objects, including recurved bowls, the clean living surfaces and efficient subterranean drainage network highlight the sense of purity, sanitation, and social and ritual distinction maintained by this resident group. These changes index a transition from relatively high rank to markedly different, institutionalized status. Together with evidence from the Akapana, they represent the emergence of an elite class and the crystallization of a rigidly defined social hierarchy in Tiwanaku. Kolata (1993a) argues that spatial and functional transformations in the city reflected the emergence of a Tiwanaku royal dynasty, an interpretation supported by Couture (Couture and Sampeck 2003). I would add that what we see is the emergence of both royal dynasties and elite castes of priests.

At roughly the same time, extensive sectors surrounding the urban core experienced massive renewal projects. In the north compound of Akapana East 1, an elaborate edifice focused around a sunken interior courtyard was constructed along the west edge of the moat. Architectural elements mimicked those in the Putuni complex and other monumental areas, as did the preparation and cleanliness of the floors and the presence of exotic and sumptuary goods. Conjoined patterns indicate that the edifice was the site of ceremonial activity associated to some extent with elites. The construction and use of the north compound points to the increasing extension of elite factions and their public activities and influence toward the edges of the urban core.

New residential patterns in Akapana East 1M, La Karaña, and Akapana East 1 present a range of new patterns, including large structures that were not strictly dwellings and a more diversified, organic spatial organization of activities. A key to understanding the deeper causes behind these urban transformations lies in Akapana East 1. Here, surrounding the north compound and its elaborate courtyard edifice were residential compounds and activities, most notably the extensive south compound. Considering Tiwanaku residential contexts as a whole, the south compound presented several unique patterns. First, a notable pattern in the kitchen structure was the appearance of a unique vessel form: a roasting bowl with opposing horizontal handles. Roasting grain mash for extended periods is an important phase in the process of producing *chicha* (Cutler and Cárdenas 1947). Moreover, archaeobotanical analysis revealed that *chenopodium* was present in great frequency and ubiquity throughout the compound. Maize was somewhat less common, but its kernel to cob ratio (2.23, N = 63) was far higher here than in any other area (Wright et al. 2003). This suggests that the unusual roasting bowl, like the contemporary *hiuk'i* vessel (Tschopik 1950:206), may have been used to roast quinoa or corn, and that corn itself entered the compound as previously shelled kernels. These patterns are parsimoniously explained if elites associated with the north compound, as the heads of a centralized redistribution system, provided corn for their neighbors, who, in turn, prepared and cooked corn and quinoa for mass or elite consumption.

At the same time, storage and fermentation vessels were becoming increasingly important throughout the urban core. Large *tinajas* with long narrow necks and opposing strap handles composed huge proportions of urban assemblages, far higher overall than they had in previous occupations. These are strikingly similar to the large *wakulla* jars that for centuries have been used to ferment and store *chicha* in Aymara communities (Janusek 2002b; Tschopik 1950:206–207). Further, they formed particularly high proportions of assemblages in areas where they were stored or used for commensal activities, such as the outdoor patio and corridor of the Akapana complex, the plaza west of the Putuni, the outdoor area in Akapana East 1M, and the corridor in the south compound of Akapana East 1.

These patterns along with the new spatial configuration of activities point to the likelihood that the south compound of Akapana East 1 was a locus for the production of *chicha* and food for elite-sponsored ceremonies. Unlike specialization in Ch'iji Jawira, production here was directly related to public, elite-sponsored ceremony. *Chicha* would have been served in ceremonies conducted in the attached courtyard edifice, and the corridor between the two compounds would have served as a preparation hall. A functional linkage between the two compounds explains the striking appearance of sumptuary and exotic goods in what is otherwise a vernacular residential complex. The social relationship between noble and retainer, forged in a time of increasing elite power, was clearly highly asymmetrical and most likely differentiated by class. As in later Andean societies, this relationship would have required periodic gestures of reciprocal patronage and gift-giving. Gifts of sumptuary and exotic goods helped forge asymmetrical social bonds framed in an ideology of reciprocity, but as in the rituals of consumption such gifts helped foster, they simultaneously fueled increasing social differentiation over the long term. Elaborate ceremonies in the courtyard edifice of Akapana East 1, as in the Putuni courtyard and in the Akapana, were sponsored by elite patrons. In sponsoring periodic ceremonies and giving sumptuary gifts, elite groups enhanced their disproportionate social power by effectively presenting themselves as generous, beneficent patrons. Though implicating the consent, participation, and skilled activities of the commons, competitive displays of wealth and mass consumption in such ceremonies disproportionately served the interests of competing elite factions.

The increasing role of ritualized, competitive feasting and drinking in Tiwanaku also helps explain the appearance in Akapana East 1 of structures with ephemeral, minimally trampled *apisonados.* In recent Andean pueblos (see Chapter 2), compounds inhabited by people with disproportionate access to wealth often have one or more auxiliary structures. In part, the auxiliary structures serve to accommodate guests and family members during important communal feasts and lifecycle festivals. In part, they also serve to store important objects or goods or serve as food preparation areas during feasts. By analogy, the small structures common in Akapana East during the Tiwanaku V Phase were used only temporarily, most specifically to house the great numbers of individuals who aided in food preparation and *chicha* production during important ceremonies. Most food preparation itself would have been done in the specialized kitchen structure.

There was a notable redundancy in the style and treatment of Tiwanaku vessels from AkE 1M and the south compound of AkE 1 during the Tiwanaku V Phase. In Tiwanaku as in smaller sites of the valley, most ceramic assemblages reflect an increasing emphasis on mass production and widespread distribution. The range of ceramic types and variants decreased overall, as many elaborate variants and production techniques became extremely uncommon (Janusek 2003a). In contrast, ceramic assemblages in the Akapana, the Putuni, and the north compound of Akapana East 1 were strikingly diverse and included high proportions of elaborate wares. Such differences imply greater control over the distribution of valued goods, and thus over the social and economic networks of many local groups. Most groups living far out in the urban periphery, meanwhile, used assemblages similar to those their ancestors had employed in Tiwanaku IV, but incorporating new stylistic patterns characteristic of the age.

Thus, interwoven with other changes, status differences increased sharply in Early Tiwanaku V. Following the reciprocal development of power relations in Tiwanaku IV, evidence from Tiwanaku and its immediate hinterland indicates that the balance of power in Tiwanaku V had shifted toward elites and state rulers. As discussed in Chapter 8, power relations were now manifested in a variety of ambitious state projects of reconstruction, productive intensification, and colonization in regions near and far. In Tiwanaku, the moat, which once encompassed most of the early city, now largely enclosed spaces serving an expanding and more powerful elite class. Among new constructions were monumental temples, palaces, elaborate courtyards associated with elite-sponsored ceremonies, and entire specialized residential compounds dedicated to the preparation and sponsorship of feasts. Although many of the groups who worked or resided in the core were not themselves of particularly high status, their daily activities revolved around elite needs and concerns.

Still, local practices and group identities continued to thrive and perhaps even solidify in the face of increasing state power. Urban sectors beyond the moat (e.g., Akapana East 2, Ch'iji Jawira) remained the province of semi-autonomous compound groups who had resided there in Late Tiwanaku IV, some of which still maintained local interaction networks and practiced embedded forms of craft production. Further, a notable increase in the number of small sites and clusters throughout the valley, and the increasing size of local centers, may reflect a simultaneous shift in population and power toward dispersed rural communities; a shift that accelerated after AD 1000. Such a shift would have strained the foundations of an increasingly centralized political economy (Mathews 1997). Even as social inequality intensified, spatial segmentation and social diversity remained elemental to Tiwanaku urban and rural society.

CHAPTER 8

Transformation in the Katari Valley and Beyond

Urban renewal in Tiwanaku and settlement expansion in the hinterland mark changes that were transforming the polity and much of the south-central Andes. Overall, in Early Tiwanaku V, the region witnessed the consolidation of a centralized state in which leaders promoted transformative policies of integration on a major scale. Not all areas once considered integral to Tiwanaku's spheres of influence were under Tiwanaku political authority. In fact, direct political and cultural hegemony in the Lake Titicaca Basin itself was selectively distributed, and even more selectively in distant, temperate valley regions. Tiwanaku was not a contiguous territorial state with hard national boundaries, but was rather a centralized polity characterized by discontinuous nodes of authority and strategic interaction or influence.

In the Katari Valley, a principal region of Tiwanaku hegemony, significant changes accompanied the reorganization of Tiwanaku's urban core. Based on excavations near Wila Kollu, Bermann (1994) first noted that changes in Lukurmata were somewhat anomalous. Rather than demographic growth, increasing complexity, and continuous occupation, Bermann found provocative evidence for the near abandonment of what until now had been Tiwanaku's second city. Recent research indicates that significant changes characterized not just Lukurmata but the entire Katari Valley. With its great potential for raised field production, the Katari region was now converted into one of the principal agricultural estates of the Tiwanaku realm. Still, changes in the polity as a whole were more complex than one would imagine.

This chapter first discusses Early Tiwanaku V period occupations at Lukurmata and changes in other sectors of the Katari Valley, and then discusses evidence for Tiwanaku hegemony in far regions of Tiwanaku's political and cultural sphere. First, I present evidence for Tiwanaku V residential activity at Lukurmata, focusing on the significance of community storage in Misiton 2. Next I discuss major changes in Katari Valley settlement networks and productive systems, followed by discussions of changes in two far regions; one in Tiwanaku's near periphery, on the Island of the Sun, and one in its far periphery, in the Moquegua Valley of Peru. Synthesizing strands of evidence drawn from vast regions, we find evidence for significant changes in Tiwanaku sociopolitical organization and imperial strategy that profoundly influenced life throughout the south-central Andes. The character and impact of such changes, I argue, established a historical trajectory that ultimately fostered Tiwanaku state collapse.

Lukurmata Residential Patterns

Willa Kollu, the Ridge, and K'atupata

Significant changes occurred at Lukurmata beginning around AD 800. The platform and sunken court of Wila Kollu may have become obsolete at this time, for there is no clear evidence for significant ritual activity in Tiwanaku V. Further, for the first time in centuries, the saddle just below Wila Kollu, the focus of Bermann's excavations, no longer was a major locus of dense residential occupation and activity. Inhabited by several clustered patio groups in Late Tiwanaku IV, the same area now comprised two burial clusters (Bermann 1994:220–223). About half of the burials were collared or capped with carved andesite blocks, precisely the kinds of blocks that would have fitted between larger blocks and pilasters of the nearby platform and sunken court. The use of blocks in local burial contexts indicates that at least some of the edifices were being dismantled and quarried by local residents (Bermann 1994:223). This in tandem with lack of evidence for Tiwanaku V ritual activity vividly demonstrates that Lukurmata's monumental complex was no longer a focus of ritual or political activity.

Excavations in other areas revealed indirect evidence for residential activity. Excavations just south of Wila Kollu revealed outdoor surfaces covered with stratified layers of midden (Bermann 1994:218–219). In K'atupata, refuse continued to collect at the north edge of the old platform, suggesting that the area to the south continued to be inhabited. Yet a dearth of evidence for primary residential occupation in Lukurmata indicates that far fewer areas were occupied in Tiwanaku V.

Specialized Storage in Misiton

Residential activity continued as before in a few excavated areas. The Misiton 1 neighborhood (or at least excavated sections of the neighborhood) was abandoned sometime in Early Tiwanaku V. As on the ridge, there is no clear evidence here for why or under what new conditions abandonment occurred, but the presence of bone flute caches on final living surfaces indicates that it occurred relatively rapidly, leaving many instruments in mid-production. Such a situation alludes to some trauma, whether for the group, the site, or the region. Just to the west, life went on in Misiton 2. In Early Tiwanaku V, or perhaps toward the end of Late Tiwanaku IV, a storage complex was built in the west compound, south of the circular dwelling. While the dwelling and the complex appear to have coexisted for a while, the circular dwelling was abandoned and eventually collapsed while the storage complex continued in use.

The storage complex bordered the edge of the large north-south foundation that divided Misiton 2 into two compounds (Figure 8.1). A smaller outer wall on its west side, consisting in part of ashlars and with a single entrance, sealed the complex from the rest of the compound. Storage structures rested on a prepared floor of red clay and they consisted of five small enclosures, set side by side, each with slightly different spatial or artifactual characteristics. Room 1, which bordered the outdoor area behind the dwelling, was a rectangular structure with cobble foundations standing two to three courses high. The surface inside contained domestic refuse, sherds of elaborate serving-ceremonial wares, and over three grams of fish bone. Room 3 was a smaller structure with a narrow entrance and stone foundations three courses high. Its floor also revealed domestic refuse, including broken implements for spinning and weaving cloth.

Rooms 4 and 5 were semisubterranean enclosures with stone foundations two to seven courses high. Each had a narrow opening, and that of room 4 was sealed with a cut stone block. The floor in each of these two rooms sank thirty to forty centimeters below the red clay floor of the complex. Although the enclosures were eventually converted into refuse deposits, the rooms must have originally served to store food goods such as tubers and grains, as similar subterranean chambers do in many contemporary communities.

Room 2 was distinct. A single entrance in the ashlar foundation facing the complex opened directly into this enclosure, which was much larger than the other rooms and included two small bins, one on either side of the entrance. Wall foundations stood three courses high. Scattered on the edges of the floor were ceramic sherds, camelid bones, lithic flakes, and a polishing stone. The floor yielded two severed long bone ends similar to by-product found in Misiton 1, and one of the bins yielded two severed ends and a broken tube. The patterns indicate that some people continued to make bone panpipes in Early Tiwanaku V, and that the storage complex was in some way linked to this craft.

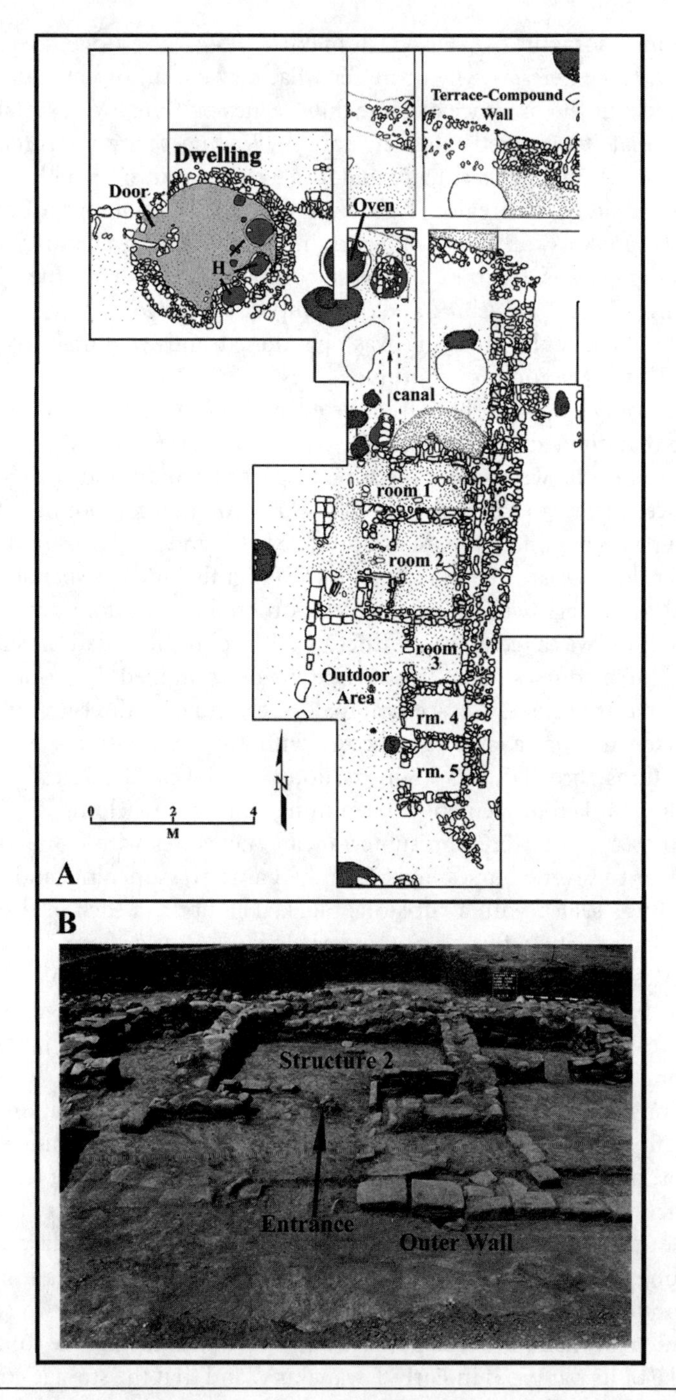

Figure 8.1 Plan (A) and view (B) of the storage complex in Misiton 2.

The floor outside of the enclosures contained two subterranean storage pits. Ceramic assemblages on the floor revealed relative high quantities of large cooking *ollas* and storage wares as well as high quantities of *kero* sherds (Janusek 1994). Refuse in front of rooms 1 and 2 contained abundant fish bone and two pieces of raw lapis lazuli. Refuse in front of rooms 3, 4, and 5 was more abundant, and it included broken weaving and polishing tools, butchered *cuy* bone, and again, high quantities of fish bone.

The size and linear arrangement of the complex, as well as its restricted access, support the idea that the complex served local storage. In layout and artifacts, Room 1 was similar to room 3, just as room 4 was to room 5. If the refuse inside of the first two rooms is any indication, some of the goods stored there included domestic supplies, but each structure had a distinct, complementary function. For instance, room 1 contained fish and ceramic vessels, while rooms 4 and 5 contained grains and tubers. Nevertheless, it is possible that many of the artifacts represent activities conducted by guardians of the complex or inhabitants of the dwellings around it.

Abundant recent research investigates the variety of ways in which storage is intimately tied to the political and economic organizations of past societies (D'Altroy and Earle 1985; Morris 1982; Levine 1992; Quilter and Stocker 1983; Smyth 1989). Storage can be differentiated as central, community, or domestic systems based on the social and economic relations in which they are embedded. Centralized polities with well-developed systems of redistribution, such as the later Inca state, required extensive central storage systems. In the Inca state, these were often massive complexes located in discrete sectors of a settlement (as in Huánuco Pampa, Morris and Thompson 1985) or outside of a settlement (as in Ollantaytambo, Protzen 1992). Inca central storage systems primarily served the elite class and its growing bureaucracies, and secondarily local populations in times of famine. Often located on prominent places outside of town, they simultaneously served as symbols of the state and the Sapa Inca, or unique ruler, in local regions.

Nevertheless, in complex incorporative polities like the Inca and Aztec states, in which much productive management was delegated to local groups, storage was required at various scales of society, and thus appeared in a variety of social and spatial contexts. Such appears to have been the case also in Chan Chan, the political and religious center of the Chimu polity on the north coast of Peru. Storage facilities here appeared in all types of social contexts, including walled elite compounds and in agglutinated residential barrios surrounding them. In the walled compounds that housed an elite group and its retainers, rows of storerooms were punctuated by large, formal *audiencia* structures, while in barrios storage facilities were associated with smaller, more vernacular *arcones.* Both *audiencias* and *arcones,* often raised on low platforms and strategically located in key access areas, were U-shaped enclosures incorporating varying numbers of bins. They are thought to have served as "supervisory structures" for administering the distribution of goods (Topic 1982:156, 2003; Klymyshyn 1982). While most *arcones* served domestic and community storage systems, *audiencias* headed storage systems that simultaneously served both central and community purposes.

The storage complex in Misiton 2 is similar in form to the barrio storage systems found in Chan Chan. Room 2 is laid out very much like an *arcon,* and may well have served some supervisory role for the complex. It was relatively large, slightly raised, and contained two internal bins, but most remarkably, it was located in front of the primary access to the complex. Quite possibly, it housed an individual who administered or guarded the storage structures. The location of the complex inside of the residential compound, and its association with domestic architecture indicates that the complex, much like the Tiwanaku IV circular structure in La K'araña, at Tiwanaku, served the resident social group as a community system. The refuse in and around the enclosures points to associated residential activities, such as broken musical instruments and their by-product, tools for weaving, and ceramic vessels for eating and drinking. Instruments, ceramics, and woven textiles may have been some of the goods that moved through the complex. Still, the form of rooms 4 and 5 and the presence of abundant fish remains indicate that cultivated food goods and lake resources also were among the resources temporarily stored in the complex. In light of changes occurring in the Katari Valley, discussed below, the construction of the storage complex may well have been linked to intensification in the collection and distribution of edible goods.

In this light, local storage and the distribution of goods undoubtedly served the broader state political economy. It is important to recall that the complex is located near a likely thoroughfare that leads directly to Tiwanaku. Location near the thoroughfare may explain why Misiton 2 remained important while other areas were abandoned or less intensively occupied. Residents may have been advantageously positioned to conduct exchanges or ship and receive goods to and from the Tiwanaku Valley. It is even possible that those who guarded the storage complex were local state functionaries. The group inhabiting the compound probably stored surplus food and durable goods over the dry season, to ward off famine. It is also likely, especially given the apparent close relation between this compound and the specialists in Misiton 1, that the storage complex at times pooled crops and goods collected form a number of related compounds, destined for redistribution to the broader community, region, or state.

The high frequency of *kero* sherds in local ceramic assemblages is striking. It is tempting to suggest that *keros* were pooled and distributed through the storage complex, but if such was the case it is unlikely that so many would be broken here. Rather, the pattern points to an important role for communal consumption, and especially drinking, in the area. The pattern is intriguing, and is reminiscent of the abundant drinking and storage vessels found around storage complexes in Huánuco Pampa, a major Inca regional administrative center where, among other roles, goods produced by local communities were pooled and stored (Morris and Thompson 1985). In the center of Huánuco Pampa, in fact spatially dominating the site, was a massive plaza dedicated to state-sponsored ceremonies and feasts. Shifting the analogy to a more intimate social scale, the high frequency of *keros* in Misiton 2, along with other evidence for consumption, may indicate that the storage complex was a central node in the redistribution of goods for a local neighborhood. Periodic events of filling and emptying storerooms, perhaps after laborers completed a quota or toward the end of a rainy season, may have been accompanied by local feasts sponsored by rotating local authorities or those for whom the goods were destined. To the extent such was the case, economic and ritual roles in the storage complex, as in many other social contexts, were intertwined.

Late Tiwanaku V Occupation in Misiton 2

Finally, a large structure was built over the old storage complex just after AD 1000, and it followed the same directional orientation (Janusek 1994). Prior to this event, the two subterranean rooms of the storage complex had been filled with ash and refuse, and the compound wall behind them leveled. A prepared floor of red clay was laid over the ruins of the complex, and it rose slightly over the large foundation. Between the structure and the terrace face to the north was a cobble pavement, set into which was an intricate drainage system.

The structure consisted of two rooms—a kitchen and a large room. Dominating the kitchen was a cluster of three hearths surrounded by *olla* sherds and splintered camelid bones. Similar to many Tiwanaku dwellings and contemporary houses, the hearths included both a deep oven and shallow fire pits. The oven was formed of baked adobe bricks and had a mouth fitted with a broken *olla*, while the shallower fire pits were filled with charcoal, camelid dung, and gray ash. The other room had a prepared floor and yielded high proportions of serving-ceremonial and large *tinaja* sherds. The size of the room and its associated artifacts are reminiscent of the large structure and outdoor area of the Early Tiwanaku V occupation in Akapana East 1M. Like this area of Tiwanaku, cooking, consumption, and the production and storage of fermented drinks may have been among some of the key activities conducted in Misiton 2. The room also contained abundant butchered camelid remains, as well as several artifacts associated with the production of camelid bone panpipes. The latter included two tuning segments, two fragmented flutes, and several severed long bone ends. Apparently, the room served in part as a work place or storage area associated with the production of bone panpipes, indicating that this type of specialized production continued, if perhaps at a smaller scale, long after Misiton 1 had been abandoned.

Associated with the structure, a well provided access to fresh water and several ash and refuse pits contained the detritus of domestic activities. Associated ceramic assemblages included a variety of *ollas*, including high volume pear-shaped *ollas*, large storage and fermentation *tinajas*, and serving wares, predominantly *tazons*, *keros*, and *vasijas*. Iconography included combinations of standard Tiwanaku and Cochabamba style elements, as did Tiwanaku V assemblages in Tiwanaku. New Lukurmata style wares also were common, and they included orange-hued tanwares with rectilinear volutes and undecorated *tazons*.

Settlement Shift and Agricultural Intensification in the Katari Valley

Changes in Lukurmata in Early Tiwanaku V appear paradoxical, especially in relation to changes simultaneously taking place in Tiwanaku. There, a conjunction of transformations reflects the increasing power, wealth, and influence of ruling elites. Precisely during this phase, many residential compounds in Lukurmata, two of which had been occupied for centuries, were abandoned or dedicated to interments and middens. Simultaneously, however, we see an increasing role for community storage, and an intensified scale of local collection and distribution for a wide range of edible and other goods. Changes occurring in the surrounding Katari Valley and in certain areas of the near and far periphery offer a better understanding of changes in Lukurmata.

Major transformations were occurring throughout the Katari Valley. Lukurmata was not the only major site to experience a dramatic decline in occupation and residential activity. The site of Qeyakuntu, settled in the lower piedmont zone eleven to twelve kilometers southeast of Lukurmata, experienced a similar decline (Figure 6.1) (Janusek and Kolata 2003). Occupations dating to Tiwanaku IV included a residential sector associated with ritual activity and monumental construction. By Early Tiwanaku V, monumental construction had ceased and the residential area, like that on the ridge in Lukurmata, was now dedicated solely to human interments. Interment, cranial modification, and ceramic assemblages still presented patterns characteristic of Lukurmata and the Katari region. Burial cists were lined with cobbles and slabs, interred individuals practiced annular cranial modification, and ceramic assemblages, even those employed as burial offerings, included Lukurmata style wares. Nevertheless, residential density had declined. Surface collections from other major towns and villages in the piedmont, in addition, revealed much higher proportions of Tiwanaku IV sherds than Tiwanaku V sherds.

Human settlement in Katari changed in other significant ways. For one thing, many small settlements in the pampa zone became more important in Tiwanaku V. They included the Quiripujo Mound Group (Figure 6.1), a cluster of sites located near the elbow of the Katari River (Janusek and Kolata 2003). These sites had been intensively occupied during the Late Formative period, with substantial residential and ritual structures associated with a variety of productive activities, including cultivation, fishing, and some herding. Excavations indicated that they were reoccupied again in Early Tiwanaku V. However, occupation no longer consisted of substantial buildings, but the remains of movable tentlike structures. These appear strikingly similar to the temporary, tarp-covered wooden and reed structures used by contemporary field guardians, or *kamani* (Kolata 1991; Winterhalder and Thomas 1978). A rotating position, *kamani* are charged with guarding crops against theft, predation, and through various ritual practices, hail and frost. The apparent importance of similar occupations in the Koani Pampa indicates an increasing concern with success in farming in Tiwanaku V.

Results of excavations conducted in raised field contexts of the pampa zone supported this settlement pattern (Figure 8.2) (Janusek and Kolata

Figure 8.2 View of the Koani Pampa showing visible fossil raised fields.

2003; Seddon 1994). Raised fields were encountered in forty-six percent of the nearly 200 excavations trenches excavated across the pampa. Of fourteen radiocarbon samples derived from strata associated with construction or use in these fields, nine (sixty-four percent) of them dated to Tiwanaku V. In line with evidence from the Quiripujo Mound Group, this indicates that raised field cultivation in the Katari Valley increased precipitously during this phase, especially after AD 900. By all accounts, the Katari Basin was being transfigured as a prime agricultural estate of the Tiwanaku core.

Transformation in the Peripheries

Tiwanaku Occupation on the Island of the Sun

Changes occurring in Katari are further clarified when viewed in relation to shifting mosaics of Tiwanaku influence and control in several more distant regions. Evidence with powerful implications for understanding changes in Lukurmata and the Katari Valley comes from intensive research in other regions incorporated into Tiwanaku's sphere of cultural, religious, and political hegemony. Areas of Tiwanaku influence outside of the two-valley core can be considered peripheral regions, and they can be geographically divided, somewhat concentrically, into a near and far periphery (Stanish 2003). Roughly, most of the rest of the Lake Titicaca basin can be considered the near periphery, and many valley areas beyond, such as Moquegua to the west and Cochabamba to the east, can be considered the far periphery. However, overall Tiwanaku influence was strategic rather than territorial, and it concentrated in settlements and regions with particular economic, political, or ritual significance.

Research on the Island of the Sun, near Copacabana in the southern part of Lake Titicaca, indicates that the nature and intensity of Tiwanaku influence changed dramatically between AD 750 and 850, precisely when major transformations were occurring in the core (Figure 8.3). In this case, state hegemony was intensified in relation to the ritual significance of the place. Under the Inca and at the time of Spanish contact, the Island of the Sun was a major pilgrimage center (Bandelier 1911; Bauer and Stanish 2001). The principal focus of Inca myth, ritual, and ceremonial pilgrimage was a bounded sanctuary at the north end of the island, which harbored the Sacred Rock known as Titikala, or Stone of the Puma. Inca myths held that it was from this stone that the sun rose for the first time (Bauer and Stanish 2001:196). Survey and excavation indicated that the island had been inhabited since around 2000 BC, during the Late Archaic period, and then first became a major focus of social and ritual activity during the Tiwanaku Period. During this time, discrete Late Formative clusters of relatively small sites disappeared as settlements both increased in number and populations

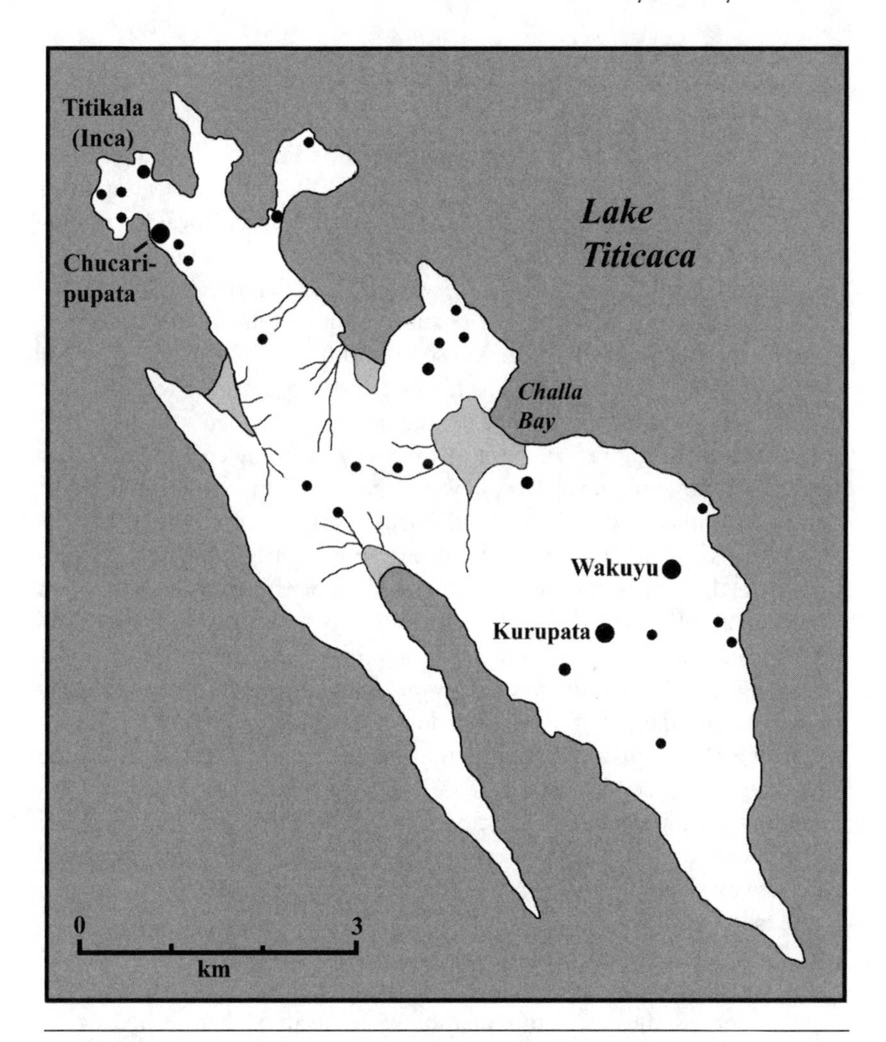

Figure 8.3 Tiwanaku V Period settlement patterns on the Island of the Sun (adapted from Bauer and Stanish 2001).

nucleated into large towns and centers (Bauer and Stanish 2001:149). Settlement became more hierarchical as political centralization intensified, and one of the most important new centers, located in a saddle just southeast of the Sacred Rock, was Chucaripupata.

Excavations by Seddon (1998) at Chucaripupata indicated that, while first occupied during the Late Formative, it became a major settlement during the Tiwanaku Period. Tiwanaku Period activity intensified over two sequential occupations. The first, dating from AD 600–800 (Seddon 1998:510) and coincident with Late Tiwanaku IV, revealed strata and features with Tiwanaku style ceramic assemblages, including elaborate serving wares associated with ritual consumption. Ceramic assemblages included both locally crafted and imported Tiwanaku vessels. Most striking, however, Tiwanaku-style wares were common only in specialized features, such as tombs and refuse pits that "appear to represent cleanup from feasting events" (Seddon 1998:245). In surrounding strata, local forms predominated. Further, tombs and storage structures were built in local styles dissimilar to those known from the Tiwanaku and Katari Valleys.

Occupation in Chucaripupata changed dramatically in the following occupation, which dated between AD 800 and 1000, or Tiwanaku V. An upper terrace previously characterized by feasting and consumption was enclosed by a massive retaining wall that simultaneously bounded and restricted access to a small interior portion of the site, effectively creating an inner sanctum. A large platform temple was constructed inside. It consisted of earth fill bounded by revetments of upright slabs alternating with larger sections of smaller fitted stones. Built in characteristic Tiwanaku architectural style, the structure mimicked other known platform structures, and in particular the Kalasasaya (Seddon 1998:361). Around it were higher proportions of valued crafted goods, including metals, turquoise beads, and a wide range and high frequency of Tiwanaku serving-ceremonial wares. On a lower terrace flanking the ritual enclosure, a residential structure was associated with ceramic assemblages that demonstrated affiliation with the Tiwanaku core. Seddon (1998:363) indicates that "Chucaripupata still maintained a certain local character," expressed in details of monumental construction and elements of ceramic style. Rather than being occupied *en masse* by populations from the Tiwanaku core, the settlement, now an important ritual locus, housed local populations who *affiliated with* the core. Tiwanaku state forms were not imposed by colonization or military force but rather were adopted among local populations (Seddon 1998:365).

Nevertheless, the nature of affiliation with Tiwanaku had shifted significantly, as the degree of interaction with the core, and thus cultural and religious influence from Tiwanaku, intensified. Simultaneous with changes witnessed at Chucaripupata, the Island of the Sun witnessed a "total reorganization of settlement" (Seddon 1998:367; also Bauer and Stanish 2001). While Chucaripupata emerged as a ritual center at the north end of the island, the site of Wakuyu may have become a primary political center at its south end. Linking the two sites, and facilitating pilgrimage to Chucaripupata for people visiting the island from the mainland, was a new road that followed the island's predominant north-south axis. Thus, after AD 800, the Island of the Sun became an integrated province of the Tiwanaku state, with road networks linking major centers and facilitating pilgrimage to a precocious ceremonial site.

Tiwanaku Occupation in Moquegua, Peru

Tiwanaku incorporated or interacted intensively with many regions far outside of the Lake Titicaca Basin, including the Cochabamba region southeast of the altiplano (Anderson and Céspedes 1998; Céspedes 2000), Azapa in northern Chile (Berenguer and Dauelsberg 1989), and Moquegua in southern Peru (Goldstein 1989, 1993). Most such regions are valley zones lower in altitude and more seasonal in climate than the altiplano, and thus amenable to producing a variety of goods—ají peppers, fruits, coca, and especially maize—to complement the rather limited range of staples available in the altiplano. In such valleys, interaction is generally considered to have been most intensive from AD 700 to 1000. Most substantial archaeological research has been conducted in the Moquegua region of the Osmore drainage, a warm, relatively small valley (900–2000 meters above sea level) surrounded by arid sierra deserts almost three hundred kilometers from the Tiwanaku core.

Abundant research in the Moquegua middle valley indicates that Tiwanaku maintained close interaction with the Osmore region, an interaction that intensified significantly after AD 800 (Figure 8.4). Interaction and trade in exotic goods had linked Moquegua with the altiplano since at least the local Late Formative, or the local Huaracane Period, driven

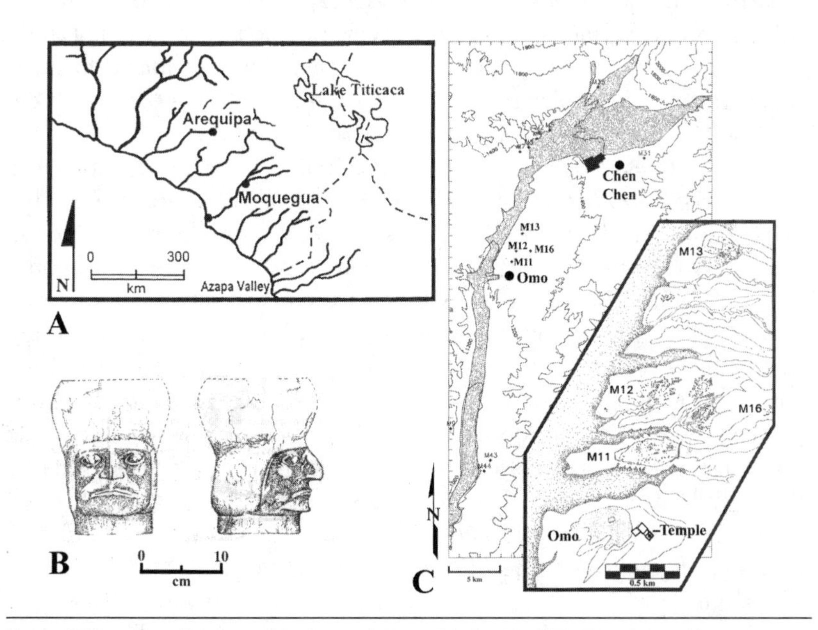

Figure 8.4 Location of Moquegua in the south-central Andes (A), a blackware vessel from the region (B), and location of Omo and Chen Chen among other Tiwanaku sites in the Moquegua Valley (B adapted from Goldstein 1989; C adapted from Goldstein 1993).

by the status-seeking strategies of local leaders and culture brokers (Goldstein 2000). However, interaction intensified qualitatively during the following Omo phase, roughly contemporaneous with Tiwanaku IV, when Tiwanaku apparently established a series of small colonies in the middle valley (Goldstein 1989). By far most ceramic serving-ceremonial vessels at these sites consisted of Tiwanaku-related assemblages, dominated by *keros* and cylindrical-neck storage and fermentation *tinajas* that were similar to those in the altiplano.

Like assemblages associated with Cochabamba and Katari, however, assemblages in Moquegua were very different from those in the altiplano (Goldstein 1989). For example, blackware vessels, including elaborate portrait vessels and *keros*, accounted for extremely high proportions of serving wares, suggesting that Moquegua was their home region (Figure 8.4B). Blackware vessels never accounted for more than five percent of any serving-ceremonial assemblage in Tiwanaku or Lukurmata. Also common were front-face *keros* depicting impassive deity faces, an iconographic motif common only on stone sculptures in the cultural heartland. Typical local forms included "coca-cola" glass *keros* with bulbous bodies, and iconography included reticulated designs and stylized birds—designs that, overall, were uncommon in the altiplano. Interestingly, certain patterns reminiscent of Katari, including the presence of feline effigy *incensarios* and continuous volutes on *vasijas*, suggest that some specific interaction network linked the two regions. In general, though, Moquegua-Tiwanaku assemblages formed a coherent stylistic complex that characterized this temperate region and distinguished it from others in Tiwanaku's sphere of influence.

Multiple lines of research in Moquegua indicate that Tiwanaku interaction and colonization intensified after AD 800, in the local Chen Chen phase (Goldstein 1989, 1993). At the site of Omo, on a bluff overlooking the valley, a temple complex was built consisting of a sequence of courts (Figure 8.4C). It consisted of a large public court that provided movement into a higher, middle court and, finally, toward a staircase leading into a smaller upper court with a small sunken enclosure in its center (Goldstein 1993). In the upper court, foundations of carved ashlar blocks, which supported a series of small rooms surrounding the sunken enclosure, rested on a clay floor that capped the terraced platform. Although associated contexts were relatively clean, they yielded assemblages with high proportions of ritual vessel sherds, including *sahumadors*, effigy *incensarios*, and most unusual, an offering cache of smashed miniature jars. Like temples in Tiwanaku, movement through the complex was a procession from more public, open space toward more intimate, increasingly sacred inner sancta (Goldstein 1993:42). Nevertheless, many specific elements of temple design, including a circular structure in the lower court, and associated activities, such as the dedication of miniature jars, alludes to the distinct local character of associated ritual activities and religious principles.

Several kilometers up the valley, the extensive site of Chen Chen became important at this time (Figure 8.4C) (Goldstein 1989; Owen 1997). Covering thirty hectares of arid desert, the site served highly specific roles in the region. It incorporated a ritual sector consisting of small ritual enclosures associated with spondylus beads and, again, concentrations of miniature vessels (Bandy et al. 1996). Also present were extensive residential sectors. Dwellings flanking the central part of the site were apparently occupied seasonally, quite possibly by rotating laborers. Closer to the site center were more permanently occupied dwellings associated with high quantities of ground stone implements for grinding grains. Most striking, near the dwelling area was a massive complex incorporating as many as 7500–11,000 storage cists, regularly arranged in rows and consisting of two standardized forms; bell-shaped pits lined with cobbles and cylindrical cists lined with cobbles in clay mortar (Bandy et al. 1996).

Also striking were thousands of burials organized into several discrete cemeteries, many set on a high ridge overlooking the site (Blom 1999; Owen 1997; Vargas 1994). Bioarchaeological analysis has revealed several significant patterns relating to the interred populations (Blom 1999; Blom et al. 1998; Tomczak 2001). First, dental and isotope analyses indicated that local populations consumed high quantities of maize. In light of other evidence from Chen Chen, this indicates that a primary function of the site was processing and storing maize. Second, nonmetric traits revealed extremely minimal biodistance measurements among local populations, those from Tiwanaku, and those from Katari. This datum confirms the hypothesis that such sites represented Tiwanaku colonies rather than, as on the Island of the Sun, local populations who affiliated with or were incorporated into Tiwanaku. Third, all local populations practiced the tabular or flattened style of cranial modification, a style that was common in Tiwanaku, if among other styles, and rare in Katari.

Moquegua clearly was an important region in Tiwanaku's far periphery, and became increasingly important in Early Tiwanaku V. Principal roles for the region at large included producing, storing, and processing maize. Chen Chen itself appears to have been dedicated to maize processing, undoubtedly in large part for shipment and distribution to the altiplano, where maize in general does not grow. Omo, meanwhile, became important as a local focus of worship, ritual activity, and politics. Ritual practices, ceramic styles, and abundant Tiwanaku-related patterns served to distinguish local populations from others in the region, on the coast, in nearby valleys, and perhaps in Moquegua itself. Nevertheless, Moquegua populations, some of whom apparently immigrated from the altiplano, maintained local practices and styles that expressed a clear regional identity in relation to highland populations. These included certain local ritual practices, ceramic assemblages, and a predominant style of body modification.

Strategic Incorporation and Local Continuity

An emerging perspective synthesizing ongoing research in the south-central Andes portrays Tiwanaku regional hegemony as highly strategic and discontinuous. While areas such as the Island of the Sun and Moquegua formed key areas of Tiwanaku power and influence, as regions incorporated into or colonized by the state, other areas indicate that Tiwanaku hegemony was highly flexible and complex. In the northern Lake Titicaca Basin, for example, local ethnic-like groups and polities thrived independent of Tiwanaku near local Tiwanaku centers (Stanish 2003). While the Puno Bay was closely affiliated with Tiwanaku, as strikingly expressed in a monumental platform complex on Estevez Island, regions north and south of the Bay have revealed little evidence for direct interaction with the state core. The northwestern basin, near the Late Formative center of Pukara, was home to an independent formation that succeeded the polity (Stanish 2003). Thus, in the Lake Titicaca Basin itself, Tiwanaku leaders established strategically located enclaves of political control, intensive production, and economic interaction.

Strategic hegemony was even more pronounced in more distant valleys, where Tiwanaku colonization and incorporation emphasized specific types of productive environments. While warm western Andean valleys such as Azapa, Chile, may also have housed small Tiwanaku colonies, others show little evidence for intensive interaction with the Lake Titicaca Basin. Just as significant, direct Tiwanaku influence in the Osmore drainage itself was limited to the Moquegua midvalley where maize grows best. No Tiwanaku sites are found on the coast (Owen 1993) and only a few are known in the less temperate upper valley, which at least until AD 800 was under Wari state control (Williams and Nash 2002). In eastern Andean valleys as well, Tiwanaku appears to have colonized the highly productive Cochabamba Valley (Anderson and Céspedes 1998; Céspedes 2000), while smaller nearby valleys regions such as Capinota remained the province of local social and political developments (Higueras-Hare 1996). Further south, in the Chuquisaca region, were drier valleys that supported independent local polities that interacted and traded with Tiwanaku-affiliated groups in the Titicaca Basin (Janusek et al. 1995). In short, Tiwanaku enclaves in the far peripheries, whether colonies or incorporated regions, were established in temperate areas where specific agricultural crops, and particularly maize, could be grown in abundance.

Transformations in Lukurmata, Katari, and Beyond: A Synthesis

Clearly, the Tiwanaku polity transformed profoundly after AD 800. In Katari, major settlements such as Lukurmata and Qeyakuntu experienced decreasing residential density just as monumental construction ceased and associated ritual activity declined. Simultaneously, specialized storage complexes in Lukurmata, in tandem with an increasing intensity of raised field production in the Koani Pampa, highlight an increasing concern with the production, distribution, and storage of cultivated goods. Associated with raised field systems in the Koani Pampa were numerous canals, dikes, and other hydrological features. It is likely that most were built or enlarged at this time to form a linked, integrated system dedicated to the production of tubers and quinoa on fieldbeds while fostering ideal microenvironments for lake birds and aquatic resources in intervening swales (Kolata 1986).

Meanwhile, changes in certain sectors of the near and far periphery point to intensification of state influence and the consolidation of Tiwanaku-affiliated regions and colonies as integrated provinces. On the Island of the Sun and in Moquegua this simultaneously involved the construction or enlargement of civic structures that incorporated specific elements of spatial design and ritual activity characteristic of monumental constructions in core political and ritual centers. Intensification of Tiwanaku influence on the Island of the Sun indicates increasing Tiwanaku ritual hegemony in certain areas of the Lake Titicaca basin. Complementing new ceremonial spaces and activities in Moquegua was a clear intensification of specialized production. Parallel with changes in Katari, the increasing importance of Chen Chen manifests an increasing concern with the production, processing, and distribution of cultivated goods, in particular maize. Producing maize and other goods with great social and ritual significance, such as coca, was a prime motive for establishing an array of far enclaves. The striking cultural and genetic affiliation between Moquegua and core Tiwanaku populations indicates that much of such lowland products were destined for the altiplano.

Productive intensification in the core and beyond was coincident with a major urban overhaul in Tiwanaku itself. A thorough reconstruction of the urban core demonstrated the increasing influence of Tiwanaku elites, as well as the increasing importance of commensalism. Combined evidence correlates remarkably well. Entire sectors of the Tiwanaku urban core were converted into specialized residential sectors, courts, or plazas dedicated to the production and performance of ritual feasting events. These areas were directly associated with Tiwanaku elite groups, which were growing in size, status, and number. Much of the impetus behind intensified production in the core and in the peripheries was the subsidization of major elite-sponsored feasting events conducted in the heartland. In Tiwanaku, botanical remains from Akapana East 1 and Putuni both indicate that such feasts involved highland crops such as tubers and quinoa, grown in altiplano raised fields, as well as lowland crops such as maize, grown and processed in colonized valleys such as Moquegua. Ceramic artifacts, including large quantities of massive fermentation *tinajas*, indicate that alcoholic beverages were an important part of elite-sponsored feasts. Such drinks included *kusa*, fermented from maize processed in colonies such as Moquegua, and *ch'ua*, fermented from quinoa grown in the altiplano. Huge quantities of such crops apparently were produced, partially processed, and temporarily stored in local regions such as Katari and Moquegua, from where they were periodically transported to Tiwanaku via trains of llama caravans.

Just as Tiwanaku leaders were implementing a range of transformative strategies of production and sociopolitical organization in various regions, Tiwanaku political economy was becoming a feasting economy. That is, a great deal of intensive farming and specialized food processing supported elite and state-sponsored feasts in Tiwanaku, as well as local rituals of consumption conducted in urban compounds and rural settlements throughout the core region. Communal consumption became an increasingly important part of life in Tiwanaku, and clearly an important domain of interaction among elite and nonelite groups. Like Andean *markas* but on a much larger scale, Tiwanaku more than ever before was now a center of social and ceremonial convergence. Tiwanaku's population must have exploded and contracted cyclically, pulsating with periodic ceremonies when the city transformed into a center of lively festival, social gathering, and economic interaction.

Why did commensalism become such a critical and ubiquitous part of culture and social interaction at this time? Several hypotheses can be forwarded. Environmental shift is one possible explanation, but there is no clear evidence for a major change at this time. Traditionally, the establishment of colonies in Moquegua in Tiwanaku V has been interpreted as a reaction to interregional political and economic crises (Browman 1981; Goldstein 1989). Browman considers colonization a reaction to the loss of key economic markets and trading partners, such as the Cochabamba Valley and the Wari state. However, there is no clear evidence for interaction between Tiwanaku and Wari outside of tense coexistence and possible military encounters in Moquegua (Moseley et al. 1991; Williams and Nash 2002), and there is to date no evidence for a shift in Tiwanaku influence or control in the Cochabamba region. Although it is conceivable that environmental and interregional political shift played some role in ongoing change, neither fully explain the increasing role and power of Tiwanaku elites or the increasing social role of commensalism.

A broader explanation draws attention to the social and cultural milieu in which transformations were occurring. Urban residential areas in Tiwanaku and Lukurmata in Tiwanaku IV manifested a tense balance of local and state power, a balance that was shifting decisively toward the state as high status groups crystallized into competing elite-led factions. Rites of consumption fostered an immediate sense of Tiwanaku community (Turner 1969), but they also remained important tournaments for competitive generosity and status negotiation among local groups, as they do in the Andes today and crossculturally. Perhaps more important, commensalism was critical for maintaining some ideal of reciprocity between elites and nonelite constituencies as elite power increased and status differences solidified. This is most clearly represented in the juxtaposition of specialized compounds in Akapana East, Tiwanaku. Much elite-sponsored ceremonial feasting was most likely motivated in part by faction-building and the desire to curry support among nonelites. By continually hosting such events, wealthy groups grew wealthier, more prestigious, and more powerful. Gestures of reciprocity enacted in feasts served to solidify relations of inequality in the face of increasing competition among elite factions, just as state strategies were seriously straining the etiquette of accepted social relations.

Regional changes in the Katari Valley, including the decline of Lukurmata, point to profound disruptions in local social organizations and economic networks. In light of other evidence, several reasons for these changes can be proposed. As Tiwanaku leaders transformed the Koani Pampa into an integrated, state-managed agricultural estate, settlement shifted as residential populations moved, perhaps forcibly, to sites best located to manage and work intensive agricultural systems (also Bermann 1994:332–333). As productive emphasis shifted from lake to agricultural resources, Lukurmata, best located to balance these two elements of Tiwanaku political economy, became less important. Lakaya, adjacent to the largest expanse of the cultivated pampa, and at the source of both a valley route that leads directly to Tiwanaku and an extensive transpampa causeway, most likely emerged as a key regional center.

Nevertheless, not only was Lakaya far less extensive than Lukurmata, other major Katari towns were declining as well. This suggests that some local inhabitants had left the region. Declining overall settlement density may mark local dissatisfaction with increasing state control, and possibly, state appropriation of productive systems in the region may have fostered social conflict and emigration. More likely, the decline in population density represents a strategic, elite-directed movement of local populations to other regions, as a resettlement and colonization policy similar to that instituted by Inca rulers several centuries later. In this scenario Tiwanaku rulers, as an astute political strategy, moved local populations with generations of experience as professional farmers, but also with strong local ties and a vigorous ethnic-like identity, to new agricultural colonies. In order to directly control the region, Tiwanaku rulers undoubtedly needed to break up or resettle social groups with vibrant identities and shared memories tied to the landscape and its resources. Until AD 800 local groups and settlement networks, though certainly transformed, were left intact as part of Tiwanaku's incorporative regional strategy. Establishing direct control in Tiwanaku V required a major restructuring of Tiwanaku political strategy, regional settlement organization, and local social dynamics.

The autochthonous population remaining in the valley may not have been large enough to provide the labor necessary for intensive raised field production in all segments of the agricultural cycle. Most likely it was of sufficient size to maintain field systems throughout most of the year, but perhaps not during peak times in the productive cycle, such as planting and harvest, which would have required massive work parties for relatively sort spans. At those times Tiwanaku or local regional authorities would have conscripted the service of rotating laborers, drawn from both local and nonlocal populations, and perhaps from the Tiwanaku Valley. At other times of the cycle many agricultural functions could have been left to rotating field guardians.

Residential occupation and activity in the Katari Valley now largely revolved around the requirements of an intensive, centrally managed productive economy. Local, strategically located storage complexes like that in Misiton 2 facilitated the collection and distribution of crops and other goods. Many other areas may represent temporary occupations for conscripted work parties. As on *kamani* mounds, temporary living quarters would have created the light middens and ephemeral surfaces now common at Lukurmata and Qeyakuntu. The Late Tiwanaku V structure in Misiton 2, which was similar in certain respects to Early Tiwanaku V structures in Akapana East 1, may have housed permanent or temporary rotating laborers. Rotating labor parties may have inhabited sites around the pampa, where they inhabited similar structures. Abundant food and sponsored feasts involving Tiwanaku serving and storage wares would have maintained morale and fostered an ideal of reciprocity between leaders and laborers. In the face of profound productive reorganization and sociopolitical transformation, in fact in part to subsidize and legitimize such state-directed changes, feasting reproduced the state system.

Still, local social identity and specific regional affiliations remained fundamental to Tiwanaku political economy and sociopolitical organization.

This is apparent in Tiwanaku outside of the restructured urban core, where life in local compounds continued much as before. It is even apparent at Lukurmata and other Katari sites, where local styles and practices continued even as new local styles emerged. Research at sites beyond the Tiwanaku core emphasizes the significance of local identity and affiliation alongside and within the ambit of Tiwanaku state enclaves. On the Island of the Sun, residents at Chucaripupata combined Tiwanaku-style material culture with an array of local materials and ritual practices. In Moquegua, residents of enclaves such as Omo and Chen Chen produced unique ceramic complexes, practiced local rituals in Tiwanaku-style temples, and practiced a specific style of body modification. Despite transformative strategies of state organization, the foundations of power remained firmly embedded in local practices, interaction networks, and social affiliations.

The clash of state and local interests in Katari and its significance in the social history of the polity should not be underestimated. With a history antedating state hegemony by several centuries, Lukurmata had been Tiwanaku's second city and the center of a highly lucrative and powerful region. Inhabitants of the Katari region maintained a distinct identity despite being an integral part of, and perhaps a complementary moiety within, the Tiwanaku core. The reorganization of Katari, and the decline of Lukurmata, was highly strategic and served to increase state productive potential and break up the local sociopolitical hierarchy. For several generations, new state strategies of production and centralized control were successful in facilitating elite power and feeding the state's massive political economy. However, alongside ongoing changes in settlement choices in the Tiwanaku Valley, the reorganization of Katari fostered a trajectory that ultimately tied into state collapse.

CHAPTER 9
State Collapse and Cultural Revolution

The decades following AD 1000 were among the most dynamic in the history of the southern Lake Titicaca basin. Late Tiwanaku V was a long, chaotic phase, and by AD 1150 Tiwanaku had been submitted to history. Like the disappearance of many civilizations, Tiwanaku collapse has fostered substantial speculation. Early ideas focused on the harsh local environment. Many early travelers and investigators considered Tiwanaku florescence to be miraculous, and thus its ultimate demise rather inevitable. As it turns out, environmental shift appears to have played a key part in Tiwanaku's disappearance. Recent paleo-environmental research reveals convincing evidence for a major shift in climate after AD 1000 (Baker et al. 2001; Binford et al. 1997; Ortloff and Kolata 1993). However, rather than interpreting collapse as the direct result of drought, in this chapter I investigate its role in catalyzing long-term social tensions and ongoing sociopolitical and demographic changes.

A view commonly held among ethnohistorians and some linguists is that Tiwanaku collapse was the product of Aymara immigration into the region (see Chapter 3). According to Espinoza (1980), Tiwanaku was a Pukina civilization that succumbed to waves of Aymara groups, which for Torero (1970, 1987) migrated into the region from Ayacucho, Peru. In light of the profound social diversity and vibrant local identities that characterized Tiwanaku throughout its history, these reconstructions of Lake Titicaca basin's prehistory appear unnecessarily static and untenable. It is more likely that different language groups coexisted in the region for centuries, as

Browman and Kolata suggest, and that Tiwanaku itself comprised diverse social groups that spoke different, and perhaps in some cases multiple, languages and dialects.

In this chapter, I examine the transition from Tiwanaku to Pacajes society and culture. First, I discuss evidence for residential decline, as well as the abandonment and destruction of monuments and icons, in Tiwanaku and Lukurmata. I then discuss post-Tiwanaku occupation and culture by examining evidence from historical documents, material culture, and settlement patterns. I conclude that Tiwanaku state fragmentation was the combined result of human agency and extrasocial forces. It was characterized by new political affiliations, productive strategies, and cultural practices. It also involved profound continuities, such as the resurgence of an ancient regional boundary of great social, ecological, and ideological significance between the Tiwanaku and Katari Valleys. Collapse was a volatile historical juncture that arose out of cumulative social practices and tensions in the face of shifting environmental, economic, and sociopolitical conditions.

Tiwanaku collapse was in part the product of a long-term trajectory in the development of power relations in which social tensions have intensified over generations. Rather than focusing on external forces as causal catastrophes, I consider the complex manners in which regional environmental and sociopolitical forces helped deflate once-sacred cultural symbols, erode once commonly held ideological values and a sense of state as community, and further exacerbate existing social tensions. Further, I shift the focus from collapse as the end of a civilization or great tradition to collapse as a cultural revolution that fostered an entirely new and equally significant range of practices and ideals. Rather than collapse in a static or absolute sense, this historical juncture was the outcome, in part, of generations of intentional actions and culturally informed practices. Collapse involved both sociopolitical fragmentation and the emergence of a new suite of symbols, values, and practices. As much as a "decline and fall" or the death of a great tradition, state collapse was simultaneously a dramatic and fascinating process of cultural genesis.

Onset of Drought

Recent models of Tiwanaku state collapse attribute partial cause to a long-term drought that began in the eleventh century and lasted several hundred years (Binford et al. 1997; Kolata and Ortloff 1996; Kolata et al. 2000; Moseley 1997; Ortloff and Kolata 1993). Lake cores taken in Lake Wiñaymarka (Abbott et al. 1997; Binford et al. 1997), the southern portion of Lake Titicaca, and ice cores taken in the Quelccaya glacier of southern Peru

(Thompson et al. 1985; Thompson et al. 1987), independently mark a major reduction in rainfall and lake levels after AD 1100, the result of severe drought conditions. The severity of the drought cannot be underestimated. Unlike normal periodic shifts in lake levels, this one caused the shores to recede several kilometers and local water tables to drop far below the surface. Such conditions would have stranded huge tracts of raised fields and left their hydraulic sustaining systems high and dry.

As recent El Niño events make poignantly clear, environmental shifts can seriously affect the lives and livelihoods of Andean people substantially, especially fishers and farmers. Nevertheless, Clark Erickson (1999) notes that directly attributing state collapse to environmental shift is in some cases plagued by "neo-environmental determinism." Environmental shift, no matter how severe, did not simply cause state collapse. Tiwanaku collapse was a long, cumulative, and periodically violent process caused by mutually reinforcing processes of environmental deterioration and sociopolitical fragmentation. Rather than single-handedly causing state collapse, climate shift exacerbated already fragile and unbalanced regional sociopolitical conditions.

Residential Abandonment at Tiwanaku

Late Tiwanaku V ushered in significant population decline at Tiwanaku and Lukurmata. There is no clear evidence for quick abandonment or violence in most residential areas. Residential compounds were abandoned sequentially, not at once. In Tiwanaku, the dwelling in Akapana East 2 collapsed sometime around AD 1000, leaving impressions of *ichu* bundles above the floor. Later, several large quarry/ash pits were excavated into the abandoned building. Akapana East 1 and 1M were abandoned gradually, and ultimately may have been reoccupied by squatters or more mobile groups. In Akapana East 1M, a final structure was built directly over the larger Early Tiwanaku V building (Figure 9.1). The new structure was relatively small and its wall foundation far less substantial than that of the earlier building. Nevertheless, it followed the same directional orientation that had for centuries characterized Tiwanaku's urban plan. The foundation incorporated recycled cut stones. As at Lukurmata in Early Tiwanaku V, the reuse of cut stones may suggest that monumental edifices were being quarried to build more vernacular, quotidian structures.

The internal living surface in the Late Tiwanaku V structure in Akapana East 1M was a simple *apisonado*, and associated artifacts represented a range of domestic activities. Artifacts included splintered and butchered camelid bones, some bird bones, lithic debitage, weaving implements, and ground stones for crushing and grinding foods. A slab served as an internal work

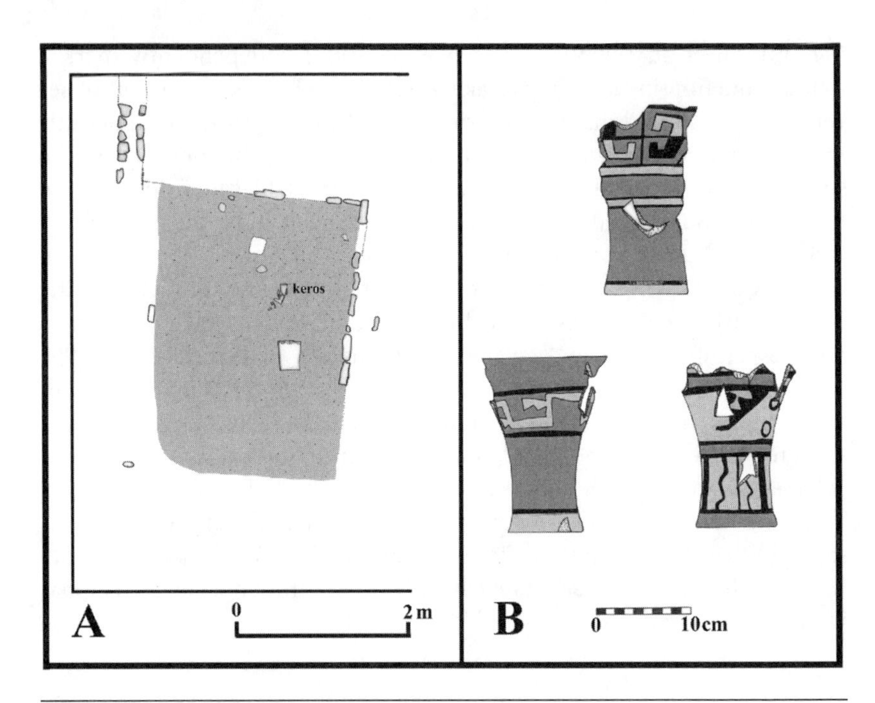

Figure 9.1 Plan of the final residential occupation in Akapana East 1M (A) with three fragmented keros found in a cache on the structure floor (B).

surface. Ceramic assemblages included high frequencies of crude serving wares—especially *tazons*—with nonburnished surfaces and roughly executed designs. Located inside of the structure was a cache of three partial *keros* decorated with stylized geometric designs (Figure 9.1). One incorporated Cochabamba style motifs, and a second portrayed a rough version of the interlocking motif found on ceremonial vessels from early Akapana offering contexts. It is likely that these elaborate vessels, which stood out in relation to other artifacts recovered from the structure, were produced to mimic those made in earlier phases of Tiwanaku's history.

The south compound of Akapana East 1 continued to be used or occupied in Late Tiwanaku V. One of the small dwellings, structure 2, eventually collapsed. A hearth above the structure foundation, set in the base of a large broken *tinaja*, represented a more ephemeral, temporary occupation. The large kitchen continued to accumulate midden, including sherds of broken cooking vessels. Among Tiwanaku sherds were bowls with transitional Tiwanaku-Early Pacajes stylistic characteristics. These included crudely molded *tazons* with convex rims, and relatively high proportions of small bowls, or *cuencos*. *Tazons* and *cuencos* tended to be roughly burnished and covered in a diluted orange or brown wash. Designs were roughly executed in black or dark brown, and consisted either of crude geometric designs or a thick wavy band along the interior rim, much like later Early Pacajes bowls. Mixed among assemblages were fragments of similarly decorated, Early Pacajes *cuencos*.

Abandonment of Monumental Complexes and Destruction of Sacred Icons

Major construction in monumental complexes had ceased by AD 1000 (Alconini 1995; Manzanilla 1992; Vranich 1999), though the timing of their eventual desuetude and destruction remains unclear. Akapana and Pumapunku, both initiated in early Tiwanaku IV, had shifted in significance and role throughout their histories, in particular during Tiwanaku V. Evidence for such a shift comes from caches and offerings superimposed on earlier contexts, many of which undoubtedly were destroyed by later Colonial quarrying and destruction. One late offering on top of the Akapana attests to such a shift (Alconini 1995; Manzanilla 1992). It consisted of disarticulated camelids strewn around the foundations of a small room in the corner of the residential patio group. Dating to Late Tiwanaku V (Janusek 2003a:Table 3.1, SMU-2473), the remains were placed around the structure once it had partially collapsed, but before it had been covered with postabandonment sediment. It appears to mark a time when the Akapana was significant as a sacred ancient shrine, or *huaca*, rather than the place of residence and ritual activity it had been through Early Tiwanaku V (Alconini 1995; Kolata 1993a).

The Sunken Temple and Kalasasaya, first built in the Late Formative period, had come to represent Tiwanaku's past history and cultural patrimony by the end of Tiwanaku IV. Akapana and Pumapunku may have come to do so later, at a time when Tiwanaku's effective influence and regional control were increasingly circumscribed. From major ritual complexes dedicated to distinct ritual cults within Tiwanaku's encompassing cosmology, it is likely that Akapana and Pumapunku became more significant as sacred icons representing Tiwanaku's past. In this regard they now served as sacred places in which, through ritual offerings and dedications, collective memory of prior glory was expressed and recharged.

As suggested in late residential sectors, many temples and monuments were intentionally dismantled, defaced, or destroyed. Some of this destruction clearly occurred toward the end of Tiwanaku's long history. In Putuni, the East and West palaces were both destroyed during or just before Late Tiwanaku V (Couture 2002; Couture and Sampeck 2003). The West Palace collapsed very quickly, suggesting that its walls were knocked down, while the East Palace was completely razed to the ground. The rapid destruction

Figure 9.2 Ritually mutilated stone sculptures from Tiwanaku: the "decapitated" Putuni monolith (A), a *chachapuma* from the west entrance to the Akapana (B), and the "decapitated" head of the massive "Gigantic Monolith" (C).

of Putuni, which had for centuries been the home of increasingly wealthy, high status groups, suggests that Tiwanaku fragmentation was at times violent. Couture (2002) hypothesizes that the destruction of Putuni indicates that Tiwanaku collapse was a rapid event in which people ran the ruling elites out of town. I suggest that this destruction indeed marked a significant turn of events in which one major Tiwanaku elite group was both concretely and symbolically disempowered. However, Tiwanaku had consisted of several elite groups, together forming a class of competing factions (Chapter 7). In addition, final radiocarbon measurements for the East Palace date well before AD 1000 (Janusek 2003a:Table 3.1). Thus, the event may have developed out of increasing factionalism in Tiwanaku, in which one elite group's place in the city and society was effectively eradicated at the hands of other groups or factions. It may well represent the ascendance of another regime, whose power, ultimately, was far more circumscribed and fragile.

Many of Tiwanaku's monumental ritual complexes also were eventually destroyed. Although we cannot determine that each act was related to state collapse rather than postcollapse events, some monuments suffered dramatic forms of destruction that appear unrelated to the opportunistic destruction of later periods. Particularly notable is the thorough destruction of Tiwanaku's key religious symbols, including stone portals and deified ancestor effigies. The frieze of an elegantly sculpted gateway lintel from the Kantatayita precinct, just northeast of the Akapana, was hammered vigorously, at least in part to remove the metal lamina that, held in place by a series of pins, had originally covered it. More impressive, perhaps, was the destruction of the large hall at the east edge of the Pumapunku platform, which had incorporated some of Tiwanaku's largest and heaviest sandstone blocks. Protzen and Nair (2000, 2002) demonstrate that a series of interlinked, massive portals once stood in this hall. The stones were not quarried, but rather the portals were pushed over and smashed in place, where most of the fragments remain to this day. Other portals show similar destruction, including a large gate currently scattered over the top of the Akapana.

Other likely evidence for selective, prehispanic destruction comes from Tiwanaku's effigy monoliths. Like Tiwanaku's portals and other architectural elements, many monoliths show clear evidence of having been defaced or destroyed at some point in the past (Figure 9.2). Located inside of the Putuni courtyard, the Putuni Monolith, a diminutive andesite sculpture depicting what was perhaps a deified ancestor for the resident elite, had been summarily decapitated and buried (Couture and Sampeck 2003). Although impossible to prove, this monolith may have been defaced and ritually interred when the Putuni palaces were destroyed. Many other Tiwanaku sculptures show similar patterns of destruction. The feline face of a basalt *chachapuma* (human-feline) recovered from the base of the Akapana, perhaps one of two that flanked its west entrance, had been intentionally mutilated before being buried. Of other monoliths, only their pedestals or shattered fragments of their bodies are known. Most impressive is the massive andesite head of a Tiwanaku ancestral deity that once crowned the so-called Gigantic Monolith, perhaps the largest effigy monolith to have stood in Tiwanaku (Ponce 1981). Like the destruction of the sculpted monolithic portals in Pumapunku and elsewhere in Tiwanaku, the ritual decapitation of the Gigantic Monolith would have required a monumental effort on the part of highly motivated zealots.

It remains possible that that many such monuments were defaced or destroyed long after state collapse. Judging from written documents, the Inca had no reason to engage in acts of destruction of monuments that, by all accounts, they appear to have held in great esteem. Moseley (2001:243) suggests that the Inca, for whom Tiwanaku was sacred, later reconstructed some of the monuments, creating a kind of park that would have reinforced their own imperial identity and collective memory. As noted in early chronicles and demonstrated in recent excavations, the Inca established a regional administrative site focused on the north side of the Pumapunku and the entire west sector of the old urban center. Thus, it is unlikely that the Inca were the highly motivated zealots implicated in Tiwanaku's ritualized destruction.

The Spanish of the Early Colonial Period better fit the bill, dedicated as many priests, *conquistadors*, and administrators were, according to documents, to transforming Andean society into a Christian world. By the 1570s carved stone blocks from monumental complexes were being hauled off to build churches, mills, and bridges as far away as La Paz. Such activity, though its specific methods are largely lost to us, was opportunistic in nature and had specific ends. The extent to which Tiwanaku portals, monuments, and monoliths suffered ritualized defacement and destruction at the hands of Spanish leaders and their followers remains unclear. However, it is perhaps diagnostic that, in the cases mentioned above, tell-tale signs of Catholic-inspired destruction are notably absent. Such signs are present on at least two other effigy monuments that remain largely intact—the Suñawa Monolith, which has an early Colonial date etched on its front torso, and the Ponce Monolith, which has a small cross etched on its shoulder. The Ponce Monolith had been buried before it was discovered by Ponce's team in the Kalasasaya in 1957 (Ponce 1995:230). Thus, at least in certain cases, potent Tiwanaku icons were put out of sight rather than destroyed in the Colonial period, and in the case of the Ponce Monolith, perhaps, given a proper Christian burial.

Thus, it is likely that some ritualized destruction and defacement occurred long before the time of Spanish contact. Recurring patterns such as facial mutilation and decapitation indicate that the monoliths had been ritually killed and literally defaced. They were destroyed while they still held great meaning and power. To the extent that the stone icons represented the primordial ancestors of Tiwanaku elites, as they had since the Late Formative, their highly patterned destruction targeted the ideological foundations of power and legitimacy of Tiwanaku's dominant groups.

Accepting that some destruction of monuments and images occurred in Late Tiwanaku V, as part of the process of Tiwanaku fragmentation, at least two scenarios regarding its chronology are possible. On the one hand, the ritual desecration of such monuments may have occurred at different times, upon the wane of successive ruling groups. On the other hand, their destruction may have occurred more or less contemporaneously in Late Tiwanaku V. In the first case, such events were directed at specific groups or factions, and in the second, they manifest an effort to efface the foundations of Tiwanaku ideology, and perhaps more abstractly, the state. In either scenario, increasing presence of elite and state power in the lives and livelihoods of constituent groups incited disaffection with Tiwanaku's dominant values and relations, which increasingly were brought to public consciousness and exposed as arbitrary and burdensome. In the overall scenario I present, Tiwanaku leaders in Tiwanaku V had begun to strain the etiquette of long-held social values, exacerbating contradictory consciousness and the potential, eventually acted out by local groups and factions, for symbolic and military violence. This was not simply a proletarian or commoner revolution, as an orthodox Marxism might lead us to believe. Rather turning away from Tiwanaku leaders and state ideals, practices, and symbols most likely involved, to some extent, factions headed by high status individuals or groups, whether or not they affiliated primarily with Tiwanaku or other societies. In this light, groups with ancestry in the Katari Valley, whether still residing in the region or now living in diaspora communities, may have played an important role in the volatile unfolding of events. Defacing and decapitating icons of Tiwanaku deities and ancestors was ritualized hostility meant to efface the power of Tiwanaku elites and destroy the ideological foundation of their identities. Burning and destroying their places of residence effectively erased their place and power in society, if not their lives.

The Rise of Pacajes Culture

By the end of the twelfth century, many practices, ideals, and settlement patterns were very different from those that had characterized Tiwanaku state culture. Tiwanaku's profound practical hegemony gave way in Late Tiwanaku V, in what was by all accounts a volatile and chaotic time, to new ideals and practices that corresponded with new forms of social identification and cultural affiliation. Emerging ideologies invoked past symbols and practices, if fragmentarily and creatively, but they involved new practices, ideals, and conditions, grounded in a sociopolitical organization consisting not in an overarching state but rather many semiautonomous communities and polities.

Historical documents indicate that profound ethnic/regional differences characterized the southern Lake Titicaca basin in the Colonial Period. As noted in Chapter 2, communities, polities, and federations were organized according to a dual principal of social and spatial order that operated at various social and geopolitical scales (Figure 9.3). (Bouysse-Cassagne 1986, 1987; Choque 1993; Izko 1986, 1992; Pärssinen 1992; Platt 1982, 1987; Rivera Cusiqanqui 1992). Sixteenth century documents place the boundary between Urkosuyu and Umasuyu somewhere in the Tiwanaku and Katari Valleys. Each region consisted of numerous *cabeceras* or *markas* and their sustaining regions. Each *cabacera* incorporated a smaller dual sociopolitical and spatial division that included members of at least two distinct ethnic-like groups, Aymara and Uru, each of which in turn comprised several kin-based *ayllus*. The boundary was reproduced following minor changes in the creation of the Pacajes and Umasuyu provinces in the late 1500s, and continues to thrive today as the boundary between the

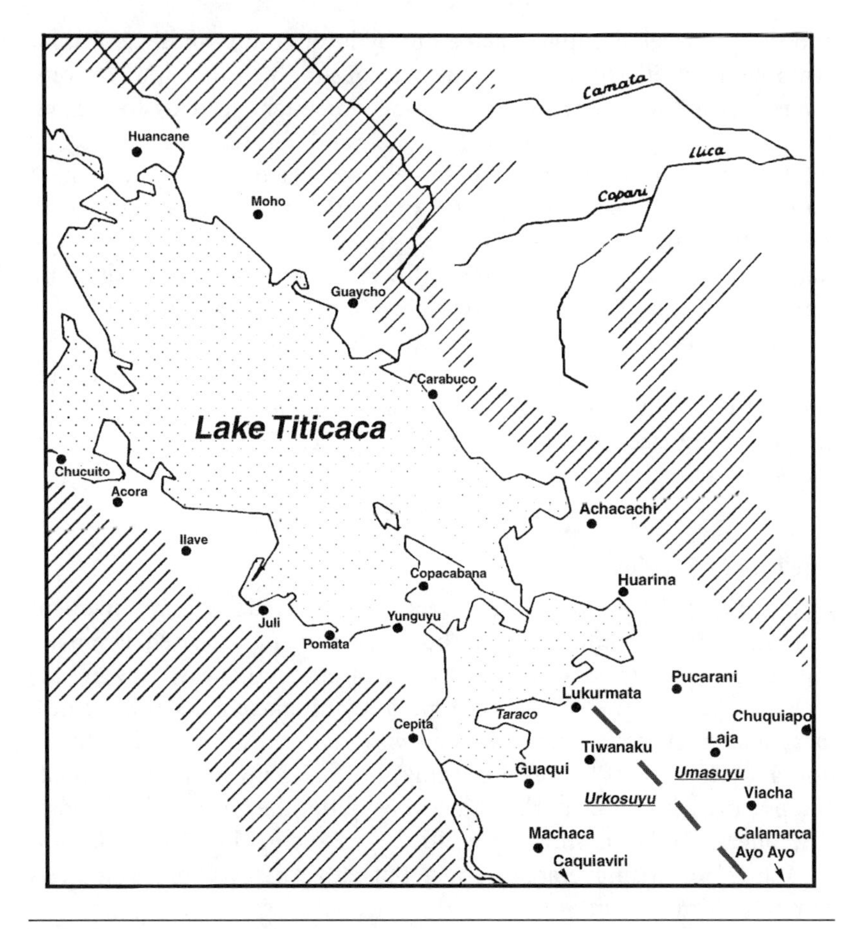

Figure 9.3 Map of the Lake Titicaca basin showing Tiwanaku and Lukurmata in relation to other major towns (marka) pertaining to Urkosuyu or Umasuyu (adapted from Saignes 1996).

provinces of Ingavi, centered in the Tiwanaku Valley, and Los Andes, centered in the Katari Valley.

Residential Patterns in Tiwanaku and Lukurmata

Settlement choices included patterns of continuity and change. Some aspects of Early Pacajes settlement followed those characteristic of Tiwanaku. In the Tiwanaku Valley, nearly all (ninety-one percent) Tiwanaku sites either continued to be occupied or were reoccupied in Early Pacajes (Janusek and Kolata 2003). In the Katari Valley, most (eighty-two percent) Tiwanaku sites, including all sites larger than one hectare, continued to be occupied. For the most part, people chose to inhabit old settlements. Even

Tiwanaku and Lukurmata were never entirely abandoned. At Tiwanaku, residence shifted to the west edge of the old urban center where the contemporary pueblo of Tiwanaku still stands. An informal surface survey I have conducted reveals a relatively extensive area of Early Pacajes ceramic distribution covering perhaps twenty hectares of the low bluff that overlooks the lower valley. Some areas of the site yield nonlocal ceramics associated with Late Intermediate Period polities (e.g., Lupaca and Qolla) north and west of the lake.

More research has been conducted on post-Tiwanaku occupation in Lukurmata. On the ridge, Bermann (1993:132–133; 1994:225–235) located the remains of a single post-Tiwanaku structure. It was occupied early in the period, only shortly after the wane of Tiwanaku-style serving-ceremonial wares (Bermann 1994:231). It was rectangular in plan, had a central hearth, and was oriented to the same direction as had been Tiwanaku-period structures. Later structures in the Katari Valley no longer followed this orientation. The structure and the activity areas around it yielded evidence for domestic activities and artifacts typical of Tiwanaku residential contexts. In later structures, characteristic Tiwanaku domestic artifacts were rare or absent (Janusek and Kolata 2003). Associated with the structure were serving wares representing what I term Urko Pacajes, Uma Pacajes (Janusek 2003a), and Mollo, a style associated with valleys east of Lake Titicaca.

An Early Pacajes residential compound occupied the north edge of Lukurmata, on a small peninsula that, when the lake is high, abuts the swampy lake edge. Karen Wise (1993) revealed two roughly circular domestic structures that were reminiscent of the Tiwanaku Period circular structure in Misiton 2 (Figure 9.4). One abutted the compound wall, and the other, just a few meters to the southeast, contained an ovoid platform of flat fieldstones covered with hard-packed clay. In the buildings and their associated refuse pits were artifacts representing domestic activities as well as the processing and consumption of fish. Unlike the early structure on the ridge and most Tiwanaku Period structures, fish bone was abundant on floors, in middens, and in associated refuse pits. This raises the possibility that the feature inside of the second structure was a fish-processing platform. All evidence suggests that inhabitants of this compound, living on the lake, specialized in the procurement of lake resources, as did most documented Uru groups.

Several offerings at Lukurmata manifest a new type of ritual activity. It consisted of buried globular jars or *ollas* (Bermann 1994:227; Janusek and Earnest 1990a:133), some with a single shattered bowl and others with lithic tools. Two buried jars, one on the ridge and one in K'atupata, contained the remains of a human infant. The offerings are reminiscent of the buried

Figure 9.4 View of the two excavated circular structures in the North Point area of Lukurmata.

incensario offerings of the Tiwanaku Period, and they most likely developed out of such dedication. They may simultaneously mark affiliations with more temperate regions to the east. Bermann (1994:227) notes that buried jars capped with small bowls were common offerings in societies in the valleys east of Lake Titicaca and near Cochabamba (see Bennett 1936:371; Rydén 1959). In such regions individuals were commonly interred in ceramic jars and urns.

Settlement Shift in the Tiwanaku and Katari Valleys

Despite continuities, settlement patterns changed remarkably in both valleys during the transition from Tiwanaku V to Early Pacajes, as conditions became drier and the centralized political system fragmented. Most notably, Tiwanaku and Lukurmata shrank considerably as settlement dispersed across surrounding landscapes. If twenty hectares is a reasonable estimate of Tiwanaku's size at this time, and this may be generous, it had decreased to three percent of its minimum extent in Early Tiwanaku V. If ten hectares is a reasonable estimate of Lukurmata's post-Tiwanaku extent, it had decreased to eight percent of its earlier extent. Both sites remained among the most important and populated in their respective valleys, and no new major centers emerged. However, rather than focusing on primate centers at the apex of regional multivalley settlement networks, settlement in the two valleys now centered on a number of well-distributed villages and towns of no more than twenty hectares in size. In effect, settlement networks became far more heterarchical.

In the Tiwanaku Valley, the number of sites increased from 339 to 964, almost three times that during Tiwanaku V, while average site size dropped considerably. Of note was a significant increase in the percentage of sites (from nine percent to fourteen percent) in the upper piedmont, including several fortified sites, or *pukaras*, at the highest edges of the valley (Albarracín-Jordan and Mathews 1990). In the southern Katari Valley, the number of sites increased from 48 to 145, again approximately three times that during Tiwanaku V. The number of sites in the upper piedmont did not increase significantly, but notably, it involved the establishment of a series of large *pukaras* in the Taraco hills between the two valleys (Janusek and Kolata 2003).

Notable in the Katari Valley was an all-out occupation of the pampa zone (Figure 9.5A). From a total of thirteen sites or twenty-seven percent of occupation during the Tiwanaku period, settlement increased to seventy-five sites or fifty-two percent of occupation in Early Pacajes. Unlike any time in the past, settlements were now well distributed across the flood plain. Approximately forty percent of Early Pacajes sites occupied the relatively high ground of raised field beds, suggesting that many of these intensive farming systems were by now obsolete (Janusek and Kolata 2003; cf. Graffam 1990). Radiocarbon measurements from excavated raised fields corroborate this pattern. Of fourteen dates recovered from raised field use contexts only two (twelve percent) unambiguously dated to Early Pacajes, while of seven postabandonment dates all but one (eighty-six percent) dated to Early Pacajes (Janusek and Kolata 2003).

Another notable aspect of new settlement patterns was the formation of clear settlement clusters. In the Tiwanaku Valley, several such clusters focused around large, widely spaced villages and towns of three to ten hectares. In the Katari Valley, many sites clustered along packed-earth roads that crossed the pampa, and one large group clustered around the limestone outcrop of Cerro Katavi. The formation of settlement clusters apparently represents the coalescence of documented coresidential *estancias* and micro-*ayllus*. In the Tiwanaku Valley, settlement dispersal in Early Pacajes was largely the continuation of a long-term process of sociopolitical fragmentation that had begun in Early Tiwanaku V (Albarracín-Jordan 1992, 1996b). In the Katari Valley, settlement dispersal was more abrupt, undoubtedly because the vast Koani Pampa had been an agricultural estate with high water tables throughout Tiwanaku V. To allow dense settlement

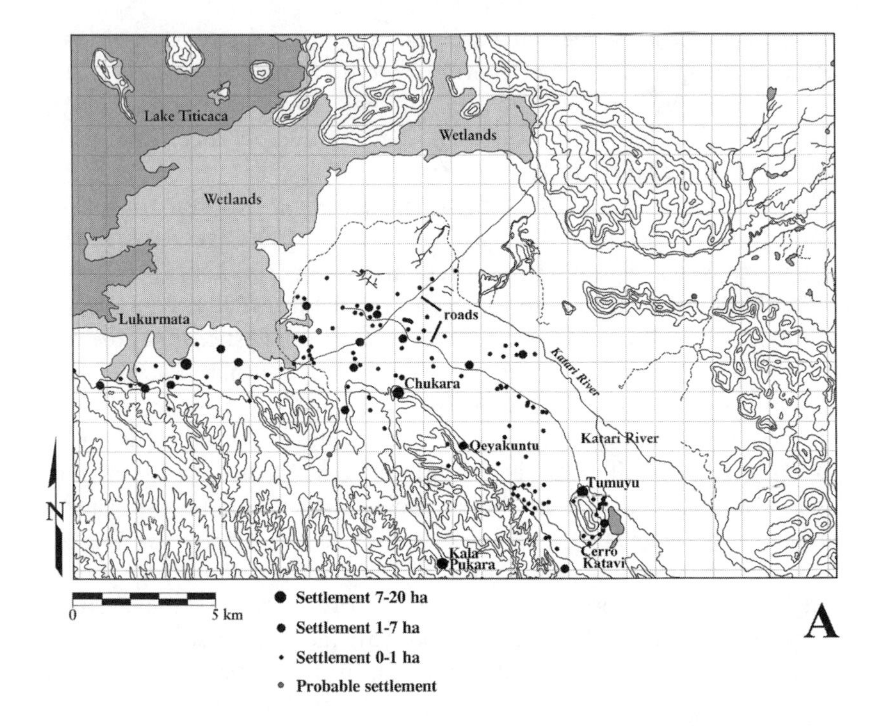

Figure 9.5 Settlement distribution in the Katari Valley during Early Pacajes (A), and a typical above-ground slab-cist burial from a site in the region (B).

in the pampa, fluctuating lake levels must have been considerably lower overall in Early Pacajes.

Of great significance, population had declined in the two valleys and remaining populations had become more mobile. The greater number of sites in the region and the expansion of settlement into new microzones such as the low pampas and high piedmont give the immediate impression that population was increasing. Many, including me, have suggested such a scenario (Albarracín-Jordan 1996a; Janusek 1994; Mathews 1992). Matthew Bandy (2001), on the other hand, convincingly demonstrates that population growth actually declined precipitously in the region during Early Pacajes. Shifting population index measures for the Taraco Peninsula and the two valleys, traced from the Early Formative through Late Pacajes, reveal not only that an ancient regional pattern of nucleated habitation disappeared in the twelfth century, but that regional population declined on a major scale for the first time. Bandy (2001:243) concludes that Early Pacajes was "a chaotic and dangerous time... including considerable localized conflict, population relocation and even famine." More patently than ethnic immigration, as hypothesized by some ethnohistorians and linguists, what occurred in Early Pacajes was significant population decline and perhaps emigration to other regions.

Driving home the point that settlement shifted dramatically is clear evidence that Early Pacajes populations were far more mobile than had been Tiwanaku populations. The living surface in the post-Tiwanaku dwelling on the ridge at Lukurmata was ephemeral, suggesting that the structure had been only briefly inhabited (Bermann 1994:225). Excavations at ten other sites in the Katari Valley revealed similar patterns (Janusek and Kolata 2003). At most sites, Early Pacajes occupations consisted of dispersed middens and isolated domestic features rather than clear dwellings, and the few clear living surfaces that have been excavated were ephemeral. Recurring evidence for evanescent occupation in Early Pacajes further supports the point that populations had declined precipitously, for the large number of settlements during the phase is thus artificially inflated by the presence of numerous short-term occupations. In tandem with evidence for drier conditions in the region, it alludes to an increasing emphasis on herding and pastoral mobility at a regional scale.

Another new pattern, noted above, also contrasted sharply with prior settlement patterns. For the first time, hill top fortresses or *pukaras*, most likely temporary refuge sites in times of military danger (Stanish et al. 1997), were established in the region (Figure 9.5) (Janusek and Kolata 2003:Figure 6.32). Most were relatively small sites surrounded by a single wall, but a series of well-hidden sites, including the massive site of Kala Pukara, were major refuge places protected by two or more walls. Such sites have been considered evidence for the immigration of waves of warlike Aymara into the region in the wake of, and in part the cause of, Tiwanaku collapse. In the southern basin, however, such sites appear almost exclusively in and along the Taraco hills, an ancient boundary between the Tiwanaku and Katari Valleys. As Stanish and colleagues found in the western basin, the location of *pukaras* suggests that most conflict and military danger in Early Pacajes was internecine rather than external. In the southern basin they appeared in, and in fact defined, the boundary between regions occupied by distinct ethnic-like groups with histories that predated Tiwanaku hegemony. Thus, the refuge sites appear to mark the resurgence of regional identities and highly volatile relations between the two valleys.

Burial Patterns in Urkosuyu and Umasuyu

Evidence for the resurgence of volatile regional identities in the southern basin appears in several new cultural patterns, including new mortuary practices. In both valleys, new burial styles included highly visible above ground chambers, each of which might hold multiple interments of a single kin-group or lineage. Further, excavations and documents indicate that the chambers housed the remains of already decomposed and curated mummy bundles (Isbell 1997). To the extent that secondary burial had been common in Tiwanaku and Lukurmata, and that above ground burial structures may have had a precedent in Lukurmata's double-chamber tombs, new mortuary practices drew on the ideologies and rituals of the Tiwanaku period (Albarracín-Jordan 1996a). Nevertheless, here and throughout the Andean highlands, visible burial structures allude to a renewed concern with visually marking the relationship between society and landscape. Sociopolitical conditions were volatile and land tenure was now an ongoing concern. Highly visible burial towers populated local agropastoral landscapes with the living ancestors of groups holding claims to the land, inhabiting them with the memories and identities of specific groups.

Significantly, and subject to future research, burial practices appear to have varied in a broad manner between macroregions. Most common in the Tiwanaku and Katari Valleys were slab-cist tombs, a form of burial with a low above-ground chamber of adobe on cobble foundations that commonly clustered together on small cemetery mounds in the pampas (Figure 9.5B). At most excavated sites slab-cist tombs appeared together with more traditional subterranean cist tombs. For example, excavations on the ridge at Lukurmata recovered sixty-five post-Tiwanaku tombs, forty-four percent of which were cist tombs similar to burials most common in the Tiwanaku Period and fifty-six percent of which were slab-cist tombs typical of other Early Pacajes sites (Bermann 1994:227–229). Most likely, slab-cist tombs gradually became more popular in Early Pacajes, but they nevertheless coexisted with cist burials for a long time. Further defining the relationship will require a better handle on the chronology of such mortuary patterns. What is clear is that various styles of slab-cist burials were common throughout Umasuyu.

In the Urkosuyu region just south and west of the Tiwanaku Valley a distinct burial practice became common. Here prominent burial towers, commonly known as *chullpas*, dotted local landscapes. *Chullpas* vary widely in technical, architectural, and decorative style, the stylistic differences corresponding with distinct macro-*ayllus* and political federations. Like slab-cist tombs, each *chullpa* might hold multiple individuals, presumably individuals of the same kin-group or lineage. In fact, at least in the Machaca range south of the Tiwanaku Valley, *chullpas* and slab-cist tombs coexisted, perhaps for people of different statuses or identities. The Tiwanaku-Taraco-Katari region forms the northern and eastern boundary of the great popularity of prominent above ground burial towers. They appear in certain regions of Umasuyu, including Cumana at the northwest edge of the Katari Valley, but they were far less common here than they were to the south and west, in Urkosuyu. Somewhere in the Tiwanaku-Taraco-Katari region, it appears, was a major cultural boundary, as corroborated by post-Tiwanaku ceramic patterns.

Urko and Uma Pacajes Ceramic Assemblages

In Early Pacajes, both the range of forms and the degree of stylistic standardization in ceramics dropped considerably. The wide range of Tiwanaku ritual and ceremonial wares disappeared. The most common Early Pacajes ceramics now included cooking vessels, storage vessels, and small serving bowls. Cooking and storage vessels were similar in size, form, and composition, suggesting that the two functions had become more interchangeable. Cooking *ollas* were on average much smaller than Tiwanaku cooking vessels, and they were far less variable in form. *Tinajas* became less common and in general were smaller than they had been during the Tiwanaku period. In particular, large fermentation *tinajas* with long cylindrical necks, which had become increasingly common throughout the Tiwanaku period, were now rare. All in all, it appears that after Tiwanaku V the role, scale, and significance of commensalism, or at least large-scale elite or state-sponsored rituals of consumption, had declined dramatically.

Early Pacajes serving and ceremonial wares consisted almost exclusively of small ellipsoid *cuencos*, by and large an uncommon type during the Tiwanaku period (Figure 9.6). The popularity of this form stands in sharp contrast to the popularity of everted forms *(keros, tazons, sahumadors)* during the Tiwanaku period. The two most common variants of *cuencos* were 1) those without and 2) those with a narrow everted lip. In later Aymara communities of the western Titicaca basin, Tschopik (1950:208) noted, cuencos with straight lips (*chuas*) were ordinary bowls for daily consumption while *cuencos* with everted lips (*platillo chua*) were for festive and ceremonial occasions. Both types demonstrate a range of stylized designs painted almost invariably in black or brown, less commonly in red or white. Decoration appeared most commonly on the interiors of bowls and less commonly on the bodies of *vasijas* and *tinajas*. Motifs for the most

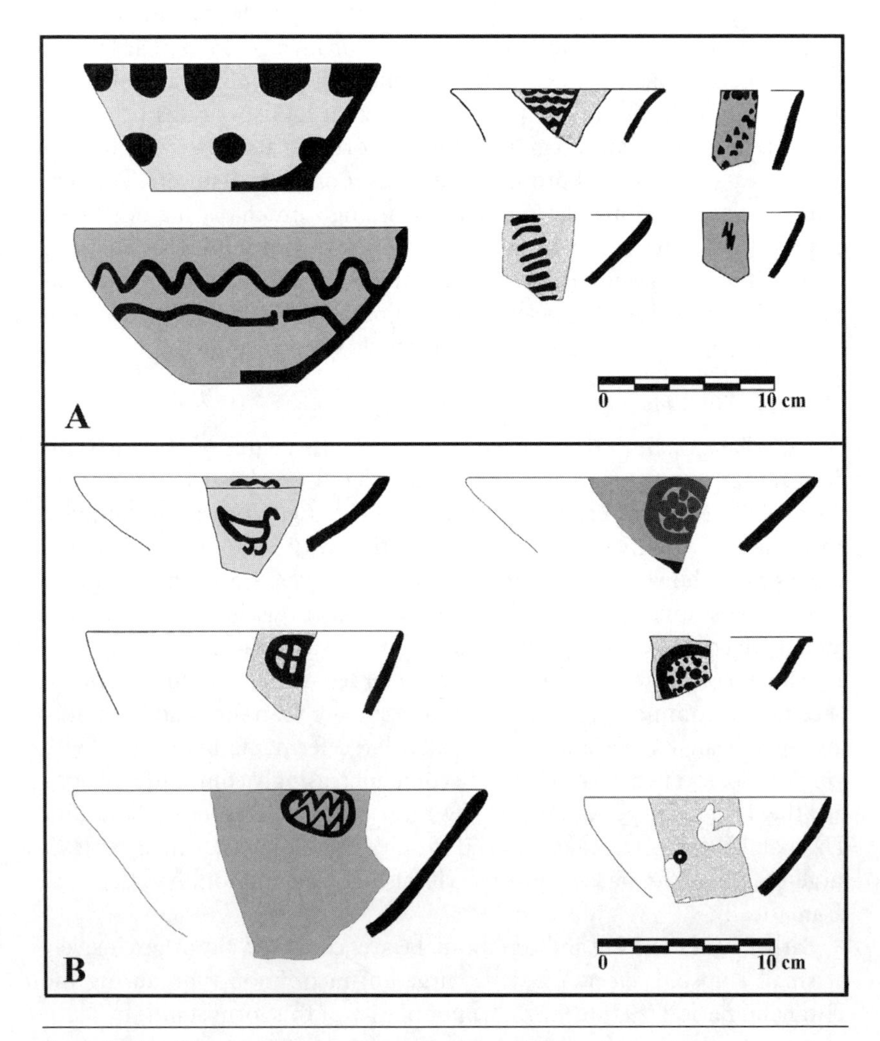

Figure 9.6 Urko (A) and Uma Pacajes (B) variants of Early Pacajaes serving bowls.

part were unlike those common in the Tiwanaku period, and their thematic range was simultaneously more restricted in design and less regulated in execution.

Roughly parallel with the distribution of new mortuary practices, Early Pacajes *cuencos* comprised two style complexes, corresponding geographically with the documented division of Urkosuyu and Umasuyu (Figure 9.6). Urko Pacajes bowls, common in the Tiwanaku Valley (Albarracín-Jordan 1996; Albarracín-Jordan and Mathews 1990) and in the Desaguadero Valley to the south, were well formed and highly burnished, with thin walls, reddish-orange slip, and stylized decoration. About seventy-five percent of these bowls had an everted lip, suggesting that they were used in festive and ceremonial contexts. On such bowls iconography often featured cross-hatched designs, plump llamas, or diagonal tracks of dots. In the Katari Valley, sites in the pampa zone almost exclusively yielded *cuencos* of another style, which shared many elements with assemblages from regions east of Lake Titicaca. These Uma Pacajes bowls, sometimes termed Omasuyus, had straight lips, thick walls, and a coarse surface finish. Decoration was less common, and when present, featured thick circles or corrals filled with rough dots or hatches, curved bands, or amorphous designs. Like mortuary practices, stylistic assemblages of serving wares define a significant cultural divide somewhere in the Tiwanaku-Taraco-Katari region, and possibly following the Taraco range.

Transformation and Continuity: The Rise of Pacajes Polity and Culture

Change and Continuity

Cultural and sociopolitical changes between AD 1000 and 1200 demonstrate a complex warp and weft of transformation and continuity. Changing environmental conditions may have catalyzed the cumulative tensions and fragile elements attendant on the social, economic, and political relations that formed the Tiwanaku state. Most immediately critical for Tiwanaku leaders, the drought diminished the viability and reliability of agricultural regimes just as valued lake resources also became scarce. Decreasing lake levels effectively stranded huge tracts of raised fields and left their hydraulic sustaining systems dry. The vast agricultural estate of the Koani Pampa, which played a huge part in subsidizing the massive feasts and ceremonies that continually reproduced Tiwanaku identity and hierarchy, and legitimized the existence of an expanding elite class, was gone. The consumable substances that fueled tournaments of competition and rank among elite groups were severely diminished. More important, the very foundation for establishing relations of generosity, patronage, and reciprocity between elites and nonelites, and for fueling tournaments of status and identity among nonelites, dwindled. In essence, in Late Tiwanaku V, the very raison d'etre of the Tiwanaku state, the lifeblood that for centuries supported its increasingly intricate sociopolitical order and reproduced its relations of mutual obligation among increasingly differentiated groups, was disappearing.

Environmental shift, however, neither single-handedly nor simplistically caused state collapse. Rather, drought conditions exacerbated fragile productive conditions and mounting tensions in an already fragmented social landscape. In Moquegua, groups heretofore closely affiliated with Tiwanaku, and some possibly descendants of altiplano groups, appear to have asserted autonomy to control local productive systems in the tenth or eleventh centuries (Williams 2002; Williams and Nash 2002). Sites such as Omo and Chen Chen were not simply abandoned but rather converted into heaping rockpiles, and thus may have been violently obliterated (Moseley et al. 1991). In the altiplano, Tiwanaku itself was depopulated gradually between AD 1000 and 1150, punctuated and perhaps in part stimulated by periodic turbulent events. These violent events appear to have been directed at specific elite groups, royal lineages, and quite possibly, a large sector of the Tiwanaku elite class. Meanwhile, major temple complexes fell into disuse and some were dismantled and destroyed. No new monuments were built, and as far as we can tell, no more monoliths depicting deified ancestors were hewn. Nevertheless, certain residential areas continued to be occupied into the twelfth century. By this time, sociopolitical structures already were disintegrating as groups left major nucleated centers to form *ayllu*-based communities. Tapping into new interregional interaction networks, groups developed new mortuary practices, adopted new styles of serving wares, and built refuge sites in the hills between differentiated regions. Many people appear to have the left the old core altogether.

Tiwanaku's disappearance involved a complex mosaic of change and continuity. On the one hand, it involved major social and economic transformations. These included more dispersed and heterarchical settlement networks consisting of communities and kin-based *ayllus* centered on smaller central villages and towns, or *markas*. Most groups abandoned the ancient nucleated centers and chose settlement locations in various microzones of the altiplano landscape, moving into areas that had been only sparsely inhabited in the past. In part, this movement reflected drier conditions and a necessary reduction in the intensity of agricultural production in wetland environments. Many populations may have left the region altogether, most likely, as discussed below, to regions that for centuries had been well adapted to dry conditions. Evidence for significant demographic decline renders the ethnic influx hypothesis unlikely, and perhaps untenable.

Much drier conditions encouraged local populations to adopt a more balanced and diversified range of productive strategies, including extensive farming, raised fields on a smaller scale, fishing, hunting, and herding. Evidence that occupation was more temporary and mobile indicates that herding, an ancient productive regime better adjusted to a drier climate than intensive farming, became increasingly important. Camelid pastoralism and most likely regional llama caravan trade now formed more fundamental aspects of the regional political economy. This point requires testing with in-depth material analysis, but we can propose that local populations began to emphasize herding in the balance of productive enterprises as the viability and role of farming systems declined and the old integrative networks comprising Tiwanaku's overarching political economy evaporated.

State collapse corresponded with new ceramic complexes. The style of high-visibility ceremonial and serving wares was transfigured completely as the specialized assemblages popular for centuries disappeared in favor of relatively homogeneous small bowls. What disappeared were the intricate assemblages associated with the production and consumption of large volumes of food and drink in large-scale ceremonial contexts. Communal feasting undoubtedly remained important in Early Pacajes, and in fact, it was primary in facilitating the rise and consolidation of the later Inca state, but centrally sponsored rituals of consumption became less common or declined in intensity. Periodic public feasts began to focus on the new towns that served as ceremonial centers for dispersed micro-*ayllus* and emerging polities.

State collapse also involved mortuary practices focused on clusters of above-ground multiple interments. Social identities and territories were routinely contested at this dynamic historical juncture. Above-ground tombs marked the areas where deceased relatives and common ancestors were interred, where rituals performed in their memory were periodically conducted, and most likely also symbolized the territories or boundaries of an ayllu's landholdings. Tomb clusters solidified and emplaced the shared memory of local groups, binding common ancestors and group identity to particular places on the physical landscape. New mortuary patterns emphasize the renewed importance of reifying group identities and exhibiting their places in the landscape.

Nevertheless, cumulative long-term transformations and even profound continuities accompanied more striking social, economic, and ideological changes. For one thing, Tiwanaku and Lukurmata like many sites in the Tiwanaku and Katari Valleys were neither rapidly nor completely abandoned. Their declines were cumulative processes that began in the Tiwanaku Period. Lukurmata and other major centers in the Katari Valley had experienced significant decline as early as the ninth century, as part of new state policies of consolidation. Such a cataclysmic shift changed profoundly and rendered far more precarious the very cultural and political foundations of the state. The shift to more dispersed settlement networks and communities also began in the Tiwanaku period and occurred over several successive generations. No doubt exacerbated by new sociopolitical and environmental circumstances, settlement dispersal and the formation of new social organizations and identities represented a long-term strategic preference for nonurban, non-nucleated—perhaps in part non-Tiwanaku—livelihoods and social networks. Mounting evidence suggests, as Mathews points out (1997:259), that "the seeds of Tiwanaku's collapse were sown during [its] apogee."

Many local practices and elements of material culture demonstrated significant continuity. For example, new mortuary practices and the treatment of ancestral remains drew on burial practices common in the Tiwanaku Period (Albarracín-Jordan 1996a, 1996c). Most interred individuals in Early Pacajes burials displayed the distinct styles of cranial modification that were prevalent in the Tiwanaku Period (Blom 1999, 2003). In regard to material style, ceramic wares other than serving assemblages and large cooking and storage vessels remained more or less the same in production and design. Thus, despite profound changes, some material patterns allude to profound continuities in certain local practices and important elements of ideology and practical hegemony.

Notably, the old social boundary between the Tiwanaku and Katari Valleys, manifested as early as the Late Formative and vibrant throughout the Tiwanaku Period, reemerged with a vengeance in Early Pacajes. In a general sense this boundary was manifested, once again, in distinct styles of ceramic assemblages. The relation of stylistic differences to the documented Urkosuyu-Umasuyu division is also manifested, in a more diffuse sense, in mortuary practices of the region. It continued to be manifested in the styles of body modification practiced by those interred in visible burial structures. Most expressly, the establishment of fortified *pukaras* in the Taraco hills manifests an increasing concern with surveillance and defense between the valleys. Like similar Late Intermediate Period sites in the Central Andes (Parsons et al. 1997), these fortresses defined a sociopolitical boundary, in this case one with an ancient history and with likely macroregional dimensions as the cultural fault between Urkosuyu and Umasuyu.

Thus, new social identities and cultural affiliations in Early Pacajes were forged and reproduced in the context of political tension and threat of conflict. Such conditions developed out of old tensions and followed deep social rifts with histories dating to, perhaps even antedating, Tiwanaku hegemony. Tensions mounted in the face of political decentralization, as old productive strategies became less dependable, and as populations developed locally based resource strategies emphasizing pastoralism. Rather than an influx of new groups to the region, the fortresses mark the development of internal political fragmentation in the old core, and the reassertion of autonomy in regions that for centuries had been under Tiwanaku hegemony. Significant tension, the product of a long history of local social, political, and cultural development, perhaps now more than ever defined the relation between the two valleys.

Collapse as Cultural Genesis

As the bases of state power eroded, the hegemonic order of things must have become increasingly burdensome and untenable. A common identity and an elegant hierarchical cosmology centered on Tiwanaku symbols, elites, and royal ancestors, once celebrated as the spiritual sources of life and regeneration for all, became increasingly difficult to justify or recreate. Instead, as conditions deteriorated and people's livelihoods were increasingly threatened, the tables slowly turned against Tiwanaku leaders. Groups with vibrant and perhaps now revitalized local identities turned away from, and to some extent against, what were now considered the sources of deteriorating conditions. Ruling residences and depictions of royal ancestors became the target for violence and destruction, and life in Tiwanaku's bustling cities gradually became undesirable.

It appears that the political and demographic balance of the southern Titicaca basin ultimately shifted south, toward the drier Desaguadero Basin. The northern part of Desaguadero had formed an important province since the end of the Late Formative, when the early center of Khonkho Wankane was incorporated into the emerging state (Janusek et al. 2003). Recent excavations at this site reveal incredibly high volumes of camelid bones in Late Formative and Tiwanaku period contexts, suggesting that herding and pastoralism had thrived for centuries as a principal element in the local productive economy. A Late Formative monolith at Khonkho depicts a winged, decorated llama, visually emphasizing the significance of herding in local life and ritual. Specialized traders from the region still load llama caravans with salt from rich local deposits, headed for valleys to the north to exchange for crops and other goods.

In Early Pacajes, settlement patterns suggest, as the Tiwanaku-Taraco-Katari region experienced demographic decline, the drier regions around Khonkho and in Pacajes, further south, experienced demographic increase. By the time the Inca administered the region the political center and major *marka* in the southern basin was Caquiaviri, capitol of the Pacajes federation some fifty kilometers south of Tiwanaku. Supporting archaeological patterns, local narratives tell not of Aymara migrations into the basin from the south, but the establishment of new societies in the region as people moved out of Tiwanaku (Paredes 1955). At a macroregional scale, state fragmentation and a climatic shift favoring pastoralism correlated with a political and demographic shift to a region where pastoralism had always predominated economically and ideologically. A shift in political balance to the south occurred just as state power was eroding. Local leaders and high status groups may well have played a causal role in state collapse.

Collapse was as much a process of cultural creation and social reformulation as it was a necessary turning away from the past. To be sure, AD 1000–1200 was a "dangerous and chaotic" time as Bandy suggests, involving sociopolitical fragmentation and a relatively rapid process of cultural amnesia. Erasing old identities and memories, however, was one dimension in the formulation of new identities and shared memories, manifested, in part, in new styles, practices, and relations to the landscape. New groups and identities, in fact, were refashioned from prior relations and identities, including those that had once characterized Tiwanaku urban compounds and regions.

To return to the "whodunit" question of state collapse, such groups, some with long narrated histories and powerful identities, are our prime culprits. Facing an exploitative and anachronistic state system, a severe drought, the development of new productive regimes, as well as new political and economic opportunities, local and regional groups crafted or adopted new styles, technologies, and values. At least for the first generations, new practices and values were forged as a negation of elite and state power, as Tiwanaku leaders and ancestors increasingly were perceived more as sources of misery than of life. In this light, dramatic reformulations in ceramic style and mortuary practices are not surprising. Such potent objects and activities had embodied Tiwanaku ideals and activities and had served to express social identity at multiple social scales. They were transformed as a symbolic negation of state power. Yet cultural reformulation was as much about creating new symbols as it was about destroying or forgetting those that were no longer meaningful. In tandem with new productive strategies, more heterarchical social orders, and emergent political centers and leaders, groups actively, and to some extent intentionally, fashioned and adopted new styles and practices to express new values and ideals. Eventually, over several generations, Tiwanaku was no longer a central part of local myths and social memories.

Conclusions

The collapse of past states and civilizations is generally considered a political process, and as "a rapid, significant loss of an established level of sociopolitical complexity" (Tainter 1988:4). Tiwanaku collapse complicates this idea in that it was neither overly rapid nor simply political. Like state collapse globally, it did involve sociopolitical fragmentation, which more than lesser complexity produced an era of less centralized integration. However, disintegration, if at times violent, was a relatively uneven process that simultaneously involved the creation of distinct cultural values, practices, and material styles. Environmental deterioration fueled this historical juncture, in part. Although changing climate did not single-handedly cause state collapse, it destroyed critical foundations on which a common identity and social relations within the state were predicated, encouraging the rise of dispersed communities, heterarchical sociopolitical systems, and a more balanced mosaic of productive strategies.

Yoffee (1988) and Cowgill (1988) correctly suggest that we should distinguish state collapse from the demise of a civilization. Yet Tiwanaku collapse involved both sociopolitical fragmentation and profound cultural shift. In part, collapse proceeded as an active, chaotic, and partly intentional destruction of its key objects, icons, and leaders. Collapse simultaneously involved the popular pursuit of new productive strategies, the formation of new political alliances and socioeconomic networks, and the adoption of new cultural traditions. In great part, Tiwanaku collapse was a cultural revolution.

PART 4

CHAPTER 10
Conclusions

Enduring several centuries, Tiwanaku was a complex and dynamic formation. Its principal core cities of Tiwanaku and Lukurmata, each comprised of diverse groups that affiliated with the overarching polity while identifying with other figured worlds and communities, cooperated and competed through time. These were dynamic centers with long histories, and their urban societies were at once integrated and diversified. The diverse groups and communities, commoner and elite, that inhabited them and the southern Lake Titicaca basin, forged and, over many generations, reproduced a common polity, identity, and culture. Yet the long trajectory of Tiwanaku rise, consolidation, and collapse, viewed from a perspective emphasizing local urban residential and ritual places, indicates that Tiwanaku's constituent groups had a limited and historically contingent tolerance for transformative state strategies, hierarchical social conditions, and centralizing policies.

In concluding this volume, I synthesize the interpretations that arise from this analysis of Tiwanaku and offer some final conclusions. First, I discuss the impact that these results have on the three perspectives of Tiwanaku that are articulated in Chapter 3. Next, I draw together as a single narrative this perspective of Tiwanaku over the long run, as it emerged, transformed, and collapsed. I then discuss predominant patterns of Tiwanaku urban centers and society in relation to later Andean societies, pointing out elements of historical continuity and transformation. Finally, I point out what I believe are some of the broader implications of this study for archaeology and anthropology.

Unifying the Three Views of Tiwanaku

This comparative analysis of Tiwanaku and Lukurmata resonates with elements of each of the three predominant intellectual traditions and its particular interpretation of the constitution, historical trajectory, and significance of the polity. It demonstrates that each benefits from consideration of elements from other traditions. Tiwanaku was for many centuries a powerful state society, as Ponce, Kolata, and others suggest. Its emergence involved the formation of hierarchical settlement networks, immense monumental complexes, a concentric gradient of social status in Tiwanaku, and a master urban orientation at both sites tied to the location and inviolable rhythms of significant natural phenomena. Residential life involved the creation, distribution, and use of valued goods in Tiwanaku style, including a range of elaborate vessels dedicated to daily consumption and commensalism. Patterns of urban conformity manifest a potent state culture that was adopted, adapted, reproduced, and held significant by everyone, structuring day-to-day life in Tiwanaku cities. Space and style took on particular significance in lively social gatherings and solemn rituals, in which an immediate feeling of common identity and an experience of community coherence, whether considered in terms of Durkheim's "collective effervescence" or Turner's *communitas*, were periodically recharged. In many such contexts, groups affirmed Tiwanaku power and identity. In addition, Tiwanaku cultural influence reached vast regions of the south-central Andes, some of which were colonized by and under the direct control of regional Tiwanaku leaders.

Nevertheless, Tiwanaku was also socially and ideologically diverse. Characteristics of Tiwanaku and Lukurmata resonate with elements of the models that emphasize local power and autonomy, including substantial social diversity, local management of craft production, and vibrant identities. Groups inhabiting residential compounds formed coherent microcommunities. Some in Tiwanaku formed urban enclaves with enduring affiliations to far regions, much like foreign barrios in Teotihuacan. Tiwanaku was in part a cosmopolitan center that incorporated semiautonomous groups. Despite vast influence and far-reaching prestige, Tiwanaku control outside of the core was highly strategic, limited to specific regions, and directed toward certain forms of production, including raised fields in the Katari Valley and maize farming in Moquegua. Autonomous polities and ethnic groups thrived alongside regions of Tiwanaku influence and control. The Tiwanaku core itself comprised at least two distinct regions, each housing a major settlement that was the political and ritual center for an ethnic-like group.

Tiwanaku cities also were profoundly spiritual places. On the one hand, Tiwanaku and Lukurmata were exemplary centers, physical symbols built and refashioned according to cosmic principles that reified, in built landscapes, Tiwanaku's dominant ideology. As many suggest, these cities and in particular Tiwanaku itself approximated the ideal order of the cosmos.

Residential and ritual places in both centers simultaneously followed the routes of inviolable cosmic cycles, such as the daily path of the sun, and they adjusted residential and ritual life to sacred natural features and celestial bodies by facilitating visual pathways and symbolic resonance with such primordial vital forces. Tiwanaku and Lukurmata were powerful, ancient symbols of the communities with which their diverse urban and rural groups affiliated.

On the other hand, Tiwanaku's multiple ritual places and monumental complexes facilitated an exciting religious experience. Tiwanaku served as a place of periodic pilgrimage and ceremonial convergence during which this concrete symbol became the lived anchor of global political unity, religious affiliation, and cultural identity. At various times and in different manners, Akapana East, the Sunken Temple, Kalasasaya, Akapana, and Pumapunku comprised ritual complexes where Tiwanaku's dominant cosmic vision was breathed life and recharged. Built in stages, each was the center of a distinct ritual cult and specific types of ritual activities, perhaps founded by a distinct elite group, priestly caste, or ruling dynasty. The religious meaning and ritual significance of most complexes changed profoundly over time. Tiwanaku was a syncretic religious phenomenon characterized by significant ritual diversity and change.

As much as they were centers of elite values and cultural hegemony, Tiwanaku and Lukurmata were places where groups of diverse statuses, backgrounds, socioeconomic networks, religious affiliations, and kin relations visited and resided. Even if all who inhabited the centers were closely related to elite groups or played some direct role in the temples or in the urban economy, as Kolata suggests, these groups clearly maintained varied ritual and domestic practices, distinct patterns of material culture, reverence to local ancestors, and enduring identities. As such, Tiwanaku, like Teotihuacan, Rome, or Chicago, was a cosmopolitan place where social identities coresided and comingled, where power relations were expressed and redressd on a day-to-day basis, and where social hierarchies were constructed, refashioned, challenged, and ultimately deconstructed. Groups with different ethnic-like backgrounds settled in Tiwanaku, plying their own trades and maintaining through time, as in Teotihuacan, enduring ties and exchange networks with their distant homelands. Lukurmata was the center for a coherent, wealthy, and powerful ethnic-like community. All such groups affiliated with Tiwanaku state culture, subscribing to and eventually internalizing, to varying degrees, its prestigious cosmology and ideological principles as a profound practical hegemony and largely unquestioned worldview. Differences of status and identity were created, affirmed, blurred, and negotiated in Tiwanaku style goods and typical domestic and ritual practices. Yet even if shaped by and expressed in representations of Tiwanaku ideology, urban group identity remained grounded in local values and unique domestic and ritual practices.

Tiwanaku over the Long Term

Tiwanaku also changed significantly over time. A long-term perspective of the polity recounts a complex narrative of prestigious ritual activity, vibrant social identities, and shifting power relations. In the Late Formative Period, Tiwanaku and Lukurmata emerged as major settlements in a regional context of interacting, fluid, and loosely coalescing multicommunity polities. Inhabitants of Tiwanaku, Lukurmata, and surrounding settlements differed in occupation, ritual participation, access to elaborate and exotic goods, and ritual knowledge. Status differences intensified throughout the period. In Late Formative 2, Tiwanaku emerged from this network of small-scale polities as the primary demographic, cultural, and political center in the basin. The precise reasons for this transformation remain unclear, and are more fully elaborated elsewhere (Janusek 2004, 2005). Several major regional changes appear to have played some part in Tiwanaku's rise. Pukara declined after AD 200, opening an economic and political vacuum in the Lake Titicaca Basin. Bandy (2001) suggests that it may be due to a shift in circum-Titicaca trade networks following rising lake levels, and Stanish (1999, 2003) hypothesizes that through competitive feasting and commensalism, Tiwanaku leaders strategically circulated social debt while accruing prestige and power. At least as critical to Tiwanaku's success, I believe, was its ability to incorporate diversity through a flexible, elegant cosmology and a range of prestigious goods and practices that gave each group good material *and* ideological reasons for being a part of and identifying with its centers, leaders, and ritual specialists. That is, at least as critical as shifting political alliances, changing trade networks, and environmental shift was the establishment of an inclusive domain of shared views and practices, a vast imagined community, with which groups with diverse ideologies, productive practices, and ethnic-like identities identified. Identity and polity were forged in ongoing projects of monumental construction, reproduced in potent ritual contexts, and replicated in the layout of ritual places, which centered on sculpted icons of mythical ancestors and embodied the familiar intimacy of mundane residential space. Tiwanaku emerged as an incorporative phenomenon grounded in ideals of tolerance, diversity, consent, and reciprocity. Such were its strength, and ultimately, its weakness. State development was an unintended consequence that formed out of the patterned practices and ideals put into action by participant groups of diverse backgrounds, interests, and statuses.

In Tiwanaku IV, by which time Tiwanaku and Lukurmata had become the primary political and cultural centers of an emergent state, leaders continued to emphasize incorporative strategies of integration. These included several interwoven policies. First, to foster the integration of diversity and popular consent, leaders promoted a prestigious state culture, embodied in a convincing worldview, and expressed in new productive technologies and highly valued material styles. In a remarkable populist shift away from ancient patterns, elaborate Tiwanaku serving and ceremonial wares were, for the most part, distributed and used across society. Second, craft specialization and even vast productive regimes, the learned practices and plied trades of specific groups, and thus key elements of local livelihoods and identities, remained firmly in the hands of local groups and communities as socially embedded practices.

Third, relations between leaders and commoners and among groups with diverse backgrounds and identities were characterized by a practical etiquette of reciprocal obligation. Social and political relations, "greasing the political wheels," as it were, demanded rituals of consumption at various scales and in varying contexts. At the public scale, elaborate feasts were lively, dramatic theaters characterized by an idiom of commensal hospitality. Through commensalism community identity was forged and felt and obligations were circulated. By sponsoring feasts, individuals and groups at all scales—households, urban compounds, regional communities, and state leaders—cultivated influence and legitimacy. By successfully hosting feasts repeatedly, power eventually concentrated to the few, as high status individuals and groups amassed substantive funds of power and promoted Tiwanaku's political and cultural hegemony.

Attention to local contexts in Tiwanaku and Lukurmata outlines a volatile sociopolitical order characterized by dynamic tensions between state institutions and strategies and local, kin-based, totemistic groups and interests. Tiwanaku emerged as a centralized, hierarchical polity founded on local identities. Tiwanaku's primary centers and their hinterlands incorporated significant heterarchy, which as much as overlapping roles included competing nodes of power and influence. The idealized relations of local groups formed the matrix from which state religious, economic, and political institutions were forged. At regional scales, communities formed salient identities with direct control over local resources and productive systems. They formed potential factions that, although participating in and benefiting from state institutions, expressed coherent identities in media such as the human body and valued ceremonial objects. Vast communities such as the inhabitants of Lukurmata and the Katari Valley had tremendous political power and cultural influence.

The tension between state and local interests shifted decisively at approximately AD 800, initiating Tiwanaku V. An elite class of administrators and priests, apparently a powerful new ruling dynasty, crystallized in Tiwanaku. Projects of urban renewal converted old residential areas into places closely tied to elite groups and their ceremonial activities. Throughout the Tiwanaku core, as strategies of transformation increased in potency and scope, feasting and communal consumption accrued increasingly important roles at all scales of society. At the public scale, commensalism became increasingly important as a mechanism for establishing relations among elites and nonelites in a world of increasing inequality. Grounded in ideals of reciprocity and generosity, it helped legitimize, or at least render livable, increasing differences in status, wealth, and power. Tiwanaku political economy quickly became a feasting economy, a shift that helps explain the implementation of transformative strategies of integration in highly productive regions. Lukurmata declined in population and importance, most likely via deliberate state strategies of transformation and perhaps colonization as the Katari Valley was converted into a prime agricultural estate. In warm valley regions such as Moquegua, distant Tiwanaku colonies were converted into highly integrated provinces dedicated to the production of maize, in great part to fuel elite-sponsored tournaments of feasting and drinking in the altiplano. Increasing state influence on the Island of the Sun indicates that Tiwanaku sought greater control over local ritual places. In the Tiwanaku core and beyond, Tiwanaku ruling groups and perhaps competing elite factions implemented transformative strategies of integration and appropriation to establish greater control over critical resources and influence in urban social networks. Perhaps not entirely a planned consequence of such specific interests and local changes, Tiwanaku became a highly centralized state.

Nevertheless, the seeds of Tiwanaku collapse were sown during its apogee. In Tiwanaku V the balance of settlement in the Tiwanaku Valley shifted to areas outside of Tiwanaku, a pattern that accelerated after AD 1000. Perhaps most significant, the decline of Lukurmata and state appropriation of the Koani Pampa in Katari shook the very foundations of state power and legitimacy. The Katari Valley comprised a powerful and productive ethnic-like community, and possibly a moiety that formed an integral part of Tiwanaku society and ideology; in essence, Tiwanaku's "better half." Increasing state control over local livelihoods and disruption of local management in productive enterprises put excessive ideological and material stresses on social conditions in the state core. In this sense, environmental shift and shifting regional political conditions exacerbated already volatile local conditions. Tiwanaku's long-term strength resided in an ideology, continually internalized as practical hegemony, that promoted diverse religious attitudes and identities. Ruling and elite strategies increasingly strained the etiquette of ancient, accepted social relations, even as age-old ideals were increasingly promoted in elite-sponsored rituals of consumption. Deteriorating environmental conditions prevented access to the resources that fueled these ideals in commensal and other ceremonial activities.

After AD 1000, contradictions between the world as represented and the world as experienced became insupportable. Local livelihoods became increasingly difficult, especially in a sociopolitical system that must have been viewed as increasingly intolerable and anachronistic. While local and countercultural expressions had previously taken the form of stylistic diversity and perhaps hidden transcripts of resistance, emergent conditions incited groups to turn violently against icons of Tiwanaku ideology and power and the elite groups they largely represented. New conditions fostered a rupture that promoted cultural amnesia in regard to Tiwanaku symbols and ideals and the adoption of new practices and material styles. This was a volatile and dangerous time that witnessed the end of the Tiwanaku state, religion, and culture. Of necessity, however, collapse proceeded as a cultural revolution in which old local practices, ideals, and identities were adapted to a transformed social context involving more heterarchical sociopolitical relations, new ritual practices, and egalitarian ideals.

Tiwanaku urban societies were diverse, and the state's long-term stability rested in great part on its attractive and redemptive vision of the cosmos and society, a vision that groups adopted, reformulated, and internalized as their own. Those who identified with Tiwanaku had something to gain, whether materially or spiritually, whether grounded in rational ends or emotional bonds, and whether in social prestige, economic opportunities, political influence, or religious inspiration. Society and ideology had to remain attractive and flexible in order for Tiwanaku's hierarchical, increasingly centralized structure to remain appealing. In changing natural and sociopolitical conditions, and as elites increasingly interfered in local livelihoods and sought direct control over local resources, Tiwanaku ultimately became insupportable. Local groups and competing factions, now mobilized as powerful factions, turned violently and publicly against state symbols and leaders. Ultimately, they adopted new symbols and affiliated with new leaders as they turned away from the past and forged a world of new meanings and practices.

Tiwanaku and Later Andean Societies

Many aspects of life, ritual, and social organization in Tiwanaku offer useful comparisons with later society in the south-central Andes. Chapter 2 details later patterns of social organization and cultural principles that

I believe shed light on Tiwanaku's character and history. Many characteristics of *ayllu*-based organization resonate with expressions of identity and power found in prehispanic material patterns. Vibrant identities and social boundaries characterized Tiwanaku's principal urban centers and in fact the entire cultural and political core. Tiwanaku and Lukurmata were comprised of discrete residential compounds, each consisting of various households that collectively formed a distinct corporate group. Some engaged in specific productive activities, crafting certain types of ceramics, musical instruments, and undoubtedly many other goods, while some clearly differed in status. Many differed in their specific socioeconomic networks and affiliations. Thus, these groups were similar in many characteristics to later micro-*ayllus*, constituent households of which were linked together via kin-based terms and principles and reverence to common ancestors.

As it was among later *ayllus*, so it was in earlier urban groups: they collectively formed complex figured worlds in which individuals and households identified with multiple broader communities. Neither *ayllus* nor the groups inhabiting urban compounds were exclusive social domains in their respective contexts. Rather their relations provided an idiom that structured social relations in other, more abstract and imagined communities. A critical element of a group's identity, as in more recent Andean societies, was its particular occupation, whether primarily farming, fishing, crafting panpipes, or making ceramic wares with tan as opposed to red exteriors. Another critical element of a group's identity was its relative place in Tiwanaku's emerging social hierarchy, and linked to this, its history in Tiwanaku and Lukurmata as well as its nonlocal origins or affiliations. By Tiwanaku V in Tiwanaku, identity and status were intertwined with spatial and temporal proximity to the now-ancient monumental temples and ceremonial areas that had become increasingly distant from the urban boundary. Also important to identity was a group's dietary regime, which was in some cases tied to its particular productive specialties. Another dimension, perhaps, was a group's affiliation with one or another built ritual complex in Tiwanaku, which were foci for distinct, complementary, and to some extent competing religious organizations or "churches." Like constituent *ayllus* of a common *marka* and macro-*ayllu*, all such groups collectively identified with Tiwanaku and some its ideals, practices, and styles.

Many of the urban compound groups in Tiwanaku and Lukurmata formed segments or enclaves of broader, far-reaching communities. In Lukurmata, the presence of circular dwellings in both Tiwanaku and post-Tiwanaku periods may represent early residence by groups identifying as Uru or a similar ethnic-like community. Early ethnographic studies determined that, while Aymara occupied rectangular dwellings, most Uru lived in homes with circular or ovoid ground plans (La Barre 1947; Metraux 1936). Shuttling such a specific correlation of architecture and identity to the Tiwanaku Period is problematic, but it correlates with other evidence supporting such an interpretation. For example, Uru communities specialized in lacustrine and riverine resources, and to date the only known Tiwanaku-Period circular dwelling in the core is in Lukurmata, a lake shore community. Further, the post-Tiwanaku circular dwellings that clustered along the shore of Lukurmata were inhabited by fishers (Wise 1993). Thus, a correspondence of evidence points to the likelihood that the southern Lake Titicaca Basin comprised resource-based identity distinctions akin to, if not directly antecedent to the documented Aymara-Uru distinction. This raises the possibility that such a distinction had a longer history in the region than is sometimes considered.

Local styles and practices simultaneously distinguished Tiwanaku and Lukurmata and their respective valleys. Tiwanaku and Lukurmata were independent or semiautonomous centers for generations preceding Tiwanaku state hegemony. Urban groups in Lukurmata, in particular, despite local differences and identities among urban compounds, formed a coherent community identity linked to a broader regional boundary. Identity at this scale, manifested in multiple dimensions of daily and ritual life, was akin to that among later macro-*ayllus*, each focused on its representative political and ceremonial center, or *marka*. Such an identity, like the Aymara-Uru distinction, had dimensions of expression and practice characteristic of ethnicity. Lukurmata and the Katari Valley, at least until about AD 800–900, formed a semiautonomous productive and political unit within Tiwanaku's core. As in later macro-*ayllus*, identity at this scale thrived on claims to common ancestors and some shared memory and mythical fabrication of its pre-Tiwanaku history. It was tied to a landscape with abundant lake resources and great productive potential, one far more amenable to raised field production than the Tiwanaku Valley. Thus, inhabitants of Lukurmata and the grater Katari Valley, grounded in shared memory, landscape, and productive concerns, and manifested in characteristic styles, practices, and bodily forms, formed a wealthy, coherent, and powerful ethnic-like group.

The boundary between the valleys approximates the cosmological, geographical, and political division of Urkosuyu and Umasuyu, documented since the sixteenth century and still alive, to some degree, in local Bolivian politics. In Chapter 9, I argued that the boundary between the regions, with a history predating the Tiwanaku state, became especially volatile in Late Tiwanaku V, as the Tiwanaku state fragmented. Volatility in the relation between the regions may have stemmed from Tiwanaku's direct appropriation of productive resources in the Koani Pampa and the disruption of local livelihoods and organizations. I raised the possibility that, in Tiwanaku IV, the Tiwanaku and Katari Valleys had been something akin to two moieties. To the extent this was the case, upon the coalescence of the state in Tiwanaku IV, sociopolitical differences between the regions were subsumed within a dual order, that ascribed to heterarchical and potentially conflictive differences an idealized relation of complementary opposition. As an effective mechanism and ideology of sociopolitical integration, duality was a common form of organization throughout the prehispanic and more recent Andes (Abercrombie 1998; Kolata and Ponce 1992). Blom points out (2004), further, that predominant differences in cranial modification styles extended well beyond the two valleys, and in fact may have characterized the entire Lake Titicaca Basin and its associated eastern and western valley regions. As in many later Andean polities, complementary opposition may have been a strategic idiom of integration that was replicated throughout the polity and across its vast regional landscapes. Whatever the case, the boundary was a significant cultural phenomenon with a long and dynamic history. Like prehispanic Maya sites in current Maya identity politics, it was an old cultural form continually given new meanings in the course of regional identity politics that antedated and postdated Tiwanaku hegemony. It remains so today.

Analogous to later *markas*, the two centers anchored the identities of their respective regional communities as places of social and ceremonial convergence. Beyond that, Tiwanaku and Lukurmata anchored the identity of the polity, in part through their embodiment of a potent and deeply rooted symbolic order. Organized around visual pathways to significant natural features and attuned to the inviolable cycles of primordial celestial rhythms, the built environments of both centers sought to approximate and appropriate the power inherent in the generative forces of the cosmos. The inner sancta of major temples were symbolic portals facilitating a connection, through ritual and offering, between living and ancestral worlds.

Tiwanaku was the political, ritual, and symbolic center of the entire polity. Characterized by frequent feasting and ceremony, several massive ritual complexes, a concentric organization of status differences, and great social diversity, Tiwanaku was fundamentally distinct from Lukurmata. Tiwanaku was a major place of pilgrimage and convergence for groups affiliated with the entire polity, and this role appears to have increased in Tiwanaku V. Periodically, following the rhythms of major feasts and rituals, plazas, courtyards, and residential compounds became nodes of dense social gathering and consumption. People from settlements in the core region and beyond, including Cochabamba and Moquegua, would have come to visit, participate, and temporarily reside in the city. Tiwanaku was a cosmopolitan center to which people came to experience, gain ritual enlightenment, or enhance their prestige. As they came to participate in the feasts and rituals sponsored by ruling and elite groups, they consumed the state's most potent expressions.

Identification with Tiwanaku and its global ideologies was compelling. Like later Andean polities, Tiwanaku was both a political hierarchy of encompassment and a prestigious imagined community. Tiwanaku was legitimized as a vast macrocommunity; as part of a political ideology that in built images and a predominant etiquette of socioeconomic relations drew on the intimacy characteristic of local settings. The notable ubiquity of Tiwanaku valued goods and the widespread participation of diverse groups in the state political economy indicate that state culture was promoted not just by ruling and elite groups but, to varying degrees, by everyone. Participation in Tiwanaku's religious, economic, and social spheres and tacit consent to its integrative strategies fortified local wealth and status. An ultimately tense and volatile situation, state power resided in the widespread adoption and internalization of Tiwanaku state culture, which in turn emboldened local identity and power.

Nevertheless, Tiwanaku was fundamentally different from later segmentary polities and federations. The scale of monumental complexes dedicated to ceremonial activities and the portrayal of religious themes and icons on elaborate material remains delineate a distinctive Andean formation. Tiwanaku's longevity, extensive urban centers, transformative strategies of production and integration, and hierarchical settlement networks were patterns by and large unknown to later Andean polities in the south-central Andes. Further, the profound transformation of social organizations and cultural principles in the process of Tiwanaku collapse indicates that local groups and communities were closely integrated with state organizations. Collapse was not the dismantling of a loosely coalescing organization, a dispersal of groups away from nucleated centers, or a simple walking away from old leaders. Rather, it was a volatile process of collapse and genesis, and of cultural amnesia and regeneration, in which distinct types of societies, polities, and practices were formulated. To be sure, the process involved the reproduction of many earlier organizations, social boundaries, and cultural principles, which ensured the continued vitality of certain traditional ideals and practices in new times and contexts. Still, the breadth of change in post-Tiwanaku society and culture, and the overall vitality of new patterns over many centuries, indicate that Tiwanaku was not simply a segmentary political organization.

Identity and Power Beyond the Andes

A perspective emphasizing local populations and historical dynamics dovetails with recent perspectives on archaic polities worldwide that seek to enhance or transcend conventional approaches to complexity in archaeology.

Among other things, it invites a nuanced consideration of the intricate relations of power and identity that linked diverse communities and fostered the rise and transformation of civilizations, whether cumulatively and gradually or rapidly and violently. Identity politics and power relations are potent dimensions of practically all social interactions in complex societies, embedded as they are in both tacit and reflexive understandings of the world. Their accepted ranges of expression form part of the generative principles that shape everyday consciousness, common sense, and activity. Intentionally or not, identity and power also inevitably transform the principles that guide their very expression in the world. An urban community or complex polity is transformed just as it is reproduced, as patterned social practices, in drawing on current ideals and symbols, adjust to changing conventions, shifting social and extrasocial conditions, and major historical events.

Tiwanaku like many other New World polities comprised diverse communities and factional interests, which were expressed in heterarchical dimensions of its built urban environments and anthropogenic regional landscapes. Increasingly through time, a common state culture, hierarchical social relations, and integrative institutions intensified in scope and influence, but they materialized in specific, if predominant patterns of life in core cities. As fundamental to state development and legitimacy were the diverse social identities and local interests out of which state institutions were forged, and with which their power and influence were always enmeshed. State forms and institutions emerged out of the ideals and practices of local kin-based groups and communities, and in great part they remained grounded in an intimate etiquette characteristic of such groups. V. Gordon Childe (1950:16) argued that in past cities there was "no room for skeptics and sectaries," or as Weber put it (1958), for the quaint "totemistic" ties characteristic of nonurban societies. Urban coherence and state power, in such views, require the submergence or disappearance of potentially cynical attitudes, conflictive interests, and cognitive dissonance. Yet Tiwanaku reminds us that relations grounded in an ideal of intimacy, and thus rooted in sectarian and totemistic ties, often formed the very cultural matrix out of which state structures were forged and constructed. Local identity and sectarian interests, given a fragile balance of power as well as volatile sociopolitical and shifting environmental conditions, also can be counted among the forces that dismantled such structures and erased for future memory their particular brands of hegemony.

Notes

Chapter 2

1. I witnessed a similar practice in Khonkho San Salvador, Bolivia (near La Paz) during the recently "invented tradition" of a winter solstice ceremony (*machac mara*, or New Year) in 2001. This ceremony takes place annually at the major archaeological site of Khonkho Wankane, now an important sacred place for the entire macro-*ayllu* of Jesus de Machaca, and to which people from micro-*ayllus* (or cantons) across the region come to participate. Upon cutting the llama's throat right after sunrise, officiants throw blood from their fingertips toward the east, onto both participants and the earth. Simultaneously, one officiant pours collected blood from a cup onto a massive sandstone monolith (the *tatakala*, or father-stone) that lies nearby.
2. In Aymara communities near La Paz, *muxsa misas*, or sweet misas, are carefully assembled by a specialist (*yatiri*), sometimes in combination with the ritual host and key participants. Kolata (1996:23) accurately points out that in Tiwanaku today, a *muxsa misa* itself (sweet misa), "once assembled, creates a map, a sacred landscape of the imagination in microcosm." Carefully formed of numerous elements infused with meaning for the local Aymara—including coca leaves, potatoes, resinous incense, candy molded into significant symbols (*misterios*), chunks of llama fat, and mummified llama fetuses themselves—they are pungent and visually sensuous, evoking the generative forces which are about to consume them in fire and smoke.

Chapter 3

1. As Albarraćin-Jordan points out (1999:19), the hypothetical Qolla race Posnansky describes is something like an "Andean Arian" race.

Chapter 4

1. Among the Wari, in Brazil, informants note that the bones of consumed ancestors were ground and buried in pits (Conklin 2001, personal communication). In this light it is not beyond reason that the small, shallow pits in Akapana East contained the pulverized remains of some portion of the bones of consumed individuals.

Chapter 5

1. This is in line with abundant evidence for distinct household cycles of construction, abandonment, and renewal throughout Tiwanaku (Janusek 1994). In many areas it is clear that abandoned houses stood for years, during which they were mined for adobe and used as refuse dumps, and inevitably, as today, provided convenient public latrines.
2. However, this estimate is based on data from surface collections analyzed before the Tiwanaku IV-V chronology was more firmly established (Albarraćin-Jordan 1996a; Janusek 2003a), and so must remain tentative. A more exact figure can be established by simply revisiting those surface collections.
3. Posnansky oversaw the construction of this modern version of the Sunken Temple in 1940, in the Miraflores sector of La Paz (Ponce 1990:161). This version is much larger than the authentic temple, and its stairway, walls (which lack pillars), and tenoned heads differ radically. As Ponce (ibid.) notes, with more than a hint of sarcasm, it is "guilty of inaccuracy" (peca de inexacta). Though much closer to excavated patterns, so does Ponce's reconstruction of the original temple at Tiwanaku.

Chapter 6

1. However, the orientation is not apparent in recent publications. Although Bennett (1936:Figure 36) was close, in Rivera (1989:Figure 19; also Bermann 1994:Figure 11.9) it is oriented exactly to the cardinal directions, and in Bermann (1994:Figure 11.1) it is several degrees *west* of north.
2. The placement of a stopper would also help control the tuning of a flute. Safford (1914:188, 190) noted that to "correct a pipe for flatness the Titicaca Indians pour either water or a little pisco (grape brandy) into it, thus shortening the vibrating column of air to the required length." La Barre (1948:113) notes that he "never observed that the Aymara were so meticulous about the absolute pitch of their instruments." This point is sharply driven home for anyone visiting a lively Aymara ritual today, particularly toward the evening, once a troop has been drinking throughout the day. In fact, it is clear that cacophany is often the desired effect, manifested both in specific songs played by a troop and, ultimately, in the simultaneous playing of different, competing troops. Having observed musicians at festivals in Aymara communities pour beer and cane alcohol *trago* into and through their instruments, I agree with La Barre that this gesture also has "a different motive" (ibid.). It is a *ch'alla*, a prayer or offering performed so that the instrument and its player will make good music (also see Langevin 1991).
3. In many double-row *sikus* each row has a similar connotation of complementary duality (Langevin 1991) A row of stopped pipes, sometimes termed *urko* referring to the masculine element and producing a crisp sound, complements a row of open pipes that provide an airy, raspier sound. The breathy element so characteristic of Andean panpipes is an integral part of a panpipe's sound, and so is sought.

Chapter 7

1. Nevertheless, as for Tiwanaku IV occupations, settlement estimates are based on ceramic analyses conducted before a firmer handle on changes in Tiwanaku style assemblages were known, and so may require some revision.

Bibliography

Abbott, M., Binford, M., Brenner, M. and Kelts, K. (1997) 'A 4500 14C yr High-Resolution Record of Water-Level Changes in Lake Titicaca, Bolivia-Peru', *Quaternary Research,* 47: 169–80.

Abercrombie, T. (1986) 'The Politics of Sacrifice: An Aymara Cosmology in Action', Unpublished Ph.D. Dissertation, Chicago: University of Chicago.

Abercrombie, T. (1998) *Pathways of Memory and Power: Ethnography and History among an Andean People,* Madison: University of Wisconsin Press.

Abu-Lughod, L. (1991) 'Writing Against Culture', in R.G. Fox (ed.) Recapturing *Anthropology: Working in the Present,* Santa Fe: School of American Research Press, pp. 137–62.

Albarracín-Jordán, J.V. (1992) 'Prehispanic and Early Colonial Settlement Patterns in the Lower Tiwanaku Valley, Bolivia', Unpublished Ph.D. Dissertation, Dallas: Southern Methodist University.

———. (1996a) *Tiwanaku: Arqueología Regional y Dinámica Segmentaría,* La Paz, Bolivia: Plural Editores.

———. (1996b) 'Tiwanaku Settlement System: the Integration of Nested Hierarchies in the Lower Tiwanaku Valley', *Latin American Antiquity,* 7: 183–210.

———. (1999) *The Archaeology of Tiwanaku: The Myths, History, and Science of an Ancient Civilization,* La Paz: PAP.

———. (2003) 'Tiwanaku: A Pre-Inca, Segmentary State in the Andes', in A.L. Kolata (ed.) *Tiwanaku and Its Hinterland: Archaeology and Paleoecology of an Andean Civilization, Vol. 2,* Washington, D.C.: Smithsonian Institution Press, pp. 95–111.

Albarracín-Jordán, J.V. and Mathews, J.E. (1990) *Asentamientos Prehispánicos del Valle de Tiwanaku, Vol. 1,* La Paz, Bolivia: Producciones CIMA.

Albó, X. (1972) 'Dinámica en la estructura intercomunicaría de Jesús de Machaca', *América Indígena,* 32: 773–816.

Albó, X. and Layme, F. (1992) *Literatura Aymara: Antología,* La Paz: CIPCA, Hisbol, and JAYMA.

Albornoz, C. de (1967[1580]) 'Instruccion para descubrir todas las guacas del Piru y sus camayos y haciendas', *Journal de la Societe des Americanistes,* 56: 17–39.

Alconini Mújica, S. (1991) 'Algunas reflexiones sobre la formación de la arqueología en Bolivia', *Etnología: Boletín del Museo Nacional de Etnografía y Folklore,* 19: 57–68.

———. (1993) 'La Cerámica de la Pirámide Akapana y su Contexto Social en el Estado de Tiwanaku', Unpublished Licenciatura Thesis, La Paz, Bolivia: Universidad Mayor de San Andrés.

———. (1995) *Rito, Símbolo e Historia en la Pirámide de Akapana, Tiwanaku: Un Análisis de la Cerámica Ceremonial Prehispánica,* La Paz, Bolivia: Editorial Acción.

Alexander, R.T. (1999) 'Mesoamerican House Lots and Archaeological Site Structure: Problems of Inference in Yaxcaba, Yucatan, Mexico, 1750–1847', in P.M. Allison (ed.) *The Archaeology of Household Activities*, London: Routledge, pp. 78–100.

Ames, K.M. (1995) 'Chiefly Power and Household Production on the Northwest Coast', in T.D. Price and G.M. Feinman (eds.) *Foundations of Social Inequality*, New York: Plenum Press, pp. 155–87.

Anderson, B. (1983) *Imagined Communities*, London: Verso.

Anderson, K. 'Omereque: A Middle Horizon Ceramic Style of Central Bolivia', paper presented at the 61st Annual Conference of the Society for American Archaeology, New Orleans, 1996.

Anderson, K. and Céspedes Paz, R. 'Tiwanaku and Local Effects of Contact: The Late Formative to Middle Horizon Transition in Cochabamba, Bolivia', paper presented at 63rd Annual Meeting of the Society for American Archaeology, Seattle, 1998.

Arellano López, J. (1975) 'La ciudad prehispánica de Iskanwaya', *Centro de Investigaciones Arqueológicas*, 6.

———. (1985) *Mollo: Investigaciones Arqueológicas*, La Paz: Imprenta Nacional.

Argollo, J., Ticcla, L., Kolata, A.L. and Rivera, O. (1996) 'Geology, Geomorphology, and Soils of the Tiwanaku and Catari River Basins', in A.L. Kolata (ed.) *Tiwanaku and Its Hinterland: Archaeology and Paleoecology of an Andean Civilization, Vol. 1*, Washington, D.C.: Smithsonian Institution Press, pp. 57–88.

Arnold, D.Y. (1992) 'La casa de adobes y piedras del Inka: género, memoria y cosmos en Qaqachaka', *Hacia un Orden Andino de las Cosas*, La Paz: Hisbol/ILCA, pp. 31–108.

Ashmore, W. and Wilk, R.R. (1988) 'Household and Community in the Mesoamerican Past', in R. Wilk and W. Ashmore (eds.) *Household and Community in the Mesoamerican Past*, Albuquerque: University of New Mexico Press, pp. 1–27.

Avila, F. de (1966 [1598?]) *Dioses y hombres de Huarochirí: Narración guichua recogida Por Francisco de Avila*, Trans. By José María Arguedas, Lima: Instituto de Estudios Peruanos.

Baker, P., Seltzer, G., Fritz, S., Dunbar, R., Grove, M., Tapia, P., Cross, S., Rowe, H., and Broda, J. (2001) 'The History of South American Tropical Precipitation for the Past 25,000 Years', *Science*, 291: 640–43.

Balkansky, A.K., Feinman, G.M. and Nichols, L.M. (1997) 'Pottery Kilns of Ancient Ejutla, Oaxaca, Mexico', *Journal of Field Archaeology*, 24: 139–60.

Bandelier, A.F. (1910) *The Islands of Titicaca and Koati*, New York: Hispanic Society of America.

———. (1911) 'The Ruins at Tiahuanaco', *Proceedings of the American Antiquarian Society*, 21: 218–65.

Bandy, M.S. (1999) 'The Montículo Excavations', in C.A. Hastorf (ed.) *Early Settlement at Chiripa, Bolivia: Research of the Taraco Archaeological Project*, Berkeley: University of California Archaeological Research Facility, pp. 43–49.

———. (2001) 'Population and History in the Ancient Titicaca Basin', Unpublished Ph.D. Dissertation, Berkeley: University of California at Berkeley.

Bandy, M.S., Cohen, A.B., Goldstein, P.S., Cardona, R.A. and Oquiche, H.A. 'The Tiwanaku Occupation of Chen Chen (M1): Preliminary Report on the 1995 Salvage Excavations', paper presented at 61st Annual Society for American Archaeology meetings, New Orleans, LA, 1996.

Bandy, M.S. and Janusek, J.W. (2004) 'Settlement Patterns, Administrative Boundaries, and Residential Mobility in the Early Colonial Period', in C. Stanish, M. Aldenderfer, and A. Cohen (eds.) *Recent Archaeological Research in the Lake Titicaca Basin of Peru and Bolivia*, Los Angeles: Cotsen Institute of Archaeology (in press).

Barrett, J.C. (1994) *Fragments from Antiquity: An Archaeology of Social Life in Britain, 2900–1200 BC*, Oxford: Blackwell.

Barth, F. (1969) *Ethnic Groups and Boundaries: The Social Organization of Culture Difference*, Boston: Little, Brown and Company.

Bastien, J.W. (1978) *Mountain of the Condor: Metaphor and Ritual in an Andean Ayllu, American Ethnological Society, Monograph 64*, New York: West Publishing Company.

Bauer, B.S. and Stanish, C. (2001) *Ritual and Pilgrimage in the Ancient Andes*, Austin: University of Texas.

Bawden, G. (1993) 'An Archaeological Study of Social Structure and Ethnic Replacement in Residential Architecture of the Tumilaca Valley', in M.S. Aldenderfer (ed.) *Domestic Architecture, Ethnicity, and Complementarity in the South-Central Andes*, Iowa City: University of Iowa Press, pp. 42–54.

Bell, C. (1992) *Ritual Theory, Ritual Practice*, New York: Oxford University Press.

———. (1997) *Ritual: Perspectives and Dimensions,* New York: Oxford University Press.
Bennett, W.C. (1934) 'Excavations at Tiahuanaco', *Anthropological Papers of the American Museum of Natural History,* 34: 359–494.
———. (1936) 'Excavations in Bolivia', *Anthropological Papers of the American Museum of Natural History,* 35: 329–507.
———. (1950) 'Cultural Unity and Disunity in the Titicaca Basin', *American Antiquity,* 16: 89–98.
Bennett, W.C. and Bird, J.B. (1964) *Andean Culture History: The Archaeology of the Central Andes from Early Man to the Incas,* Garden City: The Natural History Press.
Berenguer Rodríguez, J.R., V. Castro S. and O. Silva G. (1980) 'Reflexiones acerca de la presencia de Tiwanaku en el norte de Chile', *Estudios Arqueológicos,* 5: 81–92.
Berenguer Rodríguez, J. and Dauelsberg H., P. (1989) 'El norte grande en la órbita de Tiwanaku (400 a 1,200 d.C)', in J. Hidalgo L., V. Schiappacasse F., H. Niemeyer F., C. Aldunate Del S. and I. Solimano R. (eds.) *Culturas de Chile, Prehistoria desde sus Orígenes hasta los Albores de la Conquista,* Santiago de Chile: Editorial Andres Bello, pp. 129–80.
Bermann, M.P. (1989a) 'Una excavación de prueba cerca del Templo Semisubterraneo de Lukurmata', in A.L. Kolata (ed.) *Agquelogía de Lukurmata, Vol. 2,* La Paz: INAR, pp. 493–112.
———. (1989b) 'Vision de las Casas del Período Tiwanaku en Lukurmata', in A.L. Kolata (ed.) *La Tecnología y Organización de la Producción Agrícola en el Estado de Tiwanaku, Vol. 2,* La Paz, Bolivia: Instituto Nacional de Arqueología de Bolivia, Ediciones Pumapunku, pp. 113–51.
———. (1990) 'Prehispanic Household and Empire at Lukurmata, Bolivia', Unpublished Ph.D. dissertation, Ann Arbor: University of Michigan.
———. (1993) 'Continuity and Change in Household Life at Lukurmata', in M.S. Aldenderfer (ed.) *Domestic Architecture, Ethnicity, and Complementarity in the South-Central Andes,* Iowa City, IA: University of Iowa Press, pp. 112–35.
———. (1994) *Lukurmata: Household Archaeology in Prehispanic Bolivia,* Princeton, NJ: Princeton University Press.
———. (1997) 'Domestic Life and Vertical Integration in the Tiwanaku Heartland', *Latin American Antiquity,* 8: 93–112.
———. (2003) 'The Archaeology of Households in Lukurmata', in A.L. Kolata (ed.) *Tiwanaku and Its Hinterland: Archaeology and Paleoecology of an Andean Civilization, Vol. 2,* Washington, D.C.: Smithsonian Institution Press, pp. 327–40.
Bermann, M.P. and Graffam, G. (1989) 'Arquitectura residencial en las terrazas de Lukurmata', in Kolata (ed.), La Paz, Bolivia: Producciones Puma Punku, pp. 153–72.
Bertonio, P.L. (1984[1612]) *Vocabulario de la Lengua Aymara,* Cochabamba: CERES/IFEA/MUSEF.
Betanzos, J.de (1996[1557]) *Narrative of the Incas,* Austin: University of Texas Press, R. Hamilton and D. Buchanan (Trans.).
Binford, M.W., Brenner, M. and Leyden, B.W. (1996) 'Paleoecology and Tiwanaku Agroecosystems', in A.L. Kolata (ed.) *Tiwanaku and Its Hinterland: Archaeology and Paleoecology of an Andean Civilization, Vol. 1,* Washington, D.C.: Smithsonian Institution Press, pp. 89–108.
Binford, M.W., Kolata, A.L., Brenner, M., Janusek, J.W., Seddon, M.T., Abbott, M. and Curtis, J.H. (1997) 'Climate Variation and the Rise and Fall of an Andean Civilization', *Quaternary Research,* 47: 235–48.
Blanton, R.E. (1994) *Houses and Households: A Comparative Study: Interdisciplinary Contributions to Archaeology,* London: Plenum Press.
Blau, P.M. (1977) *Inequality and Heterogeneity,* New York: The Free Press.
Bloch, M. (1977) 'The Disconnection between Power and Rank as a Process: An Outline of the Development of Kingdoms in Central Madascar', *Archives Européennes de Sociologie,* 18:107–48.
Blom, D.E. (1999) 'Tiwanaku Regional Interaction and Social Identity: A Bioarchaeological Approach', Unpublished Ph.D. Dissertation, Chicago: University of Chicago.
———. (2005) 'Human Body Modification and Diversity in Tiwanaku Society', *Journal of Anthropological Archaeology* (in press).
Blom, D.E., Hallgrímsson, B., Keng, L., C., M.C.L. and Buikstra, J.E. (1998) 'Tiwanaku 'Colonization': Bioarchaeological Implications for Migration in the Moquegua Valley, Peru', *World Archaeology* 30(2): 238–61.
Blom, D.E. and Janusek, J.W. (2004) 'Making Place: Humans as Dedications in Tiwanaku', *World Archaeology,* 36: 123–141.
Blom, D.E., Janusek, J.W., and Buikstra, J.E. (2003) 'A Re-Evaluation of Human Remains from Tiwanaku', in A.L. Kolata (ed.), *Tiwanaku and Its Hinterland: Archaeology and Paleoecology*

of an Andean Civilization, Vol. 2, Washington, D.C.: Smithsonian Institution Press, pp. 435–48.
Bolaños, C. (1988) *Las Antaras Nasca: Historia y Análisis*, Lima: INDEA.
Bolton, R. (1977) 'The Qolla Marriage Process', in R. Bolton and E. Mayer (eds.) *Andean Kinship and Marriage*, Washington, D.C.: American Anthropological Association, pp. 217–39.
Bourdieu, P. (1977) *Outline of a Theory of Practice*, Cambridge: Cambridge University Press.
Bouysse-Cassagne, T. (1975) 'Pertenencia étnica, status económico y lenguas en Charcas a fines del signe XVI', in N. Cook (ed.) *Tasa de la Visita General de Francisco de Toledo*, Lima: Universidad Mayor de San Marcos, pp. 312–28.
———. (1986) 'Urco and Uma: Aymara Concepts of Space', in J. Murra, N. Wachtel and J. Revel (eds.) *Anthropological History of Andean Polities*, Cambridge: Cambridge University Press, pp. 201–27.
———. (1987) *La Identidad Aymara: Aproximación Histórica (Siglo XV, Siglo XVI)*, La Paz, Bolivia: Hisbol.
Braudel, F. (1980) *On History*, Chicago: University of Chicago.
Browman, D.L. (1978) 'Toward the Development of the Tiahuanaco (Tiwanaku) State', in D.L. Browman (ed.) *Advances in Andean Archaeology*, The Hague: Mouton Publishers, pp. 327–49.
———. (1980) 'Tiwanaku Expansion and Altiplano Economic Patterns', *Estudios Arqueológicos (Antofagasta)*, 5: 107–20.
———. (1981) 'New light on Andean Tiwanaku', *American Scientist*, 69: 408–19.
———. (1994) 'Titicaca Basin archaeolinguistics: Uru, Pukina, and Aymara AD 750–1450', *World Archaeology*, 26: 234–50.
———. 'Pajano: Nexus of Formative Cultures in the Titicaca Basin', paper presented at 49th International Conference of Americanists, Quito, 1997.
Brumfiel, E.M. (1991) 'Weaving and Cooking: Women's Production in Aztec Mexico', in J.M. Gero and M.W. Conkey (eds.) *Engendering Archaeology*, Oxford: Blackwell Press, pp. 224–51.
———. (1994) 'Ethnic Groups and Political Development in Ancient Mexico', in E.M. Brumfiel and.J.W. Fox (ed.) *Factional Competition and Political Development in the New World*, Cambridge: Cambridge University Press, pp. 89–102.
———. (1995) 'Heterarchy and the Analysis of Complex Societies: Comments', in Robert M. Ehrenreich, C.L. Crumley, and Janet E. Levy (ed.) *Heterarchy and the Analysis of Complex Societies*, Arlington, VA: American Anthropological Association, pp. 125–31.
Brumfiel, E.M. and Earle, T.K. (1987) 'Specialization, Exchange, and Complex Societies: An Introduction', in E.M. Brumfiel and T.K. Earle (eds.) *Specialization, Exchange, and Complex Societies*, Cambridge: Cambridge University Press, pp. 1–9.
Brush, S.B. (1976) 'Man's Use of an Andean Ecosystem', *Human Ecology*, 4: 147–66.
———. (1977) *Mountain, Field, and Family*, Philadelphia: University of Pennsylvania Press.
Buechler, H.C. (1980) *The Masked Media: Aymara Fiestas and Social Interaction in the Bolivian Highlands*, The Hague: Mouton.
Buechler, H.C. and Buechler, J.-M. (1971) *The Bolivian Aymara*, New York: Holt, Rinehart and Winston.
Burger, R.L. (1992) *Chavín and the Origins of Andean Civilization*, London: Thames and Hudson.
Burger, R., Mohr-Chavez, K. and Chavez, S. (2000) 'Through the Glass Darkly: Prehispanic Obsidian Procurement and Exchange in Southern Peru and Northern Bolivia', *Journal of World Prehistory*, 14: 267–362.
Burger, R.L. and Salazar-Burger, L. (1985) 'The Early Ceremonial Center of Huaricoto', in C.B. Donnan (ed.) *Early Ceremonial Architecture in the Andes*, Washington, D.C.: Dumbarton Oaks Research Library, pp. 111–38.
Burkholder, J. (1997) 'Tiwanaku and the Anatomy of Time', Unpublished Ph.D. Dissertation, Binghamton: State University of New York.
Caballero, G.B. de (1984) 'El Tiwanaku en Cochabamba', *Arqueología Boliviana*, 1: 67–71.
Capoche, L. (1959) *Relación General de la Villa Imperial de Potosí*, Madrid: BAE.
Casanova, E. (1934a) 'Sondeos arqueológicos en Tiahuanaco', *La Prensa (Buenos Aires)*, sección segunda.
———. (1934b) 'Hallazgos arqueológicos en Tiahuanaco', In *La Prensa (Buenos Aires)*, Vol. sección segunda.
Cereceda, V., Dávalos, J. and Mejía, J. (1993) *Una Diferencia, un Sentido: Los Diseños de los Textiles Tarabuco y Jalq'a*, Sucre, Bolivia: Antropólogos del Surandino (ASUR).
Cespedes Paz, R. (2000) 'Excavaciones Arqueológicas en Pínami', *Boletin del INIAN-Museo*, 9: 1–13.

Chang, K.C. (1983) *Art, Myth, and Ritual: The Path to Political Authority in Ancient China,* Cambridge: Harvard University Press.

Chesson, M.S. (2001) 'Social Memory, Identity, and Death: An Introduction', in M.S. Chesson (ed.) *Social Memory, Identity, and Death: Anthropological Perspectives on Mortuary Rituals,* Arlington: American Anthropological Association, pp. 1–11.

Childe, V.G. (1936) *Man Makes Himself,* London: Watts & Company.

———. (1950) 'The Urban Revolution', *Town Planning Review,* 21: 3–17.

———. (1957) *What Happened in History,* Harmondsworth, Middlesex: Penguin Books.

Choque Canqui, R. (1993) *Sociedad y Economía Colonial en el Sur Andino,* La Paz: Hisbol.

Choque Canqui, R. and Ticona Alejo, E. (1996) *Jesús de Machaca: La Marka Rebelde, Vol. 2. Sublevación y Masacre de 1921,* La Paz: CEDOIN and CIPCA.

Cieza de León, P. de (1959 [1553]) *The Incas of Pedro de Cieza de León: History of the Conquest of Peru,* Norman, OK: University of Oklahoma Press, H. de Onis (Trans.).

Claessen, H.J.M. (1984) 'The Internal Dynamics of the Early State', *Current Anthropology,* 25: 365–79.

Clarke, J.E. and Blake, M. (1994) 'The Power of Prestige: Competitive Generosity and the Emergence of Rank Societies in Lowland Mesoamerica', in E.M. Brumfiel (ed.) *Factional Competition and Political Development in the New World,* Cambridge: Cambridge University Press, pp. 17–30.

Clifford, J. (1988) *The Predicament of Culture: Twentieth-Century Ethnography, Literature, and Art,* Cambridge: Harvard University Press.

Cobo, F.B. (1956[1653]) *Historia del Nuevo Mundo, Vol. II,* Madrid: Ediciones Atlas.

———. (1990[1653]) *Inca Religion and Customs.,* Austin: University of Texas Press.

Cohen, A. (1974) 'Introduction: The Lesson of Ethnicity', in A. Cohen (ed.) *Urban Ethnicity,* London: Tavistock Publications, pp. ix-xxiv.

Cohen, R. (1978) 'Ethnicity: problem and focus in Anthropology', *Annual Review of Anthropology,* 7: 379–403.

———. (1981) 'Evolution, fission, and the early state', in Claessen and P. Skalnik (eds.) *The Study of the State,* The Hague: Mouton, pp. 637–50.

Cohen, R. and Service, E.R. (1978) *Origins of the State: The Anthropology of Political Evolution,* Philadelphia: Institute for the Study of Human Issues.

Collins, J.L. (1986) 'The Household and Relations of Production in Southern Peru', *Society for Comparative Studies in Society and History,* 28: 651–71.

Comaroff, J. (1985) *Body of Power, Spirit of Resistance: The Culture and History of a South African People,* Chicago: University of Chicago Press.

Comaroff, J. and Comaroff, J. (1992) *Ethnography and the Historical Imagination,* Boulder: Westview.

———. (1991) *Of Revelation and Revolution: Christianity, Colonialism, and Consciousness in South Africa,* Chicago: University of Chicago Press.

Conklin, B.A. (2001) *Consuming Grief: Compassionate Cannibalism in an Amazonian Society,* Austin: University of Texas Press.

Conklin, W.J. (1991) 'Tuahuanaco and Huari: Architectural Comparisons and Interpretations', in W.H. Isbell and G.F. McEwan (eds.) *Huari Administrative Structure: Prehistoric Monumental Architecture and State Government,* Washington, D.C.: Dumbarton Oaks Research Library and Collection, pp. 281–91.

Conrad, G.W. and Demarest, A.A. (1984) *Religion and Empire: The Dynamics of Aztec and Inca Expansionism,* Cambridge: Cambridge University Press.

Corrigan, P. and Sayer, D. (1985) *The Great Arch: English State Formation as Cultural Revolution,* Oxford: Basil Blackwell.

Couture, N.C. (1993) 'Excavations at Mollo Kontu, Tiwanaku', Unpublished Master's Thesis, Chicago: University of Chicago.

———. (2002) 'The Construction of Power: Monumental Space and an Elite Residence at Tiwanaku, Bolivia', Unpublished Ph.D. Dissertation, Chicago: University of Chicago Press.

———. (2003) 'Ritual, Monumentalism, and Residence at Mollo Kontu, Tiwanaku', in A.L. Kolata (ed.) *Tiwanaku and Its Hinterland: Archaeology and Paleoecology of an Andean Civilization, Vol. 2,* Washington, D.C.: Smithsonian Institution Press, pp. 202–25.

Couture, N.C. and Sampeck, K. (2003) 'Putuni: A History of Palace Architecture in Tiwanaku', in A.L. Kolata (ed.) *Tiwanaku and its Hinterland: Archaeology and Paleecology of an Andean Civilization, Vol. 2,* Washington, D.C.: Smithsonian Institution Press, pp. 226–63.

Cowgill, G.L. (1988) 'Onward and Upward with Collapse', in N. Yoffee and G.L. Cowgill (eds.) *The Collapse of Ancient States and Civilizations,* Tucson: University of Arizona Press, pp. 244–76.

———. (1997) 'State and Society at Teotihuacan, Mexico', *Annual Review of Anthropology*, 26: 129–61.
Créqui-Montfort, G. de and de la Grange, S. (1904) 'Rapport sur une Mission Scientifique en Amérique du Sud (Bolivie, République Argentine, Chili, Pérou)', *Nouvelles Archives des Missions Scientifiques*, 12: 81–129.
Créqui-Montfort, G. de. (1906) 'Fouilles de la Mission Scientifique Française à Tiahuanaco. Ses Recherches Archéologiques et Ethnographiques en Bolivie, au Chile et dans la République Argentine', *Internationaler Amerikanisten Kongress, Stuttgart 1904*, 2: 531–50.
Crumley, C.L. (1987) 'A Dialectical Critique of Hierarchy', in T.C. Patterson and C.W. Gailey (eds.) *Power Relations and State Formation*, Washington, D.C.: American Anthropological Association, pp. 155–59.
———. (1995) 'Heterarchy and the Analysis of Complex Societies', in Robert M. Ehrenreich, C.L. Crumley, and Janet E. Levy (ed.) *Heterarchy and the Analysis of Complex Societies*, Arlington, VA: American Anthropological Association, pp. 1–4.
Crumley, C.L. and Marquardt, W.H. (1987) *Regional Dynamics: Burgundian Landscapes in Historical Perspective*, San Diego: Academic Press.
Custred, G. (1977) 'Peasant Kinship, Subsistence and Economics in a High Altitude Andean Environment', in R. Bolton and E. Mayer (eds.), pp. 117–35.
Cutler, H.C. and Cardenas, M. (1947) 'Chicha, a Native South American Beer', *Botanical Museum Leaflets*, 13: 33–60.
D'Altroy, T.N. and Earle, T.K. (1985) 'Staple Finance, Wealth Finance, and Storage in the Inca Political Economy', *Current Anthropology*, 26: 187–206.
De Vos, G.A. (1995) 'Ethnic Pluralism', in L. Rmanucci-Ross and G.A.D. Vos (eds.) *Ethnic Identity: Creation, Conflict, and Accommodation*, Walnut Creek: Altamirs Press, pp. 15–47.
DeBoer, W. (1984) 'The Last Pottery Show: System and Sense in Ceramic Studies', in S.E.v.d. Leeuw and A.C. Pritchard (eds.) *The Many Dimensions of Pottery: Ceramics in Anthropology and Archaeology*, Amsterdam: University of Amsterdam, pp. 527–72.
DeBoer, W.R. (1990) 'Interaction, Imitation, and Communication as Expressed in Style: The Ucayali Experience', in M.W. Conkey and C. Hastorf (eds.) *The Uses of Style in Archaeology*, Cambridge: Cambridge University Press, pp. 82–104.
DeBoer, W.R. and Moore, J.A. (1982) 'The Measurement and Meaning of Stylistic Diversity', *Nawpa Pacha*, 20: 147–56.
Demarest, A.A. (1992) 'Ideology in Ancient Maya Cltural Evolution: The Dynamics of Galactic Polities', in A.A. Demarest and G.W. Conrad (eds.) *Ideology and Pre-Columbian Civilizations*, Santa Fe: School of American Research Press, pp. 135–58.
———. (2004) *Ancient Maya: Rise and Fall of a Rainforest Civilization*, Cambridge: Cambridge University Press.
Demarest, A.A., O'Mansky, M., Wolley, C., Tuerenhout, D.V., Inomata, T., Palka, J. and Escobedo, H. (1997) 'Classic Maya Defense Systems and Warfare in the Petexbatun Region: Archaeological Evidence and Interpretations', *Ancient Mesoamerica*, 8: 229–54.
Dietler, M. (1996) 'Feasts and Commensal Politics in the Political Economy: Food, Power, and Status in Prehistoric Europe', in P. Wiessner and W. Schiefenhovel (eds.) *Food and the Status Quest: An Interdisciplinary Perspective*, Oxford: Berghahn Books, pp. 87–125.
———. (2001) 'Theorizing the Feast: Rituals of Consumption, Commensal Politics, and Power in African Contexts', in M. Dietler and B. Hayden (eds.) *Feasts: Archaeological and Ethnographic Perspectives on Food, Politics, and Power*, Washington, D.C.: Smithsonian Institution Press, pp. 65–114.
Dietler, M. and Herbich, I. (1998) 'Habitus, Techniques, Style: An Integrated Approach to the Social Understanding of Material Culture and Boundaries', in M.T. Stark (ed.) *The Archaeology of Social Boundaries*, Washington: Smithsonian Institution Press, pp. 232–63.
Dillehay, T.D. and Núñez Atencio, L. (1988) 'Camelids, caravans, and complex societies in the south-central Andes', in N.J. Saunders and O. de Montmollin (eds.) *Recent Studies in Pre-Columbian Archaeology, British Archaeological Reports International Series 421 (Part ii)*, Oxford: British Archaeological Reports, pp. 603–34.
Dobres, M.-A. and Robb, J. (eds) (2000) *Agency in Archaeology*, Routledge: London.
Douglas, M. (1966) *Purity and Danger: An Analysis of Concepts of Pollution and Taboo*, New York: Fredrick A. Praeger.
Dumézil, G. (1973) *Destiny of a King*, Chicago: University of Chicago Press.
———. (1915) *The Elementary Forms of the Religious Life*, London: George Allen & Unwin.

Durkheim, E. (1904) *Professional Ethics and Civic Morals*, London: Routledge and Kegan Paul.

Earle, T. (1981) 'Comment on P. Rice, Evolution of Specialized Pottery Production: A Trial Model', *Current Anthropology*, 22: 230–231.

———. (1985) 'Commodity Exchange and Markets in the Inka State: Recent Archaeological Evidence', in S. Plattner (ed.) *Markets and Marketing*, Lanham: University Press of America, pp. 369–97.

———. (1991) 'The Evolution of Chiefdoms', in T. Earle (ed.) *Chiefdoms: Power, Economy, and Ideology*, Cambridge: Cambridge University Press, pp. 1–15.

Ehrenreich, R.M. (1995) 'Early Metalworking: A Heterarchical Analysis of Industrial Organization', in Robert M. Ehrenreich, C.L. Crumley, and Janet E. Levy (ed.) *Heterarchy and the Analysis of Complex Societies*, Arlington, VA: American Anthropological Association, pp. 33–40.

Eliade, M. (1959) *The Sacred and the Profane: The Nature of Religion*, New York: Harcourt, Brace & World.

Emberling, G. (1997) 'Ethnicity in Complex Societies: Archaeological Perspectives', *Journal of Archaeological Research*, 5: 295–344.

Ensor, B.E. (2000) 'Social Formations, Modo de Vida, and Conflict in Archaeology', *American Antiquity*, 65: 15–42.

Erickson, C.L. (1988) 'An Archaeological Investigation of Raised Field Agriculture in the Lake Titicaca Basin of Peru', Unpublished Ph.D. Dissertation, Champaign-Urbana: University of Illinois.

———. (1992) 'Prehistoric Landscape Management in the Andean Highlands: Raised Field Agriculture and its Environmental Impact', *Population and Environment*, 13: 285–300.

———. (1993) 'The social organization of prehispanic raised field agriculture in the Lake Titicaca Basin', in V.L. Scarborough and B.L. Isaac (eds.) *Economic Aspects of Water Management in the Prehispanic New World, Research in Economic Anthropology, Suppl. 7*, Greenwich: JAI Press, pp. 369–426.

———. (1999) 'Neo-Environmental Determinism and Agrarian 'Collapse' in Andean Prehistory', *Antiquity*, 73: 634–42.

Escalante Moscoso, J.F. (1997) *Arquitectura Prehispánica en los Andes Bolivianos*, La Paz: CIMA.

———. (2003) 'Residential Archiutecture in La K'arana, Tiwanaku', in A.L. Kolata (ed.) *Tiwanaku and Its Hinterland: Archaeology and Paleoecology of an Andean Civilization, Vol. 2*, Washington, D.C.: Smithsonian Institution Press, pp. 316–26.

Espinoza Soriano, W. (1980) 'Los Fundamentos Lingüísticos de la Etnohistoria Andina', *Revista Española de Antropología Americana (Madrid)*.

Estevez Castillo, J. (1990), Excavaciones en Lukurmata: Sitio Urbano Tiwanacota y Centro de Domino Economico Regional. Report submitted to the Instituto Nacional de Arqueologia de Bolivia, La Paz, Bolivia.

Feinman, G.M. (2000) 'Corporate/Network: New Perspectives on Models of Political Action and the Puebloan Southwest', in M.B. Schiffer (ed.) *Social Theory in Archaeology*, Salt Lake City: University of Utah Press, pp. 31–51.

Feinman, G.M. and Nicholas, L.M. (1995) 'Household Craft Specialization and Shell Ornament Manufacture in Ejutla, Mexico', *Expedition*, 37: 14–25.

Fischer, E.F. (1999) 'Cultural Logic and Maya Identity: Rethinking Constructivism and Essentialism', *Current Anthropology*, 40: 473–99.

———. (2001) *Cultural Logics and Global Economics: Maya Identity in Thought and Practice*, Austin: University of Texas Press.

Flannery, K.V. (1972) 'The Cultural Evolution of Civilizations', *Annual Review of Ecology and Systematics*, 3: 399–426.

———. (1999) 'Process and Agency in Early State Formation', *Cambridge Archaeological Journal*, 9: 3–211.

Flannery, K.V. (ed.) (1976) *The Early Mesoamerican Village*, New York: Academic Press.

Flannery, K.V., Marcus, J. and Reynolds, R.G. (1989) *The Flocks of the Wamani: A Study of Llama Herds on the Punas of Ayacucho, Peru*, San Diego: Academic Press.

Flannery, K. and Winter, M. (1976) 'Analyzing Household Activities', in K. Flannery (ed.) *The Early Mesoamerican Village*, New York: Academic Press, pp. 34–45.

Foucault, M. (1965) *Madness and Civilization: A History of Insanity in the Age of Reason*, New York: Vintage Books.

———. (1979) *Discipline and Punish: The Birth of the Prison*, New York: Vintage Books.

———. (1980) 'Power/Knowledge: Selected Interviews and Other Writings, 1972–1977', C. Gordon (ed.), New York: Pantheon

Fox, J.W. (1987) *Maya Postclassic State Formation*, Cambridge: Cambridge University Press.
Frame M. (1990) *Andean Four-Cornered Hats*, New York: Metropolitan Museum of Art.
Franke, E. (1995) 'Ceramic craft specialization at Ch'iji Jawira, Tiwanaku: organization and technology', *Journal of the Steward Anthropological Society*, 23: 111–19.
Fried, M.H. (1967) *The Evolution of Political Society*, New York: Random House.
Friedman, J. (1994) *Cultural Identity and Global Process*, London: Sage Publications.
Garcilaso de la Vega, E.I. (1869[1609]) *Royal Commentaries of the Yncas, First Part*, London: Hakluyt Society, C. Markham (Trans.).
Geertz, C. (1973) *The Interpretation of Cultures*, New York: Basic Books.
———. (1980) *Negara: The Theatre State in Nineteenth Century Bali*, Princeton: Princeton University Press.
George, K.M. (1996) *Showing Signs of Violence: The Cultural Politics of a Twentieth-Century Headhunting Ritual*, Berkeley: University of California Press.
Giddens, A. (1979) *Central Problems in Social Theory: Action, Structure and Contradiction in Social Analysis*, Berkeley: University of California Press.
Giesso, M. (2003) 'Stone Tool Production in the Tiwanaku Heartland', in A.L. Kolata (ed.) *Tiwanaku and Its Hinterland: Archaeology and Paleoecology of an Andean Civilization, Vol. 2*, Washington, D.C.: Smithsonian Institution Press, pp. 363–383.
Gillespie, S. (2000) 'Rethinking Maya Social Organization: Replacing "Lineage" with "House"', *American Anthropologist*, 102: 467–484.
Girault, L. (1987) *Kallawaya: Curanderos Itinerantes de los Andes*, La Paz: ORSTOM.
———. (1990) *La Cerámica del Templete Semisubterraneo de Tiwanaku*, La Paz, Bolivia: CERES.
Gisbert, T., Arze, S. and Cajiás, M. (1987) *Arte Textil y Mundo Andino*, La Paz: Gisbert y Cía.
Glazer, N. and Moynihan, D.P. (1975) 'Introduction', in N. Glazer and D.P. Moynihan (eds.) *Ethnicity: Theory and Experience*, Cambridge: Harvard University Press, pp. 1–26.
Goldstein, P.S. (1985) 'The Tiwanaku Occupation of Moquegua', Unpublished M.A. Thesis, Chicago: University of Chicago.
———. (1989) 'Omo, a Tiwanaku Provincial Center in Moquegua, Peru', Unpublished Ph.D. Dissertation, Chicago: University of Chicago.
———. (1993) 'Tiwanaku Temples and State Expansion: a Tiwanaku Sunken-Court Temple in Moquegua, Peru', *Latin American Antiquity*, 4: 22–47.
———. (2000) 'Exotic Goods and Everyday Chiefs: Long-Distance Exchange and Indigenous Sociopolitical Development in the South Central Andes', *Latin American Antiquity*, 11: 335–62.
Graffam, G.C. (1989) 'Una excavación de prueba en la acrópolis de Lukurmata, Bolivia', in A.L. Kolata (ed.) *Arqueología de Lukurmata, Vol. 2*, La Paz: INAR, pp. 89–91.
———. (1990) 'Raised Fields without Bureaucracy: An Archaeological Examination of Intensive Wetland Cultivation in the Pampa Koani Zone, Lake Titicaca, Bolivia', Unpublished Ph.D. dissertation, Toronto, Ontario: University of Toronto.
———. (1992) 'Beyond State Collapse: Rural History, Raised Fields and Pastoralism in the South Andes', *American Anthropologist*, 94: 882–904.
Gramsci, A. (1971) *Selections from the Prison Notebooks*, New York: International Publishers.
Grebe, M.E. (1974) 'Instrumentos musicales precolombinos de Chile', *Revista Musical Chilena*, 27: 5–55.
Guaman Poma de Ayala, F. (1992[1583–1615]) *El primer nueva corónica y buen gobierno*, Mexico City: Siglo Veintiuno.
Gutiérrez Condori, R. (1991) 'Instrumentos musicales tradicionales en la comunidad artesanal Walata Grande, Bolivia', *Latin American Musical Review*, 12: 124–59.
Haeberli, J. (1979) 'Twelve Nasca Panpipes: A Study', *Ethnomusicology*, 23: 57–74.
Hancock, G. (1996) *Fingerprints of the Gods*, Crown Publishers.
Harris, O. (1978) 'El parentesco y la economía vertical en el ayllu Laymi (norte de Potosí)', *Avances: Revista Boliviana de Estudios Históricos y Sociales*, 1: 51–64.
———. (1985) 'Complementaridad y Conflicto: Una Visión Andina del Hombre y la Mujer', *Allpanchis*, 25: 17–42.
Hastorf, C.A. (ed) (1999) *Early Settlement at Chiripa, Bolivia: Research of the Taraco Archaeological Project*, Berkeley: University of California Archaeological Research Facility.

Hayden, B. (1996) 'Feasting in Prehistoric and Traditional Societies', in P. Wiessner and W. Schiefenhovel (eds.) *Food and the Status Quest: An Interdisciplinary Perspective*, Oxford: Berghahn Books, pp. 127–47.

———. (2001) 'Fabulous Feasts: A Prolegomenon to the Importance of Feasting', in M. Dietler and B. Hayden (eds.) *Feasts: Archaeological and Ethnographic Perspectives on Food, Politics, and Power*, Washington, D.C.: Smithsonian Institution Press, pp. 23–64.

Hayden, B. and Cannon, A. (1983) 'Where the Garbage Goes: Refuse Disposal in the Maya Highlands', *Journal of Anthropological Archaeology*, 2: 117–63.

Hayden, B. and Gargett, R. (1990) 'Big Man, Big Heart? A Mesoamerican View of the Emergence of Complex Society', *Ancient Mesoamerica*, 1: 3–20.

Headrick, A. (1996) 'The Teothihuacan Trinity: UnMASKing the Political Structure', Unpublished Ph.D. Dissertation, Austin: University of Texas Press.

Hebdige, D. (1979) *Subculture: The Meaning of Style*, New York: Routledge.

Helms, M.W. (1979) *Ancient Panama: Chiefs in Search of Power*, Austin: University of Texas Press.

———. (1993) *Craft and the Kingly Ideal: Art, Trade, and Power*, Austin: University of Texas Press.

———. (1994) 'Chiefdom Rivalries, Control, and External Contacts in Lower Central America', in E.M. Brumfiel (ed.) *Factional Competition and Political Development in the New World*, Cambridge: Cambridge University Press, pp. 55–60.

Hendon, J.A. (1996) 'Archaeological Approaches to the Organization of Domestic Labor: Household Practice and Domestic Relations', *Annual Review of Anthropology*, 25: 45–61.

———. (2000) 'Having and Holding: Storage, Memory, and Social Relations', *American Anthropologist*, 102: 42–53.

Higueras-Hare, A. (1996) 'Prehispanic Settlement and Land Use in Cochabamba, Bolivia', Unpublished Ph.D. Dissertation, Pittsburgh, PA: University of Pittsburgh.

Hirth, K.G. (1993) 'The Household as an Analytical Unit: Problems in Method and Theory', in R.S. Santley and K.G. Hirth (eds.) *Prehispanic Domestic Units in Western Mesoamerica: Studies of the Household, Compound, and Residence*, Boca Raton: CRC Press, pp. 21–36.

Hobsbawm, E.J. (1983) 'Introduction: Inventing Traditions', in E.J. Hobsbawm and.T. Ranger (ed.) *The Invention of Tradition*, Cambridge: Cambridge University Press, pp. 1–14.

Hodder, I. (1982) *Symbols in Action*, Cambridge: Cambridge University Press.

———. (1990) 'Style as Historical Quality', in M.W. Conkey and C.A. Hastorf (eds.) *The Uses of Style in Archaeology*, Cambridge: Cambridge University Press, pp. 44–51.

Holland, D., William Lachicotte, J., Skinner, D. and Cain, C. (1998) *Identity and Agency in Cultural Worlds*, Cambridge, MA: Harvard University Press.

Hoshower, L.M., Buikstra, J.E., Goldstein, P.S. and Webster, A.D. (1995) 'Artificial Cranial Deformation in the Omo M10 Site: a Tiwanaku complex from the Moquegua Valley, Peru', *Latin American Antiquity*, 6: 145–64.

Ibarra Grasso, D.E. (1957a) 'Un nuevo panorama de la arquelogia Boliviana', in C. Ponce (ed.) *Arquelogia Boliviana*, La Paz: Biblioteca Paceña, pp. 235–88.

———. (1957b) 'Nuevas culturas arquelógicas de la arqueologia Boliviana', in C. Ponce (ed.) *Arquelogia Boliviana*, La Paz: Biblioteca Paceña, pp. 321–42.

Iribarren, J. (1969) 'Estudio preliminar sobre los instrumentos musicales autóctonos en el área del norte de Chile', *Rehue*, 2: 91–109.

Isbell, B.J. (1978) *To Defend Ourselves: Ecology and Ritual in an Andean Village*, Prospect Heights, IL: Waveland Press.

Isbell, W.H. (1983) 'Shared Ideology and Parallel Political Development: Huari and Tiwanaku', in D. Sandweiss (ed.) *Investigations of the Andean Past*, Ithaca: Cornell University, pp. 186–208.

———. (1995) 'Constructing the Andean Past, or "As You Like It"', *Journal of the Steward Anthropological Society*, 23: 1–12.

———. (1997) *Mummies and Mortuary Monuments: A Postprocessual Prehistory of Central Andean Social Organization*, Austin: University of Texas Press.

Izko, X. (1986) 'Comunidad andina: persistencia y cambio', *Revista Andina*, 4: 59–129.

———. (1992) *La Doble Frontera: Ecología, Política y Ritual en el Altiplano Central*, La Paz, Bolivia: Hisbol/Ceres.

Janusek, J.W. (1993) 'Nuevos Datos sobre el Significado de la Producción y Uso de Instrumentos Musicales en el Estado de Tiwanaku', *Pumapunku: Nueva Epoca,* Año 2: 9–47.

———. (1994) 'State and Local Power in a Prehispanic Andean Polity: Changing Patterns of Urban Residence in Tiwanaku and Lukurmata, Bolivia', Unpublished Ph.D. Dissertation, Chicago, IL: University of Chicago.

———. (1999) 'Craft and Local Power: Embedded Specialization in Tiwanaku Cities', *Latin American Antiquity,* 10: 107–31.

———. 'Tiwanaku: The Origins of Urbanism in the High Andes', paper presented at 66th Annual Conference of the Society for American Archaeology, New Orleans, 2001.

———. (2002) 'Out of Many, One: Style and Social Boundaries in Tiwanaku', *Latin American Antiquity,* 13: 35–61.

———. (2003a) 'Vessels, Time, and Society: Toward a Chronology of Ceramic Style in the Tiwanaku Heartland', in A.L. Kolata (ed.) *Tiwanaku and its Hinterland: Archaeology and Paleoecology of an Andean Civilization, Vol. 2,* Washington, D.C.: Smithsonian Institution Press, pp. 30–94.

———. (2003b) 'The Changing Face of Tiwanaku Residential Life: State and Social Identity in an Andean City', in A.L. Kolata (ed.) *Tiwanaku and Its Hinterland: Archaeology and Paleoecology of an Andean Civilization, Vol. 2,* Washington, D.C.: Smithsonian Institution Press, pp. 264–95.

———. (2004) 'Tiwanaku and Its Precursors: Recent Research and Emerging Perspectives', *Journal of Archaeological Research,* 12: 121–183.

———. (2005) *Ancient Tiwanaku: Rise and Fall of a High-Altitude Civilization,* Cambridge: Cambridge University Press (in press).

Janusek, J.W. and Alconini Mújica, S. 'Social Diversity and Historical Change in Tiwanaku Ceramics: Steps Toward a Tiwanaku IV-V Chronology', paper presented at 59th Annual Meeting of the Society for American Archaeology, Anaheim, CA, 1994.

Janusek, J.W., Alconini Mújica, S., Angelo, D., Aranda, K., and Lima, P. (1995) 'Organizacion del patron de asentamiento Prehispanico en la region de Icla, Chuquisaca, Bolivia', report of field operations submitted to the Universidad Mayor de San Andrés and the Instituto Nacional de Arquelogia.

Janusek, J.W. and Blom, D.E. (2004) 'Identifying Tiwanaku Urban Populations: Style, Identity, and Ceremony in Andean Cities', in G. Storey (ed.) *Population and Preindustrial Cities: A Cross-Cultural Perspective,* Tuscaloosa: University of Alabama Press (in press).

———. (2005) 'Civilization on the Andean Fringe: Verticality and Local Cultural Development in the Eastern Andes', *Latin American Antiquity* (in press).

Janusek, J.W. and Earnest, H. (1990a) 'Urban Residence and Land Reclamation in Lukurmata: A View from the Core Area', in A.L. Kolata (ed.) *Tiwanaku and Its Hinterland,* Report submitted to the National Science Foundation, pp. 118–43.

———. (1990b) 'Excavations in the Putuni: the 1988 Season', in A.L. Kolata (ed.) *Tiwanaku and its Hinterland,* Report submitted to the National Science Foundation, pp. 236–46.

Janusek, J. and Giesso, M. (1990) 'Excavations in the Akapana East, Tiwanaku: Report of Field Operations in Tiwanaku in 1989', in A.L. Kolata (ed.) *Tiwanaku and Its Hinterland,* Report submitted to the National Science Foundation, pp. 255–68.

Janusek, J.W. and Kolata, A.L. (2003) 'Prehispanic Rural History in the Rio Katari Valley', in A.L. Kolata (ed.) *Tiwanaku and Its Hinterland: Archaeology and Paleoecology of an Andean Civilization, Vol. 2,* Washington, D.C.: Smithsonian Institution Press, pp. 129–71.

Janusek, J.W., Ohnstad, A.T. and Roddick, A.P. (2003) 'Khonkho Wankane and the Rise of Tiwanaku', *Antiquity,* 77: Web publication.

Jing, J. (1996) *The Temple of Memories: History, Power, and Morality in a Chinese Village,* Stanford: Stanford University Press.

Johnson, G. (1977) 'Aspects of Regional Analysis in Archaeology', *Annual Review of Anthropology,* 6: 479–508.

Jones, S. (1997) *The Archaeology of Ethnicity: Constructing Identities in the Past and Present,* New York: Routledge.

Joyce, A.A., Bustamente, L.A. and Levine, M.N. (2001) 'Commoner Power: A Case Study from the Classic Period Collapse on the Oaxaca Coast', *Journal of Archaeological Method and Theory,* 8: 343–85.

Joyce, A.A. and Winter, M. (1996) 'Ideology, Power, and Urban Society in Pre-Hispanic Oaxaca', *Current Anthropology,* 37: 33–86.

Joyce, R. (1993) 'Women's Work: Images of Production and Reproduction in Pre-Hispanic Southern Central America', *Current Anthropology*, 34: 255–74.

———. (2000) *Gender and Power in Prehispanic Mesoamerica*, Austin: University of Texas Press.

Julien, C.J. (1983) *Hatunqolla: A View of Inca Rule From the Lake Titicaca Region. University of California Publications in Anthropology, 15*, Berkeley: University of California Press.

Kertzer, D.I. (1988) *Ritual, Politics, and Power*, New Haven: Yale University Press.

Kidder, A. (1956) 'Digging in the Titicaca Basin', *University Museum Bulletin (University of Pennsylvania, University Museum)*, 20: 16–29.

King, E. and Potter, D. (1994) 'Small Sites in Prehistoric Maya Socioeconomic Organization: A Perspective from Colha, Belize', in G.M. Schwartz and S.E. Falconer (eds.) *Archaeological Views from the Countryside: Village Communities in Early Complex Societies*, Washington, D.C.: Smithsonian Institution Press, pp. 64–90.

Kirch, P.V. (1984) *The Evolution of Polynesian Chiefdoms*, Cambridge: Cambridge University Press.

———. (1991) 'Chiefship and Competitive Involution: The Marquesas Islands of Eastern Polynesia', in T. Earle (ed.) *Chiefdoms: Power, Economy, and Ideology*, Cambridge: Cambridge University Press, pp. 119–45.

———. (2000) *On the Road of the Winds: An Archaeological History of the Pacific Islands Before European Contact*, Berkeley: University of California Press.

Klarich, E.A. 'Occupation and Offerings: Elite Household Organization at Pukara, Lake Titicaca Basin, Peru (200 BC–AD 200)', Paper presented at the 67th Annual Meeting of the Society for American Anthropology, Denver, 2002.

Klymyshyn, A.M.U. (1982) 'Elite compounds in Chan Chan', in M.E. Moseley and K.C. Day (eds.) *Chan Chan: Andean Desert City*, Albuquerque: University of New Mexico Press, pp. 119–44.

Kolata, A.L. (1985) 'El Papel de la Agricultura Intensiva en la Economía Política del Estado Tiwanaku', *Diálogo Andino*, 4: 11–38.

———. (1986) 'The Agricultural Foundations of the Tiwanaku State: A View from the Heartland', *American Antiquity*, 51: 748–62.

———. (1991) 'The Technology and Organization of Agricultural Production in the Tiwanaku State', *Latin American Antiquity*, 2: 99–125.

———. (1992) 'Economy, Ideology, and Imperialism in the South-Central Andes', in A.A. Demarest and G.W. Conrad (eds.) *Ideology and Pre-Columbian Civilizations*, Santa Fe, NM: School of American Research, pp. 65–85.

———. (1993a) *Tiwanaku: Portrait of an Andean Civilization*, Cambridge: Blackwell.

———. (1993b) 'Understanding Tiwanaku: Conquest, Colonization, and Clientage in the South Central Andes', in D.S. Rice (ed.) *Latin American Horizons*, Washington, D.C.: Dumbarton Oaks Research Library and Collection, pp. 193–224.

———. (1996a) 'Proyecto Wila Jawira: An Introduction to the History, Problems, and Strategies of Research', in A.L. Kolata (ed.) *Tiwanaku and Its Hinterland: Archaeology and Paleoecology of an Andean Civilization, Vol. 1*, Washington, D.C.: Smithsonian Institution Press, pp. 1–22.

———. (1996b) 'Mimesis and Monumentalism in Native Andean Cities', *Res*, 29/30: 223–36.

———. (1996c) *Valley of the Spirits: A Journey into the Lost Realm of the Aymara*, New York: John Wiley & Sons, Inc.

———. (1997) 'Of Kings and Capitals: Principles of Authority and the Nature of Cities in the Native Andean State', in D.L. Nichols and T.H. Chalton (eds.) *The Archaeology of City-States: Cross-Cultural Approaches*, Washington, D.C.: Smithsonian Institution Press, pp. 245–54.

———. (2003a) 'Introdcution to the Proyecto Wila Jawira Research Program', in A.L. Kolata (ed.) *Tiwanaku and Its Hinterland: Archaeology and Paleoecology of an Andean Civilization, Vol. 2*, Washington, D.C.: Smithsonian Institution Press, pp. 3–17.

———. (2003b) 'The Social Production of Tiwanaku: Political Economy and Authority in a Native Andean State', in A.L. Kolata (ed.) *Tiwanaku and Its Hinterland: Archaeology and Paleoecology of an Andean Civilization, Vol. 2*, Washington, D.C.: Smithsonian Institution Press, pp. 449–72.

Kolata, A.L. and Ortloff, C.R. (1996) 'Tiwanaku Raised-Field Agriculture in the Lake Titicaca Basin of Bolivia', in A.L. Kolata (ed.) *Tiwanaku and Its Hinterland: Archaeology and Paleoecology of an Andean Civilization, Vol. 1*, Washington, D.C.: Smithsonian Institution Press, pp. 109–52.

Kolata, A.L. and Ponce Sanginés, C. (1992) 'Tiwanaku: the City at the Center', in R.F. Townsend (ed.) *The Ancient Americas: Art from Sacred Landscapes*, Chicago: The Art Institute, pp. 317–34.

———. (2003) 'Two Hundred Years of Archaeological Research at Tiwanaku: A Selective History', in A.L. Kolata (ed.) *Tiwanaku and Its Hinterland: Archaeology and Paleoecology of an Andean Civilization, Vol. 2*, Washington, D.C.: Smithsonian Institution Press, pp. 18–29.

La Barre, W. (1947) 'The Uru-Chipaya', in J.H. Steward (ed.) *Handbook of South American Indians, Volume II: The Andean Civilizations*, Washington, D.C.: Smithsonian Institution, pp. 585–618.

———. (1948) *The Aymara Indians of the Lake Titicaca Plateau, Bolivia. American Anthropologist Memoirs Number 68*, Menasha, WI: American Anthropological Association.

Lamotta, V.M. and Schiffer M.B. (1999) 'Formation Processes of Household Assemblages', in P.M. Allison (ed.) *The Archaeology of Household Activities*, London: Routledge, pp. 19–29.

Langevin, A. (1991) 'Los Instrumentos de la Orquesta de Kantu', *Revista del Museo Nacional de Etnografía y Folklore*, 3: 11–54.

Lanning, E.P. (1967) *Peru Before the Incas*, Englewood Cliffs, NJ: Prentice-Hall.

Lechtman, H. (1977) 'Style in Technology: Some Early Thoughts', in H. Lechtman and R.S. Merrill (eds.) *Material Culture: Style, Organization, and Dynamics of Technology*, New York: West Publishing, pp. 3–20.

Lecoq, P. (1987) 'Caravanes des llamas, sel et echanges dans une communaute de Potosi, en Bolivie', *Bulletin de l'Institut Francais d'Etudes Andines*, 16: 1–38.

———. (1991) 'Sel et Archeologie en Bolivie: De quelques problemes relatifs a l'occupation prehispanique de la cordillere intersalar (Sud-Ouest Bolivien)', Unpublished Ph.D. Dissertation, Paris: Université de Paris, Pantheon Sorbonne.

———. (1999) *Uyuni Préhispanique: Arquéologia de la Cordillère iItersalar (Sud-Ouest Bolivien)*, Oxford: Archaeopress.

Lemonnier, P. (1986) 'The Study of Material Culture Today: Towards an Anthropology of Technical Systems', *Journal of Anthropological Archaeology*, 5: 147–86.

———. (1993) 'Introduction', in P. Lemonnier (ed.) *Technological Choices: Transformation in Material Culture Since the Neolithic*, London: Routledge, pp. 1–35.

Lemuz Aguirre, C. (2001) 'Patrones de Asentamiento Arqueológico en la Península de Santiago de Huatta, Boliva', Unpublished Licenciatura Thesis, La Paz: Universidad Mayor de San Andres.

Lemuz Aguirre, C. and Soria, J. Paz (2001) Nuevas consideraciones acerca del Periodo Formativo en Kallamarka, *Textos Antropológicos*, 13: 93–110.

Levine, T.Y. (1992) 'Inka State Storage in Three Highland Regions: A Comparative Study', in T.Y. Levine (ed.) *Inka Storage Systems*, Norman: University of Oklahoma Press, pp. 107–48.

Lewellen, T.C. (1983) *Political Anthropology: An Introduction*, South Hadley: Bergin and Garvey Publishers.

Lima Torrez, M. de P. (2000) 'Ocupacion Yampara en Quila Quila?: cambios socio-políticos de una sociedad prehispanic durante el horizonte Tardio', Unpublished Licenciatura Thesis, La Paz: Universidad Mayor de San Andres.

Lizárraga, F.R. de (1909[1605]) 'Descripción breve de toda la tierra del Perú, Tucumán, Río de la Plata y Chile', *Historiadores de Indias, vol. 2*, Madrid: pp. 485–660.

Low, S.M. (2000) *On the Plaza: The Politics of Public Space and Culture*, Austin: University of Texas Press.

Loza Balsa, G. (1971) 'La vivienda Aymara', *Pumapunku*, 3: 68–73.

Lumbreras, L.G. (1974) *The Peoples and Cultures of Ancient Peru*, Washington, D.C.: Smithsonian Institution Press.

———. (1981) Arquelogia de la América Andina, Lima: Editoria Milla Batires.

Manzanilla, L. (1992) *Akapana: Una Pirámide en el Centro del Mundo*, Mexico City: Universidad Nacional Autónoma de México, Instituto de Investigaciones Antropológicas.

———. (1993) *Anatomia de un conjunto residencial Teotihuacano en Oztoyahualco, Vol. 1*, Mexico City: UNAM.

———. (1996) 'Corporate Groups and Domestic Activities at Teotihuacan', *Latin American Antiquity*, 7: 228–46.

———. (2002) 'Living with the Ancestors and Offering to the Gods', in P. Plunket (ed.) *Domestic Ritual in Ancient Mesoamerica*, Los Angeles: The Cotsen Institute of Archaeology, University of California, pp. 43–52.

Manzanilla, L. and Woodard, E.K. (1990) 'Restos humanos asociados a la Pirámide de Akapana (Tiwanaku, Bolivia)', *Latin American Antiquity*, 1: 133–49.

Marcus, J. (1992) *Mesoamerican Writing Systems: Propaganda, Myth, and History in Four Ancient Civilizations*, Princeton: Princeton University Press.

———. (1993) 'Ancient Maya Political Organization', in J.A. Sabloff and J.S. Henderson (eds.) *Lowland Maya Civilization in the Eighth Century A.D.*, Washington, D.C.: Dumbarton Oaks, pp. 111–183.

Marcus, J. and Feinman, G.M. (1998) 'Introduction', in G.M. Feinman and J. Marcus (eds.) *Archaic States*, Santa Fe: School of American Research Press, pp. 3–14.

Martinez, G. (1989) *Espacio y Pensamiento I: Andes Meridionales*, La Paz: Hisbol.

Mathews, J.E. (1992) 'Prehispanic Settlement and Agriculture in the Middle Tiwanaku Valley, Bolivia', Unpublished Ph.D. Dissertation, Chicago, IL: University of Chicago.

———. (1997) 'Population and Agriculture in the Emergence of Complex Society in the Bolivian Altiplano: The Case of Tiwanaku', in L. Manzanilla (ed.) *Emergence and Change in Early Urban Societies*, New York: Plenum Press, pp. 245–74.

———. (2003) 'Prehistoric Settlement Patterns in the Middle Tiwanaku Valley', in A.L. Kolata (ed.) *Tiwanaku and its Hinterland: Archaeology and Paleoecology of an Andean Civilization, Vol. 2*, Washington, D.C.: Smithsonian Institution Press, 112–28.

McAndrews, T., Albarracin-Jordan, J. and Bermann, M. (1997) 'Regional Settlement Patterns in the Tiwanaku Valley of Bolivia', *Journal of Field Archaeology*, 24: 67–84.

McGuire, R.H. (1983) 'Breaking Down Cultural Complexity: Inequality and Heterogeneity', *Advances in Archaeological Method and Theory*, 6: 91–142.

Mehrer, M.W. (1995) *Cahokia's Countryside: Household Archaeology, Settlement Patterns, and Social Power*, DeKalb, IL: Northern Illinois University Press.

Mendelssohn, K. (1971) 'A Scientist Looks at the Pyramids', *American Scientist*, 59: 210–20.

Mendoza, F., Flores, W. and Letourneux, C. (1994) *Atlas de los ayllus de Chayanta, Vol. 1: territorios del suni*, Potosí: Programa de Autodesarrollo Campesino.

Menzel, D. (1958) 'Problemas en el estudio del Horizonte Medio en la arqueología peruana', *Revista del Museo Regional de Ica*, 9: 24–57.

———. (1959) 'The Inca conquest of the South Coast of Peru', *Southwestern Journal of Anthropology*, 15: 125–42.

———. (1964) 'Style and time in the Middle Horizon', *ñawpa Pacha*, 2: 1–105.

Mercado de Peñalosa, P. (1965 [1583]) 'Relación de la provincia de los Pacajes', in M. Jiménez de la Espada (ed.) *Relaciones Geográficas de Indias—Perú, Biblioteca de Autores Españoles (t. 183)*, Madrid: Ediciones Atlas, pp. 334–41.

Métraux, A. (1936) Contribution a l'éthnographie et a la linguistique des Indiens Uro d'Acoaqui. *Journal de le Société des Américanistes*, 28: 75–110.

Millon, R. (1994) 'The Place Where Time Began: An Archaeologist's Interpretation of What Happened in Teotihuacan's History', in K. Berrin and E. Paszstory (ed.) *Teotihuacan: Art from the City of the Gods*, San Francisco: Thames and Hudson, pp. 16–43.

Mills, B.J. (1995) 'Gender and the Reorganization of Historic Zuni Craft Production: Implications for Archaeological Interpretation', *Journal of Anthropological Research*, 51: 149–72.

Mohr-Chávez, K. (1985) 'Early Tiahuanaco Related Ceremonial Burners from Cuzco, Peru', *Diálogo Andino (Arica, Chile)*, 4: 137–78.

———. (1988) 'The Significance of Chiripa in Lake Titicaca Basin Developments', *Expedition*: pp. 17–26.

Moore, J.D. (1996) 'The Archaeology of Plazas and the Proxemics of Ritual: Three Andean Traditions', *American Anthropologist*, 98: 789–802.

Morell, V. (2002) 'Empires Across the Andes', *National Geographic Magazine*, 201: 106–29.

Morris, C. (1982) 'The Infrastructure of Inka Control in the Peruvian Central Highlands', in G.A. Collier, R.I. Roslado and J.D. Wirth (eds.) *The Inca and Aztec States 1400–1800—Anthropology and History*, New York: Academic Press, pp. 153–71.

Morris, C. and Thompson, D.E. (1985) *Huánuco Pampa: an Inca City and Its Hinterland*, London: Thames and Hudson.

Moseley, M.E. (1997) 'Climate, Culture, and Punctuated Change: New Data, New Challenges', *The Review of Archaeology*, 18: 19–27.

———. (2001) *The Incas and Their Ancestors, 2nd. ed.*, New York: Thames and Hudson.

Moseley, M.E., Feldman, R.A., Goldstein, P.S. and Watanabe, L. (1991) 'Colonies and conquest: Tiahuanaco and Huari in Moquegua', in W.H. Isbell and G.F. McEwan (eds.) *Huari Admin-*

istrative Structure: Prehistoric Monumental Architecture and State Government, Washington, D.C.: Dumbarton Oaks, pp. 121–40.

Mujica, E. (1978) 'Nueva Hipótesis Sobre el Desarrollo Temprano del Altiplano, del Titicaca y de Sus Áreas de Interacción', *Arte y Arqueologíia*, 5–6: 285–308.

———. (1985) 'Altiplano-Coast Relationships in the South-Central Andes: From Indirect to Direct Complementarity', in S. Masuda, I. Shimada and C. Morris (eds.) *Andean Ecology and Civilization*, Tokyo: University of Tokyo, pp. 103–40.

Murra, J.V. (1972) 'El "control vertical" de un máximo de pisos ecológicos en la economía de las sociedades andinas', in J.V. Murra (ed.) *Visita de la Provincia de León de Huánuco en 1562*, Huánuco: Universidad Nacional Hermilio Valdizán, pp. 429–76.

———. (1980 [1956]) *The Economic Organization of the Inka State*, Greenwich, CT: JAI Press.

———. (1985) '"El archipiélago vertical" revisited', in S. Masuda, I. Shimada and C. Morris (eds.) *Andean Ecology and Civilization: An Interdisciplinary Perspective on Andean Ecological Complementarity*, Tokyo: University of Tokyo Press, pp. 3–14.

Netting, R.M., Wilk, R.R. and Arnould, E.J. (1984) 'Introduction', in R.M. Netting, R.R. Wilk and E.J. Arnould (eds.) *Households: Comparative and Historical Studies of the Domestic Group*, Berkeley: University of California Press, pp. xiii–xxxviii.

Nielson, A.E. (2001) 'Ethnoarchaeological Perspectives on Caravan Trade in the South-Central Andes', in L.A. Kuznar (ed.) *Ethnoarchaeology of Andean South America*, Ann Arbor: International Monographs in Prehistory, pp. 163–201.

Núñez Atencio, L. (1963) 'Problemas en torno a la tableta de Rapé', *Anales de la Universidad del Norte*, 2: 149–68.

Núñez Atencio, L. and Dillehay, T.C. (1995 [1979]) *Movilidad Giratoria, Armonía Social y Desarrollo en los Andes Meridionales: Patrones de Tráfico e Interacción Económica*, Antofagasta: Universidad Católica del Norte.

Oakland Rodman, A. (1993)Tiwanaku III Ceramic Style. Report submitted to the Instituto Nacional de Arqueologia, La Paz.

Obeyesekere, G. (1997) 'Afterward: On De-Sahlinization', in G. Obeyesekere (ed.) *The Apotheosis of Captain Cook: European Mythmaking in the Pacific*, Princeton: Princeton University Press and Bishop Museum Press, pp. 193–250.

Olsen, D.A. (2002) *Music of El Dorado: The Ethnomusicology of Ancient South American Cultures*, Gainesville, FL: University Press of Florida.

Ortloff, C.R. and Kolata, A.L. (1989) 'Hydraulic Analysis of Tiwanaku Aqueduct Structures at Lukurmata and Pajchiri, Bolivia', *Journal of Archaeological Science*, 16: 513–35.

———. (1993) 'Climate and Collapse: Agro-Ecological Perspectives on the Decline of the Tiwanaku State', *Journal of Archaeological Science*, 20: 195–221.

Ortner, S. (1984) 'Theory in Anthropology since the Sixties', *Comparative Studies in Society and History*, 26: 126–66.

Owen, B. (1993) 'A Model of Multiethnicity: State Collapse, Competition, and Social Complexity from Tiwanaku to Chiribaya in the Osmore Valley, Peru', Unpublished Ph.D. Dissertation, Los Angeles: University of California.

———. (1997), Informe de Excavaciones en los Sectores Mortuarios de Chen Chen, Temporada de 1995, Dirigido por Lic. Antonio Oquiche. Report submittdd to the Museo Contisuyo, Moquegua, Peró.

Paddock, J. (1983) 'The Oaxaca Barrio at Teotihuacan', in K.V. Flannery and J. Marcus (ed.) *The Cloud People: Divergent Evolution of the Zapotec and Mixtec Civilizations*, New York: Academic Press, pp. 170–75.

Palka, J.W. (1997) 'Reconstructing Classic Maya Socioeconomic Differentiation and the Collapse at Dos Pilas, Peten, Guatemala', *Ancient Mesoamerica*, 8: 293–306.

Paredes, M.R. (1955) *Tiahuanacu y la Provincia de Ingavi*, La Paz: Edicionies "Isla".

Parsons, J.R. (1968) 'An Estimate of Size and Population for Middle Horizon Tiahuanaco, Bolivia', *American Antiquity*, 33: 243–45.

Parsons, J.R., Hastings, C.M. and Matos M., R. (1997) 'Rebuilding the State in Highland Peru: Herder-Cultivator Interaction during the Late Intermediate Period', *Latin American Antiquity*, 8:317–41.

Parssinen, M. (1992) *Tawantinsuyu: The Inka State and its Political Organization*, Helsinki: Societas Historica Finlandiae.

Patterson, T.C. 'Pachacamac: An Andean Oracle Under Inca Rule', paper presented at Second Annual Northeast Conference on Andean Archaeology and Ethnohistory, Ithaca, 1985.

———. (1991) *The Inca Empire: The Formation and Disintegration of a Pre-Capitalist State,* New York: Berg Press.

Pauketat, T.R. (1994) *The Ascent of Chiefs: Cahokia and Mississippian Politics in Native North America,* Tuscaloosa: University of Alabama Press.

———. (2000) 'The Tragedy of the Commoners', in M.-A. Dobres and J. Robb (eds.) *Agency in Archaeology,* London: Routledge, pp. 123–39.

Paynter, R.W. (1983) 'Expanding the Scope of Settlement Analysis', in J.A. Moore and A.S. Keene (eds.) *Archaeological Hammers and Theories,* New York: Academic Press, pp. 233–75.

Pizarro, P. (1965[1571]) 'Relacion del descubrimiento y conquista de los reinos del Perú, y del gobierno y orden que los naturales tenían, y tesoros que se en ella se hallaron . . . ', *Crónica del Perú, Vol. 5: Biblioteca de Autores Españoles,* Madrid: Ediciones Atlas, pp. 167–242.

Platt, T. (1982) *Estado Boliviano y Ayllu Andino: Tierra y Tributo en el norte de Potosí,* Lima, Perú: Instituto de Estudios Peruanos.

———. (1987) 'Entre Ch'axwa y Muxsa: Para una Historia del Pensamiento Político Aymara', in T. Bouysse-Cassagne, O. Harris, T. Platt and V. Careceda (eds.) *Tres Reflexiones Sobre el Pensamiento Andino,* La Paz: Hisbol, pp. 61–132.

———. Ponce Sanginés, C. (1957) 'La cerámica de Mollo', *Arqueología Boliviana,* in C. Ponce (ed.) *La Paz: Biblisteca Paceña,* pp. 35–120.

———. (1961) *Informe de Labores,* La Paz: Centro de Investigaciones Arqueologicas en Tiwanaku.

———. (1970) *Las Culturas Wankarani y Chiripa y su Relación con Tiwanaku,* La Paz, Bolivia: Academia Nacional de Ciencias de Bolivia.

———. (1971) 'La cerámica de la época I de Tiwanaku', *Pumapunku,* 2: 7–28.

———. (1978a), El Instituto Nacional de Arqueologia de Bolivia: su organizacion y proyecciones. Internal Report 26, Instituto Nacional de Arqueologia, La Paz.

———. (1978b), Apuntes Sobre Dearrollo Nacional y Arqueologia Instituto. Internal Report 25, Nacional de Arqueologia, La Paz.

———. (1980) *Panorama de la Arqueología Boliviana, 2nd edition,* La Paz, Bolivia: Librería Editorial Juventud.

———. (1981) *Tiwanaku: Espacio, Tiempo, Cultura: Ensayo de síntesis arqueológica,* La Paz, Bolivia: Los Amigos del Libro (originally published 1972, Academia Nacional de Ciencias de Bolivia).

———. (1990) *Descripción Sumaria del Templete Semisubterraneo de Tiwanaku,* La Paz: Juventud

———. (1991) 'El urbanismo de Tiwanaku', *Pumapunku: Nueva época,* 1: 7–27.

———. (1993) 'La cerámica de la época I (aldeana) de Tiwanaku', *Pumapunku: nueva época,* 4: 48–89

———. (1995) *Tiwanaku: 200 Años de Investigaciones Arqueológicas,* La Paz: Producciones CIMA.

———. (2001) *Tiwanaku y su fascinante desarollo cultural,* La Paz: Producciones CIMA.

Ponce Sanginés, C., Echazú, A.C., Salinas, W.A. and Barrau, F.U. (1971) *Procedencia de las Areniscas Utilizadas en el Templo Precolombino de Pumapunku (Tiwanaku),* La Paz: Academia Nacional de Ciencias de Bolivia.

Poole, D. (1984) 'Ritual-Economic Calendars in Paruro: The Structure of Representation in Andean Ethnography', Unpublished Ph.D. Dissertation, Chicago: University of Illinois, Urbana-Champaign.

Portugal Ortiz, M. (1985) 'Informe de la prospección arqueológica efectuada en la provincia Camacho del Departamento de La Paz, 1er Parte', *Arqueología Boliviana No. 2,* La Paz: OEA-INAR, pp. 17–39.

———. (1992) 'Trabajos arqueológicos de Tiwanaku (I. Parte)', *Textos Antropológicos,* 4: 9–50.

———. (1998) *Escultura Prehispanic Boliviana,* La Paz: UMSA.

Portugal Ortíz, M. and Portugal Zamora, M. (1975) 'Investigaciones arqueológicas en el valle de Tiwanaku', *Arqueología en Bolivia y Perú,* La Paz, Bolivia: Instituto Nacional de Arqueología, pp. 243–83.

Posnansky, A. (1914) *Una Metrópoli Prehistórica en la América del Sud (Eine Praehistorische Metropole in Südamerika),* Berlin: Editor, Dietrich Reimer (Ernest Vohsen).

———. (1945) *Tihuanacu: The Cradle of American Man, Vols. I and II,* New York: J. J. Augustin.

Protzen, J.-P. (1992) *Inca Architecture and Construction at Ollantaytambo,* New York: Oxford University Press.

Protzen, J.-P. and Nair, S.E. (2000) 'On Reconstructing Tiwanaku Architecture', *Journal of the Society of Architectural Historians,* 59: 358–71.

———. (2002) 'The Gateways of Tiwanaku: Symbols or Passages?', in H. Silverman and W.H. Isbell (eds.) *Andean Archaeology II: Art, Landscape, and Society,* New York: Kluwer Academic/Plenum Publishers, pp. 189–223.

Quilter, J. and Stocker, T. (1983) 'Subsistence Economies and the Origins of Andean Complex Societies', *American Anthropologist*, 85: 545–62.

Randall, R. (1982) 'Qoyllur Rit'i, An Inca Fiesta of the Pleiades: Reflections on Time and Space in the Andean World', *Boletin del Instituto Frances de Estudios Andinos*, 11: 37–81.

Rappaport, J. (1990) *The Politics of Memory: Native Historical Interpretation in the Colombian Andes*, Cambridge: Cambridge University Press.

Rasnake, R.N. (1988) *Domination and Cultural Resistance: Authority and Power among Andean People*, Durham: Duke University Press.

Rattray, E.C. (1990) 'The Identification of Ethnic Affiliation at the Merchants' Barrio, Teotihuacan', in Y. Sugiura and M.C. Serra (eds.) *Etnoarqueología: Primer Coloquio Bosch-Gimpera*, Mexico City: Instituto de Investigaciones Antropológicos, UNAM, pp. 113–38.

Reichel-Dolmatoff, G. (1971) *Amazonian Cosmos: The Sexual and Religious Symbolism of the Tukano Indians*, Chicago: University of Chicago Press.

Reinhard, J. (1985) 'Chavín and Tiahuanacu: A New Look at Two Andean Ceremonial Centers', *National Geographic Research*, 1: 395–422.

———. (1990) 'Tiahuanaco, Sacred Center of the Andes', in P. McFarren (ed.) *The Cultural Guide of Bolivia*, La Paz: Fundacion Quipus, pp. 151–81.

Rendon L.P. (2000) 'La Tableta de Rape de Amaguaya', *XIII Reunión Anual de Etnología, Tomo 1*, La Paz: MUSEF, pp. 89–96.

Rivera Casanovas, C.S. (1994) 'Ch'iji Jawira: Evidencias sobre la Producción de Cerámica en Tiwanaku', Licenciatura Thesis, La Paz: Universidad Mayor de San Andrés.

———. 'Inca Domination and Local Sociopolitical Dynamics: A Vision from Cinti', paper presented at 67th Annual Meeting of the Society for American Anthropology, Denver, 2002.

———. (2003) 'Ch'iji Jawira: A Case of Ceramic Specialization in the Tiwankau Urban Periphery', in A.L. Kolata (ed.) *Tiwanaku and Its Hinterland: Archaeology and Paleoecology of an Andean Civilization, Vol. 2*, Washington, D.C.: Smithsonian Institution Press.

Rivera Cusicanqui, S. (1992) *Ayllus y Proyectos de Desarrollo en el Norte de Potosí*, La Paz: Aruwiyiri.

Rivera Sundt, O. (1989) 'Resultados de la excavación en el centro ceremonial de Lukurmata', in A.L. Kolata (ed.), Arqueologia de Lukurmata, Vol. 2, La Paz: Inar, pp. 59–88.

Roosens, E. (1989) *Creating Ethnicity: The Process of Ethnogenesis*, London: Sage Publications.

Rostworowski de Diez Canseco, M. (1992) *Pachacamac y el Señor de los Milagros: Una Trayectoria Milenaria*, Lima: Instituto de Estudios Peruanos.

———. (1999) *History of the Inca Realm*, Cambridge: Cambridge University Press.

Rowe, J.H. (1946) 'Inca culture at the time of the Spanish conquest', in J.H. Steward (ed.) *The Andean Civilizations, Handbook of South American Indians, Volume 2. Bureau of American Ethnology Bulletin 143*, Washington, D.C.: Smithsonian Institution, pp. 183–330.

———. (1962) 'Stages and Periods in Archaeological Interpretation', *Southwestern Journal of Anthropology*, 18: 40–54.

———. (1963) 'Urban Settlements in Ancient Peru', *Nawpa Pacha*: pp. 1–25.

Royce, A.P. (1982) *Ethnic Identity: Strategies of Diversity*, Bloomington: University of Indiana Press.

Russell, B. (1938) *Power, A New Social Analysis*, New York: W.W. Norton & Company.

Rydén, S. (1947) *Archaeological Researches in the Highlands of Bolivia*, Göteborg: Elanders Boktryckeri Aktiebolag.

———. (1956) *The Erland Nordenskiöld Archaeological Collection From the Mizque Valley, Bolivia*, Göteborg.

———. (1959) *Andean Excavations 2: Tupuraya and Cayhuasi, Two Tiahuanaco sites. Ethnographical Museum of Sweden, Monograph Series, no. 6*, Stockholm: Ethnographical Museum of Sweden.

Sackett, J.R. (1977) 'The Meaning of Style in Archaeology', *American Antiquity*, 42: 369–80.

———. (1990) 'Style and Ethnicity in Archaeology: The Case for Isochrestism', in M.W. Conkey and C. Hastorf (eds.) *The Uses of Style in Archaeology*, Cambridge: Cambridge University Press, pp. 32–43.

Safford, W.E. (1914) 'Pan-Pipes of Peru', *Journal of the Washington Academy of Sciences* 4(8): 183–91.

Sahlins, M. (1962) 'Poor Man, Rich Man, Big-Man Chief: Political Types in Melanesia and Polynesia', *Comparative Studies in Society and History*, 5: 285–303.

———. (1972) *Stone Age Economics*, Chicago: Aldine.
———. (1981) *Historical Metaphors and Mythical Realities: Structure in the Early History of the Sandwich Islands Kingdom*, Ann Arbor: University of Michigan Press.
———. (1985) *Islands of History*, Chicago: University of Chicago Press.
———. (1996) 'The Sadness of Sweetness: The Native Anthropology of Western Cosmology', *Current Anthropology*, 37: 395–428.
———. (2000) *Culture in Practice: Selected Essays*, New York: Zone Books.
Saignes, T. (1985) *Los Andes Orientales: Historia de un Olvido*, Cochabamba: IFEA/CERES.
———. (1993) *Borrachera y Memoria: La Experiencia de lo Sagrado en los Andes*, Hisbol and IFEA.
Salles-Reese, V. (1997) *From Viracocha to the Virgin of Cpacabana: Representation of the Sacred at Lake Titicaca*, Austin: University of Texas Press.
Sallnow, M.J. (1987) *Pilgrims of the Andes*, Washington, D.C.: Smithsonian Institution Press.
Sampeck, K.E. (1991) 'Excavations at Putuni, Tiwanaku, Bolivia', Unpublished M.A. Thesis, Chicago: University of Chicago.
Sanders, W.T., Parsons, J.R. and Santley, R.S. (1979) *The Basin of Mexico: Ecological Processes in the Evolution of a Civilization*, New York: Academic Press.
Schaedel, R.P. (1988) 'Andean World View: Hierarchy or Reciprocity, Regulation or Control?', *Current Anthropology*, 29: 768–75.
Schiffer, M.B. (1996) *Formation Processes of the Archaeological Record*, Salt Lake City: University of Utah Press.
Schortmann, E. (1989) 'Interregional Interaction in Prehistory: the Need for a New Perspective', *American Antiquity*, 54: 52–65.
Schüler, W. (1988) 'Close Encounters', M.Sc. Thesis, London: London School of Economics.
Schwartz, T. (1995) 'Cultural Totemism', in L. Romanucci-Ross and G.D. Vos (eds.) *Ethnic Identity: Creation, Conflict, and Accommodation*, Walnut Creek: Altamira Press, pp. 48–72.
Scott, J.C. (1990) *Domination and the Arts of Resistance: Hidden Transcripts*, New Haven: Yale University Press.
Seddon, M.T. (1994) 'Excavations in the Raised Fields of the Río Catari Sub-Basin, Bolivia', Master's Thesis, Chicago: University of Chicago.
———. (1998) 'Ritual, Power, and the Development of a Complex Society', Unpublished Ph.D. Dissertation, Chicago: University of Chicago.
Sennett, R. (1998) *The Corrosion of Character: The Personal Consequences of Work in the New Capitalism*, New York: W. W. Norton & Company.
Service, E.R. (1975) *Origins of the State and Civilization: The Process of Political Evolution*, New York: Norton.
Shennan, S. (1989) 'Introduction: Archaeological Approaches to Cultural Identity', in S. Shennan (ed.) *Archaeological Approaches to Cultural Identity*, London: Unwin Hyman, pp. 1–13.
Shils, E. (1975) *Center and Periphery: Essays in Macrosociology*, Chicago: University of Chicago Press.
Shimada, I. (1991) 'Pachacamac Archaeology: Retrospect and Prospect', *Pachacamac: A Reprint of the 1903 Edition by Max Uhle*, Philadelphia: The University Musuem of Archaeology and Anthropology, University of Pennsylvania, pp. XV-LXVI.
Sillar, B. (2000) *Shaping Culture: An Ethnoarchaeological Study of Pottery Production, Trade and Use in the Andes*, Oxford: BAR International Series.
Silverman, H. (1993) *Cahuachi in the Ancient Nasca World*, Iowa City: University of Iowa Press.
———. (1994) 'The Archaeological Identification of an Ancient Peruvian Pilgrimage Center', *World Archaeology*, 26: 1–18.
Simmel, G. (1950) *The Sociology of Georg Simmel*, New York: The Free Press.
Smith, A.T. (2000) 'Rendering the Political Aesthetic: Political Legitimacy in Urartian Representations of the Built Environment', *Journal of Anthropological Archaeology*, 19: 131–63.
Smith, J.Z. (1987) *To Take Place: Toward Theory in Ritual*, Chicago: University of Chicago Press.
Smith, M.E. (1987) 'Household Possessions and Wealth in Agrarian States: Implications for Archaeology', *Journal of Anthropological Archaeology*, 6: 297–335.
———. (1992) 'Braudel's Temporal Rhythms and Chronology Theory in Archaeology', in A.B. Knapp (ed.) *Archaeology, Annales, and Ethnohistory*, New York: Cambridge University Press, pp. 23–34.
———. (1993) 'Houses and the Settlement Hierarchy in Late Postclassic Morelos: A Comparison of Archaeology and Ethnohistory', in R.S. Santley and K.G. Hirth (eds.) *Prehispanic Domestic Units in Western Mesoamerica*, Boca Raton: CRC Press, pp. 191–206.

———. (1994) 'Social Complexity in the Aztec Countryside', in G.M. Schwartz and S.E. Falconer (eds.) *Archaeological Views from the Countryside: Village Communities in Early Complex Societies*, Washington, D.C.: Smithsonian Institution Press, pp. 143–59.

Smyth, M.P. (1989) 'Domestic storage behavior in Mesoamerica: an ethnoarchaeological approach', in M.B. Schiffer (ed.) *Archaeological Method and Theory*, Tucson: University of Arizona Press, pp. 89–138.

Sökefeld, M. (1999) 'Debating Self, Identity, and Culture in Anthropology', *Current Anthropology*, 40:417–49.

Sollors, W. (1996) *Theories of Ethnicity: A Classical Reader*, Washington Square: New York University Press.

Southall, A. (1988) 'The Segmentary State in Africa and Asia', *Comparative Studies in Society and History*, 30: 52–82.

Spence, M.W. (1981) 'Obsidian Production and the State in Teotihuacan', *American Antiquity*, 46:769–88.

Spencer-Wood, S.M. (1999) 'The World Their Household: Changing Meanings of the Domestic Sphere in the Nineteenth Century', in P.M. Allison (ed.) *The Archaeology of Household Activities*, London: Routledge, pp. 162–89.

Spengler, O. (1934) *The Decline of the West, Vol. II*, New York: Alfred A. Knopf.

Squier, E.G. (1878) *Peru: Incidents of Travel and Exploration in the Land of the Incas*, New York: Harper Brothers.

Stahl, A.B. (1993) 'Concepts of Time and Approaches to Analogical Reasoning in Historical Perspective', *American Antiquity*, 58: 235–60.

Stambaugh, J.E. (1988) *The Ancient Roman City*, Baltimore: Johns Hopkins University Press.

Stanish, C. (1989a) 'Household archaeology: Testing Models of Zonal Complementarity in the South Central Andes', *American Anthropologist*, 91: 7–24.

———. (1989b) 'An archaeological evaluation of an ethnohistorical model in Moquegua', in D. Rice, C. Stanish and P. Scarr (eds.) *Ecology, Settlement and History in the Osmore Drainage, Peró*, Oxford: British Archaeological Reports, pp. 303–21.

———. (1992) *Ancient Andean Political Economy*, Austin: University of Texas Press.

———. (2003) *Ancient Titicaca: The Evolution of Complex Society in Southern Peru and Northern Bolivia*, Berkeley: University of California Press.

Stanish, C., de la Vega M., E., Steadman, L., Chávez Justo, C., Frye, K.L., Onofre Mamani, L., Seddon, M.T. and Calisaya Chuquimia, P. (1997) *Archaeological Survey in the Juli-Desaguadero Region of the Lake Titicaca Basin, Southern Peru. Fieldiana Anthropology New Series No. 29*, Chicago, IL: Department of Anthropology: Field Museum of Natural History.

Stanish, C., de la Vega, E. and Frye, K.L. (1993) 'Domestic Architecture on Lupaqa Area Sites in the Department of Puno', in M.S. Aldenderfer (ed.) *Domestic Architecture, Ethnicity, and Complementarity in the South-Central Andes*, Iowa City: University of Iowa Press, pp. 83–93.

Stark, M., Elson, M.D. and Clark, J.J. (1998) 'Social Boundaries and Technical Choices in Tonto Basin Prehistory', in M.T. Stark (ed.) *The Archaeology of Social Boundaries*, Washington, D.C.: Smithsonian Institution Press, pp. 208–31.

Steadman, L.H. (1995) 'Excavations at Camata: An Early Ceramic Chronology for the Western Titicaca Basin, Peru', Unpublished Ph.D. Dissertation, Berkeley: University of California at Berkeley.

Steadman, L.H. 'Ceramic Perspectives on the Yaya-Mama Religious Tradition', paper presented at 62nd Annual Meeting of the Society for American Archaeology, Nashville, 1997.

Stein, G. (1994) 'Segmentary States and Organizational Variation in Early Complex Societies: A Rural Perspective', in G.M. Schwartz and S.E. Falconer (eds.) *Archaeological Views from the Countryside: Village Communities in Early Complex Societies*, Washington, D.C.: Smithsonian Institution Press, pp. 10–18.

Stern, S.J. (1982) *Peru's Indian Peoples and the Challenge of Spanish Conquest*, Madison: University of Wisconsin Press.

Steward, J. (1955) *Theory of Culture Change*, Urbana: University of Illinois Press.

Storey, R. (1992) *Life and Death in the Ancient City of Teotihuacan: A Modern Paleodemographic Synthesis*, Tuscaloosa: University of Alabama Press.

Straughan, B. (1991) 'The Secrets of Ancient Tiwanaku Are Benefiting Today's Bolivia', *Smithsonian*, 21:38–49.

Sutherland, C. (1991) *Surface Collections at Akapana-East, Tiwanaku, Bolivia,* Chicago: University of Chicago.

Tainter, J.A. (1988) *The Collapse of Complex Societies,* Cambridge: Cambridge University Press.

Tambiah, S.J. (1977) 'The Galactic Polity: The Structure of Traditional Kingdoms in Southeast Asia', *Annals of the New York Academy of Sciences,* 293.

Terada, K. and Onuki, Y. (1982) *Excavations in the Cajamarca Valley, Peru, 1979,* Tokyo: University of Tokyo Press.

Thompson, L.G., Mosley-Thompson, E., Bolzan, J.F., and Koci, B.R. (1985) 'A 1500–Year Record of Tropical Precipitation in Ice Cores from the Quelccaya Ice Cap, Peru', *Science* 229: 971–73.

Thompson, L.G. and Mosley-Thompson, E. (1987) 'Evidence of Abrupt Climatic Change During the Last 1,500 Years Recorded in Ice Cores From the Tropical Quelccaya Ice Cap, Peru', in W.H. Berger and L.D. Labeyrie (eds.) *Abrupt Climatic Change: Evidence and Implications,* Boston: Reidel Publishing Company, pp. 99–110.

Ticona Alejo, E. and Albó Corrons, X. (1997) *Jesús de Machaca: La Marka Rebelde, Vol. 3. La Lucha por el Poder Comunal,* La Paz: CEDOIN and CIPCA.

Tomczak, P.D. (2001) 'Prehistoric Socio-Economic Relations and Population Organization in the Lower Osmore Drainage of Southern Peru', Unpublished Ph.D. Dissertation, Albuquerque: University of New Mexico.

Topic, J.R. (1982) 'Lower class social and economic organization at Chan Chan', in M.E. Moseley and K.C. Day (eds.) *Chan Chan: Andean Desert City,* Albuquerque: University of New Mexico Press, pp. 145–76.

Torero, A. (1970) 'Lingüística e Historia en la Sociedad Andina', *Anales Cientificos de la Universidad Nacional Agraria,* 8: 231–64.

———. (1987) 'Lenguas y Pueblos Altiplánicos en Torno al Siglo XVI', *Revista Andina*: pp. 329–405.

Torres-Rouf, C. (2002) 'Cranial Vault Modification and Ethnicity in Middle Horizon San Pedro de Atacama, Chile', *Current Anthropology,* 43: 163–71.

Tourtellot, G. (1988) 'Developmental Cycles of Households and Houses at Seibal', in R.R. Wilk and W. Ashmore (eds.) *Household and Community in the Mesoamerican Past,* Albuquerque: University of New Mexico Press, pp. 97–20.

Tringham, R. (1991) 'Households with Faces: The Challenge of Gender in Prehistoric Architectural Remains', in J.M Gero and M.W. Conkey (eds.) *Engendering Archaeology: Women and Prehistory,* Oxford: Blackwell Press, pp. 93–131.

———. (1995) 'Archaeological Houses, Households, Housework, and the Home', in D.N. Benjamin (ed.) *The Home: Words, Interpretations, Meanings, and Environments,* Avebury: Aldershot, Engel, pp. 79–107.

Tschopik, H. (1950) 'An Andean Ceramic Tradition in Historical Perspective', *American Antiquity,* 3: 196–219.

Tschopik, M.H. (1946) 'Some Notes on the Archaeology of the Department of Puno, Peru', *Papers of the Peabody Museum of American Archaeology and Ethnology, Harvard University, vol. 27, no. 3.* Cambridge, MA: Peabody Museum of American Archaeology and Ethnology.

Turner, T. (1996) 'Social Complexity and Recursive Hierarchy in Indigenous South American Societies', *Journal of the Steward Anthropological Society,* 1–2: 37–59.

Turner, V. (1969) *The Ritual Process: Structure and Anti-Structure,* Ithaca: Cornell University Press.

Uhle, M. (1902) 'Types of Culture in Peru', *American Anthropologist,* 4: 753–58.

———. (1903) 'Ancient South American Civilization', *Harper's Monthly Magazine,* 107: 780–86.

———. (1912) 'Review of A. Posnansky, Guía general ilustrada para la investigación de los monumentos prehistóóricos de Tihuanacu é Islas del Sol y la Luna', *Revista de la Sociedad Chilena de Historia y Geografía,* 2: 467–79.

———. (1991[1903]) 'Pachacamac: Report of the William Pepper, M.D., LL.D., Peruvian Expedition of 1896', *Pachacamac: A Reprint of the 1903 Edition by Max Uhle,* Philadelphia: The University Museum of Archaeology and Anthropology, University of Pennsylvania.

Upham, S. (1990) *The Evolution of Political Systems: Socio-politics in Small Scale Sedentary Societies,* Cambridge: Cambridge University Press.

Urton, G. (1990) *The History of a Myth: Pacariqtambo and the Origins of the Inkas,* Austin: University of Texas Press.

———. (1999) *Inca Myths,* Austin: University of Texas Press.

Van Buren, M. (1996) 'Rethinking the vertical archipelago: ethnicity, exchange, and history in the South Central Andes', *American Anthropologist,* 98: 338–51.

van den Berghe, P.L. (1981) *The Ethnic Phenomenon,* New York: Elsevier.
van Kessel, J. (1992) *Cuando Arde el Tiempo Sagrado,* La Paz: Hisbol.
van Zantwijk, R. (1985) *The Aztec Arrangement: The Social History of Pre-Spanish Mexico,* Norman: University of Oklahoma Press.
Vargas V., B. (1994), Informe Sobre Tumbas Intactas (334) Excavadas Durante el Proyecto "Rescate Arqueológico en el Cemeterio de Chen-Chen – Moquegua." Report submitted to the Museo Cuntisuyo, Moquegua, Peró.
Vellard, J.A. (1963) *Civilisations des Andes: Evolution des Populations du Haut-Plateau Bolivien,* Paris: Editions Gallimard.
Vincent, J. (1971) *African Elite: The Big Men of a Small Town,* New York: Columbia University Press.
Vom Bruck, G. (1997) 'A House Turned Inside Out', *Journal of Material Culture,* 2: 139–72.
von Däniken, A. (1971) *Chariots of the Gods?: Unresolved Mysteries of the Past,* New York: Bantam Books.
Vranich, A. (1999) 'Interpreting the Meaning of Ritual Spaces: The Temple Complex of Pumapunku, Tiwanaku, Bolivia', Unpublished Ph.D. dissertation, Philadelphia: University of Pennsylvania.
———. (2001) 'The Akapana Pyramid: Reconsidering Tiwanaku's Monumental Center', *Boletin de Arquelogia PUCP,* 5: 295–308.
Wachtel, N. (1994) *Gods and Vampires: Return to Chipaya,* Chicago: University of Chicago Press.
Wailes, B. (1995) 'A Case Study of Heterarchy in Complex Societies: Early Medieval Ireland and Its Archaeological Implications', in C.L.C. Robert M. Ehrenreich, and Janet E. Levy (ed.) *Heterarchy and the Analysis of Complex Societies,* Arlington, VA: American Anthropological Association, pp. 55–70.
Wallace, D.T. (1957) 'The Tiahuanaco Horizon Styles in the Peruvian Highlands', Unpublished Ph.D. Dissertation, Berkeley: University of California.
———. (1980) 'Tiwanaku as a symbolic empire', *Estudios Arqueológicos. Homenaje al VII Congreso de Arqueología Chilena,* 5: 133–44.
Walle, P. (1914) *Bolivia: Its People and its Resources, Its Railways, Mines, and Rubber-Forests,* London: T. Fisher Unwin LTD.
Wassén, S.H. (1972) *A Medicine-Man's Implements and Plants in a Tiahuanacoid Tomb in Highland Bolivia. Etnologiska Studier 32,* Göteborg: Elanders Boktryckeri Aktiebolag.
Weber, M. (1947) *The Theory of Social and Economic Organization,* New York.
———. (1958) 'The City', in D. Martingale and G. Neuwirth (eds.) *The City,* New York: The Free Press, pp. 65–230.
Webster, A.D. (1993) 'The Role of the South American Camelid in the Development of the Tiwanaku State', Unpublished Ph.D. Dissertation, Chicago: University of Chicago.
Webster, A.D. and Janusek, J.W. (2003) 'Tiwanaku Camelids: Subsistence, Sacrifice, and Social Reproduction', in A.L. Kolata (ed.) *Tiwanaku and Its Hinterland: Archaeology and Paleoecology of an Andean Civilization, Vol. 2,* Washington, D.C.: Smithsonian Institution Press, pp. 343–62.
Wheatley, P. (1971) *The Pivot of the Four Quarters—A Preliminary Enquiry into the Origins and Character of the Ancient Chinese City,* Chicago: Aldine Publishing Company.
White, J.C. (1995) 'Incorporating Heterarchy into Theory on Socio-Political Development: The Case for Southeast Asia', in Robert M. Ehrenreich, C.L. Crumley, and Janet E. Levy (ed.) *Heterarchy and the Analysis of Complex Societies,* Arlington, VA: American Anthropological Association, pp. 101–24.
White, L. (1949) *The Science of Culture: A Study of Man and Civilization,* New York: Farrar, Straus, and Giroux.
Wiessner, P. (1983) 'Style and Social Information in Kalahari San Projectile Points', *American Antiquity,* 48: 253–76.
———. (1990) 'Is There A Unity to Style?', in M.W. Conkey and C. Hastorf (eds.) *The Uses of Style in Archaeology,* Cambridge: Cambridge University Press, pp. 105–12.
Wilk, R.R. (1983) 'Little House in the Jungle: the Causes of Variation in House Size Among the Modern Kekchi Maya', *Journal of Anthropological Archaeology,* 2: 99–116.
———. (1991) 'The Household in Anthropology: Panacea or Problem', *Review in Anthropology,* 20: 1–12.
Wilk, R.R. and Netting, R.M. (1984) 'Households: Changing Forms and Functions', in R.M. Netting, R.R. Wilk and E.J. Arnold (eds.) *Household: Comparative and Historical Studies of the Domestic Group,* Berkeley: University of California Press, pp. 1–28.

Wilk, R.R. and Rathje, W.L. (1982) 'Household Archaeology', *American Behavioral Scientist*, 25: 617–39.

Williams, P.R. (2002) 'Rethinking Disaster-Induced Collapsed in the Demise of the Andean Highland States: Wari and Tiwanaku', *World Archaeology*, 33: 361–74.

Williams, P.R. and Nash, D.J. (2002) "Imperial Interaction in the Andes: Huari and Tiwanaku at Cerro Baul', in H. Silverman and W.H. Isbell, *Andean Archaeology I: Variations in Sociopolitical Organization*, New York: Kluwer/Plenum, pp. 243–66.

Winterhalder, B.P. and Thomas, R.B. (1978) *Geoecology of South Highland Peru: A Human Adaptation Perspective*, Boulder: University of Colorado, Institute of Arctic and Alpine Research.

Wise, K. (1993) 'Late Intermediate Period architecture of Lukurmata', in M.S. Aldenderfer (ed.) *Domestic Architecture, Ethnicity, and Complementarity in the South-Central Andes*, Iowa City, IA: University of Iowa Press, pp. 103–13.

Wobst, H.M. (1977) 'Stylistic Behavior and Information Exchange', in C.E. Cleland (ed.) *For the Director: Research Essays in Honor of James B. Griffin*, Ann Arbor: Museum of Anthropology, University of Michigan, pp. 317–42.

Wright, H.T. (1977) 'Recent Research on the Origin of the State', *Annual Review of Anthropology*, 6:379–97.

———. (1991) 'Women's Labor and Pottery Production in Prehistory', in J.M. Gero and M.W. Conkey (eds.) *Engendering Archaeology: Women and Prehistory*, Oxford: Blackwell Press, pp. 194–223.

Wright, H.T. and Johnson, G.A. (1975) 'Population, Exchange and Early State Formation in Southwestern Iran', *American Anthropologist*, 77: 267–89.

Wright, M.F., Hastorf, C.A. and Lennstrom, H. (2003) 'Pre-Hispanic Agriculture and Plant Use at Tiwanaku: Social and Political Implications', in A.L. Kolata (ed.) *Tiwanaku and Its Hinterland: Archaeology and Paleoecology of an Andean Civilization, Vol. 2*, Washington, D.C.: Smithsonian Institution Press, pp. 384–403.

Wylie, A. (1985) 'The Reaction Against Analogy', *Advances in Archaeological Method and Theory*, 8:63–111.

Xu, Y. (2000) The Chinese City in Space and Time, Honolulu: University of Hawaii Press.

Yoffee, N. (1988) 'Orienting Collapse', in N. Yoffee and G.L. Cowgill (eds.) *The Collapse of Ancient States and Civilizations*, Tucson: University of Arizona Press, pp. 1–19.

Yoffee, N. and Cowgill, G.L. (1988) *The Collapse of Ancient States and Civilizations*, Tucson: University of Arizona Press.

Zuidema, R.T. (1964) 'The Ceque System of Cuzco: The Social Organization of the Capital of the Inca', Leiden: E. J. Brill.

———. (1978) 'Shafttombs and the Inca Empire', *Journal of the Steward Anthropological Society*, 9:133–78.

———. (1990) *Inca Civilization in Cuzco*, Austin: University of Texas Press.

Index